BRITISH WAR FILMS

1939–1945

British War Films
1939–1945

The Cinema and the Services

S. P. MacKenzie

hambledon
continuum

Hambledon Continuum

The Tower Building
11 York Road
London, SE1 7NX

80 Maiden Lane
Suite 704
New York, NY 10038

First published 2001 in hardback
This edition published 2006 in paperback
Reprinted 2007

ISBN 1 85285 258 5 (hardback)
ISBN 1 85285 586 X (paperback)

Typeset by Carnegie Publishing, Lancaster
and printed in Great Britain by MPG Books, Cornwall.

Contents

Paperback Preface

The welcome decision by Continuum to publish a paperback edition of this book six years after its first appearance in hardback offers a chance for the author to make one or two additional comments on the book and its subject matter. A number of fine volumes have been published in recent years that study the commercial war films made in the UK. None of the authors, however, has been primarily concerned with the role played by the armed forces in the making of these films, which was and remains my central concern and the focus of this book.

The development of a computer catalogue at what is now the National Archives in the years after this book was researched and written seemed to offer the possibility of uncovering hitherto obscure material on cooperation between the services and the film companies that could be exploited by other scholars. Unhappily this technological development has only confirmed an old suspicion that the majority of the relevant files were destroyed for what was likely considered at the time lack of potential usefulness when material was transferred to the Public Record Office.

Major changes to this volume have therefore been eschewed. A variety of typographical and related errors have been corrected, however, and it is perhaps worth listing a number of additional wartime features with which the armed forces were involved that, for reasons of time and space, could not be worked in to the current text and were omitted from the original.

King Arthur Was A Gentleman (Gainsborough, 1942) and *Great Day* (RKO, 1945) were films for which the British Army provided men and military equipment. The Royal Navy also provided support for *Contraband* (British National, 1940) and *Perfect Strangers* (London Films, 1945), as did the Royal Air Force for *Dangerous Moonlight* (RKO, 1940), *The Day Will Dawn* (Rank, 1942), and *The Adventures of Tartu* (MGM, 1943).

Post-war films for which the services gave greater or lesser help also include *Theirs Is the Glory* (Gaumont-British, 1946), *Now it Can Be Told* (RAF, 1946), *Against the Wind* (Ealing, 1948), *Landfall* (Associated-British, 1949), *The Intruder* (British Lion, 1953), *The Quatermass Xperiment* (Hammer, 1955), and *X-The Unknown* (Hammer, 1955). It is also worth mentioning that the Royal Navy allowed US companies to film aboard RN vessels for *On the Beach* (United Artists, 1959) and *The Bedford Incident* (Columbia, 1965).

Acknowledgements

This book would not have been possible without the help of staff members at a variety of research institutions. I would therefore like to thank those who work in various departments at Boston University Library; the British Film Institute; the British Library; the British Newspaper Library; Churchill College Cambridge; the House of Lords Record Office; the Imperial War Museum; the Liddell Hart Centre for Military Archives; the National Film and Television Archive; the National Library of Scotland; the National Sound Archive; the Public Record Office; the Thomas Cooper Library, University of South Carolina; the Tom Harrisson Mass-Observation Archive; TV Ontario; and the archive of the University of Southampton. The task was also made easier through access to the extensive stock of a number of retail video outlets in North America, notably Movies Unlimited, Nostalgia Family Video, Videoflicks and Vintage Video.

I am also grateful to a number of institutions and individuals for granting permission to quote from or reproduce sources to which they hold the copyright. These include the trustees of the Liddell Hart Centre for Military Archives for the papers of Sir Ronald Adam; the Department of Special Collections, Boston University Library, for the Eric Ambler papers; the present Lord Croft for the papers of the 1st Baron Croft; D. C. Grigg for the papers of P. J. Grigg; the Imperial War Museum for the papers of Ronald Tritton and A. D. Melville, as well as transcripts of interviews with Roy Boulting, David Macdonald, Desmond O'Neill, and Hugh Stewart; Curtis Brown on behalf of the Trustees of the Mass-Observation Archive, for Mass-Observation material; the trustees of the National Library of Scotland for the Elibank and Elliot papers; the Controller of Her Majesty's Stationery Office for official papers held in the Public Record Office; and the Rank Organization for stills from various films. Stills from GPO and service unit films are Crown copyright. Efforts have been made to contact all copyright holders, and any omissions from the list are purely unintended.

Finally, I would like to acknowledge the support and critical assessments provided by my editors, Tony Morris and Martin Sheppard. It was their interest in this project which brought it to fruition. Needless to say, any errors of fact and controversial opinions are my responsibility alone.

Introduction

As historians have come to recognize in recent decades, feature films are not only an engaging form of popular entertainment but also a vital source for understanding the social and cultural makeup of modern society. Nowhere has this been more true than in reference to the Second World War, years in which cinema-going reached new heights of popularity and British film production – hitherto written off as inferior to the Hollywood product – finally came of age. Combined with the issue of state involvement in the choice of subject matter through the Films Division of the wartime Ministry of Information (MoI) this has meant that the films of the war years now rank among the most heavily studied of British pictures.[1]

With so much already written about the production, nature, and reception of these wartime films, not least within the context of state propaganda policy, one might legitimately wonder if there is anything left to say. But there is never a last word on any subject, and there happens to be at least one aspect of wartime feature production that has not yet attracted much interest: the involvement of the armed forces in the making of wartime features.[2] Most historians have tended to focus their attention on the Ministry of Information in relation to government involvement in the making of war films.

Yet while the MoI bore overall responsibility for film propaganda in the Second World War, it is important to recognize that its powers with regard to the service ministries were by no means unlimited. Security censorship remained largely in the hands of serving or retired officers, and while proposals for film productions almost always passed through the hands of the Films Division, no film involving warships, tanks, military aircraft or uniformed personnel could proceed without it first being given the green light by the Admiralty, War Office, or Air Ministry.[3]

As we shall see, proposals for feature-length films could originate from a variety of sources, including commercial companies, the services, the MoI or other government departments. For projects to come to fruition, however, they had to be seen by the service ministry concerned as useful. An ambiguous attitude towards publicity within the armed forces, coupled with the number of parties involved, often made the creation of features about the services a far from smooth process. The fact remains, however, that through involvement in filmmaking the publicity branches of the Admiralty, War Office and Air Ministry and their superiors were engaged during the war in attempts to sway public opinion in particular directions.[4]

Understanding what was being attempted, and why, necessarily involves placing events in the wider context of the evolving war situation and popular reactions to particular events. To grasp fully what was happening in the war years, however, and to appreciate the long-term significance of the wartime experience, it is also important to situate that experience in relation to the overall relationship between the services and feature film publicity. Hence, bracketing the main body of the text, chapters describing the evolution of this relationship before 1939 and after 1945.

The absence of much work to date on the services and cinema is understandable. The armed forces are rarely considered important in film history, the cinema is not often considered relevant to military historians, and above all the surviving documentary record is – to say the least – extremely patchy.[5] However, enough relevant service and other ministry files, film industry reports and publicity material, memoirs, diaries, and recorded interviews are now in the public domain for an attempt to be made to explain what was happening. Whether this particular effort is successful or not will be for the reader to judge.

1

The Services and the Cinema, 1900–1939

The emergence of cinema as a major form of popular entertainment in Britain was quite swift. Beginning life as a mere novelty attraction at fairgrounds and in music-halls in the last years of the nineteenth century, film evolved within fifteen years into a potent mass medium. As technical and other problems were overcome, an extensive cinema industry developed that both catered for and stimulated popular demand. Between 1898 and 1914 the number and length of films produced annually in Britain had increased approximately tenfold, while by the latter year picture theatres – able to capitalize on imported as well as domestic product – numbered in the low thousands. In Manchester, to take a particularly striking case, there were 111 cinemas in operation, with a grand total of 920,000 available seats: one for every eight inhabitants. With tickets ranging in price as low as threepence, 'going to the pictures' had developed into a common leisure activity for much of the working population. Contemporary estimates of weekly attendance figures in the prewar years ran as high as seven or eight million.[1]

In a jingoistic age of militant patriotism in which positive representations of the armed forces appeared on everything from postcards to cocoa advertisements, it is not surprising to find military and naval subjects featuring extensively in the new medium. In the first decade of the century, for example, scores of short boyish adventure films with titles like *A Son of Mars* (Cricks & Martin, 1912) and *Lieutenant Daring* (British & Colonial, 1912) were shot.[2]

The services, however, kept their distance from this new phenomenon. Going to the pictures was a familiar enough activity for the humble urban families from whom the army and navy drew their recruits. Those in command, however, came from a very different social environment. Commissions still went to those of gentle birth or the sons of 'respectable' middle-class professionals, while the uppermost ranks in particular tended to be dominated by the gentry or the aristocracy. Whatever their origin, and despite a growing sense of professionalism, officers maintained the habits and prejudices of county families. As gentlemen, officers were expected to hunt foxes, shoot grouse, and engage in other country house

pursuits: they definitely were not supposed to go to the cinema. As representatives of elite society, they tended to view the mass culture of the lower
orders with a mixture of incomprehension and disdain, despite – or because
of – the evident growth in the power and influence of those orders as
time passed. As one observer later put it, cinema was regarded in service
circles as 'a kind of music hall turn', both 'vulgar' and 'without serious
importance'.[3]

Public pageantry, to be sure, especially royal reviews involving the display
of traditional pomp and circumstance, had become by the early 1890s an
accepted recruitment tool and prestige builder. Representations of Jack Tar
and Tommy Aitkins on postcards, on the stage, in commercial advertising,
and eventually on celluloid, were tolerated. But for the services to engage
directly or indirectly in the manufacture of popular culture and the shaping
of mass opinion was considered by most officers to be *infra dig*.[4]

There were, nevertheless, occasional signs of a more positive official
attitude even in the early years of cinema. In particular, senior individuals
in both services proved willing to engage in episodic collaboration with the
film industry if particular circumstance seemed to demand it.

The Boer War witnessed the first instances of such collaboration. Defeats
in the first campaigns aroused a storm of criticism directed at the army in
press and parliament, while manpower demands imposed a severe strain
on army resources. The navy, meanwhile, came under attack for being
complacent in the face of public fears of a lightning French invasion attempt
while the army was occupied in South Africa. It was in this context that
the War Office and the Admiralty made their first, tentative efforts at
employing film as an instrument of propaganda.

Sir Evelyn Wood was in most respects a conventional senior army officer,
as his memoirs make clear.[5] But as Adjutant-General at the War Office he
was very much aware of both public criticism of the army's performance
in South Africa and the manpower problem. He was therefore receptive
when, sometime in the spring of 1900, he was approached by R. W. Paul,
a pioneer in commercial film production, with a proposal to make a series
of 'Animatograph Pictures' on the British Army. The idea was 'to illustrate
the life and career of a soldier, and the work of each branch of the Service'
by filming, for the first time, the real thing. In the hope that recruiting and
public esteem might be stimulated at a particularly difficult time, Wood
provided the necessary access to military facilities for the making of *Army
Life; or How Soldiers are Made*. Episodes included actuality footage of cavalry,
artillery and infantry at exercise, as well as staged scenes of soldiers joining
up, enjoying themselves off duty, charging into combat, and retiring into the
Commissionaire Corps. The War Office also authorized another successful

producer, Cecil Hepworth, to make a similar series, *The British Army* (which included scenes of tent-pegging and cavalry trotting in review). The Admiralty, meanwhile, almost certainly in an effort to demonstrate its readiness for war, gave permission for Hepworth to film sailors training ashore. *The British Navy* included shots of bluejackets at exercise and cutlass drill, probably taken at Portsmouth.[6]

Once the immediate crisis had passed, though, neither service proved eager to follow up on this first brush with cinematic propaganda. Despite plaudits in the *Morning Post, The Times, Daily Mail* and other newspapers for *Army Life*, it would be almost a decade before the War Office gave its help again to a film company, and even longer before the Admiralty made any further moves.[7]

It was another invasion scare in 1909, coupled with the usual problem of insufficient enrolment – both for the regular army and especially the new Territorial Force – that prompted the War Office to engage more actively in what the war minister of the day, Richard Haldane, termed 'modern methods of recruiting'.[8] Among other things this involved providing help for another Hepworth effort, *In the Service of the King*. Directed by Lewin Fitzhamon and released in January 1909, this was a fictional account of the successful career of a young soldier from his enlistment to his return home as conquering hero.[9] This and other publicity measures appear to have had a positive but only short-term effect, and in early 1913 the War Office came to an agreement with Keith, Prouse & Co. – who passed production on to Gaumont – to make and distribute another film 'illustrating the life of the soldier'. Approximately one-and-a-half hours long, *The British Army Film* was a mixed drama-documentary, partially staged but with no actors involved. Shot at Aldershot with over a thousand troops participating, it showed men of various army branches at work and play. The aim, as stated publicly by the war minister, J. E. B. Seely, was to 'create an interest in the Army which will be useful for recruiting purposes'. The final product would be 'subject to the final approval of the Army Council'.[10] Released in January 1914 as part of a major recruiting campaign and the biggest cinematic effort yet made with official cooperation, *The British Army Film* opened well but was rented at too high a cost to achieve wide distribution.[11] The Royal Navy, meanwhile, at least in reference to self-promotion, remained true to its motto: *acta non verba*.

That both the Admiralty and the War Office remained, at heart, seriously ill at ease with the film industry became apparent in the initial months of the First World War. As in the first phases of the war in South Africa fifteen years earlier, there was a boom in the production and popularity of commercial melodrama, comedy, and adventure films with war-related plots.

Dozens of films with titles such as *Your Country Needs You*, *England's Call*, *The Kaiser's Spies* and *The Heroine of Mons* were released in the last months of 1914 and on into 1915. Most involved characters in the services and all were resolutely patriotic.[12] Yet despite the fact that, according to a leading trade newspaper, 'Everybody is wanting Army and Navy films',[13] film manufacturers largely had to make do with prewar footage and staged scenes. Beyond allowing a few companies to shoot innocuous scenes of life in newly established training camps, neither service proved at all willing to have anything to do with the active creation of film propaganda.

The newly established government propaganda bureau at Wellington House under Charles Masterman, the Foreign Office, and the film trade – operating through a lobby group, the Kinematograph Manufacturers' Association Topical Committee, as well as through Wellington House – all argued that the image of the services could only benefit from war footage. For many months, however, both the War Office and Admiralty continued to insist that security considerations made the filming of operational units out of the question.[14] Such considerations were not entirely frivolous. But it rapidly became clear that refusal to cooperate in the making of films had to do as much with distaste for the medium as it did with worries about what the Germans would learn.

As Secretary of State for War, Field-Marshal Lord Kitchener, despite his role in raising Britain's new armies, exhibited a marked distaste for the mass media. Negotiations for the filming of military personnel dragged on so long that the setting for the London Film Company feature *You!*, sponsored by the Parliamentary Recruiting Committee and released in January 1916, had to be shifted from the army to a munitions factory.[15] Winston Churchill, serving as First Lord of the Admiralty until May 1915, was certainly more loquacious and at ease with the idea of promotional publicity than Kitchener, and may indeed have been responsible for a directive which 'instructed' the Neptune Film Co. to make a recruiting film on the Royal Naval Division (in which he had taken a great personal interest). But the senior admirals, including Lord Fisher, the First Sea Lord, and Sir John Jellicoe, Commander-in-Chief of the Grand Fleet, were just as uncomfortable as the Secretary of State for War with the whole idea of film propaganda.[16]

Service obstructiveness, indeed, could extend beyond a refusal to grant facilities. Even in the context of the super-patriotic commercial films of 1914–15, there is evidence to suggest that the War Office and Admiralty were distrustful enough of the trade to ask the British Board of Film Censors – the industry watchdog body formed a few years earlier which had been given official standing for the duration and solicited the opinion of the services in doubtful cases – to ban some commercial products either on security grounds or because in their view there were 'scenes holding up the King's uniform to contempt or ridicule'.[17] To propagandists working in other departments it was clear that to many at the War Office and Admiralty the cinema was still akin to the mass-circulation yellow press and just as nasty: 'a sort of moving edition of the "Penny Dreadful"'.[18]

By the start of the second year of war, it was clear even to some senior figures in the services that, as the propagandists and the film trade had claimed would be the case, stonewalling on film publicity was doing more harm than good. In neutral countries the strength and might of the enemy was being driven home by the images presented in exported film footage. At home the number of volunteers for the new armies was beginning to decline, while the shroud of secrecy surrounding the fleet had rendered it all but invisible. After prolonged negotiations with representatives from Wellington House and the film manufacturers' association, the Admiralty and the War Office separately agreed in the autumn of 1915 to terms under which selected cameramen would be allowed to visit and take footage of the BEF and the Grand Fleet for propaganda purposes.[19]

This was a significant development. It did not, however, imply a whole-hearted conversion of the service Establishment to the propaganda cause. Sir Arthur Balfour, the highly cultured Tory statesman appointed to succeed Churchill as First Lord of the Admiralty in May 1915, and Sir Henry Jackson, the orthodox admiral he in turn appointed First Sea Lord, had accepted that film could produce impressive images after being shown prewar footage of ships at sea by Charles Urban (head of the Wellington House cinema committee) in the late summer and autumn: quite possibly the first time either man had actually viewed a film. Balfour had in turn persuaded Jellicoe to allow a camera crew to visit the Grand Fleet. The First Lord, however, made it clear that he shared Jellicoe's distaste at having to participate in what amounted to mass advertising. Admiral Jackson, after putting his signature to the document allowing filming of the Grand Fleet to proceed, said: 'Take it away. I don't agree with any of it, though I have signed it!'[20] The War Office, meanwhile, in coming to an agreement with the Kinematograph Trade Association for filming on the Western Front, managed to delay the public appearance of films involving the BEF by insisting on an unnecessarily convoluted and time-consuming vetting process.[21] After agreements had been reached to allow filming, the task of day-to-day liaison with filmmakers was given over to censors working in the military or naval intelligence branch. These were officers whose prime function was to maintain security rather than to generate publicity, as numerous complaints from the press were already demonstrating.[22]

Nevertheless, by the last months of 1915 the way had been paved for films to be made of the services at war. In early October a three-man camera team under the direction of Charles Urban travelled up to Invergordon to take footage of the fleet, and in early November two trade cameramen were made official War Office kinematographers and set off for BEF Headquarters in France.

The quality of the resulting footage was not always very good. Quite apart from the limits imposed on what could and could not be filmed on security grounds, cameramen faced daunting technical problems in trying to shoot the services in action.[23] Enough quality footage emerged, however, for Wellington House and the manufacturer's association to produce full-length war documentary features of considerable visual power. Both *Britain Prepared* (in which the fleet played a central part) and *The Battle of the Somme* (chronicling the start of the first great offensive of the new armies on the Western Front) were both striking enough at the time to make both the Admiralty and the War Office adopt – up to a point – a more positive attitude towards film propaganda.

Britain Prepared was the first to reach audiences, premiering in London at the end of 1915 and going on general release in February 1916. Wellington House had been planning from the start to make a full-length film involving the navy, and its camera team had begun work earlier than the official cameramen in France. At a fairly late stage it was decided to incorporate footage of munitions workers supplied by Vickers and shots of troops in training at Aldershot. Projecting the power and majesty of the Royal Navy, however, remained at the heart of the enterprise.

Despite security difficulties and technical problems Urban had managed to capture scenes of submarines, minesweepers, and above all battleships ploughing through rough seas, and take footage – shot from another ship sailing astern – of the battleship HMS *Queen Elizabeth* firing her 15-inch guns broadside. Both the C-in-C Grand Fleet and the First Lord of the Admiralty were impressed enough to put aside their prejudices. Admiral Jellicoe 'threw himself into [the making of the film] heart and soul', and Balfour, though admitting that he found himself 'in rather unaccustomed surroundings', spoke to the audience at the first public showing about his commitment to the film. '[S]uch representations as you are about to see, which I have done my individual best to further, will do much in this, as in other countries, to put the great operations of the war that are now going on in their true perspective. The world has yet to know, and it does not yet know, how much it owes to the British Fleet.'[24]

Endorsement at this level meant that a galaxy of influential politicians, admirals, and others turned up for the premiere at the Empire Music Hall,

Leicester Square, on 29 December 1915. After a successful six-week run at the Empire, the film was booked at over a hundred cinemas around the nation.[25] The press was unstinting in its praise. In the *Evening News* it was described as 'marvellous, wonderful, stupendous, magnificent', while *The Times* labelled it 'the finest thing ever produced in this country'.[26] The sheer length of *Britain Prepared* – over three and a half hours with minimal titles – may have made the culminating scenes of the Grand Fleet at sea, especially the *Queen Elizabeth* firing, all the more impressive. 'I saw public shows of this film several times and noted the reaction of the audiences', Lucy Masterman, wife of Wellington House chief Charles Masterman, later wrote. 'The interest in the military half was lively, the applause enthusiastic. But there was a different quality in the deep roar that greeted the features of the naval section.'[27]

The Battle of the Somme was slower to develop but ultimately even more striking in its effects. In negotiating with the War Office for cameramen to be allowed to film the BEF at work, the film manufacturers' association committee had been thinking in terms of newsreels rather than long features. The success of *Britain Prepared*, however, combined with the patchy quality of the short topical films produced in early 1916, led both the committee and some sections of the military to think in terms of a full-length documentary. The opportunity came in the wake of the opening of the great British offensive on the Somme at the start of July 1916. As much by circumstance as design, the two official cameramen in France at the time, Geoffrey Malins (formerly with Clarendon Co.) and J. B. McDowell (formerly of British & Colonial), had been in a position to take some impressive footage. This included shots of artillery in action, elements of the 29th and 7th divisions moving up, and various facets of the actual attack of 1 July. The explosion of a giant mine, activity in front-line trenches, the killed and wounded of both sides, and even a sequence of soldiers getting hit as they scrambled 'over the top' had been captured on film. On seeing the results the trade committee, in particular the chairman, William Jury (head of his own exhibition company), realized that they had in their hands the makings of a major feature.[28]

The War Office was in turn impressed by the imagery of the full-length film (one hour and seventeen minutes long) Jury and his colleagues had assembled in less than a month. Sir Reginald Brade, who as Permanent Secretary had played a major role in the negotiations surrounding the dispatch of cameramen to France in the first place, proved willing to renegotiate the War Office share of profits in a way that enabled the trade committee more effectively to distribute the finished product. The censoring of images and the creation of titles by GHQ and the War Office was carried out quite expeditiously and with minimal interference. The new Secretary of State for War, David Lloyd George, issued a special public statement of support.[29]

Opening in London at thirty-four cinemas in the third week of August 1916, and then a week later around the country, *Battle of the Somme* was a huge success. Thousands upon thousands of people queued to see the film in its opening week, breaking box office records, with many still being turned away. The same thing later happened elsewhere, and the film was still being booked and drawing audiences in London into the autumn of 1917.[30] There were very few who did not share the view expressed in *The Times* that *Battle of the Somme* gave 'a glimpse not merely of the horrors of war but also of its glories'. King George V, after seeing the film in early September, stated that 'the public should see these pictures [so] that they may have some idea of what the Army is doing, and what it means'.[31] The public did so *en masse*, sharing the satisfaction of the *Manchester Guardian* in seeing 'the real thing at last'.[32]

Going to the cinema was by now more popular than ever. By 1917 weekly attendance at well over 4000 cinemas was up to twenty million.[33] The War Office and Admiralty, like the rest of the Establishment becoming aware of the extent to which popular support for the war could no longer be assumed, could not but be impressed by what was emerging as 'the most powerful agent for publicity now in existence'.[34]

In November 1916 the War Office set up a three-man cinema propaganda section, the War Office Cinematograph Committee, and disbanded the trade committee. Though this did not mean, as some thought, that the military authorities had taken matters entirely 'into their own hands' – the trade was still involved in the processing and distribution of official films and William Jury, chairman of the old trade committee, was a member of the new triumvirate – it did herald a more activist approach by the War Office.[35] The presence on the committee of the Sir Reginald Brade, the Permanent Secretary, was one indicator of the higher profile cinema a now enjoyed in Whitehall. Another was the choice of chairman: Sir Max Aitken, the Canadian financier, Unionist MP and temporary lieutenant-colonel who had successfully organized film and other publicity for the Canadian Corps.[36] The official cameramen seem to have begun to receive more direction from the War Office, while BEF headquarters passed the word down to unit commanders to cooperate in the making of films when called upon to do so.[37]

In January 1917 a new battle film, compiled from footage taken in the autumn of 1916, was put on general release with the rather cumbersome title *Battle of the Ancre and the Advance of the Tanks*. The War Office cinema committee evidently decided that the new film should adhere as closely as possible to the first hugely successful effort. In form and content as well as length, *Battle of the Ancre* was very much a *Battle of the Somme* sequel. Apart from shots of the first British tanks – thought to be of enough public interest to include in the title though making up only a fraction of the total film – most of the scenes, including men going over the top, were variations on themes already established.[38] Once more the public flocked into the cinemas and once more critics were impressed by the realism. According to the *Daily Mail* it was 'all real, all unrehearsed', and gave a more 'complete and coherent picture' of events than the earlier film.[39] Six months later a third feature-length film appeared: *The German Retreat and the Battle of Arras*. There were variations on by now standard themes, but the film's lineage was clear enough. It was also a critical and public success, the *Evening News* calling it 'the greatest war picture yet produced'.[40]

The Admiralty was rather slower to exploit the great success achieved with *Britain Prepared*. It did, however, allow footage of the fleet to be taken for the five-part film *Sons of Our Empire* (released in April 1917), and shortly thereafter merged its cinematic efforts with those of the War Office. Sir Graham Greene, the permanent secretary at the Admiralty, became in May 1917 the fourth member of the committee chaired by Max Aitken (elevated to the peerage as Lord Beaverbrook at the end of 1916).[41]

In bureaucratic terms, therefore, film propaganda had established a definite presence within the services by the summer of 1917. As trade and public interest in long films waned, more emphasis was placed on the sponsorship of newsreels and short documentaries focusing on specific units and tasks. Production of the latter type of film became regular, dozens of them appearing in the last year of the war. The messages being conveyed were not always subtle – especially in the naval films – but service interest seemed to have finally come of age.[42]

Old habits, however, died hard. The film industry continued to feel that those responsible for film propaganda – both at the War Office and Admiralty and at the Department of Information that had replaced Wellington House in February 1917 – lacked a true appreciation of the propaganda possibilities of commercial films. An editorial in the *Cinema News and Property Gazette* published in August 1917 complained that:

> our hidebound officials, bursting with a sense of their own dignity and self-importance, and imbued with pre-war – that is to say pre-historic – theories about what is and what is not worthy of consideration, when they are not openly sneering at 'the pictures', still maintain a semi-condescending attitude towards a new-fangled invention.[43]

The red tape encountered by filmmakers was in large part due to the lack of coordination in film propaganda work.[44] But there were also specific problems with the services.

In France, the GHQ Intelligence Department, under Brigadier-General Sir John Charteris, refused to countenance any simplification of the cumbersome vetting process for film taken on the Western Front (involving dual censorship by GHQ and the War Office). Meanwhile, as one Admiralty supporter was forced to conclude, it was clear that 'the Navy did not want publicity'.[45] Certainly neither Sir Eric Geddes (First Lord since July 1917) nor Admiral Sir Rosslyn Wemyss (First Sea Lord since late December 1917) proved particularly keen in 1918 to support the making of a major new naval film as Beaverbrook was suggesting.[46]

The end result was delay and frustration, even when some form of official consent for a film was forthcoming. *Hearts of the World*, a full-length fictional drama produced and directed by D. W. Griffith about the effect of the war on life in a French village, was so fraught with overlapping and conflicting departmental interests – including those of the War Office – that it took fourteen months to reach the screen. Equally problematic was *The National Film*, sponsored by the National War Aims Committee, which dealt with a fictional German occupation of Chester. The sheer scale and complexity of the project (which involved among other things obtaining permission to use British troops to act the part of the Prussian occupiers), along with a disastrous fire which destroyed the first version, meant that the film, initiated in the autumn of 1917, was not completed until after the war had ended a year later. Hugely expensive, it was not released and the negatives eventually destroyed on the grounds that in the postwar environment the plot was too anti-German.[47] As for the new feature-length documentary on the navy, with the support of Admiral Sir David Beatty, commanding the Grand Fleet, it did eventually get made: but was not ready for release under the title *Rule Britannia* until after the fighting had ended in November 1918.[48]

There were thus still very real limits to the services' commitment to film propaganda in the latter part of the First World War. The outbreak of peace, moreover, brought with it a return of the prewar distaste for both popular propaganda and film. With national mobilization and neutral opinion no longer at issue, propaganda appeared both redundant and – in the context of traditional liberal values – rather un-English. The Ministry of Information and other wartime bureaucracies associated with either domestic or foreign propaganda were quickly dismantled.[49]

No tears were shed over this within the senior ranks of the armed forces. Admiral (retd) Douglas Brownrigg, the chief naval censor and the closest thing to a publicity officer, in reflecting on his wartime work and the postwar navy, concluded:

> The attitude of the Navy towards publicity was very slow to change, and I think I can say to-day [1920] with a perfectly clear mind that, though the officers of the Navy may grudgingly agree that some measure of publicity is an absolute necessity, since the Fleet belongs to nation (i.e. the public) and not to the Navy, they thoroughly detest it.[50]

There was certainly no sense that the services themselves might still have a role in shaping such publicity. With the end of official censorship, the services severely reduced or eliminated their publicity machinery, those involved with film production either retiring or moving on to more traditional intelligence work. In the late 1920s the Information Section at the War Office, C6, consisted of a single civil servant with one assistant, as did the Press Section of the Air Ministry (the RAF having been created as a separate service in 1917). The Admiralty dispensed with a separate office altogether, making do throughout the interwar period with 'one passed-over Commander in NID [Naval Intelligence Directorate]', as a later Chief of Naval Information trenchantly put it.[51] This was symptomatic of a broader trend. Within both the army and navy, and even the air force, attitudes and behaviour in the 1920s were often more evocative of the Edwardian era than of the wartime period of mass mobilization.[52]

This left matters very much in the hands of the commercial film industry in the immediate postwar years; an industry that continued to find it profitable to produce adventures, dramas, and occasional comedies with characters in uniform. Most appear to have been made without service cooperation. Assistance was provided by the army and navy for a series of quite popular documentaries made by British Instructional Films on the battles of the Great War.[53] The navy, in addition, allowed Astra-National Productions to film ships as a backdrop to the 1926 version of *The Flag Lieutenant*, an imperial adventure-drama play by W. P. Drury and Leo Tover first filmed back in 1919. The Admiralty, however, was suspicious enough of what it distastefully termed 'the "romantic" type of film' (i.e. fictional plots) to insist on complete veto power. The relevant contract clauses indicate the extent to which negative control might be exercised.

> 3. The Admiralty or any authorised Officer appointed by them, shall at all times have the right of censorship in every case and no copy of any film disapproved of shall at any time be exhibited without the special approval of the Admiralty in writing. The negatives and all copies of any film so disapproved of shall if so required be handed over to the Admiralty and shall thereupon become the property of the Admiralty.

4. Prior to the exhibition of the film it shall be exhibited before Officers to be nominated by the Admiralty for the purpose and any alterations required by them to be made to the film or to the titling shall be made by the Company at their own expense. The film in its final form shall before public exhibition be submitted to the Admiralty for approval and it shall not be exhibited in public unless and until the approval of the Admiralty shall be communicated to the Company in writing.[54]

Even with these restrictions, however, sentiment was strongly against extending naval facilities for non-documentary films. By 1926 there were 3000 cinemas in operation in Britain, and it was recognized that it was the fictional film which had a truly 'wide appeal'. But the very popularity of 'the pictures' made them suspect in the minds of social conservatives. In 1927 the Board of the Admiralty was informed that 'there was strong feeling in the Fleet against using Naval personnel and material to supply a background for romantic films', and decided that in future no support should be extended.[55]

This was evidently the policy followed throughout the 1920s by the army.[56] Even the new Royal Air Force, dangerously unorthodox in terms of its officer training and structure in the eyes of generals and admirals, did little to utilize the feature film as a medium of publicity. Though keen to prevent the service from becoming 'mere chauffeurs for the army and navy',[57] senior RAF figures such as Air Marshal Sir Hugh Trenchard, the Chief of Air Staff, were at the same time anxious to establish legitimacy in reference to the older services. Hence the RAF selectively adopted existing social traditions. Dining-in nights and formal parades were for officers to be 'affairs of gentlemanly ritual and elegance', complete with dress uniforms modelled on those of the Edwardian age. Both the Boer War era uniforms and the recruit training of Other Ranks were copied from the army.[58] Thus, though willing to develop its own versions of traditional service self-promotion in the form of the annual Hendon Air Pageant as well as gymnastic and other public displays, the Air Ministry did not embrace feature film propaganda.[59]

In 1922, a year in which the future of the RAF was in doubt due to budget cuts and hostility from the army and above all the navy, the obscure promotional film *The Eyes of the Army* appeared. Taken on manoeuvres, this film was apparently designed to show that the air force was still willing to cooperate with the other services.[60] The RAF's only foray into commercial films in the 1920s came five years later in the making of *The Flight Commander*. This Gaumont feature, directed by Maurice Elvey and starring Sir Alan Cobham, the famous long-distance flier, dealt with the foiling of an attack on a British outpost in China by the bombing of a village: a none-too-subtle allusion to the kind of air control practised in Iraq. Despite the staging of the bombing scene at the Hendon Air Pageant amid much fanfare, *The Flight Commander* did not attract much public attention.[61]

This very limited output was not accidental. Film companies continued to approach the RAF with scenarios and requests for cooperation. But as one Air Ministry official put it to another in looking back on the latter 1920s, 'the Air Council are jealous of the reputation of the RAF and, as you are aware, no one has yet succeeded in satisfying their requirements'.[62]

In the following decade, however, things began to change in all three services with regard to feature film propaganda. The growing social acceptability of filmgoing among the middle classes, combined with booming attendance figures among the working classes, made the publicity value of the pictures – above all the sound-era features which drew in the crowds – harder to discount. The number of cinema tickets sold rose year by year: 903 million in 1934; 907 million in 1935; 917 million in 1936; 946 million in 1937; 987 million in 1938; and 990 million in 1939 – by which point an estimated 23 million people were going to the pictures each week.[63] Cinemas proliferated as Odeon and other chains opened dozens of new suburban 'dream palaces'. In 1935 there were 4448 cinemas in operation. By 1938 there were 4967.[64] Though still deplored by intellectuals, going to the pictures had unquestionably become the dominant social habit of the age.[65]

At the same time the anti-militarist sentiment of the late 1920s and early to mid 1930s made it clear that the services could no longer count on unquestioning public support. The Great War, in all its horror and apparent futility, had dealt a severe blow to traditional patriotic sentiment. In the first decade after the war people had tried to forget; now, as new conflicts began to loom, pacifistic sentiment replaced jingoism. These were the years in which plays such as *Journey's End* and books such as *Goodbye to All That* appeared, the Peace Pledge Union rose to prominence, and the National Peace Ballot – affirming support for international disarmament efforts – attracted over eleven million supporters. Meanwhile the major political parties competed with one another to demonstrate their anti-warmonger credentials. The armed forces, in short, were no longer popular: a sign of the times being the sharp decline in the number of films with plots involving the services.[66]

The navy was the first to act in trying to boost its public image in the 1930s through the feature film. Though still in many ways tradition-bound and suspicious of popular representation, the Admiralty could not entirely ignore signs of declining public support. In 1928 a petty and very public dispute between senior officers aboard the battleship *Royal Oak* made the navy look 'extremely foolish'.[67] Then came the Invergordon Mutiny of 1931, sparked by pay cuts, which had a definite negative effect on both the navy's image and its ability to attract quality recruits for the lower deck.[68] Hence, despite the standing policy against supporting 'romantic' films, the Board of the Admiralty in practice began – cautiously and on a case-by-case basis – to extend facilities to film companies that appeared to offer good propaganda value.

The first crack in the Admiralty edifice came in connection with *The Middle Watch*, a comedy made by British International Pictures at Elstree in 1930 based on a hit play written by Ian Hay and Stephen King-Hall. The plot ('Captain tries to hide accidental female passengers from Admiral') might not have appealed to the more sober-sided admirals; [69] but both the authors of the play, from a service point of view, possessed a good pedigree. Ian Hay (the pseudonym of John Beith) had won the MC and later been involved in wartime publicity, while Stephen King-Hall had served with distinction and risen to the rank of commander before leaving the navy to write. In any event, 'the only facilities given were for the photography of incidents in a ship's normal routine, and no film artists were allowed on board for filming purposes'.[70]

British International next asked the Admiralty if it would lend a hand in the making of *Men Like These*, a drama based on the story of HM submarine *Poseidon*, sunk in a collision with a Chinese merchant vessel in June 1931. P. C. Stapleton, the company's general manager, pointed out that the film would be good for the Royal Navy's image at a time when Hollywood was heavily promoting the United States Navy. 'We have detailed with some care', he wrote in connection with a request for permission to shoot British submarines diving, cruising, and surfacing, 'the facilities which would enable us to include in our picture a display of Naval power, and make the picture useful from the point of view of showing ... something of a Navy which is not American'.[71] In return for this, use of a test tank at Portsmouth for underwater shooting and the loan of parts from old L-class submarines to create a control room in the studio, BIP agreed to the Admiralty's decision that the story be made fictional and to its unconditional right to censor the finished product as it saw fit. Everything was covered in the contract. 'The Company shall be responsible', clause eight read in part, 'that if Naval uniform is worn by any of their employees in the production of this film, the uniforms when worn shall be complete and correct.'[72] There were no less than three naval advisors to make sure. (Captain K. Bruce, Lieutenant-Commander John L. F. Hunt and Lieutenant-Commander E. V. Hume-Spry.)[73] The film, detailing the escape efforts and general heroism of the crew of submarine 'L 56', appeared in November 1931.

Next came a request from British and Dominions Film Corporation to use some of the naval scenes from the 1926 production in a 1932 remake of *The Flag Lieutenant*. A representative of the Directorate of Naval Intelligence noted that the silent version had been popular, 'and could be considered as good propaganda in keeping the Navy before the public'. The First Lord agreed. 'I observe that in favour of granting this request the argument is used of the value of good propaganda', minuted Sir Bolton Monsell. 'With that I am strongly in sympathy.'[74]

Not all within the navy were so well disposed. Contractual complications concerning the Admiralty's fee for the 1926 version of *The Flag Lieutenant* had by 1932 produced an embarrassingly public court case. The judge commented: 'There is something to me very sordid in that our great ships and our sailors should be used for purposes of this sort.'[75] Within the Fleet many officers also felt that 'the making of romantic films is not in keeping with the dignity of the Navy'; there was a definite fear that scenes of ships at sea would be mixed in with 'silly or sentimental situations'. Reviewing the situation in June 1932, the Board of the Admiralty 'confirmed the previous decision against the encouragement of romantic films'.[76]

Nevertheless it was recognized that in peacetime film companies could take as much footage as they liked of HM ships from the shore or hired boats,[77] and permission to use the existing film taken with Admiralty approval was granted. Thus *The Flag Lieutenant* (which the Admiralty kept an eye on through their naval adviser, Commander F. W. Gleed,[78] and vetted before its release) joined *Men Like These* and *The Middle Watch* as a showcase for the navy. *The Middle Watch*, released in December 1930, was a success. 'Adapted to the film,' the *Times* critic wrote, 'this farce is no less amusing than it was on the stage. Indeed, its fun has now been heightened by a veracious but unobtrusive naval background.'[79] *Men Like These*, which appeared the following year, was also praised. The *Daily Telegraph* film critic, G. A. Atkinson, found that RN cooperation had allowed for a film of breathtaking spectacle. P. L. Mannock, writing in the *Daily Herald*, reported that the director had 'reconstructed with terrifying realism' what it must be like to be trapped in a submarine. *The Times* noted that 'every detail has a convincing air of accuracy'. Opinion on the acting was mixed; but even Ewart Hodgson of the *Daily Express* allowed that 'From a technical standpoint *Men Like These* is a superb piece of talkie making'.[80] Both the new version of *The Flag Lieutenant* and *The Middle Watch* were big enough hits with the public to be re-released some years later.[81]

The public, indeed, appeared much more willing to accept a fictitious 'romantic' plot than the kind of straightforward propaganda film with which some on the Board of Admiralty were more comfortable. When the promotional documentary *Our Fighting Navy* was released in September 1933,

it generated sporadic demonstrations from peace activists, in marked contrast to the earlier commercial features.[82]

The success of the exceptions, however, only highlighted the fact that
there was still an official ban on helping with 'romantic' films, and in late
1933 Viscount Lee of Fareham, Vice-President of Gaumont-British, wrote
to the Admiralty emphasizing the advantages of a more cooperative policy.
His main argument was that

> the case for an adequate navy needs to be kept prominently before the present
> and the rising generation, whose sympathies have to be aroused before their
> support can be counted upon. There are few ways in which this can be done
> more effectively than by the wide circulation of Naval Films which are sufficiently
> entertaining or exciting and which yet present a reasonably true and creditable
> background of life aboard His Majesty's Ships, whether in peace or war.

The Director of Naval Intelligence, conscious of the way in which a close
relationship with Hollywood, combined with the popularity of American
films, gave the US Navy a higher profile than the Royal Navy, recommended
to the Board of the Admiralty that 'the present restrictions on romantic
films should be withdrawn'. There were, however, still plenty of senior
officers opposed to this. The Commander-in-Chief Mediterranean, Admiral
Sir William Fisher, for example, argued that ships' companies had better
things to do with their time than help make 'frivolous or fantastic' films,
and thought that it was 'by no means certain that public opinion would
support the view that it is desirable for the Navy to be advertised and
exploited by means of the cinematograph'.[83] The ever-cautious Board
decided at the end of November 1933 to continue the current ad hoc
arrangements, with the Admiralty considering applications on a case-by-case
basis.

Viscount Lee's argument, however, was not entirely made in vain. The
Board also agreed that 'without binding themselves to future policy in this
matter, the Admiralty are prepared to give sympathetic consideration to
the facilities required by the Gaumont British Picture Corporation for the
Naval story that they have in view ... provided that Naval personnel is [sic]
not to be used to an undue extent or in an objectionable manner'.[84] Over
the following months terms were negotiated for full-scale RN support in
the making of the film version of the 1929 C. S. Forester novel Brown on
Resolution.[85]

This was the tale of young Leading Seaman Albert Brown, who, after his
cruiser is sunk by a German raider in the opening days of the Great War,
manages to delay repairs to the Zeithen at Resolution Island in the Galapagos
chain long enough to allow heavy units of the Fleet to catch up and destroy

it. The Admiralty liked the story. It involved individual heroism and self-sacrifice – Brown is eventually killed – as well as sea fights in which ships and men 'engaged the enemy more closely'. Best of all, the hero was an enthusiastic member of the lower deck at a time when the authorities were still having trouble recruiting enough young men. Brown could serve as a role model, while the film as a whole could showcase some of the navy's impressive-looking warships.

Having taken the plunge, there were practically no limits to what the navy would supply once the script had been approved; despite the fact that, as the director, Walter Forde, put it, 'a film unit aboard ship is better calculated to get in the way of normal ship routine than anything I can think of'.[86] Four fully crewed warships, suitably disguised to resemble vessels of 1914, were placed at his disposal: HMS *Broke*, a flotilla leader, the cruisers HMS *Neptune* and HMS *Curacoa*, and, most impressive of all, the old battleship HMS *Iron Duke* (now a gunnery training vessel). Scenes were shot at Invergordon and Rosyth, Plymouth and Portsmouth, as well as at sea along the Cornish coast, where Gull Rock stood in for Resolution Island. Facilities were also made available for shooting at the boys training establishment, Gosport, and at the gunnery school at Whale Island. Captain (retd) R. W. Wilkinson acted as naval adviser on what actor John Mills, who played the part of Brown, thought was 'the largest and most expensive production ever tackled by a British studio'.[87] As before, however, a contract was drawn up which gave the Admiralty full power to censor the finished product.[88]

Brown on Resolution, which included in its main titles a dedication 'To the Lower Deck of the Royal Navy', premiered at the New Gallery Cinema on 12 May 1935 to a distinguished audience that included the First Lord, Viscount Monsell, and several admirals. Its release coincided with a visit by warships of the Home Fleet to the Thames estuary. The film was a great success.[89] The critics also generally liked it. To Paul Holt of the *Daily Express* it was 'a simple, stirring tale of English patriotism'. R. J. Whitley, writing in the *Daily Mirror*, concurred: 'a simple story of a British sailor's heroism against odds'. *The Times* critic thought it 'displays a fine sense of naval drama', while Campbell Dixon in the *Daily Telegraph* wrote of 'brilliant battle scenes' and a 'high patriotic note'. In the *Spectator* the film was called 'unusually exciting because most of the details are unusually realistic'.[90] It was still playing at the time of the Silver Jubilee naval review in July – in which the *Iron Duke* participated – and was reissued, under the title *Forever England*, in 1941.[91]

The last major feature film in which the Admiralty took an interest that appeared before the start of the Second World War was a conventional romantic melodrama with the working title *The Navy Eternal*.[92] Sponsored by the Navy League and eventually given the same title as an earlier documentary, *Our Fighting Navy*, a Herbert Wilcox production, premiered in April 1937. It was written by 'Bartimeus' (the pseudonym of Lewis da Costa Ricci), known for his patriotic tales celebrating the traditions of the Royal Navy.[93] The plot revolved around an RN cruiser captain's efforts to use his ship, HMS '*Audacious*', to protect British nationals – in particular the pretty daughter of the British consul – during a revolt in 'Bianco', a fictional Latin American country; efforts which culminate in a successful gun duel with a rebel battleship. *Our Fighting Navy* struck critics as a rather juvenile affair, only partially saved from ludicrousness – the opening night audience broke into titters at various points – by the background presence of a real RN light cruiser (HMS *Curacoa*), a battleship (HMS *Royal Oak*), and thirteen other craft lent by the Admiralty (many of them featured at the coronation review the following month).[94] 'If this is primarily a recruiting film,' Guy Morgan concluded in the *Express*, 'then the slogan of the Admiralty should be "Join the Navy and marry a consul's daughter"'. Even a trade critic had to admit that 'In many ways the film is schoolboy stuff – the plot is naïve and the scene of much of the action [Bianco] is reminiscent of comic opera'. Yet as *The Times* put it, 'so long as the battleships are on the move and in action they are the heroes, and most impressive ones too when they are allowed to play their part'. Even the *Manchester Guardian* critic, who hated it, admitted that in reference to 'the main object of the film', which was 'to enhance an adventure story with the traditional spirit of the navy at work', *Our Fighting Navy* 'succeeds'. Campbell Dixon summed the matter up well in the *Telegraph*. 'To say that it is a good picture would be insincere', he concluded. 'It is, on the other hand, a picture that will be thoroughly enjoyed by a great many people, and as such it amply justifies its existence, and all the enterprise, private and public, lavished on it.'[95]

Success breeds confidence, and in the summer of 1939 the Admiralty cooperated in the making of two more commercial productions. *Sons of the Sea*, a British Consolidated Pictures colour production directed by Maurice Elvey and starring Leslie Banks, was a spy melodrama in which Dartmouth Naval College served as a backdrop. 'With its topically appealing title,' as the reviewer for *Today's Cinema* put it, 'its surge of espionage incident, its stirring angles of filial devotion and its panoramic backgrounds of cadets on parade performing this or that manoeuvre, the development has all the essentials which make for popular success.' Publicity material for the film stressed that *Sons of the Sea* was 'Made with full Admiralty Co-operation'.[96] The other film, *All at Sea*, a British Lion feature, was a slapstick comedy starring Sandy Powell as a bumbling chemical factory employee who accidentally joins the navy and foils unscrupulous villains out to steal a secret formula aboard HMS '*Terrific*'. British Lion made sure that the public knew that *All at Sea*, re-released in 1944, was 'produced with the full co-operation of the Admiralty.'[97] The reviews were again favourable. 'In addition to the bland hilarities of Sandy Powell,' *Today's Cinema* noted, 'this truly British picture has the advantage of authentic naval atmosphere and settings.'[98]

The War Office, meanwhile, was slower off the mark than the Admiralty in exploiting commercial feature films to boost its image, being content to allow Colonel (retd) J. C. Hanna of the British Board of Film Censors to make sure that films 'holding up the King's uniform to ridicule or contempt' were altered.[99] Thus, for example, when First National Pictures was in the process of scripting *Hail and Farewell*, a comedy based around a real incident in which a battalion returning from service overseas was dispatched abroad again within forty-eight hours, it was the BBFC rather than the War Office which intervened to make clearer the distinctions between officers and NCOs, substitute a fake regiment for the real one, and generally made sure that good order and discipline were portrayed as per King's Regulations.[100] Nevertheless by the mid 1930s the section of the Adjutant-General's branch responsible for publicity and recruiting, AG10, had also begun to recognize that, both to counteract the prevailing anti-militarism within society and in order to attract recruits, it would be a good idea to involve itself more actively with the film industry. In 1937, as the War Office prepared to coordinate its press and publicity efforts under a new Directorate of Public Relations, three films were made with full Army Council cooperation.[101]

The first was *OHMS*, a Gaumont-British feature. This was directed by an American, Raoul Walsh, who had scored a great success in 1926 with *What Price Glory?*, a film that had helped boost recruiting for the US Marine Corps.[102] *OHMS* starred another American, Wallace Ford, and featured John Mills in a reprise of his *Brown on Resolution* lower-middle-class persona. The plot involved an American fugitive who joins the British Army and dies a hero when his battalion ('1st Wessex Regiment') saves civilians under attack by 'bandits' in the British consulate at 'Kang Loo', China. 'As the character I was portraying,' Wallace Ford wrote after the film was completed, 'I had to rebel against discipline, but in the end gain a tremendous respect for the regulations and a love for England.'[103] The army's contribution came primarily in the form of 10,000 troops filmed in training and on parade at Aldershot.[104] Interestingly, the BBFC seems to have been overruled in relation to the usual complaints about military detail, the War Office perhaps realizing that a degree of artistic latitude had to be allowed in order to make the film commercially appealing.[105]

OHMS received a gala premiere at the Tivoli Theatre on 20 January 1937. In attendance were a galaxy of War Office luminaries, including the Secretary of State for War, Duff Cooper, Field-Marshal Sir Cyril Deverell (Chief of the Imperial General Staff), General Sir Harry Knox (Adjutant-General), Lieutenant-General Sir Reginald May (Quartermaster-General), Lieutenant-General Sir Hugh Ellis (Master-General of Ordnance), Sir Victor Warrender (Financial Secretary) and Sir Herbert Creedy (Permanent Under Secretary).[106] Though some critics accused Gaumont-British of propagandizing a false view of army life, most accepted that War Office participation had given the film greater authenticity.

'The co-operation of the Army Council in British picture making has been a long time coming,' *Kinematograph Weekly* commented, 'but, having broken the red tape, its members have done all that is humanly possible to invest the story atmosphere with realism.' *Film Weekly* concurred, arguing that the great strength of the film was 'the reality with which it captures and interprets the life of the barrack-rooms, the regimental concert parties, the sergeant-major's parlour'. *The Times* was also impressed by the apparent realism of it all.

> Too often films which purport to give a picture of Army life only succeed in grotesquely distorting it, but here the Army is seen not only in action against Chinese bandits but going about its routine work in the barracks and on the parade ground. Some of the shots taken of a march past the saluting base arouse a not unmilitaristic feeling of pride in watching soldiers march as soldiers should. And, once the parade is over, listening to soldiers talk as soldiers do.

The *Manchester Guardian* was somewhat less enthusiastic, but admitted that 'the military background is authentic'.[107] *OHMS* was indeed 'recruiting propaganda', both the regular and Territorial army taking advantage of its appearance to launch recruiting drives. The film undoubtedly gave a rather glossed-over image of life in the ranks; but it was successful enough as both entertainment and as a recruiting tool be re-issued five years later.[108]

Next came *The Gap*, a General Film Distributors effort only thirty-eight minutes long. Released in April 1937 with the official sanction of the Army Council and Air Council, and with technical advice from Lieutenant-Colonel J. K. Dunlop, secretary of the Territorial Army Joint Publicity and Recruiting Committee, this 'Official Air Defence Film' was a semi-documentary which sought to 'show what might happen in the event of a hostile air raid over England, owing to the gap in Britain's air defence caused by the shortage of territorials in the ground defence sections'.[109] Rather heavy-handed and inept as propaganda, the film did not much impress either the critics or the cinema-going public. 'It falls badly between the two stools of straight documentary and fiction with a moral', *Film Weekly* complained. 'The dialogue is stilted, and there is a naïve British embarrassment over handling anything so raucous as propaganda, which prevents the picture from coming to grips with its subject.' Even *The Times* thought it had problems.[110]

Rather more successful was another full-length dramatic feature, *Farewell Again*, a London Films production under Erich Pommer which appeared in May 1937. This was a new, romance-drama version of the story that had inspired *Hail and Farewell*, this time written by Wolfgang Wilhelm. Costing ten times as much as the earlier version, it involved the '23rd Royal Lancers' *en route* from India via the Mediterranean aboard a troopship, and the trials and tribulations of various officers and men with their wives and sweethearts before and during the six precious hours they have at Southampton before setting off again for Aden. As well as location shooting at Gilbraltar and Malta of the troopship *Somersetshire* – in which the Admiralty and Air Ministry also lent a hand in allowing a camera crew to film the troopship at sea from a destroyer and from an aircraft – the War Office sent elements of the Horse, Grenadier and Coldstream Guards, and other units, to act as extras at Denham Studios where dockside scenes were being recreated under the direction of Tim Whelan.[111]

Thanks to a good script and a strong cast as well as the help of the military authorities, *Farewell Again* was clearly meant to emphasize the twin themes of patriotism and imperial duty which played so great a role in almost all the prewar feature films sponsored by the War Office (and indeed the Admiralty). The centrepiece of the pressbook issued for the film succinctly laid out the main message the War Office was trying to convey:

> All over the world, wherever the Union Jack is flown, men from castle and cottage, from city and village, are on duty protecting and policing the Empire – soldiers not of War but of Peace.
>
> Some have their families with them but many serve year after year facing hardship – and danger – death – with only brief glimpses of home.
>
> Each has his own joys and sorrows, but a common purpose unites them all –
>
> THEIR COUNTRY'S SERVICE

Thanks to the help provided by the services, good writing and direction, and a strong cast that included Leslie Banks, Flora Robson and a young Robert Newton, *Farewell Again* was a hit. 'A dramatic and realistic story', was the verdict of the *Monthly Film Bulletin* critic from the British Film Institute. '*Farewell Again* is a moving tribute to the men who serve in the British Army and as a production is an outstanding achievement.' The reviews in the popular press were equally enthusiastic. 'Its rich human quality, with its many echoes of active service, make it something to appeal to the heart of every British filmgoer', enthused the *Daily Mail* critic. 'Brings you laughter, tears and at times a choking sensation', was the verdict of the *Daily Sketch*. 'This is one of those pictures', concluded the *Daily Mirror*, 'which means queues at the nation's cinemas.' [112] Campbell Dixon, writing in the *Daily Telegraph*, noted that:

> Without undue flag-wagging the sentiment is British – 100 per cent British – perhaps because the thing was written by Wolfgang Wilhelm, directed by an American, Tim Whelan, under the supervision of a German, Erich Pommer, at studios controlled by a Hungarian, Alexander Korda.

All in all it was 'first-class entertainment' – a view shared even by those critics who recognised that they were being manipulated. 'Critical investigation finds that there are no cads in a British regiment', an amused but sympathetic Paul Holt noted, 'and that the colonel is a mother to his men.' Kenneth Allot, writing for the *Spectator*, thought it 'a regimental *Grand Hotel*, slices of comedy and tragedy in the terms of the newspaper, militarism without tears or only warm, sympathetic ones. But the film is not deadly. Call it sentimental and absurd, and then add that there is much to admire.' [113] Territorial Army units were not slow to see the recruiting potential in cooperating with local exhibitors in helping publicize the film. *Farewell Again* was reissued twice, once in 1942 and again in 1944.[114]

The final two major features with which the War Office was involved before the Second World War, both by made by Korda's London Films, heavily reinforced the image of the British Army as imperial policeman already expressed in *OHMS* and *Farewell Again*. In the spring of 1938 permission was given to Alexander Korda to use troops as extras on location in India for *The Drum*. Then in 1939 British and local troops stationed in the Sudan were allowed to serve as extras in Korda's biggest imperial extravaganza, a film version of the novel *The Four Feathers*, set around the Battle of Omdurman.[115] Though the implicit racism of both caused problems abroad – *The Drum* and *The Four Feathers* had to be banned in India and the Sudan respectively[116] – they were liked by the generals and were a success with the public at home. *The Drum*, with its contemporary setting, allowed Territorial Army units to tie in their recruiting efforts with the exhibition of the film in local cinemas. Both pictures were reissued twice in the 1940s.[117]

The War Office also thought it worthwhile in 1939 to grant permission to film scenes at RMA Sandhurst for Butcher Films' *Sword of Honour*, in which a cadet proves that he is not a coward. Released in May 1939, *Sword of Honour* was successful enough to encourage Elvey to switch locations and use Darmouth Naval College for *Sons of the Sea*. The War Office was pleased. 'The military parts', M. V. O. Verney of the Directorate of Public Relations wrote, 'are very good indeed.' [118]

The Royal Air Force, perhaps because it obtained the lion's share of resources during the rearmament efforts of the 1930s and was already receiving a good deal of publicity through newsreel footage of the Hendon air pageants, was the last of the services to involve itself in feature films. There were, to be sure, recruiting films, such as John Bettes' fifty-minute *RAF* (Gaumont-British Instructional, 1935), in which were covered 'many incidents in the life of members of the RAF, from the time they enter until they take charge of aircraft'. Training scenes, 'practice flights, formation flying, parachute descents, and bombing in this country, at sea and abroad' were also depicted to a musical background played by the RAF Central Band.[119] The Royal Air Force was also involved in staged air defence documentaries such as *The Gap* (1937) and *The Warning* (1939) – the latter 'a grim and effective piece of propaganda' according to the *Monthly Film Bulletin*.[120] But it was only in 1937–38 that the Air Ministry – after a ten-year hiatus – allowed RAF personnel and machines to be involved in a commercial feature.

The renewed interest in commercial film propaganda arose from the deliberations of a special ministry committee set up by the Air Minister, Lord Swinton, in January 1937 under the chairmanship of Sir Donald Banks, Permanent Under Secretary at the Air Ministry, to conduct a major review of RAF publicity. The aim of publicity, the committee reported, ought to be threefold:

(a) Maintenance of the prestige of the RAF as an efficient instrument of defence

(b) Recruitment

(c) Make the public 'air-minded'

To achieve these objectives the committee recommended the expansion of the Press Section at the Air Ministry into a full-fledged Press and Publicity Branch. There were many specific recommendations beyond mere reorganization and expansion of the RAF publicity apparatus, one of the most significant relating to feature film propaganda. 'We are of the opinion that the use of films,' the Banks Committee stated, 'which are of ever-growing importance and influence, reaching the vast masses of the people at home and overseas, should be extended beyond the present activities, which with rare exceptions have been confined to news reel subjects.' [121]

In point of fact the RAF was involved in new features even before the Banks Committee first met. And though it took many months for the administrative recommendations of the report to be implemented – the framework for a Directorate of Public Relations was only in place by the outbreak of war – the policy recommendations concerning commercial films certainly helped spur efforts to provide support for a larger-scale effort the following year.[122]

Interestingly, two of the three commercial features in which the RAF took an interest in the latter 1930s – *Splinters in the Air* (1937) and *It's in the Air* (1939) – were both comedies; a form of cinematic entertainment the other services, especially the army, appeared to dislike.[123] Quite why the comedy film should become the preferred vehicle for RAF feature film publicity is unclear. It may simply have been that the commercial production companies had concluded that air subjects in an adventure-drama format were box office poison. Alexander Korda, for example, head of London Films, had lost money on the futuristic *Things to Come* and even more on a feature about the development of flight entitled *Conquest of the Air* in the mid 1930s. It was about this time that the British production arm of MGM apparently terminated a project entitled *Shadow of the Wing*.[124] It also seems possible, however, in light of the recruiting efforts built around the release of *Splinters in the Air* (January 1937) and especially *It's in the Air* (January 1939), that the Air Ministry thought that music-hall style comedy – one of the most popular types of British film in the 1930s [125] – would reach a wider audience, especially the young men of modest background whom the RAF needed for ground duties as it expanded.[126]

Splinters in the Air, a Herbert Wilcox production starring veteran stage and screen comic Syd Howard, was about the difficulties faced by a helicopter inventor who takes the place of his twin brother in the RAF and eventually saves the CO's wife from a cad. It was set in an RAF depot, for which the Air Ministry allowed Wilcox to film at RAF Northolt.[127]

Rather more ambitious was *It's in the Air*, a George Formby vehicle produced by Basil Dean for Associated Talking Pictures. This also centred on a case of mistaken identity, George taking the place of an RAF dispatch rider, creating havoc at an RAF airfield, and inadvertently becoming a reluctant test pilot. The Air Ministry put the men and machines of an RAF station – probably Halton – at the disposal of director Anthony Kimmins, formerly a lieutenant-commander in the Fleet Air Arm. The result was a film in which, aside from George's antics, a few jibes at NCOs, and a few ukulele-accompanied songs, the RAF was shown in a generally positive light, at work and play, on the ground and in the air, for sixty-odd minutes. Perhaps not coincidentally the biplane aircraft featured were not the latest RAF machines. But the uniforms were both contemporary and flattering. Every aircraftsman was shown either in the smart open-neck tunic with collar-and-tie plus forage cap uniform adopted in 1936 – the outfit worn by George being especially form-fitting – similar to that worn by officers, or in spotless white overalls.[128] Combined with scenes of canteen relaxation this helped to reinforce the idea that service in the ranks of the RAF was not the humiliating experience commonly attributed to service in, say, the army. The extent to which the Air Ministry saw this film as an important publicity vehicle was evident at the premiere at the New Gallery Cinema on 16 January 1939, where members of the Air Council, the RAF Central Band, a contingent of airmen from RAF Uxbridge and sundry Air Ministry officials all turned out. When *It's in the Air* went on general release, arrangements were made for the RAF to help publicize the film. In London alone the Air Ministry contributed to foyer displays in eighty-three cinemas.[129] Though Princess Margaret loved it, not everyone thought that this was a particularly dignified way for the RAF to attract publicity. But *It's in the Air* was a major commercial success, topping the charts in February 1939 and being reissued twice thereafter.[130]

The third project in which the Air Ministry took an interest was *Spies of the Air*, an espionage thriller directed by David Macdonald for British National. Spy films were very much in vogue as war approached, and the RAF agreed to lend a hand by allowing some of its aircraft to be filmed from a commercial plane. *Spies of the Air*, however, was overshadowed at the time of its release in March 1939 by a rival, *Q Planes*, which used only commercial aircraft but featured a better-known cast.[131] This was undoubtedly disappointing for all concerned, but RAF involvement was another indication that the Air Ministry was starting to take cinema seriously.

All three services, to sum up, had in the course of the 1930s learned the value for recruiting and general publicity purposes of cooperating with the commercial film industry in the making of feature films. This did not mean that the Admiralty, War Office, or Air Ministry always helped in the making of all the films in which they were featured. Indeed, the number of films where there was no evident cooperation outnumbered those where there was over two-to-one.[132] Nor did it mean that class-based suspicion of 'the pictures' had completely disappeared, as we shall see. It did mean, though, that elements within the services were taking an active interest, which in turn affected their attitude to film propaganda once the Second World War began in September 1939.

In theory all wartime cinematic propaganda was to be handled through the films division of a new Ministry of Information (MoI), planning for which began in the latter 1930s.[133] However, like other major departments with interests to defend, the Admiralty, War Office, and Air Ministry were not about to allow control over cinematic propaganda to pass entirely out of their hands. Even as the wartime MoI was being organized the service ministries, on the basis of the need for censorship, made sure that their

officers – albeit usually on the retired list – were earmarked to represent
the service interest in the new organization.[134] All three, moreover, took
advantage of the difficulties experienced by the Ministry of Information in
its first fifteen months of existence (a lack of coherence in policy, producing
press and parliamentary criticism, followed by a fairly rapid turnover in
senior personnel) to buttress their own authority.[135] The service ministries
maintained their own separate censorship and public relations sections,
guarding them jealously against any threat of subordination or amalgama-
tion.[136] The MoI, to be sure, eventually overcame its internal problems and
began to take a firmer grip on state propaganda, especially once Brendan
Bracken became Minister of Information in the summer of 1941. Jack
Beddington, for example, as head of the films division, would exert considerable influence on the film trade through his consultative 'ideas
committee'.[137] The services, though, continued to control access to their
facilities, thus providing the security and publicity sections in most cases
with de facto control over the films on service themes that either they
themselves, the commercial trade, or the films division of the MoI wanted
to see made. Moreover, the air force and army developed their own film
production units, partly at least as a counter to the growing influence of
the MoI's Crown Film Unit.[138] What all this meant in practice was that,
while the Ministry of Information was almost always a player in the making
or distribution of feature films, the views and actions of the Admiralty,
War Office and Air Ministry were of crucial importance in projects involving
the armed forces. Some features would come about at the suggestion of
the films division of the MoI, some through initiatives of film companies,
and others by way of the service ministries themselves. The fact remained,
however, that no film involving the army, navy or air force was made
without at least the tacit consent – more usually the active support – of
the relevant ministry. The manner in which they sought to influence popular
perceptions of the air force, navy, and army under wartime conditions
forms the subject of the next three chapters.

2

On Target: The Royal Air Force
and Feature Films, 1939–1945

As Neville Chamberlain mournfully announced over the wireless in the first week of September 1939 that Britain was once more at war with Germany, the immediate public concern was not what was likely to happen either at sea or on land, but rather what would happen in the air. As the possibility of a new war began to loom in the 1930s, public attention had increasingly focused on the growing range and power of aircraft. Would a future war, as was popularly supposed, involve mass aerial bombardment of cities and produce casualties and destruction on such as scale as to cause a general collapse? Could anything be done to defend against such an attack?

Air power theorists such as Giulio Douhet thought not. H. G. Wells suggested that air raids would cause civilization to collapse – an apocalyptic vision translated with graphic effectiveness onto the screen in the 1936 Alexander Korda production, *Things to Come.* Stanley Baldwin, prime minister in the mid 1930s, had gloomily told parliament that the bomber would always get through. The bombing of Guernica during the Spanish Civil War only heightened public anxiety. Was the RAF strong enough to deter or fend off German air assaults? The sounding of the air raid sirens within minutes of the outbreak of war was in fact a false alarm. But it was an ominous portent that did nothing to allay popular anxiety about the war in the air. Though no serious Luftwaffe attacks on Britain occurred in subsequent weeks, news of the German bombing of Warsaw kept public anxiety in Britain very much alive into the autumn of 1939. Despite the creation of Air Raid Precautions and other civil defence organizations, as well as the expansion of the RAF in the latter 1930s, anxiety remained. Was the country ready for aerial warfare? [1]

It was this concern which led to the first wartime feature film to focus on the Royal Air Force. The new Ministry of Information was too disorganized at this stage to serve as the brainchild of such a film. But even before the war began the flamboyant Hungarian émigré film mogul, Alexander Korda, urged on by Winston Churchill (a great film fan who had worked as an adviser and writer for London Films in the mid 1930s), had been thinking of making a patriotic feature film to reassure the public that Britain was ready in the skies. Once war began Korda approached the director-designate of the MoI films division, Sir Joseph Ball, who in turn contacted the Air Ministry. There the propaganda possibilities of such a film were recognized at once and full RAF support offered. Ian Dalrymple, an associate producer, later recalled the beginnings of what eventually became *The Lion Has Wings*.

> A few days before 3 September, some of us working at the Denham Studios – a fortuitous gaggle of directors and writers of various ages and origins, all of sadly unbellicose aspect – were summoned to Alex's office. He told us that we were to make a film to reassure the public of the power of the Royal Air Force, and that a liaison officer from the Air Ministry was on his way to assist us.[2]

The central aim of the film was 'to reassure the British public they weren't all going to be blown to pieces in five minutes: the Royal Air Force would prevent it'.[3]

With Ian Dalrymple acting as coordinator, various directors were assigned to shoot footage of Bomber Command, Fighter Command, and various staged sequences (the actors and actresses, all from the Korda stable, playing virtually for free as a public service). According to Dalrymple, there were no overt attempts by the authorities to shape the content of the picture. Squadron-Leader H. M. S. Wright, the Air Ministry liaison officer, however, always pointed Michael Powell, who took charge of many of the flying sequences, in the direction the RAF felt presented the force to best advantage. Powell was given an airborne tour of the Balloon Barrage around London, escorted round RAF aerodromes, and generally treated as a VIP. Parts from a surplus Wellington bomber and a Spitfire were provided to make studio mock-ups (the interiors suitably modified to preserve security), and Powell allowed to talk with aircrew and others. The only thing that he was not allowed to do was accompany a 149 Squadron crew from Mildenhall in a Wellington bomber to film a raid on German warships in the Kiel Canal on the second day of the war.[4]

With all concerned working at breakneck speed, old footage was combined with newly shot sequences to create a full-length feature that was part documentary and part action-drama. Seventy-six minutes long, *The Lion Has Wings* opens with a series of documentary sequences, narrated over by the familiar voice of E. V. H. Emmett of Gaumont-British News, contrasting the British way of life (peaceful, fun-loving, and progressive) with that of the Nazis (militaristic, regimented and destructive). Hitler's broken promises from 1933 onward are covered down to the occupation of Prague in March 1939, followed by a staged sequence recalling Britain's confrontation with Imperial Germany over the violation of Belgian neutrality in 1914. According to the film this was the point at which 'Britain awoke'.

Since it was clear that Hitler 'aimed at dominating the whole of Europe', and that 'Britain must defend her freedom once again', then 'Britain must be strong'. *The Lion Has Wings* then turns to examine the state of Britain's armed forces. The senior service came first, with shots of majestic battleships steaming line-ahead. 'Britain's navy in 1939', the narrator confidently asserts, 'was still the greatest navy the world had ever known.' The focus then quickly switches to the British Army, with footage of the Trooping of the Colour and references to the glorious traditions of the British soldier followed by shots of light tanks, infantry carriers and artillery to reinforce the claim that 'modern mechanization' was in full swing. But these references to the army and navy, and indeed the 'road to war' sequence, were only a prelude to the main business of the film: the power of the Royal Air Force.

Over footage of Hawker biplanes taken on the ground and in the air during the 1937 Hendon air pageant, it was admitted that, while the pictures were a bit out of date (they had in fact been taken for the aborted MGM film *Shadow of the Wing*),[5] 'since that time the air force has expanded into the magnificent force that it is today. Once again, second to none, ready for anything, no matter how difficult and dangerous.' After more Hendon footage and further references to the skill of pilots and ground staff, the scene switches to aircraft and armament factories. Quality, Emmett asserts as scenes of Hurricane fighters being assembled are shown, is the hallmark of British aircraft production. Wellingtons, shown on the factory floor, 'carry a formidable weight of bombs for an immense distance at high speed'. Britain's anti-aircraft guns are modern, while the huge number of bombs already manufactured are destined 'not for defenceless towns, not to break the morale of the civilian population, but for military and naval objectives'.

The plot then shifts to the main fictional characters, Ralph Richardson as an RAF Wing Commander and Merle Oberon as his wife, introduced briefly in the Hendon sequences and now seen reacting with a mixture of sorrow and stiff upper-lip determination to Neville Chamberlain's wireless announcement that war has broken out.

Merle Oberon: 'Darling, are we ready?'

Ralph Richardson: 'D'you mean are we prepared? We've never been better prepared!'

After further documentary footage of the German invasion of Poland and references to enemy frightfulness, the scene shifts to documentary footage of Wellingtons dispersed amid trees. 'Behind every hedgerow,' the narration continues, 'a battleship of the sky stood ready: massive, forbidding, deadly.

The symbol of modern power.' Then follows a mixture of staged and
documentary sequences in which the Air Ministry passes down the chain
of command orders for Wellingtons at 'Great Milton' aerodrome to launch
the Kiel Raid. Through a mixture of documentary and staged sequences
the plot then focuses on a fictional Wellington, captained by Anthony
Bushell, involved in the attack. Skilful editing of British and old German
documentary footage shows a low-level attack in which bombs explode on
an enemy warship, followed by a German fighter attack (with Spitfires and
Fairy Battle light bombers standing in for Messerschmitts) which is beaten
off by the Wellington's nose and tail machine gunners. There are then
scenes of the bombers returning to base. 'It was an epic of the skies,' Emmett
concludes, 'carried out with brilliant skill and matchless courage.' Once
more documentary footage, this time of real RAF aircrew climbing out of
their Wellingtons, is shown. 'And though you have been watching a
reconstruction of the raid upon the Kiel Canal,' Emmett then intones, 'the
men you now see stepping out of those bombers are the officers and men
of the RAF who actually carried out that heroic raid.' The clear implication
is that the staged sequences comprise an accurate representation of what
happened on the actual raid of 4 September 1939 (though in reality the
Wellingtons had accomplished little).[6]

Bomber Command, then, is ready to strike hard at military targets. But
as both the Air Ministry and Korda's production team knew, what concerned people the most was what German bombers might do to English
cities. Hence the final and most sustained segment of *The Lion Has Wings*
deals with a fictional German night air assault on London and how it is
utterly defeated by Fighter Command without a single bomb falling on the
capital.

Forewarned of the attack by an intelligence source and listening posts –
radar was far too secret to mention in public – 'Southern Group Command'
plots the route of the German bombers and orders '299 Squadron' Spitfires
from 'Brackstead Fighter Station', where Ralph Richardson supervises the
control room, to intercept the first raid. Footage of Spitfires taken at RAF
Hornchurch is followed by shots of nonchalant actors – plus Squadron-
Leader Wright[7] – in studio Spitfire cockpits and dastardly types in mock-up
enemy bomber cockpits ('anything would do for them,' Powell later
recalled),[8] interspersed with old footage of Fairy Battles and German
Condors, were combined to show two of the first enemy raiders being shot
down and the rest driven off. The second raid, subject to attack by AA
guns and another flight of Spitfires, also suffers losses and is forced to flee.
The third set of raiders reaches the outskirts of London; but, confronted
by a Balloon Barrage which apparently makes accurate bombing impossible,

they also turn for home, with Spitfires of '301 Squadron' in hot pursuit. The message was clear: Britain was indeed prepared for war in the air.

Viewed in retrospect, *The Lion Has Wings* seems rather crude and embarrassingly naïve. 'It was a ghastly, bloody film', documentary director Harry Watt asserted; a view which observers have tended to endorse to a greater or lesser degree ever since. Even Michael Powell, who was partly responsible for the final product, conceded in his memoirs that 'It was a hodgepodge'.[9] The idea that bombers could be turned back by barrage balloons – or easily intercepted at night – was soon rendered patently ridiculous by London's experience of German bombing in the 1940–41 Blitz. Even at the time the film was released, as a Mass-Observer noted, the point at which Richardson emphatically claims that 'we've never been better prepared' could draw an audible – and highly uncomplimentary – response from the audience.[10] The widespread use of bits from other films, including Korda's own 1937 Elizabethan epic *Fire Over England* and *The Gap* (see chapter 1), also struck some observers as jarring and incongruous. The staged scenes, furthermore, portrayed the RAF as relentlessly clean-cut and upper middle-class in outlook, with Anthony Bushell using first names with the officers but last names with the Other Ranks among his Wellington crew and Ralph Richardson talking of 'damned good chaps on this station'. As a member of the RAF asked rhetorically in a letter to *Picturegoer*, 'why do all the British pilots and crews appear as strong, healthy young men and the Germans as bearded [*sic*], tough-looking brutes?'[11] At the time it was released the last words of dialogue, spoken by Merle Oberon – 'truth and beauty and fair play and … kindliness' – struck Graham Greene and several other reviewers as ridiculously Public Schoolish and woolly. 'As a statement of war aims,' he noted in an oft-quoted review in the *Spectator*, 'one feels, this leaves the world beyond Roedean still expectant.'[12]

What needs to be borne in mind, however, is the generally positive reception *The Lion Has Wings* received when it was first released in late October 1939. The Air Ministry and Ministry of Information lent public support to the film, with Sir Kingsley Wood (Secretary of State for Air) attending the premiere at a Leicester Square theatre, *The Times* devoting a leader to the film, and the MoI making it known that the King and Queen had attended a public screening – the first film George VI had visited since his accession in 1936 – and reportedly 'enjoyed the performance very much'.[13] Aware that the film was propaganda, and recognizing its flaws, critics and public alike saw it as a laudable patriotic gesture and were consequently supportive.[14]

What was more, it was the scenes of air force bombers and fighters at work which tended to elicit most praise and – bearing in mind that they had not yet been seriously put to the test – widespread acceptance as a true picture of the RAF at war. This was as true of the quality broadsheets as it was of the trade and popular press. *Today's Cinema* claimed that 'the film provides enthralling entertainment – it lifts the veil on much of the secrecy which has surrounded the capabilities of our bombers and fighters and anti-aircraft defences'. 'The suspense of the raids is brilliantly sustained', a reader's review in *Picturegoer* enthused. Paul Holt, writing for the *Daily Express*, found the scenes depicting Britain's air defences at work 'of absorbing interest' and was stirred by the Kiel Raid portion of the film. *The Times* reviewer noted the 'wealth of detail' shown in the Kiel Raid scenes, and was even more enthusiastic about the 'exciting' Fighter Command denouement. The *Manchester Guardian* film critic agreed that 'the raid on the Kiel Canal and a partly [*sic*] imaginary German air raid on Britain' were both 'enthrallingly produced'. Campbell Dixon in the *Daily Telegraph* noted that the flying and control room sequences 'seem remarkably convincing and complete', the Kiel Raid sequence in particular being 'a marvel of realism'. As the *Yorkshire Post* concluded in describing 'a most impressive combination of documentary and fictional film production', in *The Lion Has Wings* it was the Royal Air Force, not any actor, that was 'the real hero'.[15]

In the context of its time, therefore, *The Lion Has Wings* was a great public relations success for the RAF, as well as being a money-maker for Korda and the government (which, in return for Air Ministry assistance, received 50 per cent of the profits). With local RAF units lending a hand in local cinema promotional campaigns, it topped attendance charts when it opened in November, and went on to become the second-highest grossing film of the year. The film also helped the Allied cause when it was shown in the United States. In all *The Lion Has Wings* appears to have generated over £50,000 in profits.[16]

This promising start, however, was not followed up with any alacrity. It would be almost two years before another feature film would be made with full Air Ministry cooperation. This was in part the natural consequence of a dramatically changing war situation. In the summer of 1940 German forces swept westward, knocking France out of the war and placing Britain itself in grave peril. The RAF, scrambling to try and help stem the tide of German conquest on the Continent and then defend Britain itself from aerial attack, had little time or energy to spare for the making of propaganda features. Furthermore, with the strategic situation changing so rapidly, who knew whether or not the assumptions underlying any such feature might be rendered obsolete by the time the film was released?

The fate of *Squadron 922*, a short drama-documentary made by Harry Watt of the GPO film unit in the winter of 1939–40, was instructive. The

AOC Balloon Command, Air Vice-Marshal O. T. Boyd, wanted him to make a film that would boost the flagging morale of the bored men under his command. With Boyd's help, Watt used real RAF personnel and Blenheim bombers (standing in for the Luftwaffe with appropriate changes in markings) to reconstruct an enemy air raid that had taken place near the Forth Bridge in Scotland. The action, as Boyd had envisioned, focused on the work of a balloon squadron in turning back the enemy raiders.[17] When the film was first shown to an official audience at the beginning of May 1940 at the Odeon Leicester Square, it was judged a success. By the time arrangements had been made for the general release of *Squadron 922*, however, the Phoney War had ended and its message of reassurance rendered obsolete. As the film critic of the *Manchester Guardian* put it, if the film 'had been given a general release soon after it was shown to the Cabinet and the press it would almost certainly have outranked *The Lion Has Wings* as a propaganda picture'. The delay, however, meant that it had 'lost urgency and even relevance', 'so completely have events changed the picture into which it was designed to fit'. As the director later put it, *Squadron 922* had simply become 'out of date', and rapidly sank without trace.[18]

The changing war situation, however, along with the urgency of combat operations, cannot fully explain the continuation of a hiatus in support for film propaganda into early 1941 (by which time the Blitz had rendered the propaganda message of *The Lion Has Wings* completely null and void). A combination of technical difficulties, official suspicion, and red tape difficulties created obstructions which propagandists both inside and outside the Air Ministry found difficult to overcome.

Though filming from the ground was not a problem, the added weight and space taken up by camera crews, along with the problems of filming at night inside the mostly small and cramped twin-engined aircraft available, made the taking of aerial footage a technical challenge that took time to overcome.[19] There was, moreover, little incentive to make much of an effort within the senior ranks of the RAF, where as often as not propaganda in all forms was still regarded as 'a cheapjack charlatan game' with which Officers and Gentlemen should not be associated.[20]

As the British Hollywood actor David Niven discovered when he tried to enlist in the RAF after returning to Britain in the autumn of 1939, just as *The Lion Has Wings* was appearing, the cinema and those associated with it were still regarded with extreme distaste in some quarters.

> I was directed to the office of a certain Group Captain [at the Air Ministry].
> Unfortunately, I was swept into it on the crest of a giggling wave of secretaries, clutching pieces of paper and pencils.

The man restored order and eyed me with distaste. He knew who I was. Unless he had been blind he couldn't have avoided it. Nevertheless, he went through the motions of asking my name and occupation and what I wanted to do.

When I told him, he pursed his lips, sucked in some breath with a whistling sound and shook his head.

'Ever heard of Wilfrid Lawson [an eccentric character actor]?'

'Yes ... he's a wonderful actor.'

"Maybe ... we took him on and we've had trouble, nothing but trouble, ever since ... Drink.'

I said, 'Look – all sorts of people drink, but I've come seven thousand miles at my own expense and I'd like to join the RAF.'

'So I've read [in the press],' he said nastily, 'but we don't encourage actors to join *this* service.'

Niven was understandably very angry; and his was not a unique experience.[21]

Harry Watt, in making *Squadron 922*, was struck by the contrast between the enthusiasm of Air Vice-Marshal Boyd and the apathy of the Air Ministry, where the value of film publicity was clearly still not appreciated in the winter of 1939–40.[22] Moreover, though a Directorate of Public Relations was created within the Air Ministry in May 1940 under the command of Air Commodore H. Peake, many senior officers of the RAF continued to be suspicious of publicity in general and film in particular into 1941. 'The fundamental defect from which all others spring', noted Air Vice-Marshal Richard Peck (the Assistant Chief of Air Staff responsible for publicity matters) in a May 1941 memorandum, 'is the old-fashioned attitude within the Services and in Whitehall towards "propaganda" and publicity. Officers generally regard it as unsoldierly and distasteful'.[23]

As always, security concerns could be cited as reasons to avoid cooperating on publicity and propaganda ventures. In September 1940, for example, Air Marshal Sir Arthur Harris, commanding 5 Group, had complained to Bomber Command HQ that 'much mischief has already been done by giving away valuable information to the enemy at the expense of our war effort and to the lives of our crews to make snappy photographs for the gutter press'.[24]

The creation of the Directorate of Public Relations, moreover, made it impossible for those inside or outside the RAF to engage in the kind of impromptu partnership that Boyd and Watt had forged in the making of *Squadron 922*. As the official historian of the DPR later recounted, the red tape involved in making a feature film with even minimal RAF support was quite substantial by 1941.[25] The hypothetical chain of events recounted in the official history – by no means unusually complicated – is worth reproducing in full to illustrate the extent of the red tape involved.

A film producing company writes in to say that they are engaged on a picture in which one of the characters is an RAF Officer. Practically the whole of the film will be shot in the studio but they require facilities to obtain a brief 'establishing' shot of the actor stepping into an aircraft.

The first step is to advise the company that the Air Ministry cannot grant any facilities for the production of a film until it has been sanctioned by the MoI. No action is therefore taken until the MoI's written approval has been forwarded to PR1 [the film division of the Directorate of Public Relations].

Next, the company are asked to forward a complete script of the film in order that the Air Ministry may be satisfied that there is no objection to it on the grounds of Security, Suitability, or Policy, PR1 read the script and circulate it for comments to AI6 [Intelligence] and PR4 [security] after which the company are advised if any deletions or alterations are necessary.

Any special equipment required by the actor has to be obtained from a Maintenance Unit but uniforms can be hired direct by the company from one of the recognised theatrical costumiers. A point that arises here, however, is that no uniform could be hired during the war without the special sanction of the Provost Marshal. PR1 therefore apply to the PM explaining the reason for the request and the permit is issued together with a list of special conditions governing the use and custody of the uniform.

The company are then asked to name a tentative date a few days ahead for the filming to take place and PR1 pass the request on to the Command concerned who finally agree a date with a suitable RAF Station. PR1 then asked PR9 [facilities and permits] to issue passes covering the entry on to the Station of the actor and necessary camera crew. A hitch arises when it is discovered that one of the cameramen does not appear on the Approved List; the Company therefore have to make a formal application for his name to be inserted on the list but, as the special security investigation into the man's history takes some weeks to complete his place in the camera crew is taken by another approved technician.

Finally, the film detachment arrives at the Station which is about 100 miles from London. They are met by the Command PRO who regretfully has to inform them that the filming must be postponed to a later date. The reason is that a maximum operational effort has been ordered and the Station Commander cannot spare the personnel or aircraft for filming; the film people cannot be told this, of course, and they return to London somewhat disgruntled.

Arrangements are made through Command and PR9 for another visit to be made a few days later. On this occasion they are admitted to the Station and the necessary aircraft is produced; unfortunately, however, the weather is bad and the light is so poor, photographically, that the Director refuses to shoot. The Station personnel who think the visibility is good enough for flying and should therefore be good enough for filming, wonder why the film company does not get on with the job. Luckily, overnight accommodation is secured nearby and telephone arrangements made between the PRO and PR1 for the passes to be extended; the following morning the necessary shots are obtained.

Nine months later the film is completed; the airfield shot shows for some five seconds.[26]

All this was undoubtedly both daunting and frustrating for commercial companies.

The Air Ministry, to be fair, gave its full support to the making of a *March of Time* eighteen-minute documentary on 'Britain's RAF' in the autumn of 1940. But this was in the context of strong pressure from both the MoI and Foreign Office to help in the task of shaping US public opinion (*The March of Time* was an American monthly film news magazine).[27] Domestic filmmakers usually found their requests for cooperation were either refused on security grounds or became mired in red tape. 'I am personally prepared to supply in detail, to anybody who is interested', Michael Balcon, head of production at Ealing Studios, bitterly noted in a piece for the leading trade weekly, 'particulars of RAF facilities applied for by this company which have either been refused or ignored.'[28] This may or may not have been a fair assessment in light of the security and other concerns with which the air force had to grapple. There was no doubt, though, that it produced frustration.

The problems surrounding the making of a film about the RAF's recent triumph in the Battle of Britain were a case in point. Ealing Studios in the autumn of 1940 explored the possibility of an air force drama to match the success of its recent navy film, *Convoy*. The delays and other difficulties Balcon experienced in trying to obtain facilities from the RAF, combined with a report from Mass-Observation which questioned whether people would respond to such a film, led to the abandonment of the project.[29] Twentieth Century Fox then announced at the beginning of 1941 that Carol Reed was to direct a feature entitled '*Spitfire*' at Shepherd's Bush studios. 'The story centres round the activities of a typical defence squadron of the RAF,' the press release explained, 'the members of which have been drawn from all parts of the British Empire.' Despite early Air Ministry support, nothing came of this.[30] At the same time producers George King and John Stafford took up the task by building a story around the career of the designer of the Spitfire, R. J. Mitchell. This film also ran into problems. The project, first announced in the trade press in December 1940, got off to a good start in January 1941 when permission was obtained from the Prime Minister, Winston Churchill, to paraphrase his famous tribute to Fighter Command in the film's title, *The First of the Few*. It was to be made by British Aviation Pictures, with a script by Miles Malleson based on an original story by Henry C. James. Three months later, however, a report in *Kinematograph Weekly* suggested that the producers were trying to excuse delays by making the filmmaking itself into a symbol of patriotism.

> *The First of the Few* is claimed to be the most inspiring film yet conceived by any producer, and the production of such a film at this time cannot be measured in mere terms of commercial enterprise. Rather, and as well, it is a work of the greatest possible value to the national effort, because of its inspiring theme, and the inspiration and encouragement it will afford to every man and woman engaged in the war effort.[31]

It was not until October 1941, however, that the publicity arm of British Aviation Pictures – with the production and direction both now being undertaken by Leslie Howard and starring David Niven as well as Howard himself – was able to report that scenes taken of Spitfires (from 501 Squadron) landing and taking off, a staged aerial dogfight between Spitfires and a captured He–111 (flown by 1426 Enemy Aircraft Flight), and of RAF pilots in staged outdoor scenes, had been completed.[32] Further shooting at Denham Studios meant that it was not until August 1942, almost two years after its inception, that *The First of the Few,* appeared in cinemas.

Luckily for all concerned *The First of the Few,* though somewhat less topical than would have been the case if it had appeared earlier, was a huge success with critics and public alike. The film opens and closes with staged sequences of about seven minutes each in which real Spitfire pilots are shown landing, chatting – in a rather stilted manner – and taking off again to engage the Luftwaffe during the Battle of Britain. The central plot, though, was a heavily reworked account of the career of R. J. Mitchell – played by Leslie Howard – as narrated to the pilot actors by David Niven, finally in RAF uniform while playing an RAF Station Commander who just happened to have been Mitchell's chief test pilot. In the hands of Leslie Howard – an actor of Hungarian extraction who had built his career playing fey intellectuals of gentle charm – the Mitchell saga became quintessentially English: the story of a modest genius who overcomes inertia and indifference in time to save the country by creating an artistic as well as technical masterpiece, the Spitfire, just before he dies. With a musical score written by William Walton and a cast in which Leslie Howard was ably backed up by Rosamund John as well as David Niven, and blending melodrama with semi-documentary footage, *The First of the Few* was an instant success. With hindsight it is easy to see that a lot of artistic licence – not to say outright fabrication – was taken in portraying R. J. Mitchell and his work, and the switches between semi-documentary scenes at the RAF airfield and the conventional drama on the soundstage appear far from seamless. In the summer of 1942, however, it was often taken to be the genuine article.

The First of the Few was 'a tribute and a record true', according to the *Daily Herald*. The *Daily Express* critic argued that 'officers and men of the RAF pep up the cast to actuality, and the result is a superb picture, inspiring and real'.[33] Trade reports as well as Mass-Observation and other surveys confirm that *The First of the Few* was one of the most popular films of the year.[34]

The long gestation period involved in the making of *The First of the Few* meant that by the time it was released Air Ministry attention had passed definitively from Fighter Command to other aspects of the air war – above all the strategic air offensive and Bomber Command.

Success in the Battle of Britain had meant that Hitler could not invade in 1940 and that the war would go on into 1941. Happily for the RAF, whose *raison d'être* as a separate force rested on the efficacy of strategic bombing, the collapse of France and Hitler's mastery of the Continent meant that over the winter of 1940–41 only Bomber Command possessed the means to strike back at the enemy. 'We must therefore develop the power to carry an ever-increasing volume of explosives to Germany,' Churchill informed his War Cabinet colleagues in early September 1940, 'so as to pulverise the entire industry and scientific structure on which the war effort and economic life of the enemy depend ... In no other way at present can we hope to overcome the immense military power of Germany'.[35] Thus encouraged, Bomber Command continued to launch dozens of attacks against a wide range of industrial and other centres – particularly those associated with oil production – during the winter months and on into the spring of 1941.[36]

Actions without words – and images – were not, however, nearly enough in the eyes of the DCAS(G) and members of the DPR at the Air Ministry. The work of Bomber Command, at least in comparison to the exploits of Fighter Command in the Battle of Britain, was largely invisible. Quite apart from BBC and press reports, the public knew of the successes of Spitfire and Hurricane squadrons through seeing them in the air in daylight and observing the numerous German aircraft wrecks that littered the landscape of south-east England in the autumn of 1940 (which may, in turn, partially account for the relative lack of timely support offered by the Air Ministry for domestic feature films on the subject).

Fighter Command, in short, generated its own publicity through its actions.[37] The heavy bomber squadrons of Bomber Command, however, flew mostly at night and fought beyond the horizon, and thus needed to be more actively presented before the public both in words and images. Even those, such as Air Marshal Harris, who were concerned about security and doubted the qualities of the Directorate of Public Relations could agree that the activities of Bomber Command required an 'inspiring' PR campaign to keep strategic bombing in the public eye.[38]

As early as December 1939, while *The Lion Has Wings* was still doing brisk business, Bomber Command HQ had notified Group HQs that 'full publicity should be given to our bomber operations in the fullest and most attractive light'.[39] Daily press communiqués quickly became a standard item in RAF publicity, soon joined by semi-official booklets and BBC talks celebrating wartime achievements.[40] Distrust of publicity and security fears at various headquarters, however, often limited what was passed on to the press concerning operations to the most general of statements. Visual publicity was particularly problematic. One of the best means to reinforce the message that Bomber Command was waging an effective campaign would have been to release pictures – both still and moving – taken from the air of devastated targets. The amount of photographic evidence that was released by the Air Ministry to the MoI in the winter of 1940–41, however, was very limited. Quite apart from the difficulty of acquiring suitable cameras in a period of acute shortage, senior air officers objected to requests to carry non-operational personnel – voyeuristic passengers who took up space and added weight while contributing nothing to the task at hand – on bombing raids.[41] As to the release of the flash photos taken by the bomb aimer of the target, those in the know recognized that this could do more harm than good given what such photos revealed.

Deprived of all but the most general of information and photographic evidence of air operations over Germany, the press and BBC tended to give the public what it wanted (or thought it wanted) as a counterpoint to the Blitz: news that enemy targets, not least Berlin, were being repeatedly hit hard on a large scale and to very good effect. This was a success in keeping Bomber Command in the public eye.[42] But over time problems began to develop. Month after month of optimistic reports did not seem to yield much in the way of tangible result. In particular those few target photographs released by the Air Ministry were often too unclear to support the assertions made for a particular raid. 'People were unconvinced by the material, particularly photographic,' the Ministry of Information concluded in March 1941 on the basis of its home intelligence apparatus, 'put out by the Air Ministry to prove the havoc done by the RAF.'[43] The obvious solution was to provide better photographs, and attempts were made by the DPR to obtain them from Bomber Command. Those staff officers who had regular access to such photographs, however, were not keen to release them, since this 'might produce quite the opposite effect to that expected by the Air Ministry'.[44]

The plain fact of the matter was that the successes reported in the media as normal were in fact the exception to a rule of general failure. A huge gap existed between what was being reported and what was being achieved.

A member of a heavy bomber squadron, in a far from atypical broadcast, described a September 1940 raid on Berlin in the following terms:

> We found our targets without difficulty. It was a gas-generating plant only a few miles from the centre of Berlin ... when the bombs burst, there were four huge explosions across the works ... The first four large explosions were followed by series of smaller explosions, Two huge fires started and huge tongues of flame leapt up ... then dense smoke ... The bombs had fallen about fifty yards apart. Almost immediately the fires and explosions seemed to link up and for a distance of 200 yards through the works there was this great mass of flames.
>
> Next I saw our incendiaries fall on the western edge of the plant. They take longer to get down than the heavy bombs. What part of the works they hit, I don't know, but I could see large clusters of brilliant-coloured flashes on the ground. We circled round and watched the fires blazing up. The rear gunner, I remember, shouted: 'Oh Boy, it's terrific.' [45]

This was the staple diet provided in media reports of Bomber Command operations in 1940–41: a series of accurate blows against important industrial targets.[46]

Unfortunately the reality was rather different. Though Hampden, Whitley and Wellington bombers flew hundreds of sorties over Germany in the autumn, through the winter and on into the spring, their rate of success was very small indeed. Night flying meant that the catastrophic losses of the 1939 daylight raids were avoided; but primitive navigation equipment and bad weather also meant that few aircraft actually found their targets. Journeys of many hours in unpressurised, draughty and largely unheated aircraft that were prone to icing, along with the distinct possibility of losing one's way, made for stressful flights. On one raid a Whitley had got so hopelessly lost that that it ended up bombing an RAF airfield – the crew under the impression that they were over the Third Reich. As one pilot later put it, even if navigation was successful 'in the event of cloud cover over or near the target the accuracy was pitiful'.[47] Some targets were bombed accurately, but the tendency for the crews themselves to exaggerate their success only partially masked a picture of distinct failure emerging from post-raid photos. 'As you know,' a Bomber Command HQ staff officer noted in a minute to a colleague in January 1941, 'some of the most heavily attacked targets have not shown [through photographs] any discernible damage.' [48]

What applied to still photographs would, ipso facto, apply to film. Thus while the films section (PR1) of the Directorate of Public Relations was keen 'to have more films of RAF activities presented on the Screen' in order to reinforce the message of success, what was actually happening over Germany could not be presented.[49] A suitably detailed and optimistic documentary film, however, might reassure the public that, as Churchill had told the House of Commons, 'night after night, month after month, our bomber squadrons travel far into Germany, find their targets in the darkness by the highest navigational skill, aim their attacks ... with deliberate careful precision, and inflict shattering blows upon the whole technical and warmaking structure of the Nazi power'.[50] In late 1940, therefore, either at the suggestion of director Harry Watt or – more likely – on its own initiative, the Air Ministry informed the MoI that it was 'anxious for such a film to be made as soon as possible and [lacking its own film unit at this point] would cooperate with in every way and provide the fullest facilities to the GPO Film Unit'.[51]

The original idea was for the film to trace the history of RAF Bomber Command down to the present. The central feature, however, would be to document the success of current raids. 'Night after night, in all weather conditions,' the author of the outline presented to the MoI enthused, 'our bomber squadrons rise into the sky and drone unerringly to some essential economic target in Germany.'[52] In the last weeks of 1940 the film's chosen director, Harry Watt, working under Ian Dalrymple (who headed what was transformed from the GPO Film Unit into the Crown Film Unit in January 1941), and with Flight Lieutenant Derek Twist from DPR, had undertaken some preliminary research at Bomber Command HQ (High Wycombe) and at RAF Mildenhall. After reading hundreds of post-action reports and interacting with RAF ground- and air-crew of all ranks, Watt concluded that the film ought to follow the fortunes of a single aircraft on a typical raid, with real RAF personnel acting and speaking according to a prepared script: 'the dramatising of reality'.[53] This was very much in the tradition of the documentary movement that John Grierson had pioneered, and in which Watt had worked in the 1930s within the GPO Film Unit, but was a departure from the more conventional, narrated history that the Air Ministry had in mind. Squadron Leader John Lawrence, the Public Relations Officer assigned to Bomber Command HQ, complained in a letter to Wing Commander W. T. S. Williams, head of PR1, that Watt was straying too far from his brief. Watt, however, successfully counter-argued that what was really needed was 'a prestige film of Bomber Command, not a factual resume of the long term policy'.[54]

In April 1941, script in hand, Watt and his two-man camera team travelled once more to Mildenhall to do the exterior shooting and choose a cast. In addition to a host of aircrew and groundcrew extras, Watt picked a regionally diverse crew for 'F for Freddie', to be led by Squadron Leader 'Pick' Pickard ('Dickson'). Watt also drew in the station commander, Group Captain F. J. Fogerty, as well as Wing Commander 'Speedy' Powell, 149 Squadron

CO, for briefing room and other scenes. He later even managed to persuade the Commander-in-Chief Bomber Command, Air Marshal Sir Richard Peirse, and his senior staff officer, Air Vice-Marshal Sir Robert Saundby, to play themselves briefly on a set built to resemble the operations room at High Wycombe. While at Mildenhall, Watt managed to get some good footage of Wellington Ic's flying over cloud, taking off and landing. Attempts to film the actual bombing of targets in Germany, however, ran into technical difficulties, and in the end models were used.

Having completed exterior shooting, Watt moved to sound stages at Elstree and Denham Studios to work on interior shooting. The main sets included the Bomber Command operations room, the briefing room and crew room at 'RAF Millerton', and the interior of 'F for Freddie'. This last was accomplished when a complete and pristine Wellington Ic fuselage was delivered to Denham for the director to play with. Watt, somewhat combative by nature, had several run-ins with Squadron Leader Williams, whom he thought officious and lazy. In point of fact, though, RAF facilities and personnel were provided on a scale and with a rapidity which was – for DPR at least – quite unusual; especially bearing in mind that both the length and the cost of the film became more than double what had been originally envisioned.[55]

The end result, eventually titled *Target for Tonight* after other choices ('Night Bomber', 'A Target is Bombed', and 'Bomber Command') had been mooted and then discarded, had a straightforward linear narrative plot based on a script by Watt himself that the Air Ministry had carefully vetted. It begins with the examination of reconnaissance photographs of a new German oil storage facility at 'Freihausen' and the decision by Bomber Command HQ – this was the scene in which Pierse and Saundby appeared – to divert a Wellington squadron to attack it that night. The scene them shifts to 'RAF Millerton' and the preparations for the night's operations, including a extended briefing room scene in which Group Captain Fogerty and Wing Commander Powell both figure prominently. The crew of 'F for Freddie', introduced in the briefing, are then shown, amid much banter in the crew room, climbing into their flying suits and being lorried out to their aircraft. There follows a long sequence of exterior mixed with interior shots in which Wing Commander Powell, operating from a mobile flare-path post, sees off the aircraft involved in that night's raid as they taxi out and take off. The plot then focuses on 'F for Freddie' and its crew, who – significantly – have no trouble with weather or navigation, and along with the other Wellingtons bomb the oil storage facilities with great success despite searchlights and strong anti-aircraft fire. 'As from the plane,' an early version of the shooting script explains, 'we see the bombs hitting the ground. One, two three four, and than a colossal explosion with the fifth. Sheets of flame then shoot up.' In this version of the script the rear gunner subsequently shouts: 'Oh boy, what a beauty. Right on the dot!'[56] Only after the target is wrecked do things start to go wrong: 'F for Freddie' is hit by flak, a crew member is wounded and one engine packs up, and fog develops on the ground at RAF Millerton. In the end, however, after a suspenseful return trip, 'F for Freddie' and its crew return safely. What is notable about the film from the propaganda perspective is that, through the use of models rather than combat footage, the impression is given that Bomber Command is striking regularly and with great effect at specific industrial targets.

Target for Tonight was a huge success. The Air Council approved it, personnel at RAF Mildenhall liked it, and the Prime Minister, when given a private showing at Chequers, 'chuckled when the bombs hit their target'.[57] Most importantly of all, both the critics and the public felt it was both an inspiring film and an accurate reflection of Bomber Command at war when it first appeared on cinema screens in late July 1941.

'It dramatises reality', was how the reviewer for the *Monthly Film Bulletin* put it. 'Throughout *it is the real* thing', was the verdict of *Kinematograph Weekly*, labelling the detail 'full and authentic'. *Picturegoer* agreed. 'The thrill of this picture is the reality of it. This is the real thing, not something baked up in a studio.' The daily newspapers were also laudatory, as were the weeklies. 'Authenticity, to the makers of documentaries, is its own reward', William Whitebait wrote in the *New Statesman*, 'and *Target for To-night* wins from every detail.' Edgar Anstey concluded that the film 'is the screen's best piece of factual reporting'.[58] While the film itself was making a splash the Air Ministry sought to capitalize on it by selling the serialization rights to the *Daily Express*. The story, condensed by *Express* film critic Paul Holt, then went on to appear as a sixpenny pamphlet published by Hutchinson.[59] Though there were some problems with distribution, the public flocked to see what all the fuss was about. *Target for Tonight* quickly became a sensation that took the cinema trade completely by surprise. 'It has proved a far more powerful magnet to the public than even the most enthusiastic could have hoped', *Kinematograph Weekly* noted two weeks after its release.[60] People who saw the film, eager to believe that Britain was striking back rather than just taking it, generally appear to have agreed that *Target for Tonight* was 'the real thing'.[61] As an added bonus to reassuring the public – as well as foreign observers – of the effectiveness of Bomber Command, the film also served as a recruiting tool for, and morale booster within, the RAF itself.[62]

Meanwhile, even while *Target for Tonight* was in production, the

Directorate of Public Relations had been looking further down the road. The Crown Film Unit, though it would do an excellent job of promoting Bomber Command, was part of the Ministry of Information. With MoI resources stretched thin, and no absolute guarantee that the films the Air Ministry wanted made would always be supported, it seemed to Air Vice-Marshal Peck as well as members of the DPR in the spring of 1941 that the time had come for the RAF to set up its own films section. He obtained the sanction of the Air Minister, Sir Archibald Sinclair, and went on to assure the MoI and other services that footage would be shared, explaining to the Treasury that personnel and equipment would be obtained from within the air force. In part the aim was simply to keep a film record of the RAF at war; but Peck's chief concern was positive publicity while the war lasted. 'Good men with an eye for good shots could, I am convinced,' Peck had explained to the Air Minister's private secretary in May 1941, 'produce many wonderful pictures of the day-to-day life of the air force which would be very good and valuable propaganda.' In August 1941 the RAF Film Unit began to take shape.[63]

It would take many months, however, for the film unit to recruit qualified personnel from within the air force and obtain the right type of equipment in sufficient quantity, and even longer to begin to put together its own films. By the summer of 1941 it was also becoming clear that Bomber Command might need more than *Target for Tonight* in order to reinforce public support for the strategic bombing campaign.

Though there had been some doubts about the bombing effort during the second winter of the war, it was only in August 1941 that a systematic attempt was made to evaluate the effectiveness of Bomber Command. This was at the initiative of Professor Sir Frederick Lindemann, chief scientific adviser to the Prime Minister, who asked D. M. B. Butt of the War Cabinet Secretariat to compile a statistical analysis of the flash photographs taken after bombers had dropped their loads. Based on over six hundred photographs from raids in June and July, the report Butt compiled revealed just how inauthentic the picture painted in *Target for Tonight* really was. Of those aircraft which had reported bombing German targets, only one in four had actually done so; only one in ten of those which had been sent to attack the Ruhr. In all, less than one third of all night-time sorties had got within five miles of the objective.[64]

These findings came as a distinct shock. Nobody within Bomber Command or the Air Ministry had guessed that the situation was as bad as this. Even the Prime Minister, hitherto a strong advocate of strategic bombing, began to have second thoughts. 'It is very doubtful', he sharply warned the Chief of Air Staff in September 1941, 'whether bombing by itself will be a decisive factor in the present war.' Churchill went on to assert that at best it might be 'a heavy and I trust seriously increasing annoyance'.[65]

This was not the sort of thing that air marshals wished to hear or believe. The war-winning potential of strategic bombing had always been at the heart of RAF thinking, the essential *raison d'être* for an independent air force. To cast doubts on the campaign, therefore, was by implication to undermine the Royal Air Force itself. Thus the CAS, Air Chief Marshal Sir Charles Portal, while conceding that there had been problems, concluded that success would come once large numbers of a new generation of heavy long-range bomber types were introduced along with new navigational aids. Until this happened, however, both the Prime Minister and the public would have to be persuaded that present efforts – despite all evidence to the contrary – were worthwhile. In the case of Churchill and other luminaries, this meant arguing the case for more and better equipment and pointing out that the RAF remained the only means Britain possessed of striking directly at the German war effort.[66] In the case of the public, who knew nothing of the Butt Report but whose support mattered in relation to parliamentary and press opinion, it meant intensifying the propaganda effort to convince people that the bombing of Germany was yielding solid results. The Air Ministry plan, as an internal RAF account later explained, was to improve the real effectiveness of bombing while keeping 'the British people happy' by concealing the uncomfortable truth 'under the cloak of complacent publicity'.[67]

The thrust and tone of such publicity can be gauged from surveys of the daily press and radio broadcasts, the contents of trade books sponsored by the Air Ministry, and from *Bomber Command: The Air Ministry Account of the Bomber Command's Offensive Against the Axis*, a lavishly illustrated booklet which appeared in October 1941. This was full of confident statements such as 'the attacks delivered by Bomber Command are steadily increasing in weight and severity'.[68] Meanwhile, in the wake of the success of *Target for Tonight*, it was to be expected that the Air Ministry would be eager to explore further the potential of the feature film as a propaganda tool. The film trade had certainly begun to feel that a sea-change in attitude had taken place. As a piece in *Kinematograph Weekly* put it:

> Of all the Services the RAF grant facilities with the greater fairness and will go to great lengths in their efforts to co-operate generally, both by the release of artistes and assistance to camera crews on pictures requiring flying backgrounds. This in spite of heavy operational duties undertaken by the RAF.[69]

Rex Harrison, applying to join the RAF a year after David Niven had been sent on his way, found the officer selection board he went up before to be friendly and obliging.[70]

Preliminary planning quickly began for a more ambitious picture that would supplant *Target for Tonight* as the definitive bomber film. This cinematic representation 'of the RAF's nightly smashings of German industrial towns' (as the *Express* described the project) involved a budget of £150,000 for an eighty-five minute, full-colour feature on Bomber Command based on a script by Laurence Howard. By November 1941, however, serious problems began to emerge. The Ministry of Information took exception to the way in which the Air Ministry was taking matters into its own hands without even a courtesy nod to the supposed supremacy of the MoI in propaganda matters. More importantly, PR1 at the Air Ministry itself, when presented with the script, disliked it. Reading between the lines it seems that they were made uneasy by colourful leading characters. All in all it was 'bad propaganda'. The film was abandoned.[71]

Cooperation, it seemed, still only went so far. Luckily there were several lesser projects already underway by the time of this débâcle. *Target for Tonight* would not be supplanted, but rather complemented, by features in which Bomber Command was no longer the exclusive focus of attention.

The first alternative project dated back to late 1940, when a commercial feature film on the blockade of Germany was being contemplated. Frustrated by the slowness of the official response to requests for facilities – even as it appeared *The March of Time* was being given red-carpet treatment – Michael Balcon of Ealing Films had thrown over the sponsorship of the MoI in favour of the Ministry of Economic Warfare (MEW).[72] This was to be a narrated and staged documentary celebrating the work of MEW in organizing an aggressive blockade of Germany. It involved, among several other things, demonstrating the effectiveness of the RAF in attacking the industrial infrastructure of the Third Reich. Once the financing had been arranged, and MEW had reached a modus vivendi with the MoI, the Air Ministry was more than happy to cooperate. By the spring of 1941 exterior shooting of 50 Squadron aircraft was taking place at Skillingthorpe in Lincolnshire, and in the summer a worn-out Hampden bomber was provided for interior shooting on an Ealing sound stage.[73]

More delays followed, no doubt in part the result of the need to adapt the script of what was then entitled 'Siege' to the changing war situation. (Sequences involving a Soviet commissar played by Michael Redgrave, for example, who voices concern about Hitler's military buildup in the East as well as scepticism about the non-effectiveness of the RAF, could only have been added after the Nazi invasion of the USSR began on 22 June.) By February 1942, however, what was now titled *The Big Blockade* was complete.

The Air Ministry can only have been pleased by the portrayal of Bomber Command in the film. Though there were many other aspects of economic warfare to cover, the dramatic moments in the opening segment of the film, and above all its denouement, were devoted to an RAF raid on key industrial sites in Hanover. In all, thirty minutes of a seventy-minute film were directly or indirectly devoted to Bomber Command. 'T for Tommy', crewed by 'George the pilot' (Michael Rennie), 'Tom the navigator' (John Mills), along with air gunner 'Percy' and radio operator 'David' (David Evans and Peter de Greeff), takes off with other Hampdens to attack Hanover. The squadron's specific targets are very precise: an oil refinery, an ersatz rubber factory, a railway junction, a steel foundry, and a power station. In the opening segment devoted to the RAF, narrator Frank Owen speaks of 'scores' of squadrons attacking German industry 'in raid upon raid'. By the time of the film's climax, an attack by 'T for Tommy' on a power station, claims for Bomber Command have increased. There were now 'huge fleets' of aircraft that flew to Germany. 'British bombers hammer at the heart of German industry, destroying the mechanism of war itself', Owen stressed. 'Not the overworked squadrons of 1940, but a brand new bomber force, with further range, height, and speed – and a far higher bomb load.' This was a bit of a stretch of the imagination in relation to the Hampden, a bomber of pre-war design and limited utility,[74] and may have been meant as a reference to the new generation of heavy bombers such as the Stirling, Halifax and Manchester then coming into service. Either way, Hampden crews were going to be shown as doing an excellent job of striking at the enemy. In an eleven-minute sequence involving a mixture of close-ups of the crew, models, and pieces from acquired German films, 'T for Tommy', having beaten off a German night fighter, makes a total of three runs over the target. While the first stick of bombs falls a hundred yards short, and flak causes a fire to start amidships, the Hampden goes round again twice to deliver the second and third stick at low level. These score direct hits, which in turn utterly destroy the power station. The radio operator is wounded; but 'T for Tommy', decorated near the nose with an image of St George slaying the dragon and multiple sortie marks, makes it safely home. The message was clear: Bomber Command was going from strength to strength.

In retrospect it seems clear that *The Big Blockade* was unlikely to entrance audiences. 'Blockade is a dull word,' Balcon later wrote, 'and the subject rather too abstract to be dramatic or exciting.'[75] The Hanover attack, heavily stressed in Ealing publicity material and noted by critics, might have achieved both goals if it had not been weighed down by long and somewhat tedious explanations – partly narrated, partly staged – of the evolution and work of the Ministry of Economic Warfare. Despite a wide range of acting talent and efforts to convey its message through a mix of documentary, comedy and drama, *The Big Blockade* remained obviously pedantic and – even to the uninitiated – both discordant and overly optimistic. Some critics tried to be kind when the film was released at the beginning of 1942, but the consensus was that it was a failure. Even the patriotic *Times* found it 'woefully unconvincing'. It quickly disappeared from view.[76]

Even as *The Big Blockade* was coming to grief, another commercial feature film was in production that featured the work of Bomber Command. Unfortunately, *Flying Fortress* also failed to live up to early expectations. This was a Warner Brothers (UK) effort, directed by Walter Forde and based on an original story by Brock Williams. First announced in October 1941, before the entry of the United States into the war, *Flying Fortress* was clearly meant to serve several interests. The MoI and Foreign Office would have another opportunity to influence positively the American public through film; Warner would be able to market a film with a US aircraft in the title in America as well as Britain, thereby making more money; and the RAF would have the opportunity to showcase the new four-engine bomber from Boeing that it was acquiring.

For the Air Ministry, moreover, there was the specific prospect of influencing the script to support its Bomber Command publicity efforts. This was in contrast to purely Hollywood features which, even if RAF assistance was given in order to keep up good relations with a neutral power vital to national survival, were less subject to oversight. This had been made evident in the Twentieth Century-Fox movie *A Yank in the RAF*, a Tyrone Power and Betty Grable vehicle. This had been made in cooperation with the Air Ministry, mainly in reference to allowing a British camera team (Ronald Neame, Jack Whitehead and Otto Kanturek, working under the direction of Herbert Mason) to take footage of Spitfires being rearmed and a 602 Squadron scramble, plus making suggestions concerning a version of the script sent to London by studio head Darryl Zanuck. The problem for Bomber Command was the fact that one of the scenes written and shot in California showed Tyrone Power taking part – to his evident disgust – in a leaflet raid on Berlin in early 1940. This was not an aspect of its early operations of which Bomber Command cared to be reminded, and contradicted the current message of real effectiveness as a striking weapon. Luckily, when the film was released in October 1941, those who liked it tended to recall the Spitfire scenes, while those who hated it as a caricature of life in wartime England tended to dwell on the poor attempts at English accents and its general crassness. As J. E. Sewell put it in an end-of-year film round-up for the *Telegraph*: 'Curses, not loud, but deep.'[77] The Air Ministry evidently felt the same, Wing Commander Williams making it clear in reference to a follow-up Zanuck project, *Eagle Squadron*, that after the *A Yank in the RAF* experience 'there can be no "free hand" for shooting RAF material'.[78] Though produced by a US company subsidiary and destined for the US market, *Flying Fortress* would be truly made in England and thus subject to greater control.

The plot was very similar to that of *A Yank in the RAF*. An American playboy (Richard Greene), ferries a plane to England from Canada, ends up joining the RAF, and falls for a fellow American (Carla Lehemann) during the Blitz. The hero becomes a bomber pilot who subsequently – as the studio publicity department put it – 'captains a Flying Fortress in sensational raids on Berlin'. Secure in the knowledge that bombs rather than leaflets would be seen dropping over the capital of the Third Reich, the Air Ministry laid on facilities that included a Spitfire from 12 Group, a Blenheim (from which aerial footage could be shot), and three B–17 Fortress Is of 90 Squadron operating out of RAF Polebrook in Northamptonshire.[79]

When it was released in June 1942, however, the comparatively low-budget *Flying Fortress* did not catch on. With the United States now in the war, the plot had become dated. Thus while the *Daily Mail* might claim it to be 'accurate, sympathetic, comprehensive', others papers were much less enthusiastic. As the *Daily Express* put it, 'as a portrait of the times it is unreal'.[80] With the entry of the USA into the war and the beginnings of the build-up of the US 8th Air Force in England in the spring of 1942, the B–17 – an American aircraft to begin with – was going to be associated in the public mind with the USAAF rather than the RAF. What was more, by the time the film was released, the early-model version of the B–17 supplied to the RAF had proved to be less than successful in operational terms. Within a few months those that remained of the twenty delivered were handed over to Coastal Command. *Flying Fortress*, like *The Big Blockade*, was a victim of changing circumstances. But while the film did not make much of a mark at the box office, DPR could at least take comfort from the fact that critics were very impressed by the flying scenes.[81]

The success of *Target for Tonight* had therefore been followed first by an aborted 'big' film and then two commercial flops. There remained one further chance to reinforce the cinematic message concerning Bomber Command while it was still comparatively fresh in people's minds. In the summer of 1941, basking in the success of the MoI-sponsored feature *49th Parallel*, the director-writer team of Michael Powell and Emeric Pressburger had been casting about for a new film project. Something that intrigued Powell, and which he thought could be used as a title, was the phrase used by the BBC to indicate losses over enemy territory: 'One [or some higher number] of our aircraft failed to return.' This would be the story of a bomber crew forced to bail out over occupied Holland, and would highlight the help given by the Dutch Resistance to stranded British airmen trying to get back home. Jack Beddington at the MoI Films Division liked the idea, the resistance theme being one that his Ministry was keen to promote. The Dutch government-in-exile was understandably happy to cooperate. Once it became clear that RAF airmen would not only be shown as brave and resourceful but also that the film would open with a long sequence essentially repeating the first half of *Target for Tonight* – Michael Powell told one of the lead actors that the film was really 'about the RAF' [82] – the Air Ministry once again agreed to provide all necessary facilities. Ironically, the only difficulty came in finding a financial backer. Though *49th Parallel*, the costs of which had been underwritten by the MoI, had turned out to be a great success, the giving of state funds to a private company had become too controversial to repeat. Powell therefore approached J. Arthur Rank for backing, only to discover that one of Rank's deputies, C. M. Woolf of General Film Distributors, disliked the idea of showing an RAF bomber being shot down. Eventually he was able to get the project financed – on a limited scale – through British National, and the film got underway.[83]

Perhaps remembering C. M. Woolf's conclusion that the plot was 'defeatist', or possibly because either the MoI or – more likely – the Air Ministry had expressed concern, not only was the title changed to *One of Our Aircraft is Missing*, but the bomber in question is not shown being shot down by the enemy. Instead, in a plot development which allowed for a powerful series of opening shots – a Wellington flying over the sea without anyone aboard – the crew of 'B for Bertie', aboard an aircraft hit by flak and flying on one engine, bail out just before the apparently terminal port engine picks up again, allowing the plane to fly on autopilot until it hits a pylon over England.

Other aspects of the thirty minutes of screenplay given over to the raid in which 'B for Bertie' takes part required little or no change. There could certainly be no objection to basing one of the crew on Sir Arnold Wilson (Tory MP for Hitchin) who, at the age of fifty-one, had announced in the House early in the war that he was going to set an example by volunteering to be an air gunner in the RAF.[84] A regionally mixed crew, already featured in Watt's film (and to a lesser extent in *The Big Blockade*), was more than acceptable. Nor was the choice of target – a Mercedes-Benz works in Stuttgart – in any way at odds with the official line that Bomber Command was striking with precision at industrial targets. When facilities were requested, the Air Ministry cooperated to the same lavish extent as it had over *Target for Tonight*. Powell, like Watt, was allowed to do exterior shooting – this time with 115 Squadron at Marham in Norfolk – and a complete Wellington was delivered to Denham Studios that could be taken apart for interior shots. The only intrusion by the Air Ministry was to make sure that camera angles and some equipment modification prevented the transmission of any vital information to the enemy. Nevertheless, as Powell had wanted, the scenes shot inside the Wellington appeared very authentic.[85]

One of the striking things about the first third of *One of Our Aircraft is Missing* is how closely it parallels *Target for Tonight*. In both cases a Canadian air gunner expresses disappointment at being scrubbed from the sortie and is consoled by a senior officer ('Bad luck, Catford', 'Bad luck, old man'). Powell, playing the flare path controller as the bombers taxi out to take off, was clearly imitating – if not engaging in outright parody – the accent and demeanour of Wing Commander 'Speedy' Powell in the earlier film. And the raid itself closely follows what had become a set pattern. Weather and other navigational hazards pose no problems in reaching the target, which is already ablaze from the bombs of other Wellingtons (Navigator: 'Golly, it's a wizard fire!'). Despite flak and searchlights – at which the gunners are given permission to fire in both films – 'B for Bertie' descends straight toward the target. After a bomb run filmed very much in the style of *Target for Tonight*, with tense close-ups of the bomb-aimer directing the pilot to make slight course corrections, four bomb hits are shown exploding inside the factory. Like 'F for Freddie', the aircraft is then hit by flak and limps away. The stories then diverge as the crew of 'B for Bertie' bail out over Holland and begin their evasion adventure.[86]

The Air Ministry did, however, require one late addition to the finished film in order to back up the claim made in *The Big Blockade* that a new generation of bombers was increasing the might of Bomber Command. In a final scene not present in the published booklet of the film, the crew, after successfully escaping back to England with the help of the Dutch Resistance, are shown staring up at 'the new kite' – cut to newsreel footage of a 7 Squadron Stirling bomber at Oakington[87] – followed by a dramatic moment in the Operations Room: 'Target: Berlin!'

There were also some more subtle differences between *One of Our Aircraft is Missing* and *Target for Tonight*. The crew of 'B for Bertie', though also sporting regional accents (Wales, Yorkshire and the rural south of England complementing rather than duplicating the Scottish and Northern Irish intonations heard in the earlier film), was made up of professional actors rather than genuine RAF aircrew. Supported by some of the most talented film production people in the business, including Ronald Neame (lighting), David Lean (editing), and of course Powell and Pressburger themselves, the ensemble cast – full of talented actors such as Bernard Miles (front gunner

Geoff Hickman), Eric Portman (second pilot Tom Earnshaw), Hugh
Williams (navigator Frank Shelley) and Godfrey Tearle (rear gunner Sir
George Corbett) – appeared, somewhat ironically, more 'natural' aircrew
than the sometimes uneasy but genuine RAF types aboard 'F for Freddie'.[88]

Using actors rather than Bomber Command personnel, furthermore,
allowed Michael Powell to downplay accent in relation to class. Film critics
and viewers had liked the inclusion of regional accents in *Target for Tonight*,
suggesting as it did a service in which teamwork rather than social origin
was what mattered. Unfortunately using 'the real thing' had also meant
including Wing Commander 'Speedy' Powell, who had a large speaking
part and whose accent was extraordinarily upper class. This, amidst what
was being labelled a People's War, had struck a jarring note with some
left-wing critics and audience members.[89] In *One of Our Aircraft is Missing*
the officers among the crew of 'B for Bertie' included Flying Officer John
Glynn Haggard, a diplomat's son (Hugh Burden) as well as Pilot Officer
Sir George Corbett (Godfrey Tearle). Both Burden and Tearle, however,
along with Hugh Williams (Flight Lieutenant Frank Shelley, West End actor)
speak in unremarkable, BBC-type middle-class accents. Emeric Pressburger,
what was more, with the keen ear of an émigré for idiom, had produced
a script in which the crew spoke with great naturalness.[90] There could be
no criticism of accent or character.[91]

A considerable effort was made to publicize *One of Our Aircraft is
Missing* as it was being made and at the time of its appearance in April
1942. Powell was interviewed on the set at Denham by the BBC, the plot
was recast in illustrated booklet form prior to the film's release – this time
courtesy of His Majesty's Stationery Office (price 6*d.*) – and a well-publicized
premiere arranged at the Odeon Leicester Square. The luminaries present
for this first public showing included Air Marshal Sir Charles Portal, the
Chief of the Air Staff, and Lord Sherwood, joint Under-Secretary of State
for Air.[92]

The result, from the Air Ministry standpoint, could not have been better.
Critics and public alike agreed that *One of Our Aircraft is Missing* did not
require much in the way of suspension of disbelief. It 'has the conviction
of fact' (*News Chronicle*); was 'founded on fact' (*Sunday Pictorial*); was
'realistic' (*Daily Mirror*); or, as a more up-market weekly put it, was excellent
in reference to 'verisimilitude' (*New Statesman*). In the view of a Plymouth
man contacted by Mass-Observation, it was one of those films 'absolutely
true to life' – an opinion echoed by other cinema-goers.[93] A number of
critics also noted the life-like yet unobtrusive mix of accents among the
crew.[94] *One of Our Aircraft is Missing* rapidly developed into a box-office
success.[95]

Though other means of bolstering confidence in Bomber Command would continue to be used into the following year and beyond,[96] *One of Our Aircraft is Missing* turned out to be the last feature film in which Bomber Command played a key role that was released until the war was over. At one level this appears surprising, given that the cinema was more popular than ever. A study sponsored by the MoI in 1943 revealed that 70 per cent of the population went to the cinema at least occasionally, while 32 per cent went once a week or more.[97] There were, however, a number of interrelated and compelling reasons why further films on the RAF's strategic mission were not made to match the burgeoning film audience.

First, there was the fact that war films were thought to be losing their public appeal. Trade representatives and others were claiming that, after three years of struggle, cinema audiences were tired of war pictures.[98] It was certainly true, as time passed and more easily filmed Allied war operations occurred, that the Air Ministry found it became more and more difficult to interest the public in Bomber Command efforts.[99]

Secondly, in relation to official films as well as commercial features, the new head of Bomber Command, Air Marshal Sir Arthur Harris, remained highly antagonistic toward the publicity apparatus at the Air Ministry – and indeed all representations of 'his' war that did not originate at High Wycombe. In the summer of 1942, for instance, the Air Ministry had given its stamp of approval to a stage drama dealing with a bomber station written by Terence Rattigan, based on his experiences as an RAF rear-gunner. The play, *Flare Path*, was a success, and the Chief of Air Staff personally congratulated the author on the opening night. Harris, on the other hand, who saw it shortly afterward, was furious at the theme of emotional vulnerability among bomber crews which Rattigan had explored, and was not shy about expressing his displeasure in front of the leading cast member.[100] Harris much preferred to court attention for Bomber Command through organizing record-breaking attacks, such as the first thousand-bomber raid on Cologne (May 1942), and planning raids in which conditions favoured RAF success.[101] In other words, with a more and more powerful force at his disposal, equipped with new navigation aids such as 'Gee', 'Oboe', and later H2S radar, the AOC could and did argue that Bomber Command could now deliver on its promises and that therefore there was no need to generate artificial evidence of success when the real thing would now pass muster.

The third reason for the absence of further feature films arose from a change in bombing doctrine. Even with new navigation aids which allowed then to find urban targets, Bomber Command aircraft were usually unable to bomb specific industrial sites such as factories. Instead, in a tendency that was secretly confirmed as policy in 1942, the RAF shifted to area bombing in the hope of both causing material damage to industry and undermining the morale of the urban working population through the destruction of lives and property. This meant that civilians, including women and children, were being deliberately targeted. To admit this would, by implication, be to suggest that the earlier and much publicized policy had failed. Area bombing, what was more, generated constant fears in the Air Ministry about a popular reaction against it on humanitarian grounds. The result was a deliberate effort to lull the public into a sense that Germany was being struck hard without specifying who or what in particular was being hit. A feature film in which area bombing was featured was thus a non-starter. The press campaign, however, was only partially successful: veterans of the Blitz could guess what 'heavy attacks' on German cities meant in practice. 'In the great raids on cities at night one must recognise frankly that the target area is the city, or at best an area of the city, and the destruction must be indiscriminate', Stephen King-Hall, Independent MP for Ormskirk and world affairs commentator, was writing as early as June 1942. 'The military objective is the morale of the civilian population.' [102] This in turn meant that a new feature in which precision bombing over Germany was highlighted might be viewed with a good deal less credulity than *Target for Tonight* (a film which, by 1944, was being recognized as a propaganda piece rather than an accurate representation of night bombing).[103]

The fourth and final factor militating against a new Bomber Command film in the 1943–44 period was the sheer complexity of such a task. Even if a film was to be made about an operation or operations in which area bombing did not feature, and to which Harris agreed, there were a large number of difficulties that still had to be overcome. The plot had to be approved; other departments might have to be briefed; security issues would have to be resolved; and, if and when a project was approved, the need for RAF equipment and personnel would have to be fitted into operational requirements. Even when the Air Ministry seemed keen on a particular project, the number of hurdles that a filmmaker had to overcome were daunting. American director Howard Hawks, after talking with Wing Commander Guy Gibson during a US publicity tour, was very keen to make a feature film for Warner Brothers based on the famous dams raid of May 1943 that Gibson had led. The Air Ministry was not averse in principle to such a film – precision rather than area bombing would be highlighted – but problems over personnel, the script, security matters and other issues caused months of delay. In the end nothing came of what had started out as a highly topical project, and the Air Ministry had to content itself with the much less complicated task of ordering Gibson to write his story for serial publication in 1944–45.[104] This was not an isolated case.[105]

There were, to be sure, occasional glimpses of the RAF and Bomber Command in films with other central themes, mainly involving the death over enemy territory of somebody's sweetheart.[106] There was even a short piece from Strand Films at the end of 1943 entitled *There's a Future in It* in which a Stirling pilot (Barry Morse) admits to hating operations but – something that would have doubtless won the approval of Harris – also states that bombing is both just and necessary.[107] Finally, bombers played a part in two feature-length productions started late in the war: both based around scripts produced by Terence Rattigan and both made with RAF cooperation. Yet neither *The Way to the Stars* nor *Journey Together* were regarded primarily as films about Bomber Command. Both, furthermore, were released after the war had ended, placing the action portrayed in the past rather than the present.

Drawing on the RAF motto (*Per Ardua ad Astra*) for its title, shot in part at RAF Catterick and involving RAF aircraft, *The Way to the Stars*, directed by 'Puffin' Asquith, was unquestionably a film with a strong Royal Air Force background. Yet while planes are shown taking off and landing, there are virtually no scenes set in the air nor any depictions of any raids (other than enemy bombs hitting 'Halfpenny Field'). A version of the Rattigan play *Flare Path*, heavily reworked to accommodate an MoI desire for a sub-plot showing the overcoming of Anglo-American antagonism, *The Way to the Stars* was a story of emotions on the ground rather than action in the air, and as much about civilians as about RAF personnel. Moreover, most of the RAF operational scenes were clearly retrospective, set in the Battle of Britain or – to a lesser extent – early 1942. Featuring sensitive performances by John Mills, Michael Redgrave and Rosamund John among others, *The Way To the Stars* was both a critical and a huge commercial success when it was released a month after the war in Europe had ended. Indeed, it is often labelled as the 'definitive' wartime film about the Royal Air Force. The RAF being celebrated, however, was that which had fought the Battle of Britain rather than the Battle of Berlin: hence the loan of Hurricanes and Blenheim Is rather than Mosquitos and Lancasters. Even the most enthusiastic critics recognized that *The Way to the Stars*, if for some reason the war had continued into the summer, would still have been an exercise in romantic nostalgia.[108]

Journey Together, made by the RAF Film Production Unit and featuring a cast of actors serving in the RAF, had a rather more contemporary setting, and the film's climax – nearly one-third of the film – revolved around a big raid on Berlin, shot in part at RAF Methwold in which Lancaster Xs of 149 Squadron were pressed into service. This part of the film both emulated and departed from earlier feature-film depictions of raids over Germany in interesting ways.

On one level the raid scenes of *Journey Together* was a compendium of the devices used in the bomber films of 1941–42. The crew of the Lancaster on which the plot focuses at this point is a mixture of class and region, including a Scotsman, a Canadian and two lower-class types. On the way to the target this Lancaster is attacked by a fighter, which is shot down. The face of the wounded air bomber is highlighted as he guides the pilot over the target and releases the bombs. Hit by flak as it turns away, the Lancaster limps along until engine trouble forces the pilot to ditch. In marked contrast to earlier films such as *Target for Tonight*, however, there was little attempt in *Journey Together* to suggest the strategic bombing campaign involved striking at specific industrial targets. Newspaper headlines are shown, and a BBC broadcast is heard, in which the entire cities are obviously being attacked. 'Last night', we hear the BBC announcer intone, 'for the third time this week, strong forces of RAF Bomber Command delivered another concentrated attack upon the inland port of Bremen. In addition to high explosive bombs, 200,000 incendiaries were sent down.' In the briefing scene for the Berlin raid no more specific targets other than the city itself are given, the final words of the station commander being to encourage the crews to 'prang it, and prang it hard'. Instead of using models of individual enemy facilities being hit, as had been the case in earlier features, the RAF production team used documentary footage taken on an actual raid showing entire districts in flames.

This relative lack of squeamishness may have resulted from a recognition that the public could read between the lines of official news reports and knew – if only instinctively – that the raids on cities in the latter years of the war by hundreds and hundreds of RAF bombers, night after night, could not be anything other than saturation attacks. It may also have been recognized that the war in Europe would be over by the time the film was complete and that the public would no longer care. Whatever the reason, the raid scenes of *Journey Together* were the most forthright – and dramatic – of any depicted in wartime feature films.[109]

Yet neither critics nor audiences saw *Journey Together* in terms of the raid itself when the film was released in October 1945. The journey in question was that of a young NCO (convincingly played by Richard Attenborough) and his contemporaries through the process of ground and air training in Britain, the United States and Canada, and the film itself was dedicated to 'the few who trained the many'. *Journey Together*, in short, was made, and to a considerable extent viewed, primarily in reference to the achievements of Flying Training Command rather than Bomber Command, and was in any event not as widely seen as more commercially successful films.[110]

The absence of feature films about Bomber Command in the later war years did not, it is important to note, mean that the RAF was not represented. *Target for Tonight* quickly prompted other branches of the service – fiercely competitive in terms of publicity – to agitate for features celebrating their own particular contributions to victory.[111]

First off the mark was Coastal Command. Constantly fighting with Bomber Command for resources, the AOC-in-C, the new publicity-minded Air Marshal Sir Philip Joubert, was anxious to remind both Whitehall and the public that the protection of convoys against the U-boat menace was vital to the survival of Britain. Bomber Command might help win the war, but without the long-range patrols of Coastal Command aircraft that war could easily be lost. In the spring of 1941, when *Target for Tonight* was well underway, the Crown Film Unit was given the task of producing a film to be titled – appropriately enough – *Coastal Command*.[112]

Directed by J. B. Holmes and with a score by Vaughan Williams, *Coastal Command* was a more ambitious and costly film than *Target for Tonight*, but had a number features in common with Watt's film. The main plot line concerns 'T for Tommy', a Sunderland flying boat. The actors were again drawn from operational aircrew, and, like Pierse before him, Air Marshal Joubert agreed to play himself in an Operations Room scenes. The plot is somewhat more complex than *Target for Tonight*, involving as it does several types of aircraft operating against U-boats, enemy aircraft and a surface raider over several days. Coastal Command, however, is represented as being as successful – and important – as Bomber Command. A U-boat is sunk, a surface raider is crippled and 'T for Tommy' successfully defends itself against enemy aircraft. Though the prologue emphasizes the command's 'ceaseless vigil', the amount of successful action in the film was a recognition of the fact that it was actual fighting that 'fires the imagination.'[113]

Released in October 1942, the new Crown Film Unit effort inevitably suffered a little from being the follow-up to *Target for Tonight*. Critics noted that the storyline lacked the tight focus of Watt's effort (even producer Ian Dalrymple conceded – implying RAF interference – that it was 'over-elaborate'), and there are indications that the novelty of seeing 'real' RAF personnel on screen was beginning to wear off. On the other hand most were impressed by the camerawork of Jonah Jones, liked the score, and – most importantly – regarded *Coastal Command* as authentic. 'It gives the general public', as the *Monthly Film Bulletin* critic explained, 'some idea of what the work of the aircrew is like and the conditions under which they

operate.'[114] *Coastal Command*, like *Target for Tonight*, exaggerated considerably the success of RAF operations. The chances of a patrolling aircraft
coming across a surfaced U-boat in the expanses of the Atlantic were very
slight, and a positive outcome for the attacking aircraft in a duel between
them far from certain.[115] Nevertheless the film succeeded in its aim of
raising the public profile of a type of operation less glamorous than those
of Fighter Command and Bomber Command.[116]

The next RAF commands to seek a film of their own were even less
glamorous: so much so that a short- rather than feature-length format was
adopted. There remained severe limits, however, to the dramatic potential
of stories centring on Balloon Command and Maintenance Command.

Though the Balloon Barrage had already been the subject of one film
already – *Squadron 922* – the AOC Balloon Command evidently believed
that the limited exposure of the earlier film combined with changes in the
war situation meant that now was the time for a picture built around
Balloon Command, which its senior officers felt was being neglected.[117] The
project became the first major task allocated to the RAF Film Production
Unit, Arthur Taylor directing and scripting a story based around the
relatively unfamiliar work of balloon drifters – that is, barrage balloons
tethered to small craft in estuaries. The plot of *Operational Height* follows
the crew of the balloon drifter *Comeley Bank* as it goes about its daily work,
in addition to having to cope with enemy bombs and acoustic mines. To
achieve the kind of 'staged documentary' atmosphere that had become
popular since *Target for Tonight*, service personnel rather than professional
actors were used. Though only thirty-three minutes in length, *Operational
Height* was released commercially on a limited basis in March 1943 – though
by no means to general acclaim. Edgar Anstey in the *Spectator* thought the
plot rather contrived, suspecting – correctly – that life aboard a drifter was
a matter of boredom rather than adventure. The critic for the *Monthly Film
Bulletin* also noted 'the self-consciousness of the non-professional actors'.
Even *Documentary News Letter* conceded that 'to ask ordinary, pleasant men
on a balloon ship' to act 'is surely to throw too much weight on their
shoulders'.[118]

The RAF Film Production Unit was also approached in 1942 by
Maintenance Command to make an uplifting film about logistical work.
The resulting four-reel film, *The Big Pack*, directed by John Shearman, also
had problems. Producing an engaging but accurate story about air force
logistics was bound to be a difficult task, and the result was an overly
complex script and rather dull film. Though completed in 1943, it was not
released through the MoI until 1945, by which time any topicality that it
may have had was lost.[119] *The Times*, one of the few papers to review it,

concluded that 'the film presents a picture too broad and diffuse to give full credit to Maintenance Command and its achievements'.[120]

The Directorate of Public Relations, meanwhile, had not forgotten the usefulness of the commercial film trade in projecting the RAF to the public. Ealing Studios, which under Michael Balcon had already undertaken a number of service projects, was approached to make a feature film about the Air Sea Rescue service based on a script written by the scarred Battle of Britain ace, Richard Hillary.[121] As Balcon doubtless realized, a film about launches racing to save downed airmen in the Channel had dramatic potential. Charles Crichton was assigned to direct. The story involved a new officer (Ralph Michael) coming to terms with work aboard a launch rather than as aircrew as a result of a dramatic Channel rescue in which his mentor (David Farrar) is killed. Filmed with the cooperation of both the Air Ministry and the Admiralty aboard launches based at Newhaven in July and August 1943, but using professional actors, *For Those in Peril* combined authenticity with commercial potential. For though there were the by now usual mix of class and region in the crash-boat crew, and plenty of references to the importance of teamwork, what made *For Those in Peril* exciting was the sight of high-speed launches racing against time to save lives.

The reviews were generally very positive. 'The film is almost a documentary in its factual description of the daily peril of rescue work', the *Monthly Film Bulletin* reported, 'but as a narrative it grips throughout and crew and dialogue are extremely life-like. It is as if a curtain has been lifted on one section of the war, and we are shown what men are enduring each day as long as it lasts.' Other critics were also impressed, while Ernest Betts, writing in the *Daily Express*, was quite emphatic about how exciting *For Those in Peril* really was: 'It's dynamite.'[122] Curiously, however, *For Those in Peril* was not given a splashy West End premiere. This may have been because of its short length – only sixty-seven minutes – or because of the growing claim that the public was not really interested in all-male war pictures. In any event the result was that *For Those in Peril* was put directly onto general release at the start of July 1944 with only limited coverage, and did not do as well as Farrar, among others, thought it might have done if it had been given more initial publicity.[123]

As already noted, Flying Training Command got its film in what was in many ways the RAF Film Production Unit's masterpiece: *Journey Together*. With a good script to hand, the authority and time to do location shooting not only in England but also in the USA and Canada, and a cast of professional actors (including Richard Attenborough, Jack Watling, David Tomlinson and John Justin – all in the RAF – as well as Edward G. Robinson), director John Boulting was able to create a complex, authentic yet

genuinely dramatic tribute to the work of the Commonwealth Air Training
Plan. As *Spectator* critic Alexander Shaw put it, '*Journey Together* is one of
the few really fine and exciting films to come out of the war and everyone
who worked on it is to be congratulated upon an almost impeccable and
very exciting job'.[124] Unfortunately, by the time *Journey Together* was ready
for release in October 1945 the war had ended, and with it, for the time
being at least, public interest in war themes. 'If this first-class film – it
really is a fine job of work – had been screened a year or so ago', Reg
Whitley lamented in the *Daily Mirror*, 'it would have been a wow, but now
I'm afraid it loses much of its topical appeal.'[125]

Journey Together, in fact, was only the penultimate wartime film about
the RAF. Even longer in gestation was what eventually emerged as *School
for Secrets*, a highly fictionalized account of the development of radar. The
idea for a 'radar film' dated back to 1944, at a point when technical advances
and the looming end to the war in Europe made the early history of radar
less of a secret that had to be kept under lock and key (hence the working
title 'Now It Can Be Told'). The initial plan was for the RAF Film Production
Unit to take on the job as a documentary, but after VE-Day this was dropped
in favour of a commercial dramatization. A 'little laughter, a little pathos,
a lot of hard facts and rip-roaring adventure' was what Sir Robert Renwick,
Director of Communications, wanted to see on screen.[126] Filippo Del Giudice
of Two Cities expressed enthusiasm when approached by Sir Robert and,
with the backing of J. Arthur Rank, commissioned Peter Ustinov to write a
treatment. Ustinov was known as one of the people responsible for the
success of the army film *The Way Ahead* (see chapter four), and though
technically only an ordinary soldier was given red-carpet treatment by the
Royal Air Force in the summer of 1945. 'I did all my research in [private's]
uniform at RAF stations,' he later recalled, 'often getting rooms which were
reserved for visiting air marshals.'[127] The resulting treatment, entitled 'The
Boffins Went to War', was very much what Renwick had wanted – 'adventure', for instance, appearing in the form of a heavily fictionalized account
of the seizure of enemy radar equipment in the 1941 Bruneval Raid – and
Ustinov was given the green light to produce a script for a film that he
would direct. Production, however, on what was initially called 'Top Secret',
was delayed by arguments as various parties within the RAF and also the
Admiralty sought to reshape the story to maximize their own exposure (all
in the name of accuracy, of course). The end result was that what was
eventually titled *School for Secrets*, starring Ralph Richardson as a leading
radar scientist, did not appear on screens until November 1946.[128]

Reaction to *School for Secrets*, which Ustinov later claimed he made as
'kind of parody' of stiff-upper-lip war films, was mixed. The *Guardian* critic

faulted the director for producing 'a rather trivial treatment of an exciting subject'. Leonard Mosley in the *Daily Express*, on the other hand, found it 'rich in all the human virtues – exciting, sentimental, humourous, understanding', while to Richard Winnington of the *News Chronicle* it was simply a refreshing 'frolic'. Fred Majdalany of the *Daily Mail* took it as 'a leisurely, enjoyable, and thoroughly English comedy'. Like *Journey Together*, though, it could also seem a film too late. Noel Whitcomb, in an otherwise very positive review for the *Daily Mirror*, commented that 'It is a pity this story could not have been told two years ago. It would then have been hailed as a brilliant semi-documentary.' [129]

Despite the relatively modest impact of these last films, the RAF had more cause to celebrate than to mourn its involvement in feature films as war gave way to peace. Though its public relations machinery was beset at times by bureaucratic fumbling and lack of vision, and its promotional activities in the latter half of the war had not always been entirely successful, the Air Ministry had got the message across when it counted most. It was the role of the RAF, rather than either of the other services, which had been impressed on the public mind in the first propaganda feature of the war, *The Lion Has Wings*. The messages of reassurance it conveyed did, to be sure, become obsolete in 1940; but by then the importance of the RAF was being reestablished through its paramount role in the Battle of Britain. Most importantly, in 1941–42, when the future of the strategic bombing campaign had been in doubt, *Target for Tonight* and its commercial successors had done their part in fostering the belief that Bomber Command was in fact achieving its aims. Generating the same degree of public interest in, and enthusiasm for, other branches of the RAF proved to be more problematic (in part because the semi-documentary approach adopted in *Target* and repeated in later films soon began to appear humdrum rather than novel). But the comparative failure of later cinematic efforts such as *For Those in Peril* did not, ultimately, matter that much. Almost none of the activities covered in these later films were central to the core identity and key functions of the air force. The feature films that really mattered, those which highlighted the importance of the RAF in prosecuting the war between 1939 and 1942, had helped mask real weaknesses until the time when the force was strong enough to promote itself through actions rather than manufactured images.

The degree of commitment the Air Ministry brought to promoting the RAF's public image – symbolized by successive expansions in the number of personnel working for the Directorate of Public Relations – did not go unnoticed.[130] Successive chiefs at the Ministry of Information, even when annoyed, noted that the Air Ministry was more publicity conscious than the other service departments. Brendan Bracken, who knew a fair bit about manipulating public opinion, thought that Air Vice-Marshal Peck in particular was doing a tremendous job.[131] Rear-Admiral R. K. Dickson, Chief of Naval Information at the Admiralty, was envious of the 'immense and powerful organization' the Air Ministry had developed.[132] Its success was obvious. A Mass-Observation survey of public opinion in the autumn of 1941 revealed that the RAF was the most watched and 'most admired' of the services.[133] Little wonder that the competition began to talk of the 'Royal Advertising Force'.[134] Feature films had played a key part in promoting the interests of the RAF when it counted during the war.

3

Mightier Yet: The Royal Navy
and Feature Films, 1939–1945

Despite its dealings in the 1930s with various film companies, the Admiralty was less prepared than the Air Ministry to promote itself through film when war broke out. Since 1937, publicity matters had been handled by a single officer, Commander C. A. H. Brooking, working within the Naval Intelligence Department. Not surprisingly, the senior officers within this department, along with their designated representatives at the Ministry of Information, proved much more interested in making sure that nothing was given away to the enemy than in advertising the navy during the first months of hostilities.

The Royal Navy, in consequence, began the war by living up to its reputation as the silent service.[1] Those films which did emerge in the autumn of 1939 in which Admiralty cooperation was advertised were mostly of prewar vintage. *All at Sea*, a Sandy Powell comedy vehicle from British Lion, and *Sons of the Sea*, a spy tale set at Dartmouth Naval College made by British Consolidated, though they were released in October, had finished exterior shooting before Hitler moved on Poland. Once the war started, production companies such as London Films (for *The Lion Has Wings*) and Inspiration Films (for the documentary *Cavalcade of the Navy*) had to rely on archival footage.[2] Under pressure to play its part in influencing American opinion, the Admiralty did cooperate in the making of *The Battle Fleets of Britain* for the *March of Time* series, released in November 1939. The message was comforting – the navy was ready and able to defeat the enemy on, under or over the waves – but details were few and far between, and here again much of the footage was from prewar days. Such films, nevertheless, were greeted with interest.[3]

At the beginning of the new year a more accommodating stance became discernible at the Admiralty. This was largely the result of dissatisfaction on the part of Winston Churchill, once again First Lord of the Admiralty, at the way in which the navy's achievements – and by extension his own successes as First Lord – were not being advertised. To help remedy this situation Churchill created a new Press Division within the naval staff, working under the command of Brooking (promoted to the rank of Captain). At the same time Churchill continued to take a personal interest in publicity matters, making personal radio broadcasts and orchestrating the release of important news items.[4]

The destruction of the German pocket battleship *Graf Spee* and the *Altmark* incident were cases in point. Severely damaged after a running fight with three cruisers – HMS *Exeter*, HMS *Ajax*, and HMNZS *Achilles* – off the River Plate on 13 December 1939, the *Graf Spee* took refuge in Montevideo harbour and then, four days later, scuttled herself. In a follow-up move, the First Lord personally ordered the captain of HMS *Cossack* to enter Norwegian waters and board the German provision ship *Altmark* on 16 February in order to liberate British sailors taken from the merchantmen the *Graf Spee* had sunk. These twin events were rays of sunshine amid depressing reports of mounting British shipping losses, and Churchill took full advantage of them. On the evening of 18 December, the First Lord broadcast to the nation news of the Battle of the River Plate and its significance. Two months later, when *Exeter* and *Ajax* had both returned to Plymouth and news of the *Altmark* coup was still fresh, he supervised a victory parade of the crews through Admiralty Arch and paid tribute to them in a speech at a special dinner at the Guildhall on the evening of 23 February. The parade and the speech were photographed, filmed and given heavy play in the press. 'Both these events,' Churchill later wrote, 'strengthened my hand and the prestige of the Admiralty.'[5]

The First Lord must thus have been in a receptive frame of mind when the Admiralty was approached by Gaumont-British concerning participation in a feature being made under the title *For Freedom*. A Gainsborough Picture written by Miles Malleson and Leslie Arliss, *For Freedom* was to do for the navy what *The Lion Has Wings* had done for the air force. Approximately forty minutes of the film – in the context of a superficial story featuring Scottish comedian Will Fyffe as a newsreel magnate and E. V. H. Emmett playing a newsreel narrator – was documentary footage (narrated, naturally enough, by Emmett), explaining the events leading up to the war and contrasting the British and Nazi way of life. This was a fast and inexpensive way of assembling a picture, all the more so with *The Lion Has Wings* serving as a model. Producer Edward Black, however, wanted Admiralty help in turning the final half hour of the film – the portion dealing with events after 3 September 1939 – into a celebration of the work of the Royal Navy. He got it. 'The Naval scenes in this picture', publicity material and the opening credits proudly announced, 'were made with the co-operation of the Admiralty.' Maurice Elvey – who had worked with the navy before in *Sons of the Sea* – was allowed to direct Captain C. H. L. Woodhouse (of

Ajax) and the officers and men of both *Ajax* and *Exeter* (in port) in a reconstruction of some of their actions during the Battle of the River Plate. Crew members of merchant ships sunk by the *Graf Spee*, led by Captain Dove of the *Africa Shell*, were also used to reenact scenes of their imprisonment aboard the *Graf Spee* and *Altmark*. Elvey was also able to employ Vice-Admiral (retd) J. E. T. Harper to serve as narrator, and use footage of various Royal Navy units at sea.[6]

The result was that the final thirty minutes of *For Freedom* focused on the work of the navy, culminating in the Battle of the River Plate and the *Altmark* rescue. The initial segment was a newsreel-type series of clips showing HM ships, submarines and carrier aircraft at sea, with accompanying narration by Emmett. After claiming that U-boats were being sunk at the rate of two to four a week, showing minesweepers at work, and contrasting the sinking of helpless merchantmen by U-boats with attacks on warships by British submarines, Emmett rounded out his summation the first months of the war at sea with an emphatic crescendo:

> Never before in the naval history of the world [against a backdrop of battleships in heavy seas] has a fleet spent so much time continuously at sea. There was no rest for the crews in any branch of the service. They patrolled their hundreds of thousands of miles in all weather: in North Sea, Arctic, or Atlantic. So, in the bitterest winter for a hundred years, in the storm-lashed mountains of December seas, the navy carried on! Waiting. Hunting! Hats off to the navy!

The picture then shifts gears several times, with staged scenes of Will Fyffe and members of his (fictional) newsreel company being introduced to (the real) Captain Bell, Captain Bell plus extras then reenacting the boarding of the *Africa Shell* by sailors from the *Graf Spee*, followed by Emmett – looking directly at the camera for the first time – introducing Admiral Harper as 'someone who is very qualified to give you the details of [the] action'. Harper then gives a running commentary on the action off the River Plate and the *Altmark* incident, his words accompanied by shots of moving models (to better explain movements) and footage of the *Graf Spee*, interspersed with scenes of actors playing German crewmen on the bridge of *Graf Spee*, Dove and his fellows revisiting their confinement below decks, and officers and men of *Ajax* and *Exeter* briefly reenacting various actions on the day of the battle. 'In this and subsequent scenes,' Harper proclaims just before the first of these reenactments appears on screen, 'you are watching actual men whose deeds that day wrote this splendid new page in Britain's naval history.' The freeing of the prisoners aboard the *Altmark* is also reenacted, and the film closes with a segment from Churchill's speech of thanks to the crews at the Guildhall dinner with *Rule Britannia* playing in the background.

For Freedom had a gala premiere at the Gaumont, Haymarket, on 15 April 1940, with Churchill himself in attendance. In spite of a rather too obviously contrived plot, the clashing mix of styles, occasional hyperbole, and awkwardness on the part of some of the RN personnel as they spoke their lines, *For Freedom* was generally well received by the critics and public. The chief drawing point, to judge by reviews, a Mass-Observation report and publicity material, was the promise of seeing the 'real thing' – that is, the people who had actually participated in the Battle of the River Plate. The first part of the film, which was not publicized, was often a disappointment – 'I didn't know there was all that about the beginning of the war,' as one woman put it, 'we've seen all that before' [7] – but the battle scenes had 'the ring of conviction' (*Daily Herald*) and were 'brilliantly described' (*The Times*).[8] It performed well at the box office, tying for the top moneymaker spot in May 1940.[9]

By this time the Admiralty had become involved in a much larger-scale production being made by Ealing Studios entitled *Convoy*. This had been the brainchild of producer Michael Balcon, who, after listening to an eye-witness account of an enemy attack on a convoy on the radio, had approached the MoI and Admiralty to make a feature on the subject at the start of 1940. Balcon having explained the kind of patriotic film he intended to make, with Penrose Tennyson (related to Lord Alfred and shortly to enter the navy himself) directing, the Admiralty proved highly supportive. Everything from naval searchlights to telephones were lent in order to increase the realism of the bridge, deck and cabin sets being built on soundstages at Ealing. A naval adviser, Lieutenant-Commander J. Reid, was also provided to help achieve authenticity in dress, deportment and ship routine. In February, Tennyson and cameraman Roy Kellino were allowed to take extensive footage (20,000 feet in all) aboard the destroyer HMS *Valorous* as it rode at anchor, escorted North Sea convoys and took part in wartime operations. (On the third visit, Kellino unexpectedly found himself on his way to Norway as part of a force being sent to Norway in the aftermath of the *Altmark* incident.) [10] Clive Brook, when approached to play the ship's captain, seems to have been told that it was his patriotic duty to sign on: he promptly did.[11]

Ealing, however, was a commercial operation, and naval versimilitude had to be woven into the plot conventions of cinematic drama. The central narrative involves the convoy flagship, the *Arethusa*-class light cruiser 'Apollo', protecting a convoy against the U-boat threat and engaging in an unequal gun duel with the enemy pocket battleship *Deutschland* (the course of which bears more than a passing resemblance to the *Exeter* versus *Graf Spee* portion of the River Plate engagement). There are, however, also two major melodramtic sub-plots created by Tennyson and writer Patrick Kerwin, one involving conflict with a curmudgeonly but lovable tramp steamer captain (Edward Chapman) and the other a tale of repressed emotions and misunderstanding involving the captain of the 'Apollo', Lieutenant David Cranford (John Clements), and the woman they both care for (Judy Campbell). Cranford is eventually killed while putting out a fire in one of the ship's magazines, while the raider is held off long enough for British battlecruisers to arrive and save the day. The goal of *Convoy*, as the material provided to the press made clear, was 'Entertainment plus Authenticity'.[12]

When the film was privately screened for MoI representatives they were apparently 'dubious of its propaganda value'. Balcon guessed, however, that if the Admiralty liked it, *Convoy* could be released 'without any help' from Senate House.[13] The film was shown by Tennyson to several members of the Board of Admiralty, doubtless mostly unfamiliar with feature films, who sat entranced as the main battle sequence unfolded – a mixture of model work, staged scenes and real footage – with the 'Apollo' taking hits while striving to close in to a range where its own guns could fire. One admiral finally could stand the suspense no longer. Forgetting where he was he stood up and shouted at Clive Brook's profile on the screen: '*Dammit, man, use your torpedoes!*' Opening with a dedication 'with gratitude' to 'the Officers and Men of the Royal and Merchant Navies' whose 'cheerfulness and gratitude made it possible to present the main scenes in our film', and closing to the strains of *Rule Britannia* as the ship's crew stand mustered aft, *Convoy* was certain to receive the full blessings of the Admiralty.[14]

Heavily advertised as 'the best film about the navy', *Convoy* was released to the public in July 1940 to huge acclaim. 'It is a magnificent spectacular and thrilling entertainment,' Reg Whitley wrote breathlessly in the *Daily Mirror*, 'and wonderful propaganda for the boys who sail the seas.' Paul Holt in the *Daily Express* was also euphoric: 'I found it an invigorating tonic.' The *Daily Herald* critic was equally positive. 'Stirring and splendidly handled all the way, this is the finest drama ever screened with Royal Navy background', P. L. Mannock wrote, going on to suggest that 'it embodies the human spirit of officers and men now guarding our national existence, and combines all the terrific sweep of North Sea battle with the reality of individual character under discipline.'[15] The plaudits went on and on: 'a memorable naval occasion' (*Reynolds News*); 'a first-class film and a strong tonic' (*Evening Standard*); 'fine, inspiring stuff' (*News Chronicle*); 'best navy film ever' (*Sunday Dispatch*).[16] *Convoy* was a huge hit with the public, was reproduced in print form by Marjory Williams, and went on to become the most successful British film of 1940.[17]

Encouraged by this success, Ealing and the Admiralty began collaboration on an even more ambitious commercial feature film, designed to show 'the activities of the Fleet Air Arm and its use as a striking force'. Late in 1940, while Lieutenant-Commander Reid was arranging for shooting to take place at a Fleet Air Arm station of Fulmar fighters and other aircraft on the ground and in the sky, cameraman Roy Kellino was again sent to sea, this time for two months aboard the aircraft carrier HMS *Ark Royal*, returning with extensive footage of Skua and Swordfish aircraft taking off, landing and being prepared for action, plus shots of the carrier itself and other warships taken from the air.[18] In early 1941 casting began, with numerous familiar screen faces as well as several *Convoy* veterans eventually being brought on board. Meanwhile the director, Sergei Nolbandov, in collaboration with Patrick Kerwan, Austin Melford and Dina Morgan worked on a script that was completed by the spring. There was also extensive set and model work to be carried out, this time involving the construction of aircraft and two islands as well as ships. 'Producer Michael Balcon', a fan magazine reported in May, 'believes he has another *Convoy*, only bigger and better.'[19]

The story, like that of *Convoy*, was a mixture of naval action and melodrama, only on a grander scale. The action involves the aircraft of the carrier HMS '*Invincible*' fending off Axis air attacks and carrying out strikes on an enemy-held island 'Panteria' in preparation for a British Army landing. The melodrama was evocative not only of *Convoy* but also of prewar films such as *The Four Feathers*. The hero is Dick Stacey (John Clements), an officer cashiered from the Fleet Air Arm after inadvertently causing the death of the son (Hugh Burden) of Admiral Wetherby (Leslie Banks) while trying to impress the admiral's daughter Celia (Jane Baxter) before the war. By the time war comes, Celia has married a brother officer and Stacey is working for a tiny ferry company on the Greek island of 'Parnos'. After an interlude with an old flame (Ann Todd) and some sparring with German agents (Hugh Williams and Frank Pettingell), Stacey discovers new defences around Panteria. He manages to get to the *Invincible*, and informs her captain (Basil Sydney) and Admiral Weatherby of the new dangers. In the wake of an enemy counter-attack on the carrier, Stacey redeems his honour by helping his friends, lieutenants David Grant and Peter Maxwell (Michael Wilding and Michael Rennie), succeed in a second, three-plane attack on the Panteria dam. As Clements sardonically noted to Wilding on the set, his character, as in *Convoy*, makes the ultimate sacrifice at the end of the script. Stacey dies in making sure the dam is breached by means of crashing his fighter into an enemy bomber and piloting them both into the dam wall. By the summer of 1941 both Ealing and the Admiralty were anticipating that *Ships with Wings* 'would do for the Navy what *Target for Tonight* had done for the Air Force'.[20]

As before, the authorities had to vet the film – just over one hundred minutes in length – before its release. This time it was not the MoI who objected but Churchill himself. The Prime Minister, who had numerous films regularly privately screened for himself and his entourage during the war, thought the crash scene at the end would undermine morale. Once again Balcon appealed to the navy, and Churchill agreed that the First Sea Lord, the ageing Admiral Sir Dudley Pound, should have the final say. Balcon nervously awaited the outcome.

> The day he [the First Sea Lord] saw the film I waited in Anthony Kimmins's small office at the Admiralty, biting my fingernails in anxiety until we heard the First Sea Lord's footsteps approaching along the corridor. He had an injured foot and those waiting in the office with me knew the sound of his walk. Sir Dudley entered the room and snapped out in very few words that he saw no reason why the film should not be shown. He had formed his own independent judgment and obviously was no 'yes' man.[21]

There was indeed little to which any senior officer could object. The film opens with another dedication, this time 'to HMS Ark Royal in which many of its scenes were taken, and to the officers and men of the Fleet Air Arm, whose keenness and generous assistance made the production possible', and closes with a tracking shot of the *Ark Royal* and then a fluttering Union Jack. In between, all the RN characters in the film behave decently and perform heroically. After a special showing for senior Admiralty and other distinguished personages at the Savoy (attended by, among others, Sir Victor Warrender, Financial Secretary to the Admiralty, and Lord Louis Mountbatten, the new Chief of Combined Operations), the Second Sea Lord, Vice-Admiral Sir William Whitworth, commented that during the battle scenes he had wanted to jump into an aircraft and 'have a go' at the enemy himself.[22]

There was little likelihood that *Ships with Wings*, premiering at the Gaumont, Haymarket in early November 1941, would stand much comparison with *Target for Tonight*. Despite the *Ark Royal* footage, the new film, with its lush melodrama, was about as far as one could get from the austere realism sought after by Harry Watt. Indeed, a number of film critics took exception to the sheer melodrama of much of the story. J. E. Sewell, writing in the *Telegraph*, pointed out the plot's myriad logical flaws and improbabilities. 'I am disappointed in the story of *Ships With Wings*. It is a wildly tiresome melodrama superimposed on a story that did not need it.' The *Times* critic referred to 'pseudo-adolescent flutterings', while the *Guardian* thought that 'it does not make a very compelling story'. P. L. Mannock in the *Herald* thought that 'the plot and acting lack conviction'; Jonah Barrington in the *Express* laughed at the '"Join the Navy and See Jane Baxter" stuff'; and war correspondent Noel Monks in the *Daily Mail* damned it as 'slush' and as totally inauthentic when compared to *Target for Tonight*.[23]

Viewed today, *Ships with Wings* appears all this and more, complete with poor model work and excruciatingly stereotypical depictions of Germans, Italians and Greeks. But this was not the way it was usually seen by audiences at the time. Even the most hostile film critics usually admired the documentary footage that Kellino had taken, and many of those who hated the love interest often thought the action sequences tilted the balance in favour of the film. 'You may forget the human drama', Mannock rhymed, 'in grand bombardment panorama; in piping peace or war's alarm, it's hats off to the Fleet Air Arm.' Barrington agreed. 'These graphic scenes,' he argued, 'are a valuable contribution to national self pride [and] should be shown and explained (possibly by an Admiralty expert) in every British cinema.' All in all *Ships with Wings* was 'a worthy successor to *Convoy*,' the *Times* concluded.[24]

Whatever reservations some of the critics may have had, the cinema-going public clearly thought *Ships with Wings* was terrific stuff. If anything, news of the sinking of the *Ark Royal* a week after the film opened only seems to have heightened popular interest. A Mass-Observation study of audience reactions around the country found that, across the board, the film had received 'an overwhelmingly good reception', appealing to the emotions by adhering to the conventions of popular melodrama. *Ships With Wings* was also successful propaganda, those surveyed often mentioning that it had heightened their pride in the navy, young men in particular saying that it had made them think of enlisting. Balcon was so shocked by the Monks review and a (typically) highly critical piece in *Documentary News Letter* that he consciously ditched melodrama in favour of realism in subsequent Ealing films supported by the MoI. (The Fleet Air Arm itself was recast in less melodramatic colours in a thirty-six minute documentary made by Ealing the following year incorporating some of the *Ark Royal* footage from *Ships With Wings* and released under the title *Find, Fix and Strike*.)[25] The fact remains, however, that as popular entertainment *Ships with Wings* was a great success.[26] The film was the most popular British feature in its first month on release, continued to do tremendous business as 1941 drew to a close, and was still popular enough the following January to generate profitable spinoffs such as an illustrated booklet.[27]

All in all the Admiralty had done very well out of its association with the commercial film trade. Yet there was still plenty of resistance to having the silent service sing its own praises. According to Rear-Admiral R. K. Dickson, who became Chief of Naval Information later in the war, the Board of the Admiralty regarded the job of the Press Division as being not to publicize the navy but to make sure that 'nothing should be made public which by any stretch of the imagination could help the enemy'.[28] Rear-Admiral George Thomson, chief press officer for service matters at the MoI, also complained of the 'conservatism and secrecy of the Senior Service'.[29]

What held true for the print media was even more the case for the screen. Despite his decision in favour of *Ships with Wings*, Balcon found Admiral Pound, 'like many naval men, disliked anything that smacked of publicity'.[30] It was one thing for the Admiralty to form a small film unit to make training films; it was quite another for it to directly involve itself in producing 'films of a propaganda nature'.[31] There were, to be sure, a few exceptions. In the spring of 1941, Naval Ordnance had produced a drama-documentary with the help of Paramount Newsreel entitled *The Gun*, designed to convince Americans of the importance of US-manufactured Bofors anti-aircraft guns in convoy defence. And in early 1942 two newsreel cameramen had been allowed to direct and film the submarine HMS *Thunderbolt* at Alexandra for the purpose of creating a Movietone News documentary for general consumption entitled *Submarine Patrol*. These films were successful but also exceptional, neither being associated with any effort to build an in-house film unit comparable to those of the other services or the CFU.[32] Henceforth films produced by the navy were to be for training purposes and nothing else. In the view of one of the leading members of the army film unit the conspicuous absence of an in-house film publicity arm was due to the simple fact that the silent service 'just didn't hold with it'.[33]

Those involved in the film world were often viewed in the navy as theatre folk; which is to say as highly unreliable and morally questionable. As the head of a naval officer selection board in 1941 put it on meeting Kenneth More (after rejecting Robert Newton for a commission on the grounds of the latter's general lack of sobriety – which in this particular case was a fair enough assessment): 'Oh, God, not *another* bloody actor.' Patrick Macnee thought he got through his board the following year only because the dubious profession he had chosen was counterbalanced by his having been at Eton.[34]

Several feature film projects with naval themes foundered in the course of the third year of the war. Ealing, which had done well out of naval themes, had planned in January 1942 to make a feature about minesweepers entitled *Little Ships*, but this came to nothing. So too did a British National project entitled *Mediterranean Crossing*, first announced in April 1942, after the Admiralty refused to cooperate.[35] Rather more positive, at least initially, was a proposal from the Admiralty itself that convoy protection – at a time when the public was expressing some concern over shipping losses – be highlighted in a feature film.[36] Captain C. H. A. Brooking at the Press Division had received a rough plot outline for such a feature from Owen Rutter, a naval historian, and with the support of Admiral Sir Percy Noble, the C-in-C Western Approaches, was keen to see it made. This drama-documentary, tentatively titled *HM Escort*, was supposed to show how the convoy system worked, chiefly from the viewpoint of the RN officer commanding a convoy escort screen. The aim was to 'to show how closely the ships under the White Ensign and the Red Ensign work together in time of war, and how the Royal and Merchant navies form British sea power'.[37]

After some debate over whether a special production group or the Crown Film Unit should handle the project, Ian Dalrymple and the CFU were given the green light in early 1942. By March, however, problems were looming from the Admiralty point of view. The film's director, Pat Jackson, decided to change the film from a joint White Ensign–Red Ensign plot into a story centring almost exclusively on the merchant service. The script that was circulated in June 1942 bore almost no resemblance to Rutter's outline, the focus of attention now being not an escort vessel but a merchant vessel, the '*Leander*', plus the survivors of another merchant ship adrift in a ship's boat. In this revised version, entitled *Western Approaches*, the enemy – in the shape of a U-boat – is dealt with by the Merchant Navy, not the Royal Navy. Apart from a merchant captains' conference in the Operations Room at Western Approaches headquarters, the navy would only be featured through an RN rating firing the *Leander*'s deck gun.[38] This was not what the Admiralty had asked for, and when Dalrymple asked for naval craft and personnel for the production he encountered 'an instransigent and unhelpful attitude'.[39] Some help was eventually forthcoming, chiefly in the form of permission to take footage of HMS *Graph*, a captured U-boat. But it was clear that *Western Approaches* – which in any event only reached the screen in November 1944 because of cost overruns and technical problems – was not going to be the next big navy film.[40] There was even some doubt as to whether a commercial feature in preparation in the winter of 1941–42 about a destroyer and its crew, provisionally entitled *White Ensign*, would pass muster. Luckily for all concerned, what became *In Which We Serve* made it to the screen in the autumn of 1942.

White Ensign had its origins in the friendship and mutual interest in entertainment forged in the interwar years between Noël Coward, theatre's *enfant terrible*, and a talented, handsome and highly ambitious rising young naval officer with a royal pedigree, 'Dickie' Mountbatten. The playwright had been a frequent guest in RN wardrooms in the course of his world travels, and had got to know both Dickie and Edwina, his wife, in the milieu of twenties 'bright young things'. In the mid 1930s Coward had been a guest of Mountbatten aboard the destroyer HMS *Wishart* in the Mediterranean. Harbouring the instincts of a true patriot beneath a mask of worldly cynicism, Coward had already fallen in love with the navy and was immensely impressed not only by Mountbatten's family connections – he was cousin to the King – but with his the self-confidence and boundless energy. Mountbatten in turn enjoyed the company of a first-class raconteur with 'a talent to amuse'. Coward used the Mountbattens as the basis for a couple in a one-act play, *Hands Across the Sea*, in 1936, while Mountbatten in 1938 enlisted Coward in his efforts to organize a service to provide quality feature films aboard ships at sea. Coward went on a tour of the ships of the Mediterranean Fleet in April to ascertain the film tastes of the lower deck, thereby doing his part to forward the creation of the Royal Naval Film Corporation (RNFC) in 1939. After war broke out Coward had followed Mountbatten's career as a destroyer captain and flotilla leader, and had been relieved to learn that Mountbatten had survived the sinking of HMS *Kelly* off Crete in late May 1941.[41]

Just over a month later Mountbatten was recounting the loss of the *Kelly* to Coward over dinner. 'Absolutely heartbreaking and so magnificent', Coward wrote in his diary. 'He told me the whole saga without frills and with a sincerity that was very moving.' This was a story, Coward concluded, that ought to be brought to the screen. He visited Sir Gerald Campbell, the Director-General of the British Information Service in New York, then in London, to broach the subject of 'doing a naval propaganda film myself' that would help influence American opinion. Campbell, who was well aware of 'the all-too-silent Royal Navy, which toils but does not spin yarns', reacted positively, saying he thought it 'a magnificent idea'. As for Mountbatten, he was 'wildly enthusiastic'.[42] In contrast to the First Sea Lord and other senior figures at the Admiralty, the former captain of the *Kelly*, only forty-one years of age, was fully conversant with the popularity and power of the cinema. The project also flattered his not inconsiderable ego. Mountbatten, comparatively junior in the service but well connected, set to work at once to drum up support from the Admiralty. Within a week of talking to his subject Coward, wanting to soak up the ambiance of the wartime navy, was granted full access to the naval base at Plymouth and then allowed to visit Scapa Flow and cruise aboard HMS *Nigeria* and other ships. He was the guest of the C-in-C Home Fleet, Admiral Sir John Tovey. 'Dickie's personal enthusiasm cut through many strings of red tape,' Coward later recalled, 'and set many wheels turning on my behalf.'[43]

A deal was quickly put together with film producers Filippo Del Giudice and Anthony Havelock-Allan, who had recently approached Coward to write a *Cavalcade*-type script for them. Coward, who had never made a film before, wanted the best in the business, and was advised to watch David Lean and Ronald Neame at work on *One of Our Aircraft is Missing*. He also viewed some of their earlier films, and, liking what he saw, poached them and others as soon as production on *One of Our Aircraft is Missing* had finished. According to Powell 'he took over our entire crew'.[44]

This did not, however, mean that all went smoothly in the making of the film. Numerous difficulties were in store for Coward and Mountbatten in the months ahead, and it would be a year before *In Which We Serve* appeared in cinemas. To begin with there was the script. Coward first sketched out *White Ensign* as a wide-ranging narrative of the navy starting in 1922 and ending in 1941. He had used just such a broad temporal sweep in one of his most successful plays, and in fact envisaged *White Ensign* as 'a naval *Cavalcade*'.[45] Never having written a screenplay before, Coward underestimated how much screen time would be taken up if what he put down on paper was translated onto film. Havelock-Alan, Neame, and Lean had gently to explain that what the Master proposed would take up around ten hours on screen. Eventually it was agreed that the story should focus exclusively on the destroyer and confine itself to the immediate prewar and wartime period.[46] Mountbatten, who took a close and active interest in all phases of the project, had his own objections. Though keen to see the film made, he guessed that the Admiralty, where self-publicity was heavily frowned upon, would take great exception to a plot in which there was not at least some effort to disguise the obvious resemblance of the destroyer captain to himself. 'The very first script [Coward] showed me', he later explained, 'had the captain married to Lady Celia Kinross, living in a large country house with a Rolls-Royce and a driver.' As Mountbatten told him, 'this is pointing straight at me'. Coward agreed to make Captain Kinross an 'average', middle-class officer.[47]

Casting was also problematic. Coward had written the part of Ordinary Seaman 'Shorty' Blake for John Mills, who had successfully demonstrated his capacity to play a member of the lower deck six years earlier in *Brown on Resolution*. The other parts, however, were sometimes not so easy to fill. Mountbatten wanted actors whom he thought could convincingly pass as members of the Royal Navy, and it was only after he as well as Coward had sized up actors such as Bernard Miles – who was to play Petty Officer Walter Hardy – that they were brought on board. He was so dissatisfied with the extras that he drafted sailors recovering in the naval hospital at Haslar to take their places.[48] Coward did not take exception to any of this, and indeed was very keen to make sure that his film – unlike the navy features he had heard roundly derided while surveying ships' crews three years earlier – appeared truly authentic.[49] James Mason, considered for one of the ship's officers, was rejected by Coward because of his pacifist views, while Michael Wilding, having been seen playing a junior officer in *Ships With Wings*, was again cast in that role.[50] He took great care over even small parts, such as that of an unnerved seaman that went to Richard Attenborough.[51] The one exception Coward made was for himself: he would play Captain Kinross.

This was to cause a lot of trouble. To begin with, as Coward himself admitted, his face, diction and stage persona did not make him appear a 'natural' for the part, and he was already co-directing, producing and writing the music for the film. But he could not pass up the opportunity to play the man he so admired, even though the early rushes looked awful. 'I'm a snob, I know it', Coward told Michael Powell. 'I couldn't bear to have anyone else play Dickie!' [52] Through dampening his usual stage style and adopting the mannerisms of his hero as much as he could – down to repeating Mountbatten's speeches to the crew of the *Kelly* word for word and wearing his old cap at the same angle – the Master grew a little more credible as Kinross.[53] (His face and voice, though, along with occasional witty-sophisticate pieces of dialogue, still made him stand out.)

Rumours that Noël Coward was planning to play Mountbatten in a major new film quickly circulated, however. At the end of August this became front-page news in the *Express* and questions began to be asked. At the Admiralty, where 'naval prejudice against "undesirable publicity" – especially personal publicity in any form – increased rather than decreased', the idea of anyone playing an actual serving officer was anathema.[54] Meanwhile at the MoI both Walter Monckton, the director-general, and Brendan Bracken, the minister, questioned whether, in light of the negative publicity being generated by the *Express* and (false) press reports two years earlier that he had masqueraded as a naval officer, it might not be better for Coward to bow out of the role.[55] Despite support from Captain Brooking at the Admiralty press division, as the *Express* campaign continued into September (on the 17th, 'it is wrong to have a professional actor dressed in the peaked cap and gold braid of a British naval officer'; on the 30th, more 'criticism of Mr Coward dressing in the clothes of a naval officer'), Sidney Bernstein was dispatched to try and persuade Coward to change his mind. Mountbatten, meanwhile, off in the United States to take command of the refitted carrier HMS *Illustrious*, was growing worried at the rumblings from within his own service, and wrote to Coward asking him to either alter the plot radically or drop the whole thing entirely. Coward, however, was no shrinking violet when it came to fighting for his own cause. Bernstein was rebuffed and Mountbatten persuaded that the linkage with his own story would not be obvious.[56]

Mountbatten's support continued to be of crucial importance. Jack Beddington, head of the MoI Films Division, after reading the full script, informed Coward in December 1941 that he considered it 'bad propaganda' because one of His Majesty's ships was shown sinking, and strongly hinted that Coward ought to give up his autonomy if the film was to get any backing from the MoI. This was another attempt by the MoI and elements in the Admiralty to prevent Coward from going his own way, particularly in relation to casting.[57] Mountbatten, back in London as Chief of Combined Operations, solicited a memorandum from Commander A. W. Jarrett (in charge of the RNFC) outlining Beddington's limitations, and took time out to visit both the First Lord at the Admiralty, A. V. Alexander, and Brendan Bracken at the MoI to argue in favour of the film. He also showed the script to the Vice-Chief of Naval Staff, Rear-Admiral Sir Tom Phillips, and to his cousin, King George VI. All thought the whole thing ridiculous: 'Bloody ships *do* get hit, don't they?'[58] Beddington was forced to beat a retreat. 'Dickie's militant loyalty, moral courage and infinite capacity for taking pains, however busy he is,' Coward noted in his diary on 6 January 1942, 'is one of the marvels of the age.'[59]

Mountbatten later procured two advisers to check on authenticity, Lieutenant-Commander I. T. 'Bushy' Clarke (a destroyer commander) and Able Seaman Terry Lawler (who had served as Mountbatten's batman on the *Kelly*). He was also able to obtain necessary steel from a reluctant Board of Trade for the construction of very elaborate sets, and helped defer the call-up of the chief assistant director, Michael Anderson. In return, in addition to having a say in casting, he was allowed to view rushes practically every weekend once filming began and to give unsolicited advice on dialogue, shooting and even the title.[60]

Set construction was both time-consuming and expensive as the search for authenticity continued. As well as building various scale models, David Rawnsley and Sid Streeter (both of whom had worked on *One of Our Aircraft is Missing*) supervised the construction of full-scale wooden replicas of the bridge, quarterdeck, and – most impressive of all – the entire front third or so of a K-class destroyer, the last two resting on steel hydraulic rockers. It weighed one hundred tons and was two hundred feet long and sixty feet wide by the time it was first put to use.[61] There were also a variety of interior room and cabin sets to construct. *In Which We Serve*, as it was now called, was by February 1942 eating up the funds which Del Giudice had borrowed at a prodigious rate after C. M. Woolf of General Film

Distributors pulled out when the pre-shooting costs had reached £180,000. Only the last-minute intervention of Sam Smith at British Lion Film Distributors saved the set from being closed down after ten days shooting. Throughout the long production, as John Mills noted, 'no expense was spared'.[62]

Making a film for the first time in his life, perhaps fearful of things spinning out of control, and hence eager to assert himself, the Master made it clear that he viewed the cast and crew as a team; but a team from which he would expect high standards and over which he would exert absolute authority. With this in mind, Coward took the unusual step of distributing the whole script to the entire cast and crew three weeks before shooting began in a successful bid to make them feel fully involved in what was happening (with an added note to the cast that they be word-perfect by the time they arrived on the set). On the first day of shooting, 5 February, when actor William Hartnell was fifteen or so minutes late in arriving on the set, Coward immediately tongue-lashed and then sacked him *pour encourager les autres.* (Michael Anderson, assistant director, was hastily bundled into costume and a false moustache to play a Royal Marine in his stead.) This was intimidating but, in combination with Coward's obvious desire to create a first-rate film, it had its effect. 'This is the only way to make pictures', John Mills reflected that night, '— efficiency, drive, enthusiasm and a perfect script. Actors also word-perfect.' After the first five days Coward guessed it was going to work out all right after all. 'Whole staff working well and efficiently', he noted in his diary.[63]

Coward, as he grew less anxious, came to rely heavily on the experienced production crew he had inherited from Michael Powell, particularly the man who co-directed, David Lean. Bored and out of his depth with the tedious and time-consuming job of setting up lights, cameras and other equipment for individual shots, the Master left the technical side of shooting the picture to him. 'I handled the whole damn thing', as Lean later put it. In retrospect this was clearly one of the factors that made the film a success.[64]

Even with what Coward termed 'increased efficiency',[65] however, the sheer scale of the production meant that shooting took time and costs escalated. Influenced by the big documentaries then in vogue, Coward sent Havelock-Allan and Neame up to Newcastle to take footage of ships being built and a destroyer being launched at the Hawthorne-Leslie Yard.[66] Staging the sinking of HMS '*Torrin*' involved carefully staged explosions and shots of the full-scale bridge and ship's side mock-ups heeling over with tons of water cascading over them as men jumped into the 'sea' (in fact the large studio tank at Denham). To add authenticity, Guy Green was sent to sea to take footage of real destroyers in the South Atlantic, while Lean built a mock mast at Duxford and took shots of a Ju–88 swooping down towards it.[67] Then there were the scenes of oil-soaked members of the crew clinging to a Carley float and being machine-gunned from the air, which took over two weeks to complete. This was extremely arduous for the actors involved, who spent days on end in water covered with oil and other muck ('the *stench*, I mean the *pong*, was something to be wondered at', Attenborough recalled; the Master, who was also in the tank, with perfect timing and deadpan delivery, remarked on the final day: 'There's dysentery in every ripple!').[68] It also caused problems for the special effects people, who had to come up with a reasonable facsimile of bullets striking the water and wounding John Mills. This particular technical difficulty was solved by exploding air-filled condoms just under the water. 'I am reasonably certain', Mills later wrote, 'I can claim to be the only actor in history who has been shot in the arm by a French letter.'[69] By this point, in early March 1942, the production was costing £1000 a day, and there were still several months of exterior and set shooting to be done. Only in late June was filming complete, by which time the original budget of £60,000 had mushroomed to £200,000.[70]

The end result, however, justified the cost and delay, not least from the Admiralty point of view. In the opening credits appears the following:

THIS FILM IS DEDICATED
TO THE ROYAL NAVY

WHEREON UNDER THE
GOOD PROVIDENCE OF
GOD, THE WEALTH, SAFETY
AND STRENGTH OF THE
KINGDOM CHIEFLY DEPEND

Then, as an unseen Leslie Howard announces 'This, is the story – *of a ship!*', the documentary-style footage taken by Neame of workers building a destroyer and its launch are shown, followed by studio shots of HMS *Torrin* commissioning … The scene then shifts to 23 May 1941 off Crete, where the *Torrin* is shown creating havoc among German troop transports and an enemy destroyer in a night engagement. This is followed by an air attack on the ship the following day in which several German bombers are shot down but the *Torrin* herself is hit and heels over in what was, for the standards of the day, a highly realistic series of action sequences. As men jump overboard Coward is shown clinging to the binnacle, being swept off the bridge by a great wave, and then holding his hand over his face underwater (exactly, as it happened, as Mountbatten had described his actions on the sinking of the *Kelly*).

There then comes the first of many 'flashbacks' as Kinross, in the water, recalls the whirlwind provisioning of the *Torrin* in August 1939, his address to the assembled crew about wanting 'a happy and efficient ship' (taken word for word from Mountbatten),[71] and his farewell to Mrs Kinross (Celia Johnson). Then it is back to 1941 and the men in the water, with some of the survivors, including the three principles, Captain Kinross, Petty Officer Hardy and Able Seaman Blake, clinging to a Carley float. There are then more flashback sequences, sometimes attributable to one of the three, at others not, punctuated by short scenes on the Carley Float. In these flashbacks personal triumphs and tragedies (Christmas, a wedding, deaths), and major events in the ship's career (such as a night battle with German destroyers in the Channel and disembarking tired and wounded men from Dunkirk) are recalled.

Throughout the film the officers and men of the *Torrin* – separated by class (as the personal flashbacks make clear) but united by love of the navy (as the 'ship' flashbacks emphasize) – behave with great professionalism and understated bravery. The only exception – again based on an incident aboard the *Kelly* – is when a young sailor (Richard Attenborough in his first role) panics under fire. But this is the exception that proves the rule, as the captain's speech to the assembled crew on the subject – again lifted directly from Mountbatten – demonstrates.[72]

The picture ends with a simple but moving farewell by Kinross to the other survivors after they have been picked up and taken to Alexandria. 'So ends the story of a ship,' Leslie Howard intones, 'but there will always be other ships', as an aircraft carrier is seen plunging through heavy seas. 'For we are an island race. Through all our centuries, the sea has ruled our destiny. There will always be other ships, and men to sail in them' – cut to a shot of the crew of the *Torrin* formed up on the quayside, and then of hundreds of real sailors marching on parade. 'It is these men, in peace or war, to whom we owe so much, above all victories, beyond all loss, in spite of changing values in a changing world, they give to us their countrymen, eternal and indomitable pride.' Cut to a shot of a new ship being launched and Kinross on the bridge of a cruiser: 'Open Fire!' The last words, like the first, are spoken by the unseen Leslie Howard: 'God bless our ships, and all who sail in them!' A White Ensign is the backdrop to the full cast credits. As the Master had intended, his film was most definitely a 'tribute to the Royal Navy'.[73]

When *In Which We Serve* finally appeared on the screen in the autumn of 1942 it rapidly became clear that intertwining the private lives of three members of the crew – specifically the women they love – with the story of the ship made it wildly popular. It was a story of commitment to family and navy, a romance of love and duty, in which melodrama and heavily demonstrative emotion was eschewed in favour of moving understatement (except, of course, in the coda, which was all hats-off to the navy). The film was also, thanks to the pains taken, very authentic in terms of naval routine and equipment, and very credible in terms of special effects. Coward had wanted his tribute to be both 'accurate and sincere'. His skill as a dramatist, combined with the talent of the actors and production crew he utilized, meant that he succeeded. Admirals, critics and public alike were smitten.

As was to be expected, the higher ranks of the navy were out in force for the premiere, held in aid of naval charities on 17 September. 'Towards the end,' Coward recalled, 'there was a great deal of gratifying nose-blowing and one stern-faced Admiral in the row behind me was unashamedly in tears.' Commander Jarrett was quite overwhelmed. 'Mary Tudor said that when she died they would find Calais written across her heart', the head of the RNFC wrote. 'I think "IN WHICH WE SERVE" will be written across mine.' Mountbatten himself was 'absolutely thrilled', and watched *In Which We Serve* on three separate occasions in its opening weeks (as well as many times later). 'I have now had time to hear the opinion of various officers of different ranks and outlook who have seen the film,' he informed Coward at the start of October, 'and would never have believed that one could get such shades of opinion in the Navy to be so unanimous on any subject, let alone a film!'[74]

Critics were equally in awe. 'I want to be careful about the use of superlatives, because in no industry are adjectives so misused as in the film industry', the editor of *Picturegoer* wrote. 'But I wish I could find words adequate enough to convey the power and the beauty, the pathos and the grandeur of *In Which We Serve*.' P. L. Mannock, in the *Daily Herald*, expressed his opinion that 'previous films of the Royal Navy seem insignificant beside Noel Coward's', concluding that it was a 'magnificent, inspiring' feature. Edgar Anstey, in the *Spectator*, noted that there was 'no extravagant heroism, no glossing-over of weakness, no rhetorical hatred of the enemy; the whole is informed with a native humour and a sense of professional competence which will tell the people of the world more about the British Navy than they ever knew before'. Just as impressive were the domestic scenes involving the families of Blake and Hardy. 'Here at last on the screen in a war-film are working-class men and women with integrity, wisdom and humanity.' The *Express* critic, Ernest Betts, in spite of the proprietor's campaign against Coward, labelled it a 'human, deeply moving film', and a highly realistic one too. It 'lifts the veil which has hidden the activities of the Senior Service for far too long', Reg Whitley noted approvingly in the *Daily Mirror*, then the single most popular paper in Britain. And so in went on, with hardly a negative note at all. Even the *Documentary News Letter*, normally scornful of trade features, conceded that it was 'an exceptionally sincere and deeply moving film'.[75]

As for the public, they liked what they saw. As with the occasional critic, such as William Whitebait, there were some who found Noël Coward himself a bit unconvincing, but even they were often impressed by *In Which We Serve*. To those responding to a 1943 Mass-Observation directive on cinema-going over previous months, this was among the most commonly mentioned films. It was variously described as 'sincere', 'most moving', 'inspiring', 'authentic', 'true to life' and 'a marvellous film'. It was the most successful British film of 1943 at the box office (and second overall) and continued to be viewed in polls and surveys as one of the best films of the war in 1945. 'Here you were proud of the British Navy,' a respondent to a *Picturegoer* poll after the war reflected, 'no other country could feel as the British felt over this film, it was not one long weep, or one long view of fights, blood and death, but it had a little to sober you, a little to cheer you, it gave you a glimpse of families, the men and their home lives, it made you feel strong and proud, and what could one ask for more than that?'[76]

Despite the denials Coward issued and, at Mountbatten's request, repeated in his memoirs, *In Which We Serve* was Dickie's version of the story of the *Kelly*, and was widely seen as such. This caused Mountbatten some discomfort. 'You may not realise it,' he wrote to Coward in 1953, 'but I have been greatly criticised, chiefly among my brother officers, for being a party to the making of film which apparently was designed to boost me personally.'[77] This reaction was in part because of the way in which the navy frowned on any form of self-promotion or personal publicity, but also because many officers knew that this was a rather sanitized version of Mountbatten's wartime career as a destroyer captain and flotilla leader. The film gave an impression of great professionalism and success in battle, whereas in reality Mountbatten had displayed poor judgement that had caused severe damage to the *Kelly*, as well as another destroyer, *Javelin*, which he commanded as flotilla leader while *Kelly* was being repaired in 1940. At the same time, however, even those who thought Mountbatten a poor sailor recognized that the film 'was a splendid piece of propaganda which did good for the Service' – and in a year when propaganda seemed to be needed.[78]

From the outbreak of war down through 1941, to judge by MoI home intelligence division and Mass-Observation reports, respect for and pride in the Royal Navy had been consistently strong in Britain. The service might be silent a lot of the time, but bearing in mind its long history of maritime supremacy, coupled with the news of the hunting down of German raiders such as the *Graf Spee* (1939) and the *Bismarck* (1941) and success against the Italian navy at Taranto (1940) and Cape Matapan (1941), people held it in great and mostly uncritical respect.[79] British warships sunk tended to be viewed in terms of a gallant fight against the odds, while shock over the loss of the battlecruiser *Hood* was more than counterbalanced by the sinking of the *Bismarck.* 'There is nothing but praise', the MoI home intelligence survey for the late May and early June 1941 reported as news of the ships lost around Crete filtered back, 'for the work of the Navy in evacuating the troops from the island.'[80] The sinking of the *Ark Royal* in November, home intelligence noted, while a cause for grief, 'has not been accepted as a national disaster'.[81] A special report on naval recruiting concluded that joining the RN was often a matter of perceived prestige value: 'This takes in both the personal prestige of the man concerned, and the feeling that the Navy is the Senior Service and has a high reputation for successful action in this war.'[82] Even when news was announced in mid December 1941 of the loss of the new battleship *Prince of Wales* and the old battle cruiser *Repulse* to Japanese bombers, criticism was initially quite muted. 'The regard in which the British Navy is held', Home Intelligence noted, '. . . has silenced any criticism of the strategy which resulted in their loss.'[83]

There was, however, a limit to the number of times the public could rationalize defeat at sea. 'With the passage of time,' the end-of-year summary noted, 'there is increased criticism of the naval authorities concerning the loss of the *Prince of Wales* and the *Repulse.*'[84]

Then in February 1942 came the Channel Dash, in which the German fast battleships *Scharnhorst* and *Gneisenau* broke out of Brest harbour and eluded interception while racing up the English Channel towards the safety of a German port. 'I find that people are more distressed about the escape of the *Scharnhorst* and *Gneisenau* than they are even by the loss of Singapore', Harold Nicolson, MP, recorded in his diary on the 16th. 'They cannot bear the thought that the Germans sailed past our front door.' Intelligence reports from around the country indicated that people were indeed shocked, humiliated and very angry. 'Much of this anger was directed towards the RAF, but the Royal Navy also came in for its share of accusation: *'Where Was the Fleet?'.*[85]

It was in this context that the Admiralty began to take a more positive interest in feature films. Publicity was still frowned upon. *In Which We Serve*, then still in production, had come about largely because of lobbying by Mountbatten; efforts to make films about the navy emanating from less well-placed sources, such as the Crown Film Unit, had been firmly rebuffed in the latter part of 1941.[86] In early 1942, however, long before Coward's film added to naval prestige, the Admiralty suddenly took a renewed interest in two feature proposals involving the Royal Navy: one from Gaumont-British, the other from the Crown Film Unit.

By the third year of the war there were feature films dealing with the work of cruisers, a destroyer, even an aircraft carrier: thus the number of possible vessels was somewhat limited. The battleship as a subject doubtless seemed unpromising in view of recent sinkings, the less-than-photogenic minesweeper was hardly likely to appeal to either film producers or audiences, and the corvette was about to be used as a vehicle for an American film.[87] That pretty much left the submarine, which had much to recommend it. From the producer's point of view, the cast and sets would be relatively small in scale and cost, while a story about a submarine mission would have natural dramatic potential, as Gaumont-British had discovered through the surprise success of *Submarine Patrol*.[88] From the Admiralty's perspective, there was fact that it would only have to commit to a limited number of exterior shots of submarines, which would in turn minimize operational inconvenience. In addition, HM submarines would be shown as doing damage to the enemy at a time when the public remained anxious about the U-boat scourge in the Atlantic (any film about anti-submarine convoy work being complicated by security and logistical considerations).[89] A concomitant advantage for both would be that a submarine film could be completed and released relatively quickly. So appealing was the prospect that the Admiralty, hitherto cool to the idea, suddenly turned around and authorized two.[90]

The first submarine project was a Gaumont-British (Gainsborough Pictures) production, *We Dive at Dawn*, very loosely based on the popular memoir of a submarine captain, Lieutenant-Commander Kenneth Edwards, which began shooting at Shepherds Bush sound stage in March. The Admiralty provided producer Edward Black and director 'Puffin' Asquith with advisers, old plans and hundreds of spare pieces of equipment with which to construct a credible submarine interior. The end result, after weeks of research at naval establishments by art director Walter Murton and 250 drawings, was impressive. Elaborate reconstructions of a torpedo firing chamber, torpedo stores, seamen's mess, petty officers' mess, wardroom, commander's office, galley and corridor, control room, motor room, and engine room and various other compartments were built, with the engine room and control room in particular filled with working parts and gauges 'every feature of which', *Kinematopgraph Weekly* reported, 'will have to be learned by the stars and actors under the guidance of experienced officers of these underwater craft, who are acting as advisors'.[91] A special movable cradle, built from girders taken from bombed-out buildings, was used to vary the angle of the control room set (weighing twenty-five tons) in order to simulate diving. The naval adviser on the set, a lieutenant in the submarine service, made sure actors understood the need for them to look suitably scruffy in dress and appearance if the submarine was supposed to have been at sea for several days. To give the audience a sense of the claustro-phobia of a submarine and heighten tension, Asquith planted a camera crew within the cramped hull sets to take only close-ups.[92]

Nor was this all that was done in the quest for authenticity. Over a weekend in April, Asquith, accompanied by camera crew and key cast members, was allowed to 'direct' the submarine P614 – originally built for the Turkish navy and therefore less of a security risk in being unlike the standard RN submarines – over a weekend, coming alongside and casting off from the submarine tender HMS *Forth*, entering and leaving Holy Loch, diving, surfacing and sailing at sea. John Mills, who was to play the captain, was also allowed to accompany a submarine to sea. Because he was 'deter-mined to know what it felt like when a submarine crash-dived', Mills was given a rather frightening demonstration.[93]

The plot of *We Dive at Dawn* centres on HMS '*Sea Tiger*' and its efforts to sink a new German battleship, the '*Brandenburg*'. After returning from patrol the crew of the *Sea Tiger* is given leave, and the private lives of the captain, Lieutenant-Commander Freddie Taylor (John Mills), Leading Seaman Frank Hobson (Eric Portman), and a number of chief petty officers (notably Niall MacGinnis and Reginald Purdell) and others, are revealed. Before various domestic problems can be resolved, however, the captain and crew are recalled for special duty, and the *Sea Tiger* sets off in search of the *Brandenburg*. Discovering from downed German airmen picked up in the North Sea that the battleship has already left the Kiel Canal and is into the Baltic, Taylor decides to follow. This involves breaking through anti-submarine nets and then – in the part of the film that closely resembled the memoir on which it was based – stalking the *Brandenburg*. After firing torpedoes, the submarine is in turn subjected to depth-charge attack by the escorting destroyers, only evading destruction through a ruse: the stern is allowed to break surface and then disappear, followed by jettisoned oil, clothing and the dead body of one of the German airmen. Lacking enough fuel to get home, Taylor plans to scuttle the ship off the Danish coast until Hobson suggests a plan to steal oil from a docked Danish tanker. There follows a rather *Boys Own* escapade, as a result of which the *Sea Tiger* makes it home. The crew learn that they sank the *Brandenburg*, and the domestic problems of the principal petty officers and Hobson are successfully resolved.

Like most other service films of the mid war period, *We Dive at Dawn* was written and cast with an eye to class and regional variation as well as authenticity. As the opening scenes ashore establish, the captain is an upper-middle class RN officer, Leading Seaman Hobson is Yorkshire working class, and the chief petty officers – an Englishman, an Irishman, a Scot and a Welshman – are shown to be lower-middle class. (There is also a small part for a token Canadian seaman, 'Canada', played badly by Norman Williams.) Class distinctions aboard the cramped *Sea Tiger*, though, are more blurred than aboard the *Torrin*, and among the minor characters there is even an upper-middle class conscript sailor ('Oxford'). The domestic sub-plots established at the beginning of the film are handled in a generally unmelodramatic fashion, and were clearly designed to allow audiences to relate at a class and human level to the actors on screen. The filmmakers' object was, in a sense, to set an authentic-looking war story in the context of a staged series of personal dramas, thereby telling an exciting tale while at the same time meeting the apparent desire for at least some escapism among audiences.

From the Admiralty point of view, the plot was as important as the settings. Making the submarine and crew appear authentic in a semi-documentary manner aboard ship would lead audiences to infer that the central plot – the hunt for the *Brandenburg* – was also based on reality; that British submarines were scoring significant successes against major enemy surface units. This was, in point of fact, true enough for the war in the Mediterranean, where British submarines scored a number of successes against the Italians. But it was far less true for northern waters, where no conventional British submarine had even damaged a German heavy ship since 1939. In fact the plot of *We Dive at Dawn* was in some ways a reversal of reality: it was the German submarine fleet, in the shape of the U–47 in October 1939, which had sunk a British battleship – the *Royal Oak* – in Scapa Flow.[94] It remained to be seen, however, what the public would make of the film.

The release of *We Dive at Dawn* did not take place until the spring of 1943, probably in order to avoid having to compete with the ongoing success of *In Which We Serve*. When the film premiered in May, however, it was only natural that comparisons would be drawn between it and Coward's naval epic – even the titles sounded alike – though, to judge by the fact that Asquith's effort was well into production before *In Which We Serve* was finished (to the point where John Mills was going from one during the day to the other at night),[95] *We Dive at Dawn* was not in fact influenced by *In Which We Serve*.

Kinematograph Weekly thought the early scenes of *We Dive at Dawn*, 'which peep into the private lives ... are a somewhat misguided attempt to create an *In Which We Serve* atmosphere', but went on to admit that 'there follows a thrilling and thoroughly convincing account of action at sea'. The *Monthly Film Bulletin* thought it 'has not quite the same air of sincerity [as *In Which We Serve*],' but nevertheless possessed 'a strong air of actuality'. Campbell Dixon, writing in the *Daily Telegraph*, thought it inferior to Coward's effort overall, but still worth watching – not least for John Mills as the captain and the action scenes. 'The dialogue and the technical business are exactly right, or seems so to a landlubber', he wrote approvingly, 'the captain, his eye glued to the periscope, his face glistening with sweat, his tongue repeatedly moistening lips parched by heat and the hunter's fear, is a figure to haunt the memory. Here is one scene to match the best of *In Which We Serve*, and I can think of no higher praise.' Other critics had similar reactions, including Edgar Anstey in the *Spectator*, who thought it 'well worth seeing'.

> He [Mills as captain] might have been cool, confident and phlegmatic; instead he is jumpy and anxious, nervously uncertain for a moment about the range, then a bit querulous with his crew. He behaves, in fact, like a man faced with his first great professional opportunity and driving his mind like a racehorse to guard against everything that may go wrong. As a background to this play of emotion, the intricate mechanics of submarine operation are faithfully recorded – all sight and sound dominated by sharp, impatient finger-snap of the commander calling for his periscope to be swung up [*sic*] and give him another, nearer sight of his prey. This is film-making at its very best.

The Times and *Guardian* had already expressed similar views.[96]

Meanwhile mass-circulation dailies such as the *Daily Express* and *Daily Herald*, like the fan magazine *Picturegoer*, were less inclined to make comparisons and more unreservedly enthusiastic. *We Dive at Dawn* received a '90°' rating in the *Express* and P. L. Mannock labelled it 'the best submarine story ever screened: tense, human, comic and ideally acted'. Reg Whitley, despite his vocal opinion that too many war films were being made, wrote in the *Daily Mirror* that 'I have seen one war film which I think you will like'. All in all Asquith's contribution to the war at sea on the screen was 'an entertaining slice of life ashore and afloat'.[97] Audiences, to judge by the 1943 Mass-Observation survey and other sources, also liked the film. But they too tended to place it alongside *In Which We Serve*, from whose shadow it never fully emerged.[98]

The other submarine feature, a film very much in the drama-documentary tradition of *Target for Tonight*, came about at the initiative of the Crown Film Unit. Ian Dalrymple was later to complain that director Jack Lee was not allowed to begin work on *Close Quarters* until *We Dive at Dawn* was completed, but given that the two were released within a month of each other this seems unlikely.[99] In contrast to the *Western Approaches* débâcle, the Admiralty proved very accommodating. Art director Peggy Gick was allowed to use RN blueprints in drawing up construction plans for a realistic wood-and-plaster control room and other sets, and Lee and his camera team allowed to shoot footage of a 'T' boat at sea. As in the earlier Crown Film Unit efforts for the RAF, crew roles were played by servicemen, including actual submariners such as Lieutenant-Commander Gregory, captain of the fictional HMS '*Tyrant*'.[100]

As in other Crown Film Unit features, the plot of *Close Quarters* – seventy-five minutes in length, dubbed by one of the cast as '*In Which We Submerge*' – was designed to showcase both day-to-day conditions and operational highlights aboard HM submarines.[101] *Tyrant* sets off on a patrol off Norway, and for the next two weeks nothing much happens. Then a U-boat is sighted at night and a gun duel ensues in which the enemy submarine is sunk. *Tyrant*, with a damaged exhaust valve, is forced to remain on the surface in daylight, and narrowly escapes bombs from a German plane as she crash dives. The next day three Norwegians are picked up from a small craft, and on the final day of the patrol an enemy floating dock is sunk – after which the *Tyrant* undergoes a depth-charge attack by enemy destroyers. Surviving this assault, she heads for home.[102]

The critics, some of whom were given a preview of *Close Quarters* at the Ministry of Information on 22 June 1943, were positive. *The Times* noted that, like other CFU productions, the film 'states an heroic case through the plain objective mirror of reporting rather than through the distorting lens of a cinematic fiction'. Indeed, 'this is decidedly a film in which the part is less than the inspiring and heroic whole'. The *Daily Telegraph* thought that daily life aboard a submarine had been 'reenacted with great skill by officers and men of the Submarine Service'. *The Daily Express* was even more enthusiastic, giving it a 95° rating: 'This brilliant record honours and applauds our submarine men, and you will too when you see the film.' There were, however, some doubts about the commercial viability of the film. The 'review for showmen' in *Kinematograph Weekly*, for instance, noted that the action sequences were gripping but hinted that too much time was spent on dull routine. P. L. Mannock in the *Herald* was very impressed, yet thought that 'the monotony of undersea warfare' ought to have been avoided by cuts of at least fifteen minutes. The unfortunate fact was that what had seemed novel in *Target for Tonight* was becoming somewhat *passé*, especially in relation to routine that lacked inherent drama. Coming so soon after, but reviewed and released less widely than its commercial cousin, *Close Quarters*, which premiered at the Regal at the end of June 1943, generated a meagre £13,740 in revenue – only a fifth of the figure achieved by *Target for Tonight* – and appears to have rapidly receded from public consciousness.[103]

By this time the Admiralty was taking a more progressive attitude to publicity. In late 1942 the Parliamentary Secretary, Lord Bruntisfield, had formed a committee on publicity for the navy which had recommended the creation of a new Naval Information Department separate from the naval staff.[104] Thus in early 1943 Admiral Sir William James became the first Chief of Naval Information. The First Sea Lord, meanwhile, once again proved willing to shield film productions in which the navy had an interest when called upon to do so. The Ealing feature *San Demetrio, London*, based on a documented episode in the autumn of 1940 and directed by Charles Frend, celebrated the exploits of merchant sailors who, in the face of a German battlecruiser attack on homeward-bound Atlantic convoy HX–84, had reboarded their burning and heavily damaged oil tanker and brought her home. It was thus a commercial parallel to *Western Approaches* and also involved a degree of Admiralty cooperation. Once satisfied with how HMS *Jervis Bay*, the armed merchant cruiser escorting the convoy, was to be presented – bravely steering straight for the *Admiral Scheer* despite weakness in guns and armour – their Lordships provided the limited technical assistance requested. When Churchill took exception to the film ('dastardly'), presumably because scenes showing the shattering of the convoy and men in lifeboats might adversely affect morale, the new First Sea Lord, Admiral Sir Andrew Cunningham, was prepared to defend the film to the hilt. 'I think,' he noted pointedly in a reply to the Prime Minister, 'that the British navy can take this. And a great deal more.'[105] The film, released in December 1943, was a critical success but a commercial failure (again apparently due to public fatigue with respect to war themes). The navy, though, was nevertheless portrayed in a positive light and the Board of Admiralty thanked in the titles for help 'without which this picture could not have been made'.[106]

Despite such positive signs, there were still difficulties. While supporting *San Demetrio, London*, Cunningham remained deeply ambivalent about senior commanders appearing in the major documentary features of the period. The sight of Admiral Mountbatten and General Slim in *Burma Victory* (see chapter four) 'doing film star work', he recorded in his diary, 'made me physically sick'.[107] Responsibility for publicity matters was split between the CNI (who reported to the Parliamentary Secretary) and the DPD (who reported to the naval staff), which tended to cause confusion and dissipate effort. Just as importantly, operational and security needs always came first, underlying which was a deep-seated desire to preserve the dignity of the fleet. Senior admirals, moreover, were still often ignorant of the mechanics of filmmaking and publicity.[108]

Hence, for example, the problems associated with a forty-six minute film about the Fleet Air Arm made for recruiting purposes. Doubtless impressed by *One of Our Aircraft is Missing*, someone in the Admiralty remembered in the summer of 1942 that the actor Ralph Richardson was in the Fleet Air Arm. Knowing that Richardson had worked with Michael Powell in *The Lion Has Wings*, he ordered him to get in touch and organize a project. ('We need a film, Richardson. See what you can do about it.') Powell, a true admirer of the Royal Navy, and egged on by Richardson and Pressburger, agreed to make a semi-documentary film under MoI sponsorship, but came to regret it. *The Volunteer* 'was a pain in the arse from start to finish'.[109]

The script which Pressburger wrote involved the transformation of a rather clumsy dresser, Fred Davey (played by Pat McGrath), working with Ralph Richardson in a production of *Othello*, into a gifted FAA mechanic, with past and present being brought together by a chance meeting with Richardson, now also in the FAA, aboard a fleet aircraft carrier.[110] Initially shooting was confined to HMS *Argus*, a training ship based in Liverpool. Director, writer, cast and crew, however, thought that there would also have to be work done aboard a modern fleet carrier. The Admiralty was bluntly forthright in response:

> Dear Powell and Pressburger [as the director somewhat facetiously recalled their Lordships' response], if you ask for what you want when you want it, you can't have it. Or if you could have it, it would cost … an astronomical fee. Do as we say, tell us exactly what you want, and when it is possible to give it to you, we'll tell you to come and get it, and it won't cost you or the taxpayer a penny.[111]

Eventually Powell and his cast and crew were allowed to travel by troopship to Gibraltar, where they transferred to the modern carrier HMS *Indomitable* in the autumn of 1942. Aboard *Indomitable* they were afforded a great deal of cooperation from captain and crew, including a staged air attack on the carrier by its own planes and the expenditure of large quantities of anti-aircraft ammunition. As a result of the need for the *Indomitable* to cover Allied landings in French North Africa in November 1942, however, the entire production team found themselves in the middle of the real thing and then stranded in Oran at the end of the year. Subsequently they had to make their own way back to England with some providential aid from US forces.[112]

Once the film was completed, it had to be vetted. Powell, Pressburger and Richardson waited nervously as *The Volunteer* was shown in a tiny screening room under Admiralty Arch. As Richardson later related:

They [the admirals] sat through it in silence, after which the Sea Lord got up and – while we had stood to be presented – walked straight past us in silence … not a word … till he came to the exit by the projectionist's box. He stopped. In his glass box the projectionist, a rather naughty chap, pulling faces, a cigarette dangling from his mouth, was winding the film back by hand. The Sea Lord spots him and goes straight over. 'Very fine,' he says, 'wonderful film – congratulations', and shakes him by the warmly by the hand. I think he thought the projectionist had done the whole damn thing.[113]

For all the effort put into it, *The Volunteer* had a very limited impact when it was released in November 1943. 'The film never falls below a respectable level of interest,' *The Times* concluded, 'but it is disappointing, considering the wealth of talent involved.'[114]

This was, as it happened, the last wartime feature with which the navy was directly concerned. This was doubtless in part due to the growing doubts in the commercial trade about war subjects and also because of the massive and ongoing success of *In Which We Serve*. The absence of naval features in 1944–45, however, can also be attributed to the continuing conservatism of the RN in relation to publicity and cinema. Unlike the other services, the navy viewed documentary films exclusively in connection with training; and it was only in January 1945, with the need to explain the importance of the war against Japan looming, that the First Sea Lord centralized authority for all publicity matters in the Department of the Chief of Naval Information.[115]

Viewed in retrospect, however, the navy had done well out of its involvement in feature films. Almost in spite of itself, the Admiralty had provided support for a number of popular triumphs. *In Which We Serve*, above all, had provided the public with an image of ordinary people – subject to personal triumph and tragedy, united in their commitment to their ship and country, quietly going about their vital tasks – that was immensely seductive. The reality was rather less shining, but the public clearly wanted to believe.[116] Indeed it was symptomatic of the popular faith in the navy, and the desire to see that faith vindicated, that five of the six features dealing with the work of the silent service were successes at the box office: an enviable record.

4

Civilians in Uniform: The British Army and Feature Films, 1939–1945

In terms of public relations the army was at a disadvantage in competing with its sister services. It possessed neither the glamour of the Royal Air Force nor the mystique of the Royal Navy. Never very popular in peacetime, the British Army suffered from the more immediate legacy of the First World War. Amidst the anti-war intellectual climate of the early 1930s an image emerged of a force in which millions of brave men had been needlessly sacrificed at the hands of reactionary and stupid generals. It was the army that bore the brunt of the anti-war sentiment that had flowered in the early 1930s, and even as people began to accept in the latter 1930s that Hitler would have to be stopped and that conscription was necessary, suspicion of the War Office remained. To many members of the public military leadership continued to be associated with the hidebound and backward-looking views immortalized by David Low in his famous cartoon figure, Colonel Blimp ('Gad, Sir!').[1]

Unfortunately there was some truth to this image. Though senior officers were usually less bumbling and rather more professional than imagined, the fact remained that what might be termed the cultural experience of the previous 'People's War' had been largely forgotten in the interwar years. The military legacy was studied intensively at the Staff College and elsewhere, but both at the regimental and command level the return of a small volunteer army and imperial policing role after 1918 had brought with it a return of prewar cultural attitudes. With the ranks once more being filled almost exclusively by members of the lower classes and with the officers once again drawn from the public schools, the social gulf – and attitudes – of the Edwardian age returned.[2]

In some circles, to be sure, there was some recognition that the army could not set itself entirely apart from society at large. In peacetime public opinion needed to be taken into account in relation to recruiting, while another big war would mean the return of the civilian soldier and heightened public scrutiny of how the army operated at a social as well as operational level. Hence the formation of the Directorate of Public Relations and efforts to cooperate in the making of image-boosting feature films in the mid 1930s.[3]

There were, however, serious limits to the army's ability to connect with the general public as the Second World War began. Two decades had passed since the end of the Great War, years in which public attitudes towards everything from class to state intervention had been evolving. Even for some of the more forward-thinking at the War Office the point of reference in societal terms was 1918 rather than 1939. J. H. Beith, appointed Director of Public Relations at the rank of major-general in 1937, had been a significant force in army propaganda during the Great War. Already a successful author under the pseudonym Ian Hay, he had written a series of immensely popular and very upbeat accounts of the wartime army between bouts of active service on the Western Front. This record, combined with interwar success as a theatrical writer-producer and collaboration in an informal history of the British Army, *The King's Service*, published in 1938, made him appear an ideal candidate to head up the wartime War Office publicity machine. Beith did come to recognize that the wartime conscript or volunteer could not be treated as an automaton, later declaring that 'in the Army of today ... we have to deal with men far more independent in spirit, and far more responsible in character, than the old one-class rank and file'.[4] Yet in both tone and form the approach to public relations under Beith in the first months of the war was rooted in the assumption that popular tastes and expectations had remained unaltered in the last twenty years and that breezy optimism and 'cheerful glossing' were the order of the day. This was to be the army of 'Old Bill', the long-suffering but sympathetic cartoon Tommy created by Bruce Bairnsfather in the Great War. The implications of the more contemporary but rather less lovable 'Colonel Blimp' were simply ignored.[5]

That nostalgia was likely to be a dominant theme in the first wartime features made with War Office cooperation was evident in the two-minute documentary segment of *The Lion Has Wings* that dealt with the army. 'Six hundred years of tradition, from Crecy to Compiegne', E. V. H. Emmett explains as prewar footage unfolds of the Trooping of the Colour, 'have covered the British soldier with glory.' There was, to be sure, a subsequent reference to 'modern mechanization'. But here too the emphasis was as much on tradition as innovation. 'Our famous cavalry regiments', it was explained amidst shots of Mark VI light tanks (some of them unarmed) charging forward, 'employ their qualities of dash and hard-riding in driving mobile forts at ever-increasing speed.' *The Lion Has Wings*, to be sure, was primarily about the RAF. However, the first full-length features centring on the British Army confirmed that the Directorate of Public Relations was deliberately cultivating a traditional image.

In the winter of 1939–40, Legeran Films began a production under director Ian Dalrymple based on the Old Bill character placed in a contemporary setting. The War Office not only provided access to BEF units in France for three weeks in December and lent equipment, but also released John Mills – then serving in the Royal Engineers – and another actor in the army from all military duties while the film was being made. The light-hearted plot, conceived in large part by Bairnsfather himself, involved the efforts of 'Old Bill' (Morland Graham) to join 'Young Bill' (John Mills) in France, where war is portrayed in terms of trench lines and trench raids. The aim was made clear in publicity releases. 'The high spirit and ebullient good humour with which the British soldier faces whatever difficult situation he may find himself in', it was explained, 'is the characteristic keynote of *Old Bill and Son.*' [6]

By the time this film went on general release, however, the assumptions which underlay it concerning the nature of the war had been rendered null and void. Blitzkrieg, rather than cartoon-like trench warfare, characterized the battles fought in France in the spring and summer of 1940. Defeat in France, the prospect of enemy invasion, the Battle of Britain and the Blitz rapidly combined to disperse the mood of unreality that had surrounded the Phoney War and produce a much grimmer public mood. The cheery optimism fostered by Beith was suddenly out of tune with the times.[7]

Under these circumstances it might have been expected that the War Office would seek to promote a rather more contemporary and sober image of the army. The problem was that in 1940–41 there was little positive military activity on which to base either a *Target for Tonight* style documentary or a *Convoy* style dramatic feature. In contrast to the navy and the air force, the army had seen comparatively little active service since Dunkirk. The Italians, to be sure, had been cleared from Ethiopia and driven back from Egypt far into Cyrenaica in 1940–41. But once the senior Axis partner began to take an active interest in the Balkans and North Africa, in the first quarter of the new year, fortune once more began to frown on the British Army. In March 1941 Rommel arrived in Tripolitania with the first units of what would become the Afrika Korps, and by April had pushed British forces back across the desert into Egypt. That same month a desperate bid to help rescue Greece from Nazi invasion ended in more losses and hasty evacuation of British and Commonwealth units, while in May the garrison of Crete succumbed to a German airborne assault. This did nothing to improve the army's public standing and was certainly not the stuff of which celebratory films were made.[8]

The Army Film Unit, set up in the summer of 1940, found itself taking footage of the garrisoning of Iceland and the occasional commando raid

for short documentaries of dubious quality, while the commercial trade
continued to view the army primarily as a setting for low-brow music-hall
type comedies making light of the trials and tribulations of civilians being
turned into soldiers. The DPR was aware that army life was not agreeing
with all those who had volunteered or been called up in 1940–41, but thought
that a lot of the criticism appearing in the press was 'well-meaning but
over-sentimental'.[9] Having co-written and helped mount a number of successful stage comedies about the forces in the interwar years, Beith hoped
that improving the army's morale and image remained a matter of better
NAAFI facilities, more ENSA concerts and encouraging people to 'laugh it
off'.[10] He certainly took no exception to films such as *Somewhere in Camp*,
produced by Butcher Films and described as a naive 'comedy of camp life
with a very slight romantic plot upon which to hang a series of amusing
gags, accompanied by pithy cross-talk'.[11]

Though such films could do reasonable business at the box office,[12] the
realities of the army at home seemed rather less humorous to those donning
khaki for the first time. Army life, for many, seemed to consist of a pointless
round of square-bashing, inspections, parades and fatigues unleavened by
any news of victory overseas or likelihood of Home Forces going over to
the offensive. Officers often seemed either unconcerned with the welfare of
their men or excessively class-conscious. The attitude of the officer in charge
of an Officer Cadet Training Unit, Lieutenant-Colonel R. C. Bingham, who
wrote a letter to *The Times* complaining that too many lower middle-class
types were being given commissions, was widely thought to be typical.
Service pay and allowances were also seen as inadequate, and even the
nondescript uniform seemed to mark the soldier as more lowly than either
the sailor or airman. 'Words cannot describe the wretched appearance of
a soldier in a new battle-dress', Spike Milligan wrote in his memoirs, adding
that some men were so humiliated by their appearance that they refused
to 'walk out' in public. The fact that the public rated the army much lower
than either the navy or RAF only made matters worse. Service in either
was seen as preferable to being sent into the army, where the mood remained
depressed. 'It was clear in the Autumn and the Winter of 1941–1942', as the
Adjutant-General, Lieutenant-General Sir Ronald Adam, diplomatically put
it, 'that the morale of the Army at home was not as good as it should be.'
More trenchant was the verdict of an Ack Ack gunner who chose to break
King's Regulations by writing a highly critical analysis of his experiences
since volunteering in 1940. 'The Army to-day is grumbling and mumbling,
murmuring and muttering, simmering with tales of discontent.'[13]

The fact that the army was either not fighting at all or losing only made
matters more difficult for the Directorate of Public Relations. 'Today I saw

the Minister of Information, who wants more publicity for the Army', the director complained at the end of August 1941. 'In fact everyone wants more publicity for the Army, but as the Army isn't doing anything it is difficult to achieve.'[14] The Crown Film Unit, to be sure, had begun work on a full-length documentary on the victory over the Italians that had occurred in Libya before Rommel arrived on the scene. However, based on newsreel and some service unit footage, *Wavell's 30,000* turned out to be factually inaccurate and, rather more important, very limited in its public impact when it was released in early 1942 through MGM. Reviews were respectful but there were distribution problems and there was no getting away from the fact that the story bore little relation to the current situation in the Western Desert (where the Eighth Army was once again being pushed back into Egypt by the Afrika Korps). It was soon withdrawn.[15]

News of retreats in the Far East and North Africa, culminating in the fall of Singapore (February 1942) and then Tobruk (June 1942), made the army even less popular. 'Scepticism and despondency about our military leadership' were noticeable everywhere, MoI Home Intelligence noted in summarizing reports from the regions in February. Stories 'told by men on leave of inefficient officers and of waste of time and materials' were quoted as deepening this feeling. The difference in the bearing of the army – 'dull, dejected and bored' – was compared unfavourably with the bearing of the naval men – 'proud and confident'. Tobruk was an even greater blow. 'Disappointment, exasperation, shame and rage were only some of the reactions', another summary noted.[16]

Beith had been replaced as Director of Public Relations in January 1941 by Colonel Walter E. Elliot, who as an MP was perhaps more aware of the vagaries of public opinion than his predecessor.[17] What was more, there were those within the War Office, notably the Adjutant-General, who were keen to promote and publicize policies that would give both soldiers and civilians a sense that the army was in fact adapting to the conditions of modern war and responsive to the needs of citizen-soldiers. Hence, for example, the setting up of a special committee to monitor morale and the establishment of the Army Bureau of Current Affairs to help foster a sense of commitment among the troops. Adam, however, was regarded as a 'serious menace' by his more traditional peers, officers who did not want to pander to 'listless and lazy' conscripts.[18] Modern ideas about public relations were anathema to such traditionalists. Ronald Tritton, in charge of the DPR films section, PR2, noted in his diary how one such officer, a regular working in the Directorate of Military Training (DMT), was not shy about stating that he 'disapproves of all PR work and army publicity, and thinks everything should be shrouded in secrecy'. Newsreel footage of soldiers off parade was, in the view of General John Hawkesworth, the man in charge of DMT, 'showing the army in an unmilitary manner'. Among 'senior regimental officers and less enlightened members of the General Staff', publisher Michael Joseph noted after spending a year as a company commander in the Queen's Own, there was a tendency to 'shun the glare of publicity, a word which it is fashionable in officers' messes to detest'.[19]

Such officers, whether holding staff or command appointments, continued to view both stage and screen with great disdain. Roy Boulting, when called up, remembered the officer who interviewed him asking:

> 'Now Boulting ... what do you do?'
> I said, 'I direct films, sir'.
> He said, 'Yes yes yes, but I mean what do you do that's useful?'

Actors were even worse. Stewart Granger, whose father was a regular officer and who had served in the ranks of the Gordon Highlanders, was commissioned into the Black Watch in early 1941. He later recalled his first encounter with the decorated but Blimpish colonel in charge of the battalion depot at Perth:

> 'Stewart. I hear you used to be an actor.'
> 'Yes, sir.'
> 'Strange. I thought all actors were either conscientious objectors or pansies.'

Granger was posted away as quickly as possible. Dirk Bogarde, called from the ranks of the Signal Corps to appear before a War Office Selection Board later that year in order to ascertain whether he would make a suitable officer, found that being an actor placed him at a distinct disadvantage: 'This, I gathered, was a sign of an unstable temperament.' Being a member of the chorus in musicals was worse yet. 'A sudden hush. A red-tabbed one cleared his throat and echoed "Chorus boy" as if I had said "child molester".' Only the fact that Bogarde's father worked for *The Times* saved him from being sent back at once to his unit. Even when actors were employed as such in the army for entertainment purposes old-fashioned attitudes prevailed. 'Officers were not allowed to act in the plays we produced,' Bryan Forbes noted of his time with the Combined Services Entertainment Unit, 'acting being considered infra dig by the War Office brass: the squalid stuff was confined to the other ranks.' [20]

Despite such attitudes, even a conservative officer such as General Hawkesworth could see some purpose in cooperating with filmmakers if the subject was congenial. On the need to promote security-mindedness and the need to watch out for enemy agents, for example, the War Office could see nothing but good arising from MoI or its own approaches to Ealing Studios.

Paradoxically, however, the resulting three feature films, which appeared in 1942–43, may have reinforced the public image of an army with serious problems.

The first was *The Foreman Went to France*, an Ealing Studios production based on the true story – written up by J. B. Priestley – of a Midlands works manager, Leboune Johns, who had travelled to France during the collapse of 1940 in order to retrieve important tooling machinery before it fell into enemy hands. 'The importance of this story', producer Michael Balcon explained (doubtless echoing the MoI view), 'was that it showed how the civilian population, particularly those engaged in the manufacture of essentials for wartime purposes, were just as much in the front line as the troops.'[21] The foreman in question, played by Clifford Evans, goes over to France in the face of opposition from numerous authority figures, outwits several French turncoats, and makes his escape with the vital equipment in the company of a two-man lorry crew (Tommy Trinder and Gordon Jackson) cut off from their unit, in aid of which a vehicle and machine gun were provided by the military authorities. When it premiered in April 1942 *The Foreman Went to France* was greeted favourably by both critics and audiences. Jonah Barrington of the *Daily Express*, for instance, called it 'arresting' and 'real'.[22]

So far so good. But, as later commentators were quick to observe, the Blimpishness of the traditional upper- and upper middle-class authority figures in the film is in marked contrast to the practical patriotism of the lower middle-class foreman and his two soldier friends (a Cockney and a Scot).[23] The implied critique, moreover, included military as well as civilian officialdom. The two Army Service Corps privates meet the foreman while on the obviously frivolous job of bringing back tins of curry powder to season the stew of a certain 'Major Morrison'. Later, they and the foreman only narrowly escape the clutches of a bogus captain working for the enemy (John Williams). The captain's mannerisms are correctly upper middle-class English but one of the soldiers, recalling the recent capture of an enemy agent in the uniform of a Guards major, notes that the man's Oxford and Buckinghamshire Yeomanry badges are not quite right. Whether this captain is a masquerading German or an outright traitor is left unclear. The military authorities appear to have viewed all this as a Good Thing in terms of promoting security-mindedness. In the context of the Bingham affair and further defeats, however, *The Foreman Went to France* might have been internalized by viewers in support of the populist position, paraphrased by Harold Nicolson in reference to the opinions of various Labour MPs, that 'our "class army" can never fight'.[24]

Then there was *The Next of Kin*, another Ealing production in which the military authorities took a more active part.[25] This project dated back to December 1940, when the Directorate of Military Training had approached Michael Balcon about the possibility of producing a film on the subject of security. Balcon agreed, and Thorold Dickinson was brought in to direct. In early 1941 it was agreed that a full-length film that could be shown commercially as well as for training purposes, and that the War Office would contribute £20,000 to the cost as well as provide necessary personnel and equipment. (The Royal Navy eventually contributed three motor boats and the RAF – for three hours – various aircraft). Formulating a good story on the subject of security, however, proved problematic, the War Office apparently having given no thought as to the plot. Dickinson found himself bogged down in apparently endless bureaucratic wrangling over this and various other matters. A script, written by Dickinson and Angus McPhail, was finally accepted. Filming, which generated its own problems and frictions between the army and filmmakers, took place in the summer and autumn of 1941.

Though involving many characters and much detail, the basic plot of *The Next of Kin* – the title an effort to capitalize on the phrase 'the next of kin have been informed' that followed news of losses on the wireless – was comparatively straightforward. It was the story of the lead-up to a brigade-size raid on a German-occupied port in France, 'Norville' (Mevagissey in Cornwall), in which vital information is unintentionally provided to enemy agents, information that allows the Germans to reinforce the port and inflict very heavy casualties on the '95th Brigade' (officers and men of the Worcestershire Regiment and Durham Light Infantry, plus some commandos) when the raid takes place. Careless talk will indeed cost lives, as the title introduction makes clear.

> SECURITY
> This is the story of how
> YOU – unwittingly worked for the Enemy
> YOU
> – without knowing gave him the facts
> YOU
> – in all innocence
> – helped to write
> those tragic words
> 'THE NEXT OF KIN'

What followed was a finely crafted film based on a screenplay by Dickinson and McPhail with help from John Dighton and the supervising military officer, Captain Basil Bartlett, as well as Combined Operations HQ. An ensemble cast of service personnel – who did not have to be paid[26] – and character actors show how apparently innocent details, thoughtlessly given away to innocent-looking spies in private letters, public conversation, and through generally lax security, could provide the enemy with enough intelligence to anticipate and prepare for a major military operation. Involving as it did no stars or obvious protagonists and many real soldiers, *The Next of Kin* was at certain points almost a drama-documentary. Observers were struck by the realism of many scenes, not least those of the raid itself that form the film's climax.

The Army Council, given a special screening at the War Office in February, was so impressed by *The Next of Kin* that attendance by staff officers at future showings was made compulsory.[27] The Prime Minister, however, when shown the film at Chequers, was worried that it was so graphic that 'it would cause unnecessary alarm and despondency to a great number of people'.[28] Only after an actual raid on the port of St-Nazaire – uncomfortably similar in its aims to the fictional attack on Norville – had been carried off successfully did Churchill allow the film to be seen by the public. With eighty feet of the most graphic shots cut to avoid undue distress, the film premiered at the Carlton in mid May 1942 with Sir James Grigg (War Minister), Lord Croft (Under-Secretary of State for War) and a host of senior officers in attendance. The critics were generally most impressed. 'Production, direction, and acting are first rate', the reviewer for the *Daily Herald* enthused. 'It is the best film of this kind yet made.' The *Express* thought it good entertainment, while the *Sunday Chronicle* went as far to as call it one of 'the finest pictures ever made'. The quality press concurred, C. A. Lejeune of the *Observer* calling it 'a masterly team job, slick, unself-conscious, and about as dull as dynamite', and Dilys Powell calling attention in the *Sunday Times* to the way in which 'the final sequences of the landing are rendered with an absence of heroics which is quite heartbreaking'.[29] The public was equally enthralled. *The Next of Kin* was seen by about three million people in June and the first half of July alone, and by the end of 1942 the film had generated nearly £89,000 in revenue.[30]

A Mass-Observation survey in central and north London confirmed that, as a cautionary tale about the need to 'keep it under you hat', *The Next of Kin* was a great success. The problem was that in conveying this message the film also appears to have confirmed in viewers' minds the idea that the British Army was poorly led. The Mass-Observation report noted that 'there is a definite feeling that the officers in the film were more to blame for what had happened than the men, and that the officers ought to have set a better example'. In point of fact *The Next of Kin* showed how ordinary soldiers could breach security, but audiences 'were much more indulgent where the men were concerned', presumably on the premise that officers possessed more sensitive information.[31]

Finally there was *Went the Day Well?*, another Ealing film highlighting official concerns. Worried in early 1942 that the public was confused as to the likelihood and nature of a German invasion, the Ministry of Information appears to have approached Michael Balcon about a film dealing with an enemy raid. The result, directed by Alberto Cavalcanti, was based on a heavily reworked short story by Graham Greene. It showed the occupation of the village of 'Bramley End' (Turville in Buckinghamshire) over a weekend in May 1942 by a squad of German parachutists disguised as Royal Engineers who, assisted by a traitorous gentleman in the Home Guard (Leslie Banks), attempt to disrupt British radar as a prelude to a full-scale German invasion. At first all goes well for the invaders. But their true identity is inadvertently discovered and, despite several tragic setbacks and the taking of hostages, the inhabitants of Bramley End manage to raise the alarm and organize themselves to disrupt enemy activity long enough for relief forces to arrive and wipe out the bogus major and his men.[32] Added realism was achieved through the use of the men and vehicles of the Gloucestershire Regiment, placed at the disposal of the director by the War Office at the request of the MoI.

By the time *Went the Day Well?* premiered in the late autumn of 1942, an enemy invasion had in fact become extremely unlikely, as a number of critics pointed out. It did not do much business at the box office.[33] This may have been just as well, since it could be read to suggest, like *The Foreman Went to France* and *The Next of Kin*, that the British Army might be being betrayed from within. Contemporary analysis has tended to focus on the class implications of the traitor played by Leslie Banks. Yet what is also striking is the way in which the enemy paratroopers appear more authentic as Englishmen in the first section of the film than they do as almost caricature Nazis later on. Basil Sydney and David Farrar appear more real as, respectively, politely authoritative Major Hammond and Lieutenant Maxwell, Royal Engineers, than as scowlingly dictatorial *Kommandant* Ortler and drunkenly sadistic *Leutnant* Jung of the German 5th Parachute Regiment. Farrar subsequently received a large number of letters from fans indicating that they found it hard to accept him – a handsome young English leading man – playing a Nazi.[34] Yet from the very start of the film it is clear that Basil Sydney and his party are the enemy. What, one could ask, did this imply about the reliability of the gentlemanly officer on whom the characters of Hammond and Maxwell were based?

Public criticism of the army continued to be voiced over the summer and into the autumn of 1942. Pay and allowances generated protest, especially when compared to what American servicemen – now beginning to appear in some numbers in the UK – were receiving. The retreat of the Eighth Army, and in particular the fall of Tobruk, continued to rankle. Inadequate leadership was a common complaint, an attitude subconsciously reflected and reinforced in the cinema. The men themselves, however, were not escaping censure. According to a Home Intelligence report, for example, defeat in the Western Desert had given rise to 'some doubts as to the fighting quality of our men ...' [35] Little wonder that the War Office committee on morale should conclude that 'it has become increasingly evident that the soldier suffers from a lack of respect for himself as a member of the Army'.[36]

What to do about this state of affairs, however, was still very much open to debate in the press, parliament and the army itself. There were those who thought that the military authorities had yet to fully recognize that in a citizen army the Other Ranks needed to be treated as individuals forming part of a common war effort, not merely as a mass of faceless automatons led by an aristocratic caste with whom they had nothing in common. There were also those who drew the opposite conclusion. If there was a problem with the army it derived from the '*listless* and *lazy*' nature of modern youth, 'ruined by twenty years of soft living'. Suppression of ill-informed carping in the press and more emphasis on traditional discipline were what was needed.[37]

Traditionalists, often senior in age and rank, tended to be against promoting the idea of a 'New Model Army', either on film or off.[38] To the CO of the 5th battalion, Northamptonshire Regiment, for instance, a film project celebrating the citizen-soldier through the lives of his men was cause for disquiet. As Ronald Tritton recorded in his diary in late July 1942, 'he couldn't see why anybody wanted a film about the British Army and anyway why call it "The People's Army" as if this was the USSR?' Lieutenant-General Sir Archibald Nye, Vice-Chief of the Imperial General Staff, and Sir Frederick Bovenschen, the War Office permanent under-secretary, to take another example, disliked the populist content of newsreels featuring the army, complaining on more than one occasion to PR2 that they were 'vulgar'.[39]

For those who saw some need to create a more positive popular image of the army, this was the whole point. '40 odd million people are "vulgar"', Major-General E. F. Lawson, the former *Daily Telegraph* general manager and Territorial Army commander who had succeeded Elliot as Director of Public Relations remarked tartly in March 1943. 'The newsreels are not prepared for *Times* readers.' [40] The fact remained, however, that advocates of change, even moderate change, had few friends in high places beyond the Adjutant-General. Lawson and Elliot, both very much a part of the Establishment, were unlikely to support the kind of revolutionary shifts advocated, for example, by Tom Wintringham, ex-International Brigade officer and military correspondent of the populist *Daily Mirror*. In terms of experience, furthermore, the new DPR was far better equipped to deal with the press than with feature filmmakers. The ways of Fleet Street were familiar; those of Wardour Street were not. 'I don't think he [Lawson] had much sense of film', Roy Boulting remembered.[41] What this meant in practice was that, while most projects would have to get at least a modicum of high-level consent if they were to obtain military support, much of the groundwork would have to be done by those for whom the world of film was less of a *terra incognita*.

Unfortunately the first feature about the army for which War Office support was sought in the third year of the war was practically guaranteed to generate opposition. Having touched on the contrasting outlooks of young and old in a scene eventually cut from *One of Our Aircraft is Missing*, writer Emeric Pressburger and director Michael Powell were keen to explore this theme more fully through the prism of the tradition-versus-innovation debate being played out in the press and parliament in the first months of 1942. And what better symbol of the old-fashioned than Colonel Blimp? As Powell later explained, 'the thought of dramatising the life of Colonel Blimp appealed enormously, because at that time Blimp was a household word'.[42] Permission was obtained from David Low and Pressburger set to work on a plot outline entitled *The Life and Death of Colonel Blimp*, covering the army career of Clive 'Sugar' Candy from his dynamic subaltern days down to his retirement as an out of touch major-general.[43]

Any film dealing with the army would, perforce, be easier to make with official support, so in the second week of May 1942 the scenario was submitted to the War Office as well as the Ministry of Information. P. J. Grigg, the Secretary of State for War, was less than enchanted at the idea. As a former career civil servant with plenty of experience at the War Office, he disliked what he regarded as the ill-informed and unfair attacks on the army being made in the press and parliament.[44] Accusations of lack of imagination and dim-wittedness were often couched in terms of 'Blimpery' and 'Blimpishness'. Why on earth should the War Office cooperate in the making of a film in which the central character, through the title alone, branded the army as impossibly backward? Grigg made his position clear in his reply to Powell: this was not 'the sort of film to which the War Office could give its support'.

Its chief weakness seems to me that it revolves around a character that is more fictitious than real. I suppose it may be possible, if you look far enough, to find an officer who bears some resemblance to Major-General Candy, but I must confess that after three years in the War Office I have still to meet him. I cannot help thinking that at a time when public confidence in the Army and its leaders is justifiably increasing, it would be a pity to divert attention to a caricature. And after all Colonel Blimp *is* only a caricature!

Grigg ended by suggesting that Powell get in touch with General Lawson at DPR and Paul Kimberley, Director of Army Kinematography, to gain a better appreciation of what was needed 'if you are really anxious to make a film about the modern Army'.[45]

Powell and Pressburger remained convinced that the primary message of the plot they were developing – the need to acknowledge a 'new spirit in warfare',[46] in which traditional sporting instincts had no place – was something that the War Office ought to be promoting. Powell was willing to change the title to *The Life and Death of Sugar Candy*, but surely it was obvious to the War Minister that fair play and sympathy for the underdog 'can become absolute vices unless allied to a realistic acceptance of things as they are, in modern Europe and in Total War'. Grigg remained equally convinced that, even without 'Blimp' in the title, the story implied that generals of the British Army were retrograde and out of touch. 'To be quite frank,' he wrote to Powell in June, 'I am getting rather tired of the theory that we can best enhance our reputation in the eyes of our own people or the rest of the world by drawing attention to the faults which the critics attribute to us, especially when, as in the present case, the criticism no longer has any substance.'[47] The Ministry of Information, made aware of War Office objections, refused to help get Laurence Olivier released from the navy to play the part of Clive Candy.[48]

Powell and Pressburger decided to go ahead anyway. They had the backing of J. Arthur Rank, and a budget of £208,000. Roger Livesey could play the lead part instead of Olivier, uniforms and equipment from the wardrobe department at Denham could be utilized, and anything lacking – up to and including army lorries – could be obtained through the black market.[49] That, however, was not the end of the story. By late summer word of the 'Blimp film' had reached the ears of the Prime Minister, offering Grigg an opportunity to restate his objections.

The War Office have refused to give their support to the film in any way on the ground that it would give the Blimp conception of the army officer a new lease of life at a time when it is already dying from inanition. Whatever the film makes of the spirit of the younger soldier of today, the fact remains that it focuses attention on an imaginary type of Army officer which has become an object of ridicule to the general public. In the opening scene Candy is shown as Blimp

himself complete with towel and everything ... there is inescapable suggestion
that such a man is a type or at any rate an example of those who have risen to
a high command in the Army preceding this war.[50]

Churchill was so incensed by this that, in his most notorious intervention
in wartime filmmaking, he tried to get *The Life and Death of Colonel Blimp*
suppressed. Brendan Bracken, however, was not enthusiastic at the thought
of being given 'special authority' to do what had hitherto not been in the
MoI's power and would be bound to raise a storm of public protest once
it became known. In the end the War Cabinet decided that any action
should be deferred until the finished product had been viewed.[51]

By the time this had come to pass, in the spring of 1943, *The Life and
Death of Colonel Blimp* seemed much less dangerous to the War Office. For
one thing the finished product turned out to be far less damning than
expected. Though Clive Wynne-Candy is depicted on several occasions as
being behind the times, he remains an immensely likeable character. As
written by Pressburger and played by Livesey, he is brave, decent, and a
rather innocent romantic. Conversely, the characters who stand for a 'new
way of war' with no holds barred come across as quite sinister: Major Van
Zijl (Reginald Tate), an Afrikaner willing to beat up German POWs to
obtain information in 1918; or as mindlessly brutal – 'Spud' Wilson (James
McKechnie), the young British Army lieutenant who humiliates the elderly
Candy in 1942. The message of the film is thus ambiguous, 'Blimp' in this
case representing as many virtues as liabilities. As many film critics were
to point out, Clive Candy in the film was a far cry from the original cartoon
character.[52]

Even more importantly, the 'Blimp Factor' had abated considerably as a
result of improvements in the war situation. In late October 1942, at El
Alamein, had begun the decisive Eighth Army victory over Rommel, followed
in November by the successful Anglo-American landings in Algeria. By
April 1943, after a tough struggle in Tunisia, the last Axis forces had been
cleared from North Africa. The British Army was winning, not losing, and
parliamentary and press criticism was consequently more muted.[53] Hence,
after representatives from the War Office and MoI saw the picture in early
May 1943, Grigg accepted their verdict that *The Life and Death of Colonel
Blimp* was 'unlikely to attract much attention or to have any undesirable
consequences on the discipline of the Army'.[54] Churchill, who was given a
special screening before the premiere on 10 May, still disliked what he saw
and was instrumental in delaying the export of the film. But with the
War Office no longer objecting, the PM did not push any further for a
domestic ban.[55]

Though Grigg was wrong about *The Life and Death of Colonel Blimp* not attracting much attention – it was, after all, a major Technicolor production that had been given good deal of advance publicity – he was largely correct in guessing that the film would not seriously affect the image of the army. On the right, to be sure, there was some disquiet. The *Daily Mail* took great exception to the film on the grounds that to 'depict British officers as stupid, complacent, self-satisfied and ridiculous' was 'disastrously bad propaganda in times of war', particularly in reference to foreign audiences. Self-styled sociologists E. W. and M. M. Robson went even further, publishing a diatribe in pamphlet form, *The Shame and Disgrace of Colonel Blimp*, in which, among other things, the impulsive actions of Lieutenant Wilson were criticized as being contrary to good order and discipline. A number of left-wing critics, on the other hand, regretted the fact that Low's reactionary cartoon character had been transformed into a sympathetic figure. The *New Statesman* was disappointed, as was *Documentary News Letter*, the latter going so far as to call the film 'an apologia for the upper-class specialists who misguided this country into the mud of Munich and the disasters of 1939–40'.[56] Most critics, apart from being struck by the sheer length of the film (over 160 minutes), thought that Powell and Pressburger had been far too ambiguous, or 'muddled', in trying to convey their supposed message.[57]

There were plenty of positive comments as well; the *Daily Express*, for example, describing the film as 'a marvel of pictorial beauty and technical finish', and dismissing the Blimp issue by insisting that 'everybody knows the British don't make professional soldiers until there's a war on'.[58] Audiences poured into the cinemas to see it. *The Life and Death of Colonel Blimp* became the second most popular British film of 1943, and broke all previous box office records for the Rank-owned Odeon circuit. The results of the Mass-Observation survey of that year strongly suggested that high production values (above all the use of Technicolor, still very rare), fine acting, and engagingly human main characters were what struck people about *The Life and Death of Colonel Blimp*.[59] The film, in short, did not stoke any anti-army fires in people's minds. Thus, despite their run-in with the War Office, Powell and Pressburger apparently did not have any trouble arranging for the loan of Bren carriers for a few scenes in their next film, *A Canterbury Tale*.[60]

Not all outside interventions proved so problematic. At about the same time as the Blimp affair began in 1942, the War Office had approached Ealing Studios to see if a feature could be made from the synopsis for a projected training film. The synopsis was written by Gerald Kersh, loosely based on his account of recruit training in the Guards, *They Died With Their Boots Clean*. The idea seems to have been to try and counteract the

negative image of life in the army by making a film in which army training
and routine were illustrated in an upbeat, patriotic manner.

Harry Watt, who had recently moved to Ealing from the Crown Film
Unit, was asked by screenwriter Angus MacPhail if he thought he could do
anything with it. Watt thought he could and, with the approval of Michael
Balcon as head of production, put together a draft treatment within a
month.[61] Judging by the differences between the book and the film, Watt
evidently decided that the approach Kersh had adopted was too traditional.
Writing the screenplay as well as acting as director, Watt ditched most of
what Kersh had written in favour of a reworked version of the 1937 Soviet
film *The Thirteen* (situated in the Russian Civil War) reset in the Western
Desert. As reworked by Watt, the idea was to show how individual soldiers,
drawn from a variety of class and regional backgrounds, operate as a fighting
unit. In spite of the plot's left-wing origins, an indirect but positive reference
to the International Brigades, and a fair amount of earthy dialogue, the
War Office evidently decided that here was an opportunity to showcase
how military professionalism transcended individual foibles and class differences. In marked contrast to *The Life and Death of Colonel Blimp*, the
script of *Nine Men* was passed without objection and military facilities and
personnel were provided. Eager to make the film as realistic as possible,
Watt chose mainly unknowns for his ensemble cast.[62]

Initially given the rather odd title *Umpity Poo* – the British NCO's
rendition of the French phrase *un petit peu*, that little bit extra – but changed
just before shooting began in August 1942 to *Nine Men*, the story involves
Sergeant Watson (Jack Lambert) recalling for the benefit of recruits in
England a particularly tough fight in Libya a year or so earlier. An infantry
squad is stranded in the desert after their lorry is straffed by a German
fighter. The officer (Richard Wilkinson) is fatally wounded, and Sergeant
Watson assumes command as the small group take shelter from a sandstorm
in the semi-ruined tomb of a sheik. Once the men have settled in, Watson
as narrator gives a brief character sketch of each man as the camera focuses
on each face. 'There was old Bill Parker [Bill Blewitt] who'd seen a lot of
service in India. Good soldier he was too, but every time he'd get a stripe
he'd wet it and then he'd be back where he started.'

> 'And the young 'un [Gordon Jackson]. He said he was nineteen. I think he was
> an apprentice in Edinburgh before he joined up.'

> 'And Banger Hill [Frederick Piper]. He ran a coffee stall in Civvy Street but the
> blackout beat him.'

> 'And Joe Harvey [Jack Horseman]. He was a Durham miner until he went to
> the Spanish War. He took a bad beating in prison there.'

'And Gordon Lee from Cambridge [Eric Micklewood]. We sometimes called Lee the Bookie because he'd never had a bet in his life or because he read a lot, I can't remember.'

'And Jock Scott [Grant Sutherland], or Scotty, who used to be a Glasgow policeman but got slung out. He was a wild man, was Jock.'

'And poor Dusty Johnson [the officer's runner, played by John Varley, seriously wounded in the air attack and shortly to expire].'

It is this group, directed by the harshly professional sergeant, who go on to defend the tomb against successive assaults by superior numbers of Italian troops over the following twenty-four hours.

At one level this is about simple heroism, epitomised by the hand-written instructions Watson pins to a wall.

Orders for the Day

1. To hold the hut until relieved.

2. If no relief comes to go on holding the hut.

At a deeper level, *Nine Men* is about the grim business of killing the enemy. With Watson in charge, the emphasis throughout is on practical fighting and fieldcraft as opposed to parade-ground drill and arms exercises. At one point, as the sergeant and some of the men prepare for a night raid on the enemy by camouflaging their faces and equipment, the Young 'Un jokes about his own recruit training:

'I wonder what "old spit and polish" would say about this? Remember he used to say [Jackson here adopting an officious English accent] "A soldier always goes into battle clean and properly dressed"!'

To which Sergeant Watson responds: 'At the present moment, to hell with spit and polish.'

The comparatively graphic combat sequences, involving close-up shots of desperate men working their rifle bolts as fast as possible, and on occasion engaging in quite vicious hand-to-hand fighting with bayonets, underscores the point that learning the soldier's trade can make the difference between death and survival. About to be finally overwhelmed by superior numbers, Watson and his men are saved at the last moment through the timely arrival of British tanks (courtesy of the Royal Tank Regiment) and lorried infantry (courtesy of the South Wales Borderers). As the flashback ends, Watson bids his new charges good night in their barrack hut.[63]

Nine Men was shot on a 'shoestring budget' of £20,000.[64] But thanks to a good script, a solid cast, fine location work on beach dunes at Margam in South Wales – providing a surprisingly effective rendition of the Western Desert – and assistance from army units (including men from the London Irish Rifles playing themselves in the opening and closing barrack sequences), it appeared highly realistic.

Opening at the New Gallery and Marble Arch Pavilion at the end of January 1943, and then put on general release in February, *Nine Men* was met with universal acclaim – both in its own right and as a tribute to the Eighth Army arriving on the screen at an opportune time. 'It is impossible to go on doing successful PR work for something which is not seen to succeed', Ronald Tritton had accurately observed in June of the previous year. 'It is like trying to sell an inferior product or publicize a lousy hotel.'[65] By the time *Nine Men* appeared the situation in North Africa had changed radically.

In July and August 1942, two successive thrusts by Rommel in Egypt had been successfully parried. Two months later a heavily reinforced Eighth Army went over to the offensive at El Alamein, driving what remained of the Afrika Korps into headlong flight after three weeks of heavy fighting. In early November 1942 a new front to the west was opened in the wake Anglo-American amphibious landings in French Morocco and Algeria. Hard fighting would continue over the winter, but by the time *Nine Men* appeared it was clear that it was only a matter of time before the last Axis forces in Tunisia would be forced to surrender.

Victory in the desert made victory on the screen more plausible, and in combination with the realistic feel of the film led reviewers – and audiences – to conclude that *Nine Men* was very much true to life ('looks like the real thing', as the *Daily Express* pithily put it).[66] 'I have never seen a film in which the behaviour of soldiers in battle was so naturally and vividly depicted', William Whitebait wrote at greater length for the *New Statesman*; 'it is as though a front-line glimpse from a newsreel had been expanded and given unity'. Edgar Anstey in the *Spectator*, in another long review, was struck by how the dialogue was 'scrupulously true to Army life', Watt having captured the outlook and manners of 'citizens in uniform'. At the same time, as *The Times* noted, the film 'tells a heroic story', and through the grim professionalism of the sergeant which saves the sometimes fractious Other Ranks could be 'interpreted as a lesson in the value of discipline'. *Nine Men*, in short, celebrated both traditional martial virtues (bravery and discipline) and the heterogeneous nature of the wartime army (citizen-soldiers with distinct personal identities), the aspect being highlighted depending on the outlook of the viewer. As *Kinematograph Weekly* observed:

The picture accomplishes many tasks – it is at one and the same time a pep talk for fed-up troops and civilians, an exciting illustration of the science and practice of modern desert warfare and a worthy tribute to the men who have been and are still doing the fighting.

'One feels that justice has been done in a film', the *Monthly Film Bulletin* summed up, 'to all those qualities in the British character in wartime of which we are most proud.' [67]

Though costing a mere £20,000, and making a tidy sum for Ealing, *Nine Men* was a short film (only sixty-eight minutes long) that was released on a limited scale.[68] It was quickly overshadowed by the first full-length documentary effort of the Army Film and Photographic Unit (AFPU), *Desert Victory*, which premiered in March 1943 with the War Minister and a galaxy of War Office generals in attendance.[69]

The origins of *Desert Victory* lay in the late summer of 1942, when the director Roy Boulting, then a captain with the AFPU, had learned at the War Office from Major Sir Leonard Woolley – a highly distinguished archeologist who kept a close watch on events in the Middle East – just how crucial the coming clash between the Eighth Army and Afrika Korps would be. Eager to capitalize on success, General Lawson as head of DPR had given the green light for the making of what was initially called *The Battle of Egypt* as soon as the breakthrough at El Alamein had been carried off. By this point in the war the AFPU, capitalizing on the expertise of the numerous technicians, directors and other film people called up into the army, had developed to the point where such a project could be carried out with a high degree of professionalism and polish. Based at Pinewood Studios alongside the Crown and RAF film units, the AFPU had no less than eighty cameramen working in four separate units – including twenty-six in the Middle East. At the cost of over a dozen casualties, they had recorded a great deal of highly dramatic front-line footage under the direction of Major David Macdonald. This, along with film obtained from other sources, including German newsreel footage captured at Mersa Matruh and RAF film unit footage, was to be edited into a coherent whole by Roy Boulting. A desire to make a truly impressive documentary – as opposed to a newsreel-type quickie – in addition to bureaucratic wrangling, meant that *Desert Victory*, covering events from the fall of Tobruk through to the capture of Tripoli, was not completed until the end of February 1943. The wait, however, did little to diminish the timeliness of the film, appearing as it did just as the last enemy forces in North Africa were being defeated at Tunis.[70]

Edited for maximum dramatic effect, nicely scored by William Alwyn, and effectively narrated (mostly by actor Leo Genn from a script by journalist

J. L. Hodson which eschewed histrionics),[71] *Desert Victory* made a deep impression on all who saw it. Though it in fact included dubbed sound effects and footage from other times and places – including a small number of scenes staged for the camera where appropriate actuality footage was not available – it was so well constructed that film critics universally hailed it as the closest thing yet to reality on film. 'No fictional film has ever embodied scenes of greater intensity than does *Desert Victory*', Elspeth Grant wrote for the *Daily Sketch*. 'This is real cinema – and this is real warfare.' It was a 'magnificent close up of modern war', according to Reg Whitley of the *Daily Mirror*. For Ernest Betts of the *Express*, clearly bowled over by the experience, it was 'history exploding' on the screen. The quality press was equally enthusiastic. *Desert Victory* was 'one of the greatest factual war films ever made', Campbell Dixon of the *Daily Telegraph* wrote for example, 'and is more thrilling than any fiction I have ever seen'.[72] The cinema-going public wholeheartedly concurred. 'I was deeply impressed by the reality of it', a chief electrician from Blackburn replied in response to a Mass-Observation survey in which *Desert Victory* emerged as the third most popular film of the year. 'Seldom do we get a chance to *see* History', was how a housewife from Potter's Bar stated in a far from atypical explanation of the film's appeal.[73] Fourteen months after its release *Desert Victory* had generated an impressive £77,250 in commercial receipts.[74]

Tribute was paid at appropriate points in the film to the Allied air forces and Royal Navy as well as civilian workers in both Britain and the USA. But *Desert Victory* was – as the title dedication indicates – first and foremost about 'the desert rats ... the men of the Eighth Army' from the fall of Tobruk to the capture of Tripoli. More specifically, however, it is the story of the force 'recreated' for victory. Stress is laid on the arrival of new equipment and new units (the 51st Highland Division and 44th Home Counties Division), and of a new general, Montgomery, to command the 8th Army ('a man who lives as sternly as a Cromwell – and who is as much a part of his modern Ironsides'). This was to be an army in which officers and men fought as one. 'General Montgomery,' the unseen Leo Genn explains as commanders are shown briefing their men, 'realizing that a citizen army fights best when it knows exactly what's going on, saw to it that the plan of battle was known to everybody, from general to private soldier; and it came down from one rank to another, until the chain was complete.'[75] At the same time the script balanced the new with the old, innovation with tradition. Soldiers are said to have fought 'as dogged as our infantry at Waterloo' to defeat the enemy, and references to Montgomery are matched by coverage of the new Commander-in-Chief Middle East, General Alexander, and the importance of traditional aspects of training such as PT. 'Physical fitness and hardness of an army', Alexander explains in the only scene in which anyone addresses the camera, 'is one of the biggest battle-winning factors in war', going on to explain that when contenders are equally matched victory goes to the side which shows the greatest endurance. 'Fighting fit, and fit to fight!' *Desert Victory*, in other words, like *Nine Men*, presented a composite picture of the British Army, offering different aspects to different constituencies. It was a well-crafted film, the victory it celebrated strongly buttressed by the ongoing success of the Eighth Army. The DPR would have been happy to read the response of a young London architect on seeing the film: 'Made you feel that at last the army was a worthwhile thing.'[76]

The success of *Desert Victory* immediately spawned plans for further 'victory' films, the tide of war now turning decisively against the Axis. These, however, ran into long delays. There were, to begin with, struggles over content and overall production control waged by the services and MoI. Even more problematic were clashing British and American expectations and approaches once covering Allied operations made joint Anglo-American productions seem necessary. *Tunisian Victory*, for example, did not appear until March 1944, by which time public interest had moved on to more contemporary events. Reviews tended to highlight the fact of Anglo-American cooperation on the film as much as the film itself, and it was not a box-office success. And as a number of British officials privately noted, the end product bore the stamp of Hollywood sentimentality and – from a British perspective – overplayed the US contribution to the campaign.[77] In the meantime, the British Army still had public relations problems to deal with at home.

There was, for one thing, the image problem of the women's branch of the army, the Auxiliary Territorial Service. Set up in 1938 on a voluntary basis with a very limited role, the ATS had by 1941–42 become a vital part of the war effort. As the demand for front-line troops grew, so did the importance of the Auxiliary Territorial Service. Using women in khaki as lorry drivers, searchlight operators and anti-aircraft fire predictors, for example, meant that the men who had hitherto done these jobs in Home Forces could be moved into 'sharp end' units. At the same time it was evident that many women were far from happy at the thought of going into the ATS. Uniforms, pay, living conditions and work were all considered inferior in comparison to the WAAF (air force) and WRENS (navy). To middle-class women and their parents, moreover, the Auxiliary Territorial Service suffered from a reputation for immorality and general coarseness. The introduction of conscription in 1942 increased the size of the ATS but did little to improve its image.[78]

Knowledge of this state of affairs led the War Office and Ministry of Information to cooperate in measures designed to improve the image of the ATS.[79] A central aspect of the publicity campaign was a feature film. Two Cities Films, it was announced in June 1942, were going to turn a treatment by stage producer Moie Charles entitled *We're Not Weeping* into a feature. Derrick de Marney and Del Giudice were to produce and Adrian Brunel to direct this ensemble piece. The importance attached to the film was evident in the way production was quickly moved to the big studios at Denham, the high-profile Leslie Howard brought in as principal director, and the high level of ATS cooperation. Two ATS officers were assigned to liaise with the production, and cast and crew were allowed in August 1942 to shoot extensive exterior and interior scenes at an ATS recruit training centre and use numerous ATS and army personnel as extras. They were also allowed to shoot scenes at an Ack Ack battery.[80]

The resulting film, now entitled *The Gentle Sex*, in which Leslie Howard interjects occasional commentary, follows the fortunes of seven women from diverse backgrounds who either volunteer or are conscripted into the ATS. There is warm-hearted Maggie Fraser (Rosamund John), from a Scottish fishing family; Anne Lawrence (Joyce Howard), confident daughter of a army colonel; Betty Miller (Joan Greenwood), a sheltered middle-class girl leaving home for the first time; the happy-go-lucky Dot Hopkins (Jean Gillie), a beautician; Erna Debruzki (Lillie Palmer), a deadly serious Czech refugee; an irascible Joan Simpson (Barbara Waring), a dancing teacher; and finally the voluble Gwen Hayden (Joan Gates), a Cockney waitress. Despite their differences, they almost all become fast friends in the course of recruit training, and go on to jobs as lorry drivers and as range-finder operators and communication specialists on a 3.7 inch AA gun battery. Even Gwen, initially relegated to the job of mess orderly at the depot, eventually manages to become a telephonist.

The importance of the ATS to the war effort is then illustrated. There is a long truck convoy sequence in which the women are shown to have both the endurance and the skills necessary to drive lorries carrying vital material 400 miles across country to a port where ships are waiting (First soldier: 'Core, stone me off a branch! Women working all night!' Second soldier: 'This *is* a woman's war!'). The film's climax, when all seven come together again, centres on the way in which technically adept and courageous ATS personnel provide vital assistance in the downing of a German bomber. There are personal tragedies involving the death of loved ones, but the two women involved, Ann and Gwen, carry on. Efforts are also made to show that joining the ATS does not mean losing one's femininity. New-pattern uniforms, for example, once fitted, are shown off to advantage most of the time, and none of the actresses looks anything other than attractive. At an all-ranks dance Anne and Maggie respectively attract the attention of a handsome commissioned RAF pilot (John Justin), and a kilted Highland corporal (John Laurie). *The Gentle Sex*, in short, sought to make service in the ATS seem both important to civilians in general and appealing to women in particular.[81]

From a modern perspective elements of *The Gentle Sex*, in particular the commentary by Leslie Howard, can appear embarrassingly chauvinist.[82] When it was released in the spring of 1943, however, it came across well both as propaganda and as entertainment. A 'first rate film, most sure-footed' was the verdict of a colonel on the CIGS's staff.[83] 'The ATS cheered their own film *The Gentle Sex* at a private view in London yesterday', the *Daily Express* critic Ernest Betts noted on 7 April. 'It is a film that will give men a new respect for women at war'; adding three days later that 'Every women in the country will want to see it'. P. L. Mannock in the *Daily Herald* was equally enthralled. 'It is an inspiring record,' he wrote, 'and I was assured by several of the high-ups in that astonishing service (could they be called Brass ATS?) that it is absolutely authentic in detail and spirit.' Reg Whitley of the *Daily Mirror* thought it 'real and convincing', while Elspeth Grant of the *Daily Sketch* labelled it 'first rate entertainment' and 'an inspiring picture'. Reviews in the quality press were also positive. *The Gentle Sex* was 'half fact, half fiction, and wholly true to life', Campbell Dixon noted in the *Daily Telegraph*. To the *Manchester Guardian* critic it was both 'a well-deserved tribute' and 'good entertainment.' Even Edgar Anstey, who wondered in the *Spectator* whether life in the ATS was really quite as spectacular and exciting as suggested, had to admit that 'the film does succeed in giving us a lot of welcome facts and feelings about women in uniform'.[84] It was among the most popular four films mentioned in the 1943 Mass-Observation survey of cinema favourites, especially among women. 'A film about life as it is', 'real and natural', 'realistic portrayal of service life', and 'very like real life' were some of the responses. A Birmingham stenographer, who thought the portrayal 'too neat and trim', went on to write that it made her – despite being ineligible – 'wish for quite a few minutes that I could join one of the Women's Services'.[85]

It was not just the women's branch of the army, however, that suffered from an image problem in middle years of the war. Home Forces as a whole continued to rate poorly in popular estimation. It was true that public confidence had been increased by success in North Africa; but, as the War Office morale committee discovered, there were limits to how much the glory of the Eighth Army reflected on Home Forces (still very much the bulk of the army).

Esprit d'armée, lack of which was pointed to in the last quarter's Report, is still deficient. Recent successes in the field have certainly sent up the Army's stock in the general estimation, have dispelled the bogey of inaction to a considerable extent, and have provoked livelier interest in the war, but they are felt to be the achievement rather of a particular part of the Army than of the Army as a whole, and they cannot be said to have produced in the ordinary soldier serving at home that instinctive pride in himself as a member of the Army which is the main-spring of military morale.[86]

Though confidence had improved somewhat by the early months of 1943, conscripts remained alienated from military life, and complaints about the extension of the call-up, pay, allowances and pensions, and conditions of service, continued to make their way into MoI Home Intelligence reports and the press. 'In the public estimation,' as one private in the Black Watch put it to the morale committee, 'the soldier's status is the lowest of the three Services, and he is often treated accordingly.' Or as another private was overheard to say on a train: 'You've got to admit now, most soldiers are treated like [expletive deleted] dogs'.[87]

Among those most aware of the problem were those working in the Directorate of Army Psychiatry. Morale committee and unit reports, the higher number of requests for compassionate discharge, plus mounting desertion figures, all pointed to a potentially serious lack of self-esteem. With the blessing of the director, Brigadier J. R. Rees, Lieutenant-Colonels Ronald Hargreaves and Tommy Wilson, deputy directors, decided in the summer of 1942 to commission the Army Kinematograph Service (responsible for in-house training productions) to make a film for 'an unusual military purpose'. The idea was to make something that would make disgruntled new recruits understand that primary training, while tough, had a real purpose. An agreement was reached whereby the film, using professional actors, would be directed by Carol Reed from a script written by Eric Ambler and Peter Ustinov.[88]

The plot of *The New Lot* followed the progress of a group of reluctant new recruits through their initial training – the hardships of which would not be underplayed – to the point where they take pride in being soldiers. As Ambler later explained, the forty-minute film, designed to be shown to new recruits, 'was to be about self-respect and the consolations of an *esprit de corps*'. Ambler and Ustinov were qualified to write on this subject, having both suffered the indignities of recruit training and futility of army life as ordinary soldiers. Ambler, though now a captain, had started out as a Royal Artillery gunner in 1940, while young Ustinov, called up in 1942, remained an unhappy private in the Royal Sussex Regiment. At the same time they were both true patriots at heart. With a solid script and an ensemble cast that included Raymond Huntley, James Hanley and Geoffrey Keene, as well as Robert Donat in a cameo role, Carol Reed was able to direct a film in which patriotism allied with professionalism eventually overcomes bloody-mindedness on the part of the recruits.[89]

Those involved in its production thought *The New Lot* a fine piece of work. Unfortunately, others did not. When it was shown at the War Office the DMT became almost speechless with fury. 'You can't call those men soldiers,' he spluttered, 'they do nothing but grumble. Real soldiers don't grumble.' *The New Lot* was condemned as 'subversive stuff verging on the Bolshy'.[90] Analysis of audience reaction in a special public preview arranged by the DPR through the MoI in April 1943 showed that, while people had enjoyed the film, 'it was not clear how far it increased the warmth of their feeling for the Army'.[91] According to Ambler *The New Lot* was never shown to the recruit audiences for which it had been intended.[92]

The film did, however, have admirers. Apart from the psychiatrists who had commissioned it, both the DPR and Adjutant-General thought *The New Lot* had tackled a very real problem with great skill. Audiences would empathize with the complaints of the screen recruits; but by that very fact would be likely to come around gradually to a more positive view of the army as 'the new lot' become real soldiers. If it could not be shown to recruits, perhaps it could be released as a second feature in civilian cinemas? AKS productions, unfortunately, were officially classified as for army use only, no mechanism existing for their distribution on regular circuits. The only option, Colonels Hargreaves and Wilson suggested, was for someone else to remake the film – preferably a commercial company that would turn it into a full-length production comparable to *In Which We Serve*.[93]

It was at this point that David Niven entered the picture. Having been rejected by the RAF in 1939, he had with some reluctance rejoined the army (having resigned his commission in the early 1930s out of sheer boredom and gone to Hollywood). The contrast between the Other Ranks in peace and war, he found, was striking. 'Conscripts,' he recalled, 'particularly cockney ones ... were very different from the peacetime Jocks of the Highland Light Infantry and it took me a while to get used to the grumbling of bored soldiers who resented being pulled out of good jobs and warm homes to train in acute discomfort.' Over time, however, as he rose to command a company in a special reconnaissance unit, he observed the fact that 'bank clerks, burglars, shop assistants, milkmen, garage mechanics, school masters, painters, bookmakers, stockbrokers and labourers', despite their grumbling, could be turned into good solders. Niven was, however, increasingly worried about the effect on morale of the army's ongoing image problem. In the autumn of 1942, after seeing *In Which We Serve* and thinking 'isn't it time somebody did something about the Army', he sent a proposal that a film be made up the chain of command that eventually arrived on the desk of the Adjutant-General.[94]

To those involved in trying to sell a feature version of *The New Lot*, this intervention came at an opportune moment. For one thing, the actor could help enormously in selling the project to a commercial company. With the public supposedly growing tired of films with war themes, producers and exhibitors were leery of taking on new war-related stories. Stewart Granger, for example, knowing nothing of *The New Lot*, wrote a script at about this time dealing with the development of *esprit de corps* among a group of recruits, based on his experiences in the Gordon Highlanders and Black Watch. He hoped that his current employer, Maurice Ostrer of Gainsborough Pictures, would agree to produce it. Ostrer, however, turned it down because there was no love interest.[95] Niven, though, with his Hollywood background, was one of Britain's few recognised film stars, liked by women as well as men.[96] The prospect of a film in which he would take the leading role was one that film companies would find much harder to pass up. Moreover, Niven's fame and charm as a raconteur meant that he had many contacts in high places, up to and including the Prime Minister. Finally he had a genuine (if sometimes chequered) military pedigree, so it would be less easy for critics within the War Office to be dismissive about 'actors playing at soldiers'.[97]

Niven was therefore summoned to the War Office to meet the Adjutant-General. Typical of his generation and class in that he did not know who Niven was, General Adam had nevertheless been made aware that this was an officer whose input could prove crucial to the making of a commercial version of *The New Lot*. The encounter, as Niven explained in a TV interview many years later, was memorable.

> So I was announced 'Major Newman'. Major Newman?
> So anyway I went in [to Adam's office]. He called me 'Newman' all the time.
> He said, 'Newman, you were an actor before the war?'
> And I said, 'Yes'.
> And he said, 'Well, look, um, we want a film about the Army, so fall out and get it started.'
> I said, 'But sir, they don't start like that!'
> He said [brusquely] 'Don't stand about!'
> And the original title of *The Way Ahead* [the new version of *The New Lot*] was *Don't Stand About!*
> So then I said, 'Well, look sir, if you give me a couple of weeks leave, or something, I'll get together with some people who *really* know how to make movies and are in the Army and we'll come up with a synopsis – an idea for a

film – and if you like it get behind it with some military help and we'll get it made, somehow.'[98]

His first port of call was the Directorate of Public Relations, where Eric Linklater, who wrote stories for the public on various aspects of army – some of which were blocked by traditionalists on grounds similar to those raised against *The New Lot* – gave him 'the germ of an idea' as to the plot.[99]

Paul Kimberley, the Director of Army Kinematography, met Filippo Del Giudice, managing director of Two Cities Films, to discuss the possibility of a feature with the box-office and publicity value of Two Cities' *In Which We Serve*. Del Giudice also met Ambler and Reed, and later Niven. He was enthusiastic and wrote to Jack Beddington, head of the MoI Films Division, proposing that he lend his support to those within the War Office pushing for such a film. Since the Minister of Information, Brendan Bracken, had already been thinking along these lines – he had unsuccessfully approached Noël Coward about making an army version of *In Which We Serve* – Beddington, on whom Niven also paid a call, agreed that it was 'very desirable to produce a good feature film with an Army background'.[100]

A memo written by Niven for the Adjutant-General's office in late November 1942 laid out what he and the others involved in the project had in mind. It would have to be a commercial feature film made 'on a really important scale', which, through being 'first-class entertainment' rather than overt propaganda, would draw in audiences and make then feel proud of the British Army. 'The movie-going public', he stressed, '... after three years of war can smell pure propaganda a mile off.' The film would therefore have to be a commercial feature 'of first-class entertainment value with benefit to Army prestige coming as a natural result of the "story"'.[101]

The next stage was to produce a treatment. If *The New Lot* was to be the model, it made sense to use the same writing team. After some string-pulling, Private Ustinov and Major Ambler met daily for three weeks in the lavish London hotel suite of Captain Reed. Major Niven, meanwhile, entertained the group with reports from 'the brigadier belt' and made himself useful smoothing out the occasional administrative wrinkle. Remembering the fate of *The New Lot*, Ambler included the full text of 'a strong rousing, hurray-for-us speech' – originally to be delivered by the platoon sergeant – on the distinguished battle history of the regiment.[102] Once the treatment was complete it was nervously taken by Niven to the War Office for comment in January 1943.

Despite the efforts to balance grumbling with patriotism, official reaction to what would become *The Way Ahead* was decidedly mixed. A senior DMT general scrawled across the jacket 'Tripe! Why can't we have a full-blooded story by a full-blooded soldier?'[103] Even the Adjutant-General, a prime mover in the whole affair, was quite taken aback: 'Well these bloody fellows all hate the Army!'[104] According to Niven – then working for DPR – there ensued a lot of 'double-crossing', 'apathy' and general 'fiddling'; but in the end, after some wire-pulling by Ronnie Tritton and Jack Beddington, among others, the green light was given for further development – on the understanding that Niven would play the officer.[105]

By the end of March 1943 negotiations between the MoI and War Office on the one hand and Del Giudice and J. Arthur Rank (as head of General Film Distributors) on the other had produced the outlines of an agreement. The script would be purchased by Two Cities for £250 and made into a film costing in the region of £80–150,000. Two Cities would receive 66.6 per cent of the profits over seven years. The remainder would go to the Crown, to which all rights would revert at the end of the seven-year period. The War Office and MoI would have the right to ask for changes at every stage of production.[106]

Supervised by Carol Reed, and protected by Niven, Ambler and Ustinov began work on revising and expanding the script of *The New Lot* with the same cast in mind. There were ongoing contractual problems over using Niven in the lead role – who was under contract to Sam Goldwyn – that were not resolved until the autumn. Ambler found one of the two military advisers assigned to the film (Captain R. Fellowes of the Rifle Brigade) less than helpful, and later quarrelled with Reed about the 'honour of the regiment' speech being made by the platoon officer – Niven's part – rather than the platoon sergeant. Colonel A. C. Bromhead, a veteran of film pro-paganda from the First World War and currently an honorary advisor to the MoI films division, went on record to express his view that a feature about reluctant recruits was out of date, even 'insulting', given that the army was now on the offensive and the war might be over by the time the film was released. The production did go ahead, with shooting beginning at Denham Studios in the summer of 1943. It was to take a year to complete. The screenplay was comparatively lengthy (the film would run 115 minutes), and there was a good deal of exterior shooting at Aldershot and on Salisbury Plain to be done that was dependent on good weather and available equip-ment. There were also the many extra weeks spent on location work in North Africa over the winter of 1943–44. It was therefore not until the spring of 1944 that *The Way Ahead*, having cost £252,000 to make, was ready for its premiere.[107]

The main thrust of the plot is the transformation of a disparate group of disgruntled civilians into a coherent body of trained fighting men. As in the 1943 'pulling together' films, including *Nine Men* and *The Gentle Sex*, there is an ensemble cast of characters hailing from a variety of class and regional backgrounds.[108] There is Ted Brewer (Stanley Holloway), working-class boilerman and 'complete barrack-room "lawyer"'.[109] There is Beck (Leslie Dwyer), an ex-travel agent and sunny optimist. There is also Lloyd (James Donald), the moody landlord's agent, as well as Herbert Davenport (Raymond Huntley) and Bill Parsons (Hugh Burden), a middle-aged floor manager and worried sales clerk from the same department store. There is Luke (John Laurie), a resigned Scottish farm labourer, and finally Geoffrey Stainer (Jimmy Hanley), a young car salesman given to bragging. Also introduced are the men who will train and lead them as members of 'The Duke of Glendon's Light Infantry': the tough and professional Sergeant Fletcher (William Hartnell) and the former garage attendant and TA ranker, Second-Lieutenant Jim Perry (David Niven).

It is made clear from the start that the conscripts are not – with the partial exception of Beck – happy to have been called up. They had civilian jobs and personal commitments, or wanted to join one of the other services, and are prepared to believe the worst. ('I'll tell you something about the Army', a belligerent Stainer tells his glum fellow conscripts as they wait for a train. 'Full of people who want to make you suffer because you're no good at polishing buttons.'). Life will be mindlessly demeaning and harsh, and comforts few in the extreme. At first this seems to be the case. Spartan barrack arrangements, including a lack of sheets, prompt the fastidious Davenport to remark 'These living conditions are most unsanitary.' As for the food, Brewer pithily defines it as 'Terrible!' Then there is the uniform. When the platoon first go on parade, many of them have blouses, trousers and caps which do not fit and which make them look humiliatingly foolish. Though Lieutenant Perry fixes this problem, khaki battledress still seems somehow demeaning. 'I wish we had a collar and tie,' Davenport laments after seeing the uniform of a glamorous RAF sergeant pilot, 'this makes you feel like a convict.' And above all there is the constant hectoring by the platoon sergeant (brilliantly played by Hartnell, who had spent weeks observing the real thing at work in a training camp at Pirbright).[110]

Sergeant Fletcher appears a heartless martinet, constantly shouting orders, refusing requests for forty-eight-hour passes after the men have been in 'only a month', and pushing them hard in an apparently vindictive round of drill, fatigues and guard duty. A complaint by Lloyd to Lieutenant Perry about Fletcher's behaviour – which he and his fellows believe is due to the hostility they displayed towards the then-unknown sergeant at Crewe Station during the journey to the training depot – only seems to lead to a round of battle drill. By the eighth week of training the majority of the group have become so 'Us' against 'Them' that they sullenly refuse Perry's request for volunteers for the camp concert (Perry: 'I was almost knocked down in the rush'). Then, on Lloyd's initiative, they deliberately expose themselves to enemy fire in an exercise so as to get some rest sooner rather than later.

At the same time, however, the audience is given the other side of the picture. Early on in the film, as one Chelsea Pensioner from the 'Dogs' derides the softness of the modern army, we are shown Perry and others going over a battle-training assault course of formidable proportions. This puts the lie to the old soldier's complaints while – as with a similar sequence at the start of *Nine Men* – it makes soldiers look virile. David Niven's well-bred screen persona makes it easier to believe in him as an officer than as a garage mechanic, but it is nevertheless made clear that Perry's origins are comparatively humble. He has risen to command through commitment (disregarding the scepticism of his boss in March 1939 concerning the Territorial Army and the suggestion that they develop a comfortable position in case of war) and ability (he was a sergeant in France in 1940 before going on an officer's course in 1941) rather than social connections.

Unfamiliar with conscripts, he seeks out Fletcher in the sergeants' mess to discuss Lloyd's complaint. At this point Fletcher shows himself to be paternal and surprisingly philosophical. Perry learns that his sergeant had vigorously resisted efforts by a specialist section to pinch men from the platoon, and Fletcher himself, on hearing about Lloyd, smiles, then says good-naturedly:

> Well all soldiers like a bit of a grumble, don't they, Sir. After all, it's not very funny to have to run when you feel like walking, or to stand up when you feel you could do with a sit-down; or to have someone shouting at you when you're doing your best. No, I think it does men good to let off steam a bit.

The sergeant admits that his men are having difficulty, but stresses to Perry that training will eventually turn them into soldiers: 'We haven't got a dud there, Sir!'

Then there is the way Bill Parsons is treated after being caught trying to desert. It turns out his wife is being hounded by debt collectors working for a furniture hire-purchase firm. The platoon expect him to receive the harshest of punishments. But though he is severely reprimanded by the CO and confined to barracks, Perry – who sees the underhandedness of the firm's practices – helps make arrangements for an emergency war grant and special forty-eight-hour leave. 'You know, being in the Army has a lot of disadvantages', he tells Parsons as he works out what to do. 'But there's one compensation – you're not alone anymore against anyone: Germans or furniture shops.' Officers care about the welfare of their men and the British Army has mechanisms to help them out when in trouble.

The irrepressible Beck, meanwhile, has been occasionally reminding his grousing fellows that they are in fact exaggerating their guard and other duties as against those of other sections. By the time they decide to mess up their part of the exercise in week eight of their training, what earlier had seemed complaints with which audiences could sympathize have become sheer selfishness and laziness.

> Lloyd: 'This is too stupid for words!'
> Stainer: 'Think of the other blokes, they'll be home by now, cushy.'
> Lloyd: 'I am thinking of them. What's the point of our staying out here for hours? Why can't we get back?'

The five-minute scene that follows, almost half way through the film, is the key turning point.[111]

Perry, who has guessed what they have done, dresses the men down in their barrack hut, angrily pointing out that they have let down both the rest of the battalion and – pointing to the Penninsular War and other battle honours on the DOGS cap badge – their illustrious forebearers in the regiment ('… Salamanca, Orthez, Waterloo, Alma, Sebastopol, Tel-el-Kebir, Mons, Ypres, Somme …'). 'If you ever get near any real fighting', Perry concludes, '—I don't suppose that you'll ever be good enough, but *if* you do – you'll find that you're looking to other men not to let you down. If you're lucky, you'll have men like Captain Edwards [the company commander, Leo Genn] and Sergeant Fletcher to look to. If they're lucky … *they'll be with another company.*' Lloyd and the others clearly feel guilty and ashamed; and though grumbling continues, they are more philosophical as Perry and Fletcher, running alongside, drive them hard over the assault course and through the rest of their initial training. The ice is finally broken between Perry and the men when they unexpectedly bump into one another while seeking baths at the house of Mrs Gillingham who lives in the nearby village. By the time the platoon gets its first spell of proper leave they have begun to take some pride in their new profession – and their officer in them.

As Mrs Perry (Penelope Dudley Ward) meets her husband on the station platform as they all disperse, she asks: 'Are they the awful men?', to which Perry replies 'No, different lot'. When an acquaintance at a pub disparages the importance of footsloggers in modern war, Lloyd's response reveals how committed he has become to his role as an infantryman:

> Listen Sam: An infantryman is one of the most highly skilled technical men in the modern army. He has to be a mechanic, a gunner, an explosives expert, and an athlete to begin with. He has a greater variety of weapons than all the rest of

the army put together. And he has to be trained in not just one sort of tactics but in every sort – street fighting, tank hunting, wood clearing, and all the rest.

As Sergeant Fletcher had predicted in his mess conversation with Lieutenant Perry, Lloyd is eventually promoted to the rank of corporal.

A final symbol of the new unity achieved in the platoon is a brief sequence involving a singalong during a battalion concert set in July 1942. In marked contrast to the tensions and disasters of the first company concert, this is a happy occasion. The camera pans across the faces of all the main characters in the audience, lustily singing, as it were, from the same hymn book.

Finally, it is time for the Duke of Glendon's Light Infantry to go to war. Fully trained and eager for action, No. 9 Platoon embarks with the rest of the battalion on a troopship which, it emerges, is part of a convoy involved in Operation Torch, the Allied landings in French North Africa in November 1942. In the real operation there were no losses at sea, but in *The Way Ahead* the troopship is torpedoed. As fires rage, water pours in and the ship lists, Perry and his men coolly go to work assisting the crew (including Trevor Howard in his first role – a merchant navy officer) in moving and ditching scout cars and Bren carriers from the upper and lower decks. Sergeant Fletcher, whose foot is trapped by shifting cargo, is saved by Luke and Perry. In the end all the passengers and crew – the captain leaving last – are taken off safely by a destroyer before the ammunition explodes. The lesson of this fifteen-minute episode, filmed with the cooperation of the navy and on a scale (in terms of sets, equipment, and location work) dwarfing even *In Which We Serve*, is that No. 9 Platoon is made up of trained men who know how to act even in the most unexpected crisis situations.

The scene then shifts to March 1943 and North Africa, where we see the newly arrived DOGS arriving in a fly-blown village to take up a reserve position. Though winning the friendship of the initially suspicions proprietor of the local café (Peter Ustinov) by interesting him in darts, the men of No. 9 Platoon grow bored and homesick as they wait for something to happen. Suddenly the enemy breaks through and the battalion has to defend its positions against German infantry and tanks supported by aircraft. Assisted by six-pounder anti-tank guns, Perry and his men drive the enemy off, but a break elsewhere in the line forces the battalion to retire to the village. Taking up position amid buildings partially or completely wrecked by enemy bombing and artillery, No. 9 Platoon holds the superior force of advancing enemy at bay with rifle and Bren gun fire. A particularly effective enemy mortar is put out of action when Perry, ordering Luke and Brewer to provide covering fire with a Vickers heavy machine gun he spots (the crew dead), takes Beck with him and gets a six-pounder (whose crew is also dead) back into action. Modern infantry, it seems, really do have to know how to operate a variety of weapons.

The village battle scenes, it should be noted, shot on location in North Africa with the help of men and equipment from a Scots Guards battalion and other units, are as impressive as the troopship sequence. Able to use live ammunition for the anti-tank gun so as to produce a genuine recoil, plus quantities of explosives to simulate artillery shells landing and further wreck genuinely war-torn buildings, Carol Reed and cameraman Guy Green produced images which were as close to the kind of documentary realism present in films like *Desert Victory* as it was possible to achieve in a dramatic feature.

After further fighting Perry and his men are ordered to fix bayonets and advance under cover of a smoke screen. Though they are low on ammunition, and the Germans have said they will all perish (since they have spurned a demand that they surrender), the men of No. 9 Platoon display nothing but professionalism as they prepare to move out into the open. The camera pans across the faces of each of the main characters – all set in grim determination – as they move through the smoke. This is the penultimate scene, the film ending with the Pensioners reading about the exploits of the DOGS and (in the released version) 'The Beginning' on the screen rather than 'The End'.[112]

As already noted, there did exist some concern that, by the time it was ready to be shown, the issues *The Way Ahead* was designed to address would have disappeared as a result of a rapidly improving war situation. But there was also much to be said in its favour. For one thing, the British Army had lately tended to be overshadowed on screen by the US Army, not only in *Tunisian Victory* but also in a Hollywood rendition of the *Thirteen/Nine Men* story. In *Sahara*, directed by Zoltan Korda for Columbia Pictures, it is an American sergeant (Humphrey Bogart) who is the authority figure who finds himself leading a group of disoriented Commonwealth soldiers as well as his tank crew. The film was a hit, but not one that showed the British Army to particularly good advantage. It was a pity, Campbell Dixon wrote in the *Telegraph*, 'that the only character who behaves badly – he takes more than his share of water and at first argues against a pretty hopeless attempt to defend the well – should be English'.[113]

Rather more importantly, there were still unresolved perceptual issues in the ranks and among the public at large which *The Way Ahead* might help resolve. Military success in 1943 had done much to raise spirits within Home Forces, but there was still disquieting evidence of poor officer-man relations and an unwillingness among Other Ranks to commit to their role. A morale committee report, surveying the late summer and early autumn of 1943, detected

> an attitude of antagonism to an impersonal 'they', variously identified with 'the War Office', 'the authorities' and (by the rank and file) with 'the officers' or even 'the Army' generally, which militates against solidarity, cooperation and esprit de corps in the Army as a whole. It makes the soldier think of the Army as an institution of which he is not fully a member, administered by those who do not in any real sense lead or represent him.[114]

By the spring of 1944, according to Home Intelligence reports, waning public interest in promotional efforts such as the annual 'Salute the Soldier' campaign was matched by anxiety about likely heavy casualties in the coming cross-Channel invasion.[115]

The Way Ahead, in short, could still do some good. Whether it would or not remained to be seen. Bearing in mind the kind of hostility *The New Lot* had produced, plus the time, money and resources poured into the new production, Niven, Ambler and Reed were understandably nervous as they travelled down to Staines in late May 1944 for a special public showing at the Majestic designed to gauge public reaction. According to Ronald Tritton, the director 'was almost incoherent with nerves' as he sat down in the cinema. As it turned out, they need not have worried. Thanks to an excellent script, combining humour, drama and occasional pathos, very good direction and excellent acting by all members of the ensemble cast, *The Way Ahead* was seen for what it was: a truly fine film. It was 'enthusiastically received with much spontaneous applause', Tritton noted in his diary. 'I felt very elated and happy afterwards. We all did.'[116]

By the time of the official premiere, 6 June 1944 – D-Day in a much more important sense, as it turned out – the film's pressbook was ready. *The Way Ahead*, it was made clear, was meant to be a tract for the times. It was 'a plain tale of typical Britons of this generation' – 'your husband, my son, their brother, the man next door, the chap over the way' – the story of 'the Tommy of To-day'.[117] While few reviewers proved willing to mine the pressbook for such turns of phrase, most thought the picture highly realistic and very true to life. *The Way Ahead* received lavish and near-universal praise from the critics.

'At long last,' Reg Whitley wrote for the *Daily Mirror*, 'here is a worthy tribute to the PBI and a thundering screen salute to the soldier.' *The Way Ahead* was the 'best film yet about the British footslogger', according to the *Sunday Express* review, while the *News of the World* found it 'true to life'. The quality press was equally enthusiastic. The film was 'without affectation', according to *The Times*, and also funny. The *Daily Telegraph* thought the training scenes 'brilliantly done' and the humour 'rich and unforced'. The appearance of the film on the same day British troops were wading ashore on the beaches of Normandy – probably a coincidence – made it seem particularly timely. 'Dead on the dot of D-Day,' C. A. Lejeune wrote for the *Observer*, 'the British studios [*sic*] have brought out a film about the training of a civilian into an invasion soldier that is not only stirringly in step with the times, but a superb piece of film-craft at any time; one of the splendours of the British cinema.' It was generally considered to be the army's answer to *In Which We Serve* and was thought by at least some critics to be superior to *Nine Men* and even *Desert Victory*. Only the use of the Chelsea Pensioners came in for criticism as a rather shop-worn device.[118]

There was also much satisfaction in official circles in the wake of an obviously successful premiere in which the front rows were occupied by top brass. 'It is an absolutely first-class production from every point of view,' Lord Burnham, the DPR, wrote to Reed on 9 June, 'and I am sure will be a very big success.' Lord Alanbrooke, the Chief of the Imperial General Staff, was reported to have said that it was one of the best films he had ever seen, as were other senior figures. 'I think it is magnificent', wrote Jack Beddington, '(and I'm not inclined to use such words).' The Minister of Information was equally impressed. 'It is a superb film, the best I have seen about the war.'[119]

Though not a smash hit beyond the first month, and appearing many months after the problems it was designed to address had been most acute, *The Way Ahead* did solid business at the box office, grossing over £233,000 in the UK alone by the end of 1945.[120] A *Picturegoer* survey, moreover, revealed that those who had seen it tended to rank *The Way Ahead* alongside *In Which We Serve* as among the best films they had seen in recent years.[121] It was also authentic enough to be enjoyed by soldiers – usually very critical of screen representations of army life – and in the post-bellum decade was used a training film for officer cadets at Sandhurst on the problems of commanding National Service conscripts.[122]

The Way Ahead ranks as the premier wartime film about the British Army. It was not, however, the last wartime feature in which the army played a significant role. Though planned and partially executed while fighting was still going on, the last of the big campaign documentaries, *The True Glory* and *Burma Victory*, did not appear on screen until, respectively, the war in Europe and the war against Japan were over. This had certainly not been the original intention in either case. *The True Glory*, an Anglo-American production, had begun life as a film project that would chronicle Operation Overlord, the Allied landings in Normandy. With literally hundreds of cameramen from various Allied service film units at work during the lead-up to D-Day and the subsequent campaign in Normandy, film footage was not a problem. Competing ideas, interservice rivalries, and bureaucratic in-fighting involving a host of Allied organizations and figures, however, generated serious delays. By the autumn of 1944 it was becoming clear that the slow pace of development under the Joint Anglo-American Film Production Committee, combined with the swift progress of Allied operations on the Continent in the late summer, meant that a feature about the Normandy campaign – still only in the planning stages – would no longer be useful as topical propaganda. In October 1944 it was therefore decided to shelve this idea in favour of a film covering not only Normandy but all subsequent events down to the final German surrender. The fact that this latter event did not occur until May of the following year, along with further bureaucratic delays, meant that *The True Glory* – a title derived from the prayer Sir Francis Drake delivered before he sailed out to meet the Armada – was not ready to be shown to the public until August 1945.[123]

Despite the number of people and organizations involved and the breadth of its subject, *The True Glory*, as directed by Garson Kanin (USA) and Carol Reed (UK), turned out to be coherent and was edited with great skill over eighty-seven minutes. With the overall course of the campaign narrated in Shakespearean-style blank verse with the aid of maps, a wide variety of operations and events were given a genuinely human touch through accompanying footage with the words – spoken by actors employing an array of regional and class accents – of some of the ordinary servicemen and women involved.[124] Despite fears on both sides of the Atlantic, *The True Glory* was also remarkably even-handed in its treatment of the relative contributions of the United States and United Kingdom. Interventions by American General Dwight D. Eisenhower as Allied Supreme Commander, for instance, were balanced by the fact that the title, narration and narrator (Robert Harris) were very English in character. The quiet fortitude and achievements of the British Army (as well as the other services) were justly celebrated and the reviews were very positive. It was 'a magnificent account' (*The Times*) that was 'magnificently put together' (*Daily Herald*) and told 'a great story greatly' (*Daily Telegraph*).[125] Yet there was no gainsaying the fact that while *The True Glory* could generate retrospective pride, with the war finally over it did not have the direct propaganda value of a film like *Desert Victory*. As P. L. Mannock explained, it was a current film that was made 'for posterity'.[126]

It was much the same story with *Burma Victory*. The idea for this feature dated from July 1944, when Lord Mountbatten, as supreme commander in

South East Asia, had floated the idea of an Anglo-American film that would celebrate the success of Allied forces in the region. Once more friction arose over the direction the feature was to take and over spheres of authority, and in March 1945 it was agreed that two separate films should be made. *The Stilwell Road* was the US contribution, *Burma Victory* the British.

Made by David Macdonald and Roy Boulting of the AFPU and narrated by Frank Harvey, the sixty-two minute *Burma Victory* was in many ways a jungle version of *Desert Victory*. Both films, for example, emphasized the difficulties presented by an extreme climate, and both also focused on the doings of particular armies (Eighth and Fourteenth). Even without foreign sensibilities to contend with and with a successful model on which to base the film, however, *Burma Victory* encountered delays. Logistical and other problems, not least interventions by Mountbatten and others, meant that the film was not ready for release until late October 1945.[127]

Despite this late date – the original intention had been to get a film out before *The True Glory* – *Burma Victory* was greeted with enthusiasm by the critics. This was partly due to the undoubted merits of the film itself, but was also influenced by the fury that *Objective Burma*, a Hollywood feature starring Errol Flynn, had created in the British press the previous month. The Flynn film had seemed to indicate that the campaign in Burma was primarily an American affair; *Burma Victory* showed beyond a shadow of a doubt that Fourteenth Army played the major role. Unlike a certain film which had 'travestied' the truth about the war in Burma, this was 'exciting, moving, and above all honest', Campbell Dixon wrote in the *Telegraph*. Despite being occasionally 'sketchy and a little lacking in conviction', *The Times* noted, *Burma Victory* was 'a powerful piece of work' that eschewed entirely 'the romantic licence of *Objective Burma*'. Military observers, invited to assess the authenticity of what was presented, disputed minor points but were on the whole very supportive.[128] Still, the fact remained that *Burma Victory* appeared months after the Japanese surrender in August 1945, which naturally changed its function. It was now 'a record, a portrait, a history, rather than an urgent plea to command public support'.[129]

It had taken the War Office longer than the other service ministries to involve itself in feature films through which both soldiers and civilians could take pride in the British Army. In part this had been due to the course of events in the first half of the war, a period when the army had little to celebrate. Bad luck and poor timing also played a role. The time lag, however, was in large part the result of deeply ingrained prejudices and difficulties in adjusting to the realities of the People's War among senior figures inside and outside the War Office. Nevertheless, by the end of the war, with the help of commercial film companies and industry personnel in uniform, more flexible figures such as Sir Ronald Adam and Lord Burnham had been able to oversee the development of features in which aspects of the new citizen army were integrated with a more traditional patriotic emphasis.

5

The Services and the Cinema, 1945–1970

As wartime conditions gave way once more to peace, the prospects for promoting the armed forces on the screen appeared bright. Though the feature work of the service film units was quickly wound up, the three service ministries did not dismantle their PR apparatuses as they had after the First World War. The Air Ministry within a few years closed its Directorate of Public Relations, but replaced it with an Information Division of over twenty officers and officials. At the War Office the DPR remained, headed by a succession of brigadiers and major generals and with an executive staff of over fifteen. Only the Admiralty seriously trimmed back, but even so the Chief of Naval Information had half a dozen officials under his command. All three, what was more, agreed in 1946 that the definition of what constituted useful film publicity for the services should be expanded from the rather narrow prewar emphasis on direct propaganda value to include subjects that could be considered as promoting a wider service interest.[1]

Approaches by film producers seeking assistance, therefore, were to be seen as potential publicity opportunities rather than regarded with automatic suspicion. At the same time, however, it was universally agreed that the companies concerned would, as in prewar days, have to cover insurance and other costs and allow the ministry concerned veto power over the results. The standard contract produced by the Air Ministry, for instance, specified that the RAF would retain 'strict control' over the resulting footage, and that permission to use it could be 'conditional upon the excision of certain portions'.[2]

The commercial film industry, meanwhile, had emerged from the war in a position of relative strength. Going to the pictures was more popular than ever – between 1939 and 1946 annual cinema admissions had increased from 990,000,000 to 1,635,000,000 – while the high quality of recent features no longer automatically made British films seem inferior to the Hollywood product in the public mind. Surveys suggested greater public faith in domestic films, a trend reflected in the successful reissue of wartime hits (including *In Which We Serve*, *The First of the Few*, *One of Our Aircraft is Missing* and *The Way Ahead*).[3]

What was more, the commercial industry was soon to discover the apparently insatiable public interest in hitherto untold stories about the recent struggle in which, perforce, the services tended to hold pride of place. Popular war stories published in the latter 1940s and early 1950s, along with original screenplays, were quickly transferred to the screen in what became a boom decade for British war films. Explanations for this phenomenon, ranging from interest in hitherto untold episodes to a kind of public nostalgia for the nation's finest hour in the midst of Britain's postwar retreat from world power, remain a subject of considerable debate.[4] Whatever the reasons, the service ministries were ready and able to take advantage of the flow of requests emanating from Wardour Street as the decade advanced and the number of young male cinemagoers came to significantly outnumber female cinemagoers.[5]

In a few cases two or even all three of the services gave assistance, as with the rather unsuccessful *They Who Dare*, a 1954 Mayflower film directed by Lewis Milestone about a Special Boat Service raid on enemy airfields on Rhodes in 1942 for which the army provided pack training for the cast, the navy a submarine, and the Air Ministry liaison advice with the Lebanese air force.[6] For the most part, however, films involved help from one force at a time.

As it happened it was the army that was the first to be approached for help in a postwar film. As soon as the war had ended, Ealing Studios began preparations for *The Captive Heart*, a romance-by-letter story set in a German POW camp and starring Michael Redgrave. Thanks to Ealing's head of production, Michael Balcon, the director, Basil Dearden, was able to use hundreds of men from the 51st Highland Division as extras on location in Germany. Both parties gained from this collaboration. In the screenplay all the prisoners come to display exemplary fortitude and moral courage, which reflected well on the army. In the shooting phase the large number of real soldiers present in what really had been a German POW camp gave the film a realistic air. *The Captive Heart*, which appeared in the spring of 1946, was a big success.[7]

Rather more directly relevant to the army was *They Were Not Divided*, a Two Cities film produced by Herbert Smith and both written and directed by Terence Young that appeared a few years later.[8] This followed the fortunes of several volunteers who join the Welsh Guards from their depot training through the Normandy campaign and the Battle of the Ardennes in 1944, where two of the principals (Edward Underdown and Ralph Clayton) die gallantly. To add to the realism of a story which, as one observer put it, was 'a worthy tribute to the Brigade's war record',[9] the Directorate of Public Relations arranged for filming to take place at the Guards depot at

Caterham – where the formidable RSM Brittain played himself in the square-bashing scenes – and for war-vintage tanks to be crewed for the battle scenes. Critical reaction to *They Were Not Divided* when it appeared in March 1950 was muted. Leonard Mosley, for instance, writing for the *Express*, thought it 'a goodish film', but rather superficial. Other reviewers criticized it for occasionally descending into formulaic sentimentality. William Whitebait, while admitting that it had 'solid merit', concluded his review for the *New Statesman* by calling the film 'a rambling, jerky, commemoration number'. The public, however, was less discerning. *They Were Not Divided* made a considerable amount of money at the box office and was successful enough to be reissued in 1961.[10]

The next film with which the War Office was involved had a roughly similar recruit-to-veteran-soldier plot, but with the 1st Airborne Division instead of the Welsh Guards on parade. This was *The Red Beret*, again directed by Terence Young, though this time for Warwick Films. It starred – to help the picture in the US market – Alan Ladd as an American who joins the Paras and, under the guidance of his RSM (Harry Andrews) and commanding officer (Leo Genn), goes on to serve with distinction in the Bruneval Raid. The official contribution to this project came primarily in the form of access to the Parachute Regiment itself, whose facilities and personnel were used as background and extras during filming. Long before the premiere in August 1953, there was criticism in the press of the choice of an American actor to star as the hero in a film about a British force, and reviews of *The Red Beret* tended to focus on the shortcomings of Alan Ladd. Whether the film as a whole was 'a bit of a bore' (*Daily Herald*) or 'interesting' (*Spectator*), it was accepted that *The Red Beret* was a 'well-meaning' (*Daily Express*) effort to highlight the 'brave and masculine virtues' (*The Times*) of the 1st Airborne. It also made money at the box office.[11]

For the army such pictures were proving useful. Units could associate recruiting drives with the films while more generally they presented a positive image of the soldier to the public. By the mid fifties, amidst the war-film boom, the War Office found itself in the happy position of not having to sponsor the kind of official publicity films produced for the other services 'because of the relatively large number of commercially produced entertainment films on Army subjects'.[12] There were, naturally enough, plenty of requests for official help in the making of these films.

In 1956, *The Steel Bayonet*, a grim combat drama from Hammer Films directed by Michael Carreras and starring Leo Genn and Kieron Moore, was filmed on a set built on the tank training grounds on Salisbury Plain to represent a farmhouse in 1943. Only the mobilization arising from the Suez Crisis prevented the War Office from fulfilling its promise to provide tanks for the production.[13] When demand was at its peak, in 1957–58, the army was helping with no less than six separate productions. In Libya, reactivated Cromwell as well as serving Centurion tanks from the 2nd Dragoon Guards were placed at the disposal of Warwick Films in the making of *No Time To Die*, again with Leo Genn, about the capture and escape of a tank crew set in 1942. At the same time an ambulance and other vehicles were lent to Associated British for *Ice Cold in Alex*, the story of a small and very mixed group of army personnel led by John Mills who are trying to get back to Egypt during the retreat to Alamein, and various other vehicles to Tempean Films and director Guy Green for a story about the Long Range Desert Group entitled *Sea of Sand* that featured Richard Attenborough and John Gregson. Back in the UK, vehicles and some personnel were provided for a Marksman Films project, *I Was Monty's Double*, the story of M. E. Clifton-James's effort to mislead the Germans as to the field marshal's whereabouts in 1943–44, as well as a Royal Artillery battery and hundreds of men from the 29th Infantry Brigade for the beach and other scenes in Ealing's *Dunkirk*, in which John Mills once again appeared. In all these cases Major-General A. C. Shortt, Director of Public Relations, made sure that the shooting script provided to the War Office presented the army in a positive light before committing to provide facilities.[14]

Reviews were usually lukewarm for all war films by this time, but the public was still keen to see the better ones as they came out over successive months in 1958. *I Was Monty's Double*, in which Clifton-James played himself, did not leave much of a mark, but *No Time to Die* made money, *Ice Cold in Alex* was a huge success, and *Dunkirk*, chosen for the Royal Command performance in March, became the third biggest box-office attraction of the year.[15]

At the same time, however, the DPR was running into image problems associated with films for which help had been refused but that had gone into production anyway or films where official help was never sought in the first place. If the subject demanded only period uniforms and small arms, it was relatively easy for a production company to go it alone, thereby sometimes placing the British Army in a decidedly negative light.

It was comedy that first got the War Office into serious trouble. In 1955 the Boulting Brothers were planning to make a film version of an Alan Hackney novel, *Private's Progress*, that chronicled the wartime military service of an innocent and rather bumbling undergraduate called up into the ranks, and asked the Directorate of Public Relations for help. PR2(b), the relevant section, was horrified at what it read. The protagonist, Stanley Windrush, is a something of a square peg in a round hole as a private soldier, but learns a variety of useful dodges from Private Cox and other more worldly types he meets at a holding unit. Still innocent, Stanley gets caught up in an art theft operation on the Continent organized by his uncle, a shady regular who has risen to the rank of brigadier at the War Office. *Private's Progress* shows the army to be 'all bull', a hypocritical institution governed by petty regulation and officiousness where those who prospered were those who knew how to play the system rather than the brave and true. For the War Office to contemplate with equanimity converted stage farces was one thing;[16] to support satire of such a biting kind was quite another. 'No! You can't make fun of the army!' was the immediate response when the film's producer, Roy Boulting, first approached the military authorities. Though the ending was changed so that the crooks get caught, he was told that the War Office still 'strongly objected to the film' and would offer no assistance; the hope evidently being that, like others before him, he would abandon the project.[17]

The Directorate of Public Relations, however, underestimated its opponent in this matter. Though he had made a success of his time with the AFPU during the war in helping to create *Tunisian Victory* and *The True Glory*, Roy Boulting had found the army 'absolutely ghastly' as a creative setting, since coping with military bureaucracy was 'immensely tedious and time-consuming.'[18] Rather than trying to persuade PR2(b) to change its mind or simply give up on *Private's Progress*, the Boultings decided to thumb their noses at the War Office. Period uniforms and equipment could easily be obtained through surplus stores or manufactured by the costume department, and there were enough barracks and wartime camps that had been sold into civilian hands since 1945 for plenty of appropriate settings to be found. Moreover, the War Office position could be turned to advantage by the British Lion publicity machine with catchlines like 'The film THEY didn't want made.'[19]

Insult was added to injury in the film's title credits, where against a cartoon drawing of three generals as the three brass monkeys – hands over eyes, mouth and ears respectively – it is announced that the producer wished to acknowledge 'the official help of absolutely nobody', and in the end credits, where there is a dedication 'to those who got away with it'. Small wonder that the War Office maintained its hostile attitude by intervening to prevent the Devonshire Regiment and Wessex Brigade from using the film's premiere in Exeter as part of a planned recruiting campaign.[20]

Private's Progress, with a cast that included Ian Carmichael (Stanley Windrush), Richard Attenborough (Private Cox), Denis Price (Brigadier Tracepurcel) and William Hartnell (reprising his role as a tough sergeant), was ready for release in February 1956. The reviews were mostly hostile, many critics finding it distastefully cynical. But at a time when young men were still experiencing the mixed blessings of National Service, *Private's Progress* was enormously popular with the public. Much to the industry's surprise the film became the third biggest box office attraction of the year.[21] Nor was this the end of the matter. The success of *Private's Progress* meant that it inspired others to take up the on-the-fiddle theme, the film itself living on in modified form through Sid Colin's *The Army Game*, the very popular ITV (Granada) series that ran from 1957 to 1962.[22] At the War Office it was acknowledged that a mistake had been made. A more accommodationist – or at least less overtly hostile – attitude was to be taken towards several subsequent requests for help.

During an early stage in the making of the POW drama *The Bridge Over the River Kwai*, for example, efforts were made to get producer Sam Spiegel to alter the script in order to make the character of Colonel Nicholson less of a fool when it seemed official help would be needed for location shooting in Malaya. But when it was clear that no changes along the lines DPR wanted were going to be made, the War Office did not raise any objections and the film went on to be directed by David Lean in Ceylon. Even when Lieutenant-General (retd) A. E. Percival, head of the Far Eastern POW Association, pressured the War Office to denounce the film publicly, the DPR refused to act. 'If we had objected it would not have prevented the film being made', General Shortt explained in a letter to Percival in May 1957, 'and might well have given it undue publicity – as indeed happened in the case of a recent film made by the Boulting Brothers.'[23]

The War Office even managed to repair some of the damage done by *Private's Progress* through taking a positive approach to the spinoffs. Peter Eton, producer of *The Army Game*, made it known that the War Office made no attempt to censor the programme and indeed offered a lot of useful help.[24] The same attitude applied to the next barrack-room comedy on the big screen. *Carry on Sergeant*, a low-budget effort by Anglo-Amalgamated to capitalize on the success of one comedy (*The Army Game*) and the title of another (*Carry on Admiral*), involved the comic trials and tribulations of a platoon of misfit new National Servicemen under the baleful eye of their drill sergeant, played once more by William Hartnell. The ending is significant: despite their earlier misgivings and problems the members of the platoon eventually become quite soldierly in their bearing and behaviour, thus making *Carry on Sergeant* more like a comic version of *The Way Ahead* than the more cynical *Private's Progress*. Bearing this in mind, DPR was willing to offer quiet assistance – there would be no words of thanks to the War Office in the credits – to producer Peter Rogers and director Gerald Thomas. A regular NCO, Company Sergeant Major Fairbanks of the Queen's Royal Regiment, was posted to Pinewood in order to teach the actors close-order drill, and the march used for the graduation scene – for which troops and a Women's Royal Army Corps band were provided as marching extras – recorded in the studio by the band of the Coldstream Guards.[25]

Carry on Sergeant, which appeared in the late summer of 1958, was virtually ignored by the critics, yet had a public impact equal to that of *Private's Progress*. Made at the very modest cost of £74,000, it developed into the third-highest grossing British film of the year and provided the impetus for a host of sequels in other settings.[26]

This did not mean that army comedies of a slightly more subversive nature were not made. But films like *The Square Peg* (Rank, 1958), *Operation Bullshine* (Associated British, 1959), *Desert Mice* (Artna, 1959) and *Light Up the Sky* (Criterion, 1960) were all set during the war, which by this point made them less significant as reflections on the contemporary British Army. *I Only Arsked!* (Hammer-Laurie, 1958), a spin-off from *The Army Game* set in the Middle East, was so farcical that it was impossible to connect it with the real army. Even *The League of Gentlemen* (Allied Film Makers, 1960), a major critical and commercial success in a contemporary setting (in which characters played by actors known for their conventionally stiff-upper-lip roles are exposed as frauds and thieves), all the principals were former rather than serving officers. The contemporary army is only lampooned directly – and only in the most innocuous jokes-about-the-food manner – when a fake inspection tour of a National Service training centre is staged as a cover for an arms heist.[27]

Rather more troubling was the shifting tone of some of the service dramas being made around the turn of the decade, a time when British institutions were beginning to be questioned, and when fifties-style positive portrayals of the army were no longer necessarily as successful as some of the more critical features. In the fifties the sub-genre of British war films about small groups of soldiers might either affirm the military virtues, as in *A Hill in Korea* (Wessex, 1957), or question them, as in *Bitter Victory* (Transcontinental, 1957).[28] By the turn of the decade the latter type was very much in the ascendant. In 1959 director Val Guest, working for Hammer Films, made a screen version of a play by Peter Newman, *Yesterday's Enemy*, in which a serious war crime is committed by a British officer (Stanley Baker) during the war in Burma in the name of military necessity. It was an immediate critical and commercial success, possibly inspiring Michael Balcon to produce a film version of another stage play with a similar setting about the moral ambiguities of war, *The Long and the Short and the Tall*, which appeared in early 1961 and though disliked by the critics did well at the box office.[29]

Mindful of the lesson provided by *Private's Progress*, the military authorities kept mum about these films.[30] They both, after all, were set in a time and place far removed from the modern army. The same could not really be said about *Tunes of Glory* (United Artists, 1960), in which the setting was a postwar regimental depot in Scotland. Based on the James Kenneway novel and directed by Ronald Neame, the film followed the evolving confrontation of style and personality between the new CO of a Highland regiment (John Mills) and his second-in-command (Alec Guinness), a battle of wills that eventually results in one committing suicide and the other going mad. Initially DPR proved to be open-minded about the project and even agreed to assist, since personal flaws rather than the army itself were shown to be at the root of the tragedy and the routines of garrison life were portrayed with a good deal of affection. Cooperation was withdrawn, however, after a photograph appeared in the press of the dancing scene being shot, a scene in which the Alec Guinness character behaves a bit loutishly. After that, John Mills recalled, 'We were the bad boys who were taking the Mickey out of the army'.[31] When it appeared in the summer of 1960, *Tunes of Glory* was lauded by the critics and did well at the box office.[32]

In marked contrast to the success of *Tunes of Glory* was the fate of a feature film for which large-scale army cooperation was obtained, *The Queen's Guards* (Imperial, 1960). In the summer of 1959 Michael Powell had been approached by a friend with an idea for a father-son drama in which the Trooping of the Colour forms the centrepiece. 'I am a sucker for stories about the services', Powell later wrote of his willingness to produce and direct based on a script by Roger Milner. Told in flashback, this involved a young officer (Daniel Massey) recalling his career while the Guards are being inspected by the Queen. He is the younger son in an army family, always in the shadow of his dead elder brother hero and his embittered father (Raymond Massey), who is finally accepted by his parents after he discovers the truth about his brother's death during a deployment to uphold the government of a friendly Arab state. Very much in the mold of *The Four Feathers*, this was a story that even the most hidebound of generals could approve. In contrast to the delays and script changes that had surrounded official involvement in *Dunkirk* – where even the Chief of the Imperial General Staff had got involved – the War Office was quick to approve the project, PR2(b) even offering to make arrangements to fly a camera crew to Libya where a major NATO exercise was being staged. Though not able to 'direct' unit movements and indeed pretty much on his own with his team, Powell was able to take some impressive Technicolor footage. The resulting film, however, released through 20th-Century Fox in December 1961, did not go over well with any but the most patriotic of viewers. 'The Queen's Guards', Powell later admitted with considerable chagrin, 'is the most inept piece of film-making that I have ever produced, or directed.'[33]

The senior service, meanwhile, had been receiving its fair share of cinematic attention, beginning with Morning Departure, directed by Roy Baker and produced by Leslie Parkin, which premiered in February 1950. This was a Jay Lewis adaptation of a 1946 play by Kenneth Woolward that followed the fate of the surviving crew members of a crippled submarine (S14) sitting on the bottom.[34] Admiralty help was freely given once it was clear that the submarine service ultimately was going to be portrayed in a positive light. As adapted by William Fairchild, the four trapped survivors of HMS 'Trojan' are all too human in their initial reactions yet, with the captain (John Mills) setting an example, display exemplary restraint and quiet heroism as rescue attempts fail and it is clear that they are going to die. The event which causes the disaster is shown to be an unavoidable accident – the Trojan strikes a drifting wartime mine – rather than the result of human error on the part of the captain, who does his best to evade contact in the few seconds remaining before the explosion occurs. The failure of rescue efforts is the result of bad weather, not poor judgement on the part of naval personnel. Morning Departure was very much a drama of human emotions, including fear and anger, but one in which the honour and traditions of the navy are upheld, including those of rank. As the director recalled in an interview, 'even at the end of the film, the two officers are still officers and the two others are still the other ranks. They are never on a classless level, although they are on an equal level in that they know they are all going to die at any moment.'[35]

Despite the not always admirable reactions of men under stress and the unhappy ending, there was therefore much in Morning Departure that the Admiralty could applaud. The filmmakers, though, believed that the whole thing would fall through when a real submarine disaster occurred. On the night of 12 January 1950, HMS Truculent collided with a small Swedish steamer in the Thames estuary and sank with considerable loss of life. Given these events, it was assumed that the Admiralty would say 'no' on reading the script. To the surprise of all there was no objection, as the Admiralty decided the message 'was uplifting rather than depressing'.[36]

Official support was thus provided in the form of permission to use submarine equipment for interior shooting, a serving 'T'-class submarine for surface shots, and personnel going through escape drills in the water-filled escape tower at Blockhouse Creek, the submarine training establishment at Gosport. All this added greatly to the verisimilitude of the film.

When *Morning Departure* opened at the Gaumont and Pavillion Marble
Arch in late February 1950, film critics were impressed both with the
characterization and with the film's air of authenticity. 'I have never seen
a film of the sea that seemed, to my landsman's eye, more real', Dixon
enthused in the *Daily Telegraph*; going on to add: 'Or better acted'. *The
Times* thought the director had 'eschewed false emotion and heroics and
has produced a genuine and impressive tribute to the Royal Navy'. The
Guardian was equally positive: 'beautifully restrained', *Morning Departure*
was 'a memorial fit in every way to represent a Service which goes about
its business with undramatic zeal'. The popular press was just as enthusiastic,
Paul Holt, for example, explaining in the *Daily Herald* that it was 'splendidly
simple and relentlessly tragic', a chronicle of understated heroism on film
'that the British do best of all'. Even William Whitebait, who disliked war
films, grudgingly admitted in the *New Statesman* that 'within its limits' the
film 'achieves a modest triumph'.[37] The public flocked to it in droves, in
a few cases going so far as to write subsequent letters to the Admiralty
detailing how the crew might have been saved. *Morning Departure* was in
every way 'an immense success'.[38]

The Admiralty was somewhat less fortunate in the reception given to the
next film production with which it was involved in a major way. This was
entitled *The Gift Horse*, a Molton Films production about one of the fifty
rather ancient US four-stacker destroyers passed to Britain in the dark days
of 1940 – hence the title – in which the climax was loosely based on the
dock-ramming exploit of HMS *Campbeldown* during the 1941 St-Nazaire
Raid.[39]

There were aspects of *The Gift Horse* story, written by William Fairchild
(responsible for the adaptation of *Morning Departure*), Hugh Hastings and
William Rose, which might have caused anxiety within the Admiralty. There
is a good deal of friction between the disciplinarian captain and the mostly
hostilities-only crew of the 'Gift Horse', HMS '*Ballantrae*', a ship which
becomes something other than a well-oiled fighting machine. She keeps
breaking down at inopportune moments, while the ship's officers make
poor decisions which result, among other things, in the ship running
aground, fouling torpedo nets, and – the captain's fault – missing a rendezvous with a merchant ship in fog that might have prevented that vessel
being sunk by a U-boat. What is more, it emerges that the captain,
Lieutenant-Commander Hugh Fraser, was found guilty by court-martial in
1932 of negligence in the collision of two ships and was only brought back
into the service because of a wartime shortage of experienced RN officers.

Under prewar conditions all this negative imagery would have been
enough to ensure a refusal to lend assistance to the production. But in the

wake of the wartime films, and a greater sense of the value of cinema within the Department of Naval Information, these drawbacks were more than counterbalanced by the fact about half way through the film the captain and crew develop an effective working relationship.⁴⁰ The captain proves to be compassionate as well as stern, covering for the mistakes of his navigation officer during a court of inquiry called to investigate why the *Ballantrae* struck a wreck, granting compassionate leave to a sailor worried about his mother, and personally convincing a publican not to press charges against crewmen involved in a pub brawl. With the crew united and in fighting trim, a U-boat is then tracked and sunk, and the film reaches its denouement as the officers and men of the *Ballantrae* perform with exemplary coolness and bravery during the St-Nazaire Raid. The honour of the Royal Navy, in short, is ultimately upheld.

The Admiralty therefore agreed to lend its support to the production. Help was given in turning a mothballed four-stacker into a serviceable ship, a submarine was provided to act the part of a U-boat, motor launches were made available for the commando raid sequences, the dropping of depth charges was filmed, and the shooting of naval dockyard and quayside scenes allowed at Porstmouth. Overseeing the production was a service technical adviser, Commander R. S. Abram (retd). The Admiralty was formally thanked for its cooperation in the opening credits, which appear against a background representing an RN officer's cap badge.

Produced by George Pitcher and directed by Compton Bennett, *The Gift Horse* features an excellent performance by Trevor Howard as the captain, ably supported by Richard Attenborough as an ex-trade unionist now in the navy and Bernard Lee as a veteran rating. What the critics were most struck by, however, was the similarity to the wartime films about the navy. There was an obviously conscious effort to represent regional differences, the Chief Engineer being Welsh, the First Officer a Canadian (played by a disastrously miscast James Donald). Even more reminiscent of wartime naval films were the 'hearth and home' sub-plots involving respectively the son, wife, sweetheart and mother of each of the leading players. Though it now seems altogether a more sombre affair, *The Gift Horse* tended to be viewed at the time as too close to an earlier destroyer film for comfort and thus 'the mixture as before'.⁴¹

As *The Times* put when the film premiered in July 1952, 'if there had been no *In Which We Serve*, *Gift Horse* (Empire Cinema) would doubtless have seemed an adequate enough film; but ... *In Which We Serve* was produced, and *Gift Horse* cannot survive the competition'. Campbell Dixon, writing for the *Telegraph*, was slightly more sympathetic but agreed about the general point: the film was 'frankly not as good' as the Noël Coward

version. The London critic of the *Manchester Guardian* commented that
'the theme [the ship as unifier] remains so very much the same', and that
'everything it does was better done a decade ago'. The popular dailies were
also less than overwhelmed. To Leonard Mosley of the *Express* it was like
'too many films before', barring Trevor Howard's fine performance. 'We
have seen this done so often before', Paul Holt noted in *Herald*, 'that it is
a wonder why again.'[42] The film did, however, do reasonably well at the
box office.[43]

Even before *The Gift Horse* was released work was well underway on an
Ealing Studios film that would deeply impress both critics and public alike.
The Cruel Sea was an adaptation by Eric Ambler of the semi-autobiographical
bestseller of the same name by Nicholas Monsarrat, a book which spared
the reader little in its depiction of the harshness of the long Battle of the
Atlantic. Most of the plot is set at sea aboard a corvette – eventually sunk
– and then a frigate, which made the initial move obvious to Michael Balcon
as head of production. 'The first step in the planning of the film', he
recalled, 'was to approach the Admiralty for cooperation and facilities.'[44]

There were many reasons for the navy to refuse to give such help.
Monsarrat's book, after all, depicted the war in brutally realistic terms. It
did not flinch from the graphic depiction of serious burn cases and men
choking to death on fuel oil, and stressed the general nastiness – the cold,
the fatigue, the heavy pitching and rolling – of life aboard a corvette in the
North Atlantic. The ship's officers, what was more, are a decidedly mixed
bunch. Besides the captain they are all essentially amateurs when they
join the ship, some of them proving themselves unequal to the task. The
corvette's first Number One, for instance, is portrayed as totally without
redeeming features, a lazy and bullying oaf who puts the ship at risk by
sleeping during his watch. Perhaps worst of all, the captain, an RNR officer,
intentionally drops depth charges while pursuing a submerged U-boat in
an area where the blast is certain to kill the survivors of a torpedoed ship
floating in the water. He is tormented by this decision, but becomes steadily
more callous as the war continues. Feelings counted once, but 'we've got
to win before we can pick and choose about moral issues'.[45]

It was all a far cry from the automatic competence and heroism depicted
in wartime and prewar films featuring the navy. Yet, as the decision to help
with *The Gift Horse* indicated, the Admiralty of the 1950s was inclined to
be more broad-minded about what constituted negative publicity than in
the days of *Lieutenant Daring, RN*. Episodes in which characters behave
badly are balanced by those in which they or others act with competence
and even heroism, as for instance after the corvette '*Compass Rose*' is
torpedoed. Though the weakness in the number and quality of escort vessels

is stressed, as the war goes on the book shows how new devices (principally radar) and more and better ships (the frigate) gradually turn the tide against the enemy. In the first part of the book a submarine kill is finally achieved by *Compass Rose*, after many lost contacts, that appears the result of luck as much as skill. In the latter part of the book, however, set in the second half of the war, a U-boat is sunk in almost textbook fashion through the use of superior sonar and box search techniques by the frigate '*Saltash*'. 'This is the story of a dedication to a purpose', Eric Ambler noted in a pre-production memorandum to director Charles Frend, '— the winning of a battle.'[46]

Ealing, moreover, had considerable wartime experience in working with the Admiralty. *Convoy, Ships With Wings, For Those in Peril* and *San Demetrio, London* had all turned out well from the Admiralty's perspective, and Balcon doubtless made it clear that the film would not seek to denigrate the navy. Even if the studio was not already so inclined, the British Board of Film Censors could be counted on to make sure that the film was much less graphic – and thus more acceptable – than the novel.[47]

Balcon found 'considerable enthusiasm for the project' when he approached the Admiralty. HMS *Porchester Castle*, a wartime frigate still in service, was placed at the disposal of director Charles Frend, complete with RN crew in July 1952, along with support at Devonport for the corvette that Ealing had saved from the breaker's yard (the decommissioned *Coreopsis*) to play *Compass Rose*.[48] The navy also provided an S-class submarine to masquerade as a U-boat and two destroyers for a few days shooting. On the recommendation of the Admiralty, Captain Jacky Broome, RN (retd) and later Lieutenant-Commander R. S. Abram – who had worked on *The Gift Horse* – were hired as naval advisers. Even the damage caused by the corvette in an accidental collision in Plymouth Harbour with a moored destroyer, HMS *Camperdown* – 'Who the flipping hell's driving your boat – Errol Flynn?'[49] – did not result in any lessening of support once Ealing's insurance company had handed over £10,000 to cover the cost of repairs.[50] 'The Admiralty', as Charles Frend happily reported in a letter to the book's author, 'are being absolutely marvellous.'[51]

The choice of lead actors, meanwhile, in combination with the script itself, allowed the wardroom of *Compass Rose* to seem rather more genteel and officer-like than was the case in the book. This was apparently deliberate. The rather moon-faced Bryan Forbes was turned down after his screen test on the grounds that 'you're not officer material', as was Dirk Bogarde because his previous roles had largely been working-class youths in trouble with the law.[52] The result was that, as played by Donald Sinden, Denholm Elliott and John Stratton, the junior officers appear much more uniformly

upper middle-class in appearance and speech than in the book. The bullying
and uncouth first lieutenant, who soon disappears, was clearly *not* meant
to be viewed as belonging to the same league, having been – according to
the script rather than the novel – a second-hand car salesman in civilian
life. Stanley Baker, who came from a working-class background, was so
compellingly boorish in his screen test that he was chosen to play Bennett
even though another actor – presumably less obviously 'non U' on screen
– had been allocated the part.[53] As for the captain, the choice of Jack
Hawkins – already beginning to be typecast as the model senior officer –
made it easy to forget that he was supposed to be from the merchant service
rather than the Royal Navy.[54]

Though the Duke of Edinburgh had to cancel at the last moment due
to the death of Queen Mary, the upper ranks of the senior service were
out in force for the film's full-scale premiere. Monsarrat remembered how
pleased he was 'to meet, for the first time, so many beaming admirals'.
They had good reason to be smiling: the audience had given the picture
a standing ovation.[55] Even the high-end critics, by and large, had been
mightily impressed by the combination of unusually stark realism and
typically understated heroism at the press showing in March 1953. As
Virginia Graham put it in the *Spectator*, the horror of war, 'crowned with
the quietly burning light of heroism, is presented with objective clarity,
and the strain imposed on the Royal Navy as the years mount and the
ships go down – the bad tempers and nerve-storms and desperate fatigue
– is stated baldly without comment'. Even William Whitebait, who saw it
as merely 'a discreet improvement on the films of ten years ago – on
Western Approaches, say, and *In Which We Serve* – rather than an achievement in its own right', grudgingly admitted in the *New Statesman* that its
'extra ounce of realism' in combination with the acting of Jack Hawkins
made *The Cruel Sea* 'unusually good'.[56] The public agreed and, in return
for the outlay of £200,000, Ealing Studios found itself with the top British
moneymaker of the year.[57]

The Cruel Sea was such an enormous success that it almost completely
overshadowed the other navy film to which the Admiralty was then lending
its support: *Single-Handed*, which appeared in cinemas a few months later.
This was a 20th Century-Fox remake of *Brown on Resolution* by the direc-
tor/producer team of Roy and John Boulting, starring Jeffrey Hunter. Given
the success of the original, this new film – in which the story is altered to
allow the hero to survive – appeared a natural winner to the navy. Three
warships in the Mediterranean – HMS *Manxman*, HMS *Cleopatra* and the
cruiser HMS *Glasgow* – were placed at the Boultings' disposal, the technical
details being overseen by once more by R. S. Abram.[58] Positively but not

widely reviewed, *Single-Handed* did not make a mark at the box office and quickly vanished.[59]

The ongoing success of *The Cruel Sea*, however, was establishing beyond a doubt that there was an audience for films about the navy in action. As it continued its run of success at the box office, the Admiralty was agreeing to lend a hand with another project proposed by a British company.

This was to be another submarine epic, this time based on a book by C. E. T. Warren and James Benson detailing how midget 'X-craft' were used to cripple the German battleship *Tirpitz*. Adapted by Robin Estridge for the screen, the story was one in which the Royal Navy – now that X-craft were no longer a closely guarded secret – could take pride. A London Independent production directed by Ralph Thomas and produced by William MacQuitty, *Above Us The Waves* was made possible through the Admiralty lending several X-craft (and yet another S-class submarine to tow them) and allowing shooting to take place aboard a submarine tender and in the escape tower at Fort Blockhouse, Gosport. There was nothing questionable about either script or cast. The redoubtable John Mills had worked with the navy on and off for twenty years, while newcomer Donald Sinden had recently played his first major film role in *The Cruel Sea*. Commander Donald Cameron, a submariner who had taken part in the original exploit, oversaw the production as naval adviser. *Above Us the Waves* was an almost textbook example of the kind of film that the Admiralty was most happy to see made, an unambiguous celebration of naval heroism and technical mastery.[60]

Above Us the Waves, though not widely reviewed when it was released in the spring of 1955, was generally welcomed. It was a 'gripping saga of the sea' in which 'there is no false sentiment' according to the *Daily Mirror*, and the *Manchester Guardian* thought it 'all the more effective for the understatement'. A number of critics, among them William Whitebait in the *New Statesman*, complained that the film was unduly flat and conventional – yet another stiff-upper-lip tribute in the style of wartime films – but the public was satisfied enough to make it a reasonable success at the box office.[61]

The mid-fifties were also years when the Admiralty became involved in the making of mostly colour and/or widescreen films backed by American companies that were aimed at the US as well as UK market and in which Americans played the leading roles. In 1954 technical help was provided in the making of *Seagulls Over Sorrento*, an unsuccessful Boulting Brothers adaptation for MGM British of a hit stage play about torpedo warhead testing starring Gene Kelly.[62] The following year support was given to Columbia Pictures (Warwick Films), in the making of the more successful *Cockleshell Heroes*, which starred José Ferrer – who also directed – and

Trevor Howard. This recounted in somewhat fictionalized form a Royal Marine commando raid on Bordeaux harbour. For this the Commandant-General gave every possible assistance, including courses in drill and canoe-handling for the cast and a marine detachment for background shots. Lieutenant-Colonel H. G. Hassler, who had led the actual raid, was seconded to act as technical adviser. Shown to the Duke of Edinburgh, Lord Mountbatten and a host of senior officers in November 1955, *Cockleshell Heroes* – Technicolor and CinemaScope – was well received and made money.[63] In 1956 came *The Man Who Never Was*, a Sumar Films (20th Century-Fox) CinemaScope adaptation of the Ewen Montagu memoir concerning the effort to fool the Germans about Allied intentions in the Mediterranean. This was directed by Ronald Neame with Clifton Webb in the lead role, and also received Admiralty assistance This was even more of a hit, Josh Billings noting in his end-of-year round-up for *Kine Weekly* that it had 'scored fluently' at the box office.[64] Finally there was *The Key*, a major 1958 Open Road (Columbia) production, also in CinemaScope but filmed in black and white, dealing with the pressures of commanding ocean-going rescue tugs during the war that starred William Holden. In this case naval help was central to the main plot, director Carol Reed being given permission to shoot extensively aboard HM Tug *Restive* and allowed to film and direct – not without some difficulty – HM submarine *Trespasser*.[65] According to Josh Billings, *The Key* 'fell short of expectations, but nevertheless made a lot of money'.[66]

In the meantime the Admiralty continued to be approached for support in the making of more directly British naval films. In the summer of 1956 a cruiser of the Mediterranean Fleet masqueraded as HMS '*Gillingham*' in the British Lion colour farce *The Baby and the Battleship*, directed by Jay Lewis. Based on the novel of the same name by Anthony Thorne, the story revolved around the accidental presence of a baby aboard a warship and the frantic efforts of a group of ratings to keep it hidden and healthy. With a script poking only the gentlest of fun at naval authority and a cast that included two leading actors with a good track record in ratings' uniform – John Mills and Richard Attenborough – *The Baby and the Battleship* was the kind of light-hearted nonsense ('high jinks with nappies on the high seas') that the postwar navy could accept.[67] The preview audience found it uproariously funny, even if some high-brow critics did not, and *The Baby and the Battleship* went on to earn big money for British Lion.[68]

Meanwhile a bigger navy film was coming to fruition. Casting about for a bankable subject two years earlier, director/writer team Michael Powell and Emeric Pressburger began to look at the sinking of the German pocket battleship *Graf Spee* while on a trip to South America. 'As a boy,' Powell wrote later, 'the Royal Navy had been my first love, and I'd always wanted to make a film about the navy.'[69] For an epic on the scale that the two men envisioned, however, official backing would be essential. By the mid-fifties, though it could appear self-effacing to the point of invisibility in some contexts, the Naval Information department was by now adept at identifying the pros and cons of particular film ventures for the Admiralty. The events that Powell and Pressburger were proposing to recreate on film could hardly have appeared more suitable. Though faded from public consciousness, the destruction of the *Graf Spee* in 1939 had been one of the navy's proudest wartime moments, a surface action fought and won against the odds with great tenacity and skill. It would be no bad thing to remind people of this achievement (which among other things did not lend itself to the representation of command stress that had become almost *de rigueur* in films dealing with the U-boat war).[70] The fact that the two men had made a film for the navy a decade earlier – *The Volunteer* – that the Admiralty had liked made their Lordships even more favourably disposed to offer help, and by August 1954 the green light had been given.

Powell met with Captain (retd) A. W. Clarke, the Chief of Naval Information, to lay out his requirements. Their conversation, as recalled by Powell many years later, illustrates the extent to which the Admiralty was prepared to argue rather than dictate the extent of naval support:

> 'What about the movement of ships?' enquired Foxy-Face [the director wrote in his memoirs]. 'I suppose you'll be using models a lot, and animation?' he added, knowledgeably.
>
> But I had already made up my mind about this. 'No,' I said firmly, 'all movements of ships will be at sea.'
>
> He was impressed. 'And I suppose you want us to supply them? Don't you realise that most of the ships afloat in 1939 are now at the bottom of the sea, or in mothballs?'
>
> 'Then you'll have to help us get them out of mothballs,' I retorted. 'I'm not going to have a lot of stupid models in our big, beautiful film.' He grinned, but I could see he would help.[71]

Clarke did indeed pitch in, greatly aided by the fact that the First Sea Lord was now none other than the film-conscious Lord Mountbatten, father-in-law to the production's manager, John Brabourne. Anyone who had actually fought in the battle was encouraged to talk to Powell and Pressburger so as to heighten the authenticity of the project, with Captain (retd) F. S. 'Hooky' Bell serving as chief technical adviser. Arrangements were then made in 1955 for a camera party to travel to the Mediterranean and for Powell to direct for a few days the movements and range shooting of three cruisers – *Sheffield* (playing HMS *Exeter*), *Jamaica* (playing HMS *Ajax*), and the *Delhi* (formerly HMNZS *Achilles* and now in Indian service). The cruiser HMS *Glasgow*, based at Invergordon, was later employed in scenes representing the pocket battleship refuelling at sea, and yet another cruiser, HMS *Cumberland*, was used for some scenes as herself. Last but not least the CNI was instrumental in obtaining permission for the USS *Salem*, a heavy cruiser of the Sixth Fleet based at Malta, to be used to impersonate the *Graf Spee* in wide-angle shots. The director was well pleased: 'all doors were opened to me. I moved, arrived and departed with all the authority of the Admiralty.' [72]

So too were Mountbatten and other senior staff officers when in August they were shown a rough assemblage of the Technicolor VistaVision footage taken in the Mediterranean. 'We started with a dozen scenes on the normal screen,' Powell remembered, 'which was already better than anything they had ever seen, and then, suddenly, in the middle of a shot, we opened up the big screen and switched to the other projector – and the whole three rows of naval dignitaries pressed hard back in their chairs for, really, the great ships seemed about to sail out into the theatre. It was colossal. They were like children at a tea party ...' [73] With much work on sets at Pinewood yet to be completed, *The Battle of the River Plate* was not ready until late the following year, with a cast of thousands and at a cost of well over £280,000. Human interest elements had been inserted into the story by Pressburger, chiefly the mutual respect that develops between Captain Langsdorff (Peter Finch) of the *Graf Spee* and captured merchant navy master Captain Dove (Bernard Lee), in order to prevent the film from becoming 'a super-documentary'. But the picture was still very much a naval spectacle which – thanks to heavy advance publicity by the Rank Organization – generated a good deal of public interest in the lead-up to the release. Its patriotic elements – 'made by the British about a great British victory' explained the *Daily Express* – meant that *The Battle of the River Plate* was chosen to premiere at the Royal Command Performance at the Empire, Leicester Square, on 29 October 1956. [74]

Press reactions to the film were mixed, in large part because of its stitched-together three-part dramatic structure (the Dove and Langsdorff exchanges plus the battle exclusively from the British perspective plus negotiations in Montevideo and the scuttling of the damaged *Graf Spee* as related by an American radio reporter). Nevertheless the senior service came off well, the critics finding that the well-shot footage of ships at sea in combination with the 'semi-documentary' rendering of the principal RN characters – Commodore Harwood (Anthony Quayle), Captain Bell (John Gregson) and Captain Woodhouse (Ian Hunter) – generally impressive. And the public loved it, turning *The Battle of the River Plate* into the third biggest box-office attraction of 1957. As the fan magazine *Picturegoer* put it, whatever faults the film had one could 'discount this against the roaring VistaVision battles and magnificent seascapes', going on to conclude that it 'sails home victorious'.[75]

The reaction to the Powell and Pressburger epic was so great, indeed, that it largely overshadowed the other naval film production with which the Admiralty had been heavily involved in 1956: *The Yangtse Incident*. This was also based on an event in which the navy took pride, the escape downriver of the frigate HMS *Amethyst* in the face of hostile Communist forces in 1949. When producer Herbert Wilcox approached the First Sea Lord for help, he was told that 'You can count on the full cooperation of the navy'.[76]

The 'official blessing' of Lord Mountbatten having been obtained, Wilcox and director Michael Anderson were given everything they asked for. The *Amethyst* was de-mothballed, Commander J. S. Kerans – who had commanded the ship at the time – became naval adviser-cum-ship's captain (his 1949 role being played by Richard Todd), and extensive help provided by various warships and shore establishments. There were some red faces when the *Amethyst* was holed below the waterline on the River Orwell when one of the staged explosions went wrong in mid September 1956 but, thanks to prompt action by Kerans to save the ship from sinking and a personal intervention by Mountbatten, filming continued using HMS *Magpie* and HMS *Essex* as stand-ins.[77]

By the time *Yangtse Incident* was premiered in April 1957, many serious critics were growing tired of the steady stream of stiff-upper-lip service films that had appeared since the decade began. Except for *The Times* and *Daily Telegraph* reviewers, they treated the film with a certain sourness. William Whitebait, for instance, who had long argued that war films ought to be given a rest, claimed that it sent him to sleep. 'Bombardment at sea', he concluded in the *New Statesman*, 'is the film critic's paraldehyde.' But as Ken Gay gloomily wrote in *Films and Filming*, supporters 'of naval tradition (and patriots) will find all they want here', and lower-brow critics such as Emery Pearce of the *Daily Herald* were enthusiastic about 'a film and a story for us to be proud of'.[78]

Certainly the Lords of the Admiralty, given their own private showing before the official premiere with Prince Philip in attendance, were more than satisfied. Mountbatten ordered that a print be sent to every RN training establishment, arguing that it was a film 'that shows without frills how an ordinary seaman behaves under stress and adversity'. When it was shown at the Cannes Film Festival, the cruiser HMS *Birmingham* rode at anchor nearby 'to show the flag'.[79]

Despite the fears of the critics and the confidence of the producer and the distributors, British Lion, *Yangtse Incident* did not catch on. Perhaps after Suez people were uneasy at the sight of gunboat diplomacy. Perhaps the more spectacular *Battle of the River Plate* had saturated the market for naval drama that year; though it is worth noting that *The Silent Enemy*, a British Lion feature dealing with the work of 'Buster' Crabb (played by Laurence Harvey) in foiling the efforts of Italian frogmen to sink ships in Gibraltar harbour, was a hit the year after. Whatever the reason, *Yangtse Incident* failed to make money and in the end bankrupted Wilcox.[80]

This does not seem to have diminished the belief within the Admiralty that such projects were worth supporting, the Second Sea Lord, Vice-Admiral Sir Deric Holland-Martin, commenting the following year that 'Films like *The Amethyst* [*sic*] achieved a great deal of good.'[81] More troubling, from the Admiralty point of view, was the runaway success of dubious naval comedies made without any help or approval from the senior service in the latter fifties.

As *The Baby and the Battleship* had most recently demonstrated, the Admiralty was not averse to providing support for comedies as well as dramas. As long as the navy was not overly maligned, a certain amount of fun at the navy's expense had been tolerated. Mostly the jokes were at the expense of the lower deck, and the navy's professionalism was always upheld. Wardroom comedies were rarer, the Admiralty favouring translations of stage farces by reliable types such as Ian Hay and Stephen King-Hall. Hence the Portsmouth background and scenes aboard various frigates in the successful *Carry On Admiral* (Renown, 1957), based on their play *Off the Record*; and the presence of HMS *Jamaica* in the forgettable *Girls at Sea* (Associated British, 1958), a rendition of *The Middle Watch*, a prewar bedroom farce play filmed once already in 1939 with Admiralty support.[82]

All this was fine from the navy's point of view. But the runaway success of *Private's Progress* in 1956 inspired other 'subversive' service films. One of the things which the Admiralty would never accept in a navy film made with official cooperation was any hint of corruption. The only apparent exception had been help in making *The Ship That Died of Shame*, adapted from the Nicholas Monsarrat short story by Ealing Studios and released in 1955. The plot revolved around a motor gunboat of wartime renown whose officers (Richard Attenborough, George Baker and Bill Owen) use it for smuggling purposes after the war. MTBs and various other naval craft had been leant by the navy for the early scenes, and R. S. Abram served once more as naval liaison. But the whole premise of the story was that the offending characters eventually receive their just desserts after the boat in question 'revolts' and upholds the honour of the service.[83]

No such ending graced *Up the Creek*, an Exclusive Films production released in April 1958. The story revolves around the machinations of the skeleton crew of a mothballed sloop, led by their crooked Chief Petty Officer (Peter Sellers), who are engaged in a variety of private business ventures using purloined RN property and equipment. Coopting the silly-ass lieutenant sent to take command (David Tomlinson), they get away with it. Knowing that the Admiralty would never accept such a story, producer Henry Halstead and director Val Guest used a civilian ship as HMS 'Berkeley' rather than asking for an RN sloop. *Up the Creek*, made on a small budget, was a major hit; so much so that an equally cheeky sequel – *Further Up the Creek* – immediately went into production and appeared on screens in October of the same year, the original being re-released in 1961.[84]

Once the send-up genre had started it proved impossible to stop, as an official refusal to cooperate could be used as a marketing ploy. It was probably for this reason that the Admiralty took no exception to two Rank Organization films, *The Navy Lark*, a comedy with a plot very similar to *Up the Creek* that appeared in 1959, and *The Bulldog Breed*, a Norman Wisdom slapstick success of 1960 in which at least some of the humour – shot aboard RN frigates – was very much at the expense of the wardroom.[85]

By the start of the 1960s the serious naval war film, like its army and air force counterparts, was becoming a thing of the past. Within Whitehall the publicity value of such films was certainly recognized in the mid 1950s,[86] but by the end of the decade doubts may have begun to arise over how much the celebration of events almost twenty years past influenced views of the contemporary armed forces. If anyone at Naval Information cared to look, it would have become apparent that even in the 1950s only the comedies had a modern-day setting among the naval films. As for the war dramas, even if they were indeed good for the modern navy's image, there was less and less the navy could do to assist productions as war-era vessels were retired from service.[87] Many critics, moreover, had long chaffed at the number of heroic war films, arguing that they had become too conventional and respectful of wartime traditions.[88] What did in the traditional war film, however, was the continued rise of television and concurrent shrinkage in British the film industry. In the course of the fifties the number of TV licenses had more than doubled, while annual cinema admissions figures had shrunk by over 36 per cent, with disastrous consequences in terms of cinema closures and declining production.[89]

There was, however, to be one last hurrah for the big naval war film made with Admiralty cooperation. This was of course *Sink the Bismarck!*, a 20th-Century Fox production centring on another great triumph of the surface war with Germany. Like *The Battle of the River Plate*, it was to be a widescreen spectacular. Unlike its predecessor, however, it was to be filmed in black and white. This may have been in an effort to make the audience nostalgically identify it with earlier British war films, most of which were not in colour. It may also have been necessary in order to integrate newsreel footage and to make the models used in a tank at Pinewood look more realistic – there being no big warships still in active RN service that resembled those of 1941.

Either way the Admiralty was willing to help producer John Brabourne and director Lewis Gilbert – both of whom had worked with the navy before – as much as it could. Various technical advisers were assigned to the film, including Lieutenant-Commander Peter Peake (retd), who had served as adviser on several other naval projects. In addition, as Kenneth More remembered, the producer's father-in-law, now Chief of Defence Staff, 'gave us the benefit of his immense knowledge and experience throughout the making of this film'. The company was allowed to film aboard Britain's last remaining mothballed battleship, the *Vanguard*, and aboard a cruiser at sea for a number of deck and gun turret establishing shots. The navy also allowed Gilbert to take an old Swordfish torpedo plane aboard one of its older aircraft carriers and film it taking off to supplement newsreel footage and model work, and permitted him to simulate battle damage to the *Bismarck* by staging explosions and billowing smoke on the deck of the decommissioned cruiser *Newcastle* (an event which caused a minor panic in Portsmouth).[90]

The resulting film, starring Kenneth More and featuring a host of faces familiar from earlier films, was premiered at the Odeon Leicester Square in February 1960 before an audience that included the Duke of Edinburgh and Lord Mountbatten. Predictably, it was attacked by the anti-war film critics and applauded in patriotic venues such as the *Telegraph*. The public, however, turned *Sink the Bismarck!* into the second biggest box-office attraction of the year.[91]

In many respects the experience of the Air Ministry paralleled that of the Admiralty in its dealings with the postwar film industry. Wardour Street in the 1950s was eager to cash in on the public demand for war stories, and the Information Division was in turn willing to lend a hand in publicizing the wartime exploits of the RAF.[92]

The process began with a story set on an RAF fighter station during the Battle of Britain, for which the RAF provided Templar Productions with technical advice and help in obtaining a handful of Hurricane fighters from the Portuguese air force. Centring on the evolution of a raw pilot (John Gregson) into an experienced ace with the help of more mature officers (Jack Hawkins and Michael Denison), *Angels One Five* emphasized the value of teamwork and self-sacrifice in the pursuit of the greater good. When the picture was premiered in March 1952 the critics, while not particularly hostile, were still somewhat disappointed, even the *Telegraph* reviewer wondering if stiff-upper-lip understatement had not for once been overdone.[93] The public was much more enthusiastic, and *Angels One Five*, as Josh Billings reported at the end of the year, 'made a packet of money.'[94]

It was so successful, in fact, that it seems to have inspired *The Malta Story*, a Rank Organization feature released the following year for which the Air Ministry provided late-model Spitfires and a Wellington for taxiing purposes. The scene shifts from Britain in 1940 to the Mediterranean in 1942 but the plot and characters remain quite similar, with Jack Hawkins reprising his role as the senior RAF officer and Alec Guinness playing the part of the problematic newcomer pilot who eventually makes the ultimate sacrifice in the air. The reviewers were less than overwhelmed when *The Malta Story* appeared in the summer of 1953, but like its predecessor it did well in terms of ticket sales.[95]

Fighter Command having been given its due, Bomber Command came into focus. In early 1952, representatives of Mayflower Films approached the Air Ministry for help in the making of a film whose plot revolved around the efforts of Wing Commander Tim Mason (played by Dirk Bogarde) to hold himself and his heavy bomber squadron together in the face of mounting losses and fatigue *circa* 1943. A story in which the central RAF character is shown to be suffering from battle fatigue and buckling under the pressures of command might have caused the Air Ministry to turn its back on the project. But in light of the climax – Mason successfully conquering his own demons while leading a successful night raid on a German industrial town – and the fact that the screenplay was being written by John Woolridge, a highly decorated ex-RAF bomber pilot, and co-produced by Maxwell Seaton, who had won the DFC, the Information Division gave Mayflower the green light for *Appointment in London* to proceed. In June and July 1952 shooting took place at RAF Upwood in Huntingdonshire, an active aerodrome where air force crews serviced and flew the four Lancaster bombers specially reactivated for the picture, as well as the Avro Lincolns of 7, 148, and 214 Squadrons.[96]

Reviewers tended to dwell on the picture's obvious debt in terms of dialogue and character style to other films. 'Every character in *Appointment in London*', the critic for *The Times* wrote after the picture's premiere in February 1953, 'has appeared in every other British film of the war.' Visually, however, it was impressive, and even the doubters agreed that the climactic bombing raid was very exciting and that the acting was uniformly solid.

Made on a quite modest budget by a small company, *Appointment in London*
– the title referring to the date on which three of the principals are due to
receive decorations from the King – was a hit in the theatres.[97]

Though the plot of *Appointment in London* was fictional, Woolridge had
based elements of his central character on his former squadron commander,
Guy Gibson, who had been killed in action the year after he had led the
dams raid.[98] In a much bigger production undertaken by Associated British
the following year, Gibson would once again appear – this time without
disguise. The film was of course *The Dam Busters*, produced by Robert
Clark, directed by Michael Anderson, and based on a script by R. C. Sherriff
that chronicles the trials and tribulations of the scientist Barnes Wallis
(Michael Redgrave) in inventing the famous bouncing bomb and the
problems of learning to use it – climaxing in the dams raid – experienced
by Gibson (Richard Todd) and his aircrews. This was a straightforward tale
of ingenuity and old-fashioned heroism, and the Air Ministry had no
hesitation in agreeing to participate once it was agreed that the bouncing
bombs shown in the film would be modified so that they did not look too
much like the real thing (then still on the secret list).[99] Five RAF Lancasters
and a Wellington were taken out of storage for the film, four of the
Lancasters being modified to look like the aircraft that had actually carried
the bouncing bomb. Principal exterior shooting took place at RAF Scampton
– the wartime base of 617 Squadron – in May 1954, with air force crews
once again flying and servicing the aircraft. The Air Ministry also assisted
by providing film taken of the early tests of the weapon and allowing an
RAF flying instructor to teach Richard Todd the proper control movements
in a reassembled cockpit used for close-ups on one of the sound stages at
Elstree.[100]

When *The Dam Busters* appeared at the Empire Leicester Square in May
1955, the reviews were for once mostly positive, especially in the popular
press. Paul Holt, for example, writing for the *Daily Herald*, called it the
best British war film since *The Cruel Sea*. In the words of John Minchinton
in *Films and Filming*, it 'mainly avoided the ghastly stiff upper-lip technique', so that even William Whitebait liked it. As for ordinary cinemagoers,
they turned *The Dam Busters* into the top-grossing picture of the year in
Britain.[101]

The idea for *The Dam Busters* had come from the book of the same name
by Paul Brickhill, and it was but a short step from this to a film version
of another of his bestsellers, this one the story of Douglas Bader, the legless
air ace. A Pinnacle (Rank Organization) production directed by Lewis Gilbert
and starring Kenneth More, *Reach for the Sky* was supported by the RAF
principally in the form of a handful of Spitfires and Hurricanes used for

ground shots. Though the story suggested that at times the air force could be overly bureaucratic, it gains credit for allowing Bader to fly again – having lost his legs in a pre-war aerobatic accident – and yet again for the Battle of Britain, which is perhaps the most important dramatic moment of the film aside from the near-fatal accident and its consequences. Given the astonishing triumph against the odds the subject of the film had pulled off, it was difficult for even the most jaundiced critic to be too damning, though Anthony Carthew did note in the *Herald* that 'the film [has] an obsession with our famous British capacity for understatement'. The public, of course, loved it, and *Reach for the Sky* went on to become the most profitable film of 1956 at the box office.[102]

Association with a string of very popular feature films, each of which had been judged to have, as an Information Office memo put it, 'a strong RAF publicity angle', was cause for satisfaction at the Air Ministry.[103] Yet by the mid 1950s it was also becoming apparent that almost all of this publicity was tied to wartime events which, as the years passed, had less and less of a direct connection with the contemporary air force.

There had been, of course, *The Sound Barrier* back in the summer of 1952, the London Films picture directed by David Lean based on a fictional plot devised by Terence Rattigan about the testing of ever-faster jets, in which the Supermarine Swift, due to go into RAF service, had played the key prototype. This had done very well both critically and at the box office. But here the emphasis was on the private development stage rather than air force operations, confining the presence of the RAF to opening scenes set back in the Second World War.[104]

The one true exception to the 'wartime RAF only' rule was *Conflict of Wings*, a Group 3 production released in the spring of 1954. Based on a novel of the same name by Don Sharp, the plot deals with the struggle between villagers trying to preserve an unofficial bird sanctuary and an RAF low-level attack squadron which has been assigned the Norfolk land as a target range. On the surface this might not appear a promising subject for Air Ministry support. Yet the script was even-handed in presenting the case for as well as against the air force, and the ending, in which an official enquiry is launched, leaves neither side victorious. The rather selfish parochialism of the villagers could even sway an observer in favour of the RAF position (national security comes first). In any event the Information Division decided to take a risk when approached for help by producer Herbert Mason. A camera crew under director John Eldridge was allowed to shoot extensively at RAF Leconfield in Yorkshire, a base for squadrons equipped with the De Havilland Vampire jet fighter. There were occasional problems, as when the producer wanted a shot of a fighter nearly crash-landing after a bird strike – 'What, and risk pranging a Vampire?', was the incredulous response of the officer to whom the request was put – but these were quickly smoothed over. It was agreed, for instance, that instead of filming a ropey and potentially dangerous landing, the crew could take shots of a Vampire coming in on approach that appeared to be in trouble. In return film publicity material, rather than stressing the environmentalist aspects, made much of the RAF connection with press catchlines such as 'a "bang-on" film about the boys of the air!', and 'join the peacetime RAF in a high-speed romantic adventure!' [105]

Shot in Eastmancolor, and starring John Gregson, Muriel Pavlov, Kiernon Moore and Niall MacGuiness, *Conflict of Wings* drew mostly favourable reviews, a number of which came down in favour of the RAF over the villagers. To Reg Whitley, writing in the *Daily Mirror*, the film 'gives a convincing answer to people who complain when jet planes fly over their homes'. 'The RAF *must* train somewhere', Fred Majdalany put it in the *Daily Mail*, '—and this unit has a month in which to prepare itself for serious business overseas.' Virginia Graham of the *Spectator* thought that while the writers 'try hard to be objective one feels that at heart they are on the side of the angels-one-five'. For her this was not a problem. 'People who appreciate quiet punctuated by a little birdsong deserve sympathy, of course, but time is marching on and only under the cover of aluminium wings can England safely build her nest.' [106]

Despite the good notices, *Conflict of Wings* did not have much of an impact at the box office in the year it appeared. As before and after, people seemed to prefer stories about the wartime RAF. *The Purple Plain*, a psychological drama shot in colour about a Canadian pilot, played by Gregory Peck, who overcomes his inner demons after being shot down over the Burmese jungle in 1945, for which the RAF had supplied a Mosquito and sundry camp equipment for shooting in Ceylon, did well. So too did *The Sea Shall Not Have Them*, a more conventional air-sea rescue epic, for which the Air Ministry allowed location shooting aboard RAF rescue craft based at Felixstowe.[107]

In February 1957, Sir Norman Bottomley, retired air marshal and BBC administrator, was commissioned by the Permanent Under-Secretary at the Air Ministry to assess RAF publicity efforts. Bottomley stressed in his report that there was 'considerable value in offering film production companies for representing the interesting and attractive sides of [current] air force life and air force operations'.[108] The Information Division could in response point to the fact that it was now involved in the making of a Warwick Films colour picture about the jet-age RAF. The film, produced by Phil Samuel and directed by John Gilling, involved a young and rather rebellious cadet crossing swords with his superior officer during training but finally learning to act responsibly as a good service pilot. The Air Ministry allowed filming to take place at the officer training college at Cranwell, and a second unit under directors Max Varnel, Anthony Squire and Bernard Mainwaring to take footage of RAF jet fighters on the ground and in the air. There were distinct hopes in Whitehall that *High Flight*, starring Kenneth Haigh and Ray Milland, would prove an 'outstanding' example of how a commercial feature could 'do a public relations job for the Services'.[109]

In this *High Flight* was successful, though with the public rather than the critics. After the film was premiered in September 1957 the reviews were uniformly awful, and in the right-of-centre press often tinged with xeno-phobia. The critic for *The Times* thought the film had gone Hollywood in its stress on youthful conflict with authority. 'This film was made by Warwick, officially a British company but with a marked American influence', the *Glasgow Herald* reviewer wrote. 'I wish they would leave us to tackle our national subjects in our way. Then we might be spared travesties like *High Flight*.' Others simply thought it a mass of clichés. The aerial sequences were admirable but could not disguise the fact that, as Margaret Hinxman put it in the *Herald*, the end result was 'a diabolically dreary film'. *High Flight*, nevertheless, did well at the box office that year, and was reissued in 1961.[110]

This was cause for satisfaction, especially as by the end of the fifties the RAF, like the army and navy before it, was becoming a setting for the inexpensive anti-authoritarian service comedies made without official as-sistance that had been spawned by the success of *Private's Progress*. Luckily, however, they were fewer and less successful.

A picture such as *The Night We Dropped a Clanger*, a Four Star production starring Brian Rix, Cecil Parker and William Hartnell, could cause little offence. The plot of this farce involved a latrine orderly accidentally trading places with an RAF hero and getting dropped as an agent into German-occupied France by mistake. As the *Telegraph* put it when the film appeared in the autumn of 1959, it was 'good for some simple-minded laughs'.[111] Rather more problematic was *On the Fiddle* in 1962, in which two RAF airmen, a cockney spiv (Alfred Lynch) and his gypsy 'oppo' (Sean Connery), evade official efforts to crack down on their various schemes to make money selling RAF supplies. Happily for the air force, *On the Fiddle* was a complete bust in cinemas.[112]

By the early 1960s it was becoming increasingly clear that television rather than the cinema was the medium in which to publicize the RAF.[113] Though the focus on the Second World War became something of a mixed blessing, in retrospect the Air Ministry did rather well out of its dealings with

Wardour Street in the last decade in which going to the cinema was a
central feature of popular culture.

By the middle and late 1960s cooperative ventures involving the services
and the film industry were growing few and far between. The number of
cinemas in operation and films being made continued to decline, with
annual cinema admission between 1965 and 1970 shrinking from 327 million
to 193 million.[114] Meanwhile the continuing transatlantic interest in Second
World War themes had less and less connection with armed forces that
had re-equipped several times over the previous twenty years.

Air war films were a case in point. In the mid fifties the producer of *The
Purple Plain* could still obtain Mosquitoes with relative ease. In 1963 the
Mirisch film corporation were able to obtain the few remaining mothballed
Mosquito target-tugs from the RAF but had to supplement these with
aircraft from other sources for *633 Squadron*, released in the spring of 1964.
A few years later, when production was underway on a sequel, *Mosquito
Squadron*, and work was starting on the larger-scale *Battle of Britain* – both
released in 1969 – there were no Mosquitos at all to be had from the RAF
and only a few Hurricanes and Spitfires from the Heritage Flight. Period
aircraft either had to be obtained from private sources or less advanced
foreign air forces. Increasingly the best option was to build replicas on a
greater or lesser scale, as was done for some of the Spitfires featured in
The Battle of Britain and the Lancasters in the TV drama series of the early
70s, *The Pathfinders*.[115]

There were, to be sure, still occasional pictures made with some help
from the forces with more contemporary settings. Both the air force and
the navy cooperated in the making of the Bond film *Thunderball* (United
Artists, 1965), the RAF allowing footage to be taken of 101 Squadron Vulcan
jet bombers taking off from Waddington and the Royal Navy putting the
frigate HMS *Rothesay* at the disposal of director Terence Young for the
final sea-chase sequence. As for the army, the previous year Richard Attenborough had been allowed to join recruits of the Coldstream Guards being
drilled by the ferocious RSM Brittain – 'This marvellous man yelling at me,
screaming at me' – in order to be able to play a similar character, RSM
Lauderdale, with authority and conviction in *The Guns at Batasi* (20th
Century Fox, 1964).[116] On the surface this was a film from which the military
authorities ought to have distanced themselves, as the plot, centring on
reactions among British training personnel to a coup in a former African
colony, questions the relevance of Lauderdale's traditional concept of honour and makes his honest-soldier bravery appear futile. But at another level
The Guns at Batasi suggested that these values, however anachronistic, were

worth something. The film was a success, the review by Ian Crawford in the *Sunday Express* indicating that the leading player had taken full advantage of his 'training' and his character's sympathetic qualities. 'The film belongs to Richard Attenborough, who gives a magnificent performance as Lauderdale, full of stuffy fire, regimental bombast, and a kind of glory behind the closed mind and the Service-burnished exterior. He makes the Regimental Sergeant-Major a man who touches your heart even when every liberal instinct urges you to hate everything he represents.' [117] The last scene shows the RSM, his shaken confidence restored, marching off into retirement with full pomp and circumstance.

The British Army had a mixed image thereafter in British film portraits of the sixties. In an effort to appeal to modern youth, the Ministry of Defence (MoD) agreed to lend troops and vehicles for a musical scene on Salisbury Plain in Richard Lester's second Beatles film, *Help!* (United Artists, 1965). Though the Fab Four and Centurion Tanks made strange bedfellows, even in an intentionally surreal picture, this was innocuous enough. Other films, made without MoD involvement, were more troubling as the decade advanced and anti-establishment attitudes grew more prevalent. [118] Films about the abuses of army authority in the First World War such as *King and Country* (British Home Entertainments, 1964) were perhaps not overtly relevant. But *The Hill* (Seven Arts, 1964), set in a 1942 military prison, *How I Won the War* (United Artists, 1967), a black comedy of military manners set *circa* 1943, and the *The Bofors Gun* (Everglades, 1968), involving the collapse of order in a 1954 guardroom, were all clearly meant to suggest the apparently timeless stupidity of the British Army as an institution. [119] These, however, were essentially serious films for serious cinephiles. What remained of the mass audience seems to have preferred the sixties trans-atlantic Second World War spectacles such as *The Guns of Navarone* (Columbia, 1961), *Operation Crossbow* (MGM, 1965) and *Where Eagles Dare* (MGM, 1969), all action-adventure films featuring daring commando-type operations. [120]

By this point, however, forces participation – or lack thereof – in British films was rapidly becoming irrelevant. The Admiralty and War Office, for example, were thanked for 'their generous advice and assistance' in the credits for *The Guns of Navarone*, but it was the Greek armed forces that provided the more-or-less period equipment for the picture. The producers of *Operation Crossbow* and *Where Eagles Dare* obtained what they needed from foreign and private sources. Moreover, quite apart from the equipment considerations already mentioned, it was clear to the Ministry of Defence that the near-complete displacement of the cinema in people's lives by television meant that the future of service publicity lay with the small rather than the large screen. In the fourteen years after 1960 the number of TV licences had grown by over seven million, while annual cinema admissions shrank to less than a quarter of what they had been.[121] The provision of an RN frigate for *Warship*, a popular and contemporary BBC drama series that ran from 1973 to 1977, was symbolic of the shift in focus.[122]

The last hurrah for the war film as a public relations medium for the services came and went in the mid seventies, when Richard Attenborough was allowed to use the 1st battalion, Parachute Regiment, along with a Royal Artillery battery, in the making of *A Bridge Too Far* (United Artists, 1977), the biggest British war film since *Dunkirk* back in 1958. In the late fifties the War Office had still thought the war recent enough to make sure that the army was not blamed for defeat in 1940. By the middle seventies the Ministry of Defence apparently did not object to a script about a defeat in 1944 in which the finger of blame was pointed directly at a British general. The Second World War had finally become history, the MoD helping out mainly in the hope that footage of the Paras engaged in a mass drop – one of the most breathtaking sequences in the entire film – might stimulate recruitment.[123] Since then it has been almost exclusively TV projects that have occupied the military authorities.[124]

Conclusion

The Second World War marked a watershed in the attitude of the armed services toward feature-film publicity. Though attitudes were undergoing incremental change throughout the century, the contrast between the pre- and post-war years is stark. Before the war the need to actively publicize the army, navy, and air force through the mass media had not been widely recognized. The human and other resources devoted to publicity had been minimal, and the attitude toward the cinema had ranged from wariness to outright hostility. The Admiralty, indeed, had at one point made it official policy to turn down all approaches for help in the making of screen dramas on the ground that this was a sheer waste of time. After the war the need for service publicity was widely accepted, with all three service ministries maintaining significant PR sections and taking a serious interest in the commercial cinema as a means of positively influencing public opinion. The willingness of Vice-Admiral Sir Charles Evans to sign on as president of the British Film Producers Association after his retirement from the navy in the mid sixties was a sign of how much things had changed.[1]

The wartime experience was a key factor in this transformation. The growth of interest in the production of feature films about the services between 1939 and 1945 was in part a matter of bureaucratic imperative. In theory the Films Division of the new Ministry of Information was supposed to oversee the development of all feature films with publicity value. In practice the service ministries fought to retain and augment control over how their forces were portrayed through exercising security censorship prerogatives, taking the initiative in sponsoring film projects before the MoI became involved, and in the case of the War Office and Air Ministry setting up their own film production units as a counterweight to the Crown Film Unit. But this was by no means the only – or even the central – motive behind the wartime growth in service involvement with feature films. Even after the Crown Film Unit and its rivals had been wound up in the wake of the disappearance of the Ministry of Information, the service ministries – in marked contrast to the period after the First World War – maintained a strong involvement in the making of commercial features.

Of equal if not greater significance was the growing realization that public perceptions of the armed forces were significant and that feature films were a possible means of influencing opinion. And what people thought and felt was significant. Low morale could have an adverse effect on job performance, not least within the armed forces, and even have an impact on high policy. Though the state was far more powerful in wartime than in peace, it was not omnipotent. Dissatisfaction with the direction the war was taking could express itself through the defeat of government candidates in by-elections, through awkward questions by backbench MPs on behalf of their constituents, and of course through leading articles and letters to the editor in what was still an essentially free newspaper press. How people were interpreting events and viewing the services in light of wartime events mattered, in short, because it could affect both service morale and the allocation of resources. And in a period when the percentage of the total population going to the cinema every week began at roughly 40 per cent (1939) and went as high as 60 per cent (1945), film was obviously a significant medium through which to project a particular image. Apart from raising the public profile of a particular branch of the service, be it submarines in the navy or flying boats in the air force, war films became, as we have seen, an important means of reassuring the public that strategic bombing worked, that the senior service could still be counted on, and that modern soldiering was rooted in the present rather than the past. There was, as we have seen, a good deal of resistance within the services to engaging in such self-promotion, and the process by which pictures such as *In Which We Serve* and *The Way Ahead* emerged was often complicated and fraught with competing interests. Ad hoc as it must have seemed at the time, involving different organizations and people, there was a pattern to the development and content of features in which the armed forces played a central role. And once one service got in on the act in a big way – *Target for Tonight* was one significant catalyst – the others were quick to follow. By the end of the war feature films had become an accepted aspect of service PR, and through a happy confluence of commercial and military interests, would continue to be significant over the next twenty years.

Clearly senior figures such as Air Marshal Peck, Admiral Mountbatten, and General Adam believed in the importance of feature film propaganda, and were satisfied with the results of their support. But just how influential *were* films in terms of shaping public perceptions? In terms of changing people's minds, getting them to believe in something which they had hitherto been unwilling to accept, pictures probably achieved little. 'The British public were well aware of the score', as one keen young filmgoer recalled of the war years. 'They had a fair idea of what was true and what was false and what was glamourised and what was slanted …'[2] Hence, for example, the evident scepticism surrounding the message of a film like *The Big Blockade*.[3] Yet as we have seen, many of the wartime films with which the armed forces were associated *were* immensely popular.

Some big hits, to be sure, were attractive for reasons other than pure content. The success of *Target for Tonight*, for example, owed much to its novelty value – it was the first time most cinemagoers had seen real people act – which in turn helps explain the diminished audience for *Coastal Command* and other docudramas. What first drew people to *The First of the Few*, conversely, was star attraction, the expectation that the R. J. Mitchell character would be a variation on the standard and very popular Leslie Howard screen persona: the sensitive, vulnerable, yet resolute English intellectual.[4]

Yet the fact remains that most of the war films were hits because they and the publicity surrounding them presented an image of the forces in which people at the time wanted to believe: an air force striking back, a navy guarding the seas, an army turning the corner to victory. The much-admired 'realism' present in many of them – the depiction of quite ordinary people of all classes and backgrounds coming together with stoic humour and quiet courage to defeat the enemy – was in fact a somewhat artificial and period-specific ideal; but an ideal which added to the appeal for both critics and much of the public.[5]

Audiences, in short, were receptive to films which did not stray too far from the obvious facts but that held up 'a mirror for England' in which they could see reflected what was then commonly thought to be best about themselves and the country.[6] The writer George Macdonald Fraser, while dismissing the idea that war films 'imbued my generation with martial ardour', went on to stress how much as a young soldier in Fourteenth Army he had liked *The Way Ahead* because of the way it managed to be both realistic and attractively idealistic. The film

> is just beautifully done; every character is right, and every incident rings true. Niven is the perfect subaltern, keen, energetic, not totally sure of his ability to be a mixture of fighting leader and mother hen; as for Hartnell, he doesn't play the part [of platoon sergeant], he *is* it: the pared-to-the-bone immaculate figure, the hard eye, the cold barking voice – how you hated it, and how you missed it later when you realised what a good man was underneath. The others are perfect types …

When *The Way Ahead* appeared on screens 'it had to stand the immediate test of exposure to relentless critics like me; we found no fault with it'.[7] Quality of dialogue and acting as well as production values did of course matter; but the success of films about the armed forces was ultimately dependent on the extent to which they conformed to public desires and expectations.

This was also true of pre- and post-war films. Pictures like *OHMS* and *Brown on Resolution* had done well in the mid thirties in part because audiences expected and got a story in which soldiers and sailors of the King acted with nobility and self-sacrifice as a Shield of Empire. As for the post war period, it was the popular appetite for pictures about wartime exploits that fuelled the fifties boom in service-assisted films like *The Cruel Sea* and *The Dam Busters*, audiences expecting and receiving a story of British ingenuity, courage, and self-sacrifice featuring a relatively narrow range of principal players mostly in officer roles.[8]

This is not to suggest that the films had no impact on audiences, and that therefore the time and energy spent on this aspect of public relations in Whitehall was totally wasted. In presenting images of the armed forces in which audiences wished to believe, filmmakers were bolstering those images on an emotional level. The pre-war films buttressed traditional patriotism and its military associations. The successful wartime pictures with contemporary themes may have been 'the equivalent of a pat on the back' for audiences,[9] but they were nevertheless sufficiently satisfying psychologically to remain 'deeply impressed on the memory of the audiences who saw them' for years afterward according to a post-war study.[10] The celebratory films of the fifties reinforced the sense of victory achieved – 'listen, we've won, you know'[11] – which in turn reflected well on the contemporary armed forces while memory of the war was still fresh and before the inevitable sixties counter-reaction set in.

The service ministries, in short, definitely benefited in terms of public esteem from involvement in feature films in an age when popular opinion had begun to matter a good deal. Class and other barriers between the services and society were still present as the age of the dream palace came to an end. But the evolution of attitudes towards the cinema and the importance of public relations within the Admiralty, War Office, Air Ministry, and latterly the unified Ministry of Defence, indicate that the need to come to grips with popular society and its culture had finally come to be understood; a process in which the Second World War experience played a vital part.

All that said, it is worth remembering that in cooperating with film companies the armed forces bequeathed to posterity a host of films ranging from the forgettable to the classic. Tastes and expectations do of course change over time, and there is no doubt that in one way or another the war films under discussion have become dated; but some have definitely stood the test of time better than others.

Of the features released during the war that the public chose to ignore, such as *Flying Fortress*, most remain deservedly interred. *The Lion Has Wings*, quickly rendered obsolete by a war situation radically different from the one it posited, has value as an historical document but little contemporary resonance (except perhaps as an unintended comedy).

Target for Tonight and its progeny, films in which servicemen were used instead of stage and screen professionals, long ago lost their novelty value. A daring experiment at the time, this casting technique did not last and yielded an isolated cadre of RAF drama-documentaries which now seem embarrassingly amateur in terms of acting. (*Journey Together*, on the other hand, which came too late to have much of an impact, today comes across as one of the most polished of the wartime pictures produced by the various official film units, in large part because trained actors already serving in the RAF were used instead of 'real' people.) The straight documentaries, from *Desert Victory* onward, though not entirely accurate in light of later research, have aged rather better, with some of the techniques used – and indeed bits of the actual footage – becoming commonplace in the age of the television documentary.[12]

Among the commercial features that were hits at the time of first release there are several from the first half of the war whose popularity appears baffling to audiences fifty years on. Conventions of language, setting and action in melodramas have changed substantially, so that not only a film such as *Ships With Wings*, which even the critics of the day disliked, but also *Convoy*, a critical as well as commercial success, seem excruciatingly stagey. The grittier, often less class-bound, and more thoughtful dramas of the later war years have matured more successfully. Some indeed have proved themselves to have an enduring impact on audiences.

Though Noël Coward as Captain Kinross seems even more incongruous now than he did when the film was released, and some of the class lines – accurate though they were – are too sharply drawn for contemporary taste, the deftly handled emotional content of *In Which We Serve* still has the power to engage. Overshadowed at the time by Coward's film and saddled with a highly melodramatic title, *We Dive at Dawn* deserves – and now occasionally gets – more credit than it first received.[13] The views on womanhood expressed by Leslie Howard in *The Gentle Sex* make it seem very much a period piece, but *The Way Ahead* has largely withstood the test of time. Good direction, an excellent ensemble cast, and above all an unusually naturalistic script have meant that those born long after the war can still identify with Sergeant Fletcher's awkward squad. Despite its popularity at the end of the war and reputation as the air force answer to both *In Which We Serve* and *The Way Ahead*, the nostalgia-laden *Way to the*

Stars no longer resonates in the way it once did. Though its contains scenes which are still striking, its trademark emotional understatement has become something of a cliché (largely through overuse in the 1950s). Rather more robust is *One of Our Aircraft is Missing*. Despite its now obvious limitations as a piece of war reportage, this well-acted ensemble piece contains enough plot movement, humour and mystery to sustain interest, even if it is not in quite the same class as *The Way Ahead* and *In Which We Serve*.[14]

Service involvement certainly added to the versimilitude of these features. Ironically, however, the most enduringly impressive of the films discussed in this book was the one which was made in spite of official opposition. *The Life and Death of Colonel Blimp*, a major hit at the time of its release and now an established classic, continues to attract admirers. A complex blend of romantic and martial ideals and ideas acted out by a splendid cast in lush Technicolor, it continues to have something for everyone. It is hard to see how War Office cooperation could have improved on the final product.

Audiences and critical reactions change along with society, and it may well be that the status of the major Second World War features – high from the time they were first identified as forming part of a 1940s British film renaissance [15] – will at some point begin to shift. Whatever their ultimate fate, however, they will remain milestones on the armed forces' road to greater engagement with the British public.

Notes

Notes to Introduction

1. The now classic examination written by Anthony Aldgate and Jeffrey Richards, *Britain Can Take It: The British Cinema in the Second World War* (Oxford, 1984), was followed by a host of further studies. Dozens of articles on particular wartime films and genres have been published in academic journals and as chapters in edited collections, while several new books on the films in general or specific aspects have appeared. The amount of secondary as well as primary research undertaken by James Chapman for his meticulous study *The British at War: Cinema, State and Propaganda, 1939–1945* (London, 1998) is a clear indication of the extent to which wartime films have been put under the microscope. Other general studies include C. Coultass, *Images for Battle: British Film and the Second World War* (Cranbury, NJ, 1989); R. Murphy, *Realism and Tinsel: Cinema and Society in Britain, 1939–1948* (London, 1989); P. M. Taylor (ed.), *Britain and the Cinema in the Second World War* (London, 1988), and a second, expanded edition of Aldgate and Richards (Edinburgh, 1994). See also List of Sources.

2. This is touched on in some of the works cited above, notably Coultass, *Images for Battle*, while the RAF of the 1930s is given detailed attention in K. R. M. Shortt's *Screening the Propaganda of British Air Power: From RAF (1935) to The Lion Has Wings (1939)* (Trowbridge, 1997). The current book, however, is more wide-ranging than the latter and more subject-focused than the former. It should be emphasized that this book does not deal with the development of distribution organizations within the services such as the Royal Naval Film Corporation, a subject still awaiting exploration.

3. There were, to be sure, a few rogue films, but *The Gun*, made by the Admiralty without the knowledge of the MoI, and *The Life and Death of Colonel Blimp*, made without the assistance of the War Office, were the exceptions that proved the rule.

4. As Nicholas Cull and Mark Glancy (see Bibliography) have shown, wartime films made or set in Britain sometimes were constructed with an American audience in mind. My concern here is to discuss the domestic aspects of the films with which the services were associated.

5. Probably because they were not considered of historical importance, most of the service files relating to film policy were not preserved at the time of transfer

to the Public Record Office. The surviving records of the many defunct British film companies are even scantier.

Notes to Chapter 1: The Services and the Cinema, 1900–1939

1. R. Low, *The History of the British Film, 1906–1914* (London, 1948), ch. 1; R. Low and R. Manvell, *The History of the British Film, 1896–1906* (London, 1948), chs 2–4; D. Gifford, *The British Film Catalogue, 1895–1970* (Newton Abbot, 1973); J. Barnes, *The Beginnings of the Cinema in England, 1894–1901*, 6 vols (Exeter, 1996).

2. Ibid; Low, *British Film, 1906–1914*, p. 164; J. M. MacKenzie, *Propaganda and Empire: The Manipulation of British Public Opinion, 1880–1960* (Manchester, 1984), p. 71; see R. Opie, *Rule Britannia: Trading on the British Image* (Harmondsworth, 1985), pp. 58–73.

3. L. Masterman, *C. F. G. Masterman: A Biography* (London, 1939), p. 283. On the social origins and attitudes of army officers see E. M. Spiers, *The Army and Society, 1815–1914* (London, 1980), ch. 1; G. Harries-Jenkins, *The Army in Victorian Society* (London, 1977), ch. 7; C. B. Otley, 'The Social Origins of British Army Officers', *Sociological Review*, 18 (1970), pp. 213–39. On the gentleman-officer attitudes towards the lower classes within the RN see A. Carew, *The Lower Deck of the Royal Navy, 1900–39* (Manchester, 1981), chs 1–2, especially p. 49.

4. Masterman, p. 283; PRO, INF 4/6, Boon minute, 8 June 1918. On sponsored public spectacle, see E. M. Spiers, *The Late Victorian Army, 1868–1902* (Manchester, 1992), pp. 188–89; A. R. Skelley, *The Victorian Army at Home: The Recruitment and Terms and Conditions of the British Regular, 1859–1899* (London, 1977), p. 243; A. J. Marder, *The Anatomy of British Sea Power: A History of British Naval Policy in the Pre-Dreadnought Era, 1880–1905* (New York, 1940), p. 45. The service leagues occasionally talked about reaching the working man, but were essentially upper- and middle-class in orientation. See ibid., pp. 48–55; M. J. Allison, 'The National Service Issue, 1899–1914' (unpublished Ph.D. thesis, University of London, 1975).

5. E. Wood, *From Midshipman to Field Marshal* (London, 1912). One of his complaints about the extra work the Boer War entailed was the way in which it cut into the number of fox hunts he could attend (ibid., p. 405n.). See also his *Winnowed Memories* (London, 1917).

6. On the Paul and Hepworth films, see Low and Maxwell, *British Films, 1896–1906*, p. 55; J. Barnes, *The Beginnings of the Cinema in England, 1894–1901*, v, 1900 (Exeter, 1996), ch 1. On the naval scare of 1900 see Marder, *Anatomy of British Sea Power*, ch. 18.

7. Even as *Army Life* was being mooted, pioneer filmmaker William Dickson was having trouble persuading Sir Redvers Buller, the commanding general in the early stages of the Boer War, to allow him to take footage behind the lines in South Africa. Even after Buller had given permission, Dickson found

that another 'military officer in high authority has done everything to block my path'. W. K. -L. Dickson, *The Biograph in Battle: Its Story in the South African War Related with Personal Experiences* (reprint edition, Trowbridge, 1995), pp. 63–64; see also J. Barnes, *Filming the Boer War* (London, 1992).

8. *Parliamentary Debates*, 5th Series, vol. 1, army estimates debate, 4 March 1909, col. 1597.

9. Low, *British Film, 1906–1914*, p. 164; Gifford, *British Film Catalogue*, entry 2147; Spiers, pp. 278–79.

10. *Parliamentary Debates*, 5th series, vol. 56, oral answers to questions, 7 August 1913, col. 1757.

11. N. P. Hiley, '*The British Army Film, You!* and *For the Empire*: Reconstructed Propaganda Films, 1914–1916', *Historical Journal of Film, Radio and Television*, 5 (1985), pp. 166–69; Low, *British Film, 1906–1914*, p. 164.

12. Gifford, *British Film Catalogue*, August 1914 – May 1915; R. Low, *The History of the British Film, 1914–1918* (London, 1948), pp. 29, 34, 146, 182–83; On the patriotic commercial films of 1914–15 see Low, *British Film, 1914–1918*, pp. 150–51; C. Haste, *Keep the Home Fires Burning: Propaganda in the First World War* (London, 1977), p. 45.

13. *Bioscope*, 20 August 1914.

14. See PRO, FO 395/37, Gowers to FO, 29 May 1916; P. Towle, 'The Debate on Wartime Censorship in Britain, 1902–14', *War and Society: A Yearbook of Military History*, B. Bond and I. Roy, eds (London, 1977), pp. 102–16; Masterman, *C. F. G. Masterman*, p. 283. On the development of wartime propaganda see G. S. Messenger, *British Propaganda and the State in the First World War* (Manchester, 1992); M. L. Sander and P. Taylor, *British Propaganda during the First World War* (London, 1982); Haste, *Home Fires*.

15. On *You!* see Hiley, 'Reconstructed Propaganda Films', pp. 169–73. On War Office obstruction see PRO, INF 4/2, J. Brooke Wilkinson TS, 'Film and Censorship in England, ch. 11: The War Years'; N. Reeves, *Official Film Propaganda during the First World War* (London, 1986), pp. 48–52; Towle, 'Wartime Censorship', p. 112.

16. On *The Royal Naval Division at Work and Play* see *Bioscope*, 22 April 1915. On Churchill and the RN Division, see M. Gilbert, *Winston S. Churchill*, iii, *1914–1916* (London, 1971), pp. 50–52, 111–30, 451.

17. J. C. Robertson, *The British Board of Film Censors: Film Censorship in Britain, 1896–1950* (London, 1985), p. 10.

18. PRO, INF 4/6, J. Boon minute, 8 June 1918, in report of War Cabinet committee on propaganda production and distribution.

19. Senior army officers who supported film propaganda for recruiting purposes included the first C-in-C of the British Expeditionary Force, Field-Marshal Sir John French; see Hiley, 'Reconstructed Propaganda Films', pp. 171–72. At the Admiralty the chief press censor, Rear-Admiral Sir Douglas Brownrigg, acted as a tactful advocate for other departments seeking naval publicity; D. Brownrigg, *Indiscretions of the Naval Censor* (New York, 1920); Messenger, *British*

Propaganda, p. 111. On the decline in army recruiting see P. Simkins, *Kitchener's Army: The Raising of the New Armies, 1914–16* (Manchester, 1988), ch. 4. On the problem of neutral opinion and the domestic invisibility of the Grand Fleet see Sanders and Taylor, *British Propaganda*, pp. 124–25; PRO, ADM 116/1447, Balfour to Jellicoe, 19 August 1915.

20. Brownrigg, *Indiscretions*, p. 64. On Balfour and Jellicoe, see ADM 116/1447, Balfour to Jellicoe, 6 September 1915, Jellicoe to Balfour, 15 September 1915; Brownrigg, p. 52. On the private film showings see Science Museum Library, Charles Urban papers, URB 4/3, Urban to Jury, 1 Sep. 1915, and 'How the Somme Battle was Photographed' TS; Reeves, *Official British Film Propaganda*, pp. 53–54. On Jackson at the Admiralty see M. H. Murfett, 'Admiral Sir Henry Bradwardine Jackson (1915–1916)', *The First Sea Lords: From Fisher to Mountbatten*, M. H. Murfett, ed. (Westport, CT, 1995), ch. 6.

21. On the delays, see Reeves, *Official British Film Propaganda*, p. 110. On the vetting process, see G. Malins, *How I Filmed the War* (London, 1993 reprint), p. 182.

22. Reeves, *Official British Film Propaganda*, pp. 57, 64. On press censorship see Towle, 'Wartime Censorship', pp. 112–14; P. Young and P. Jesser, *The Media and the Military: From the Crimea to Desert Strike* (New York, 1997), pp. 31–35; P. Knightley, *The First Casualty* (London, 1975), ch. 5. Some officers working in censorship, such as Admiral Brownrigg, clearly tried to act with fairness towards the media; see *Lord Riddell's War Diary, 1914–1918* (London, 1933), pp. 26–27; Brownrigg, passim. Others, such as J. C. Faunthorpe at GHQ France, were clearly as disdainful of the film trade representatives as they were of the press. Knightly, *First Casualty*, p. 96; PRO, FO 395/37/103810/8404, J. C. Faunthorpe, Report on Film Propaganda, 15 May 1916. On the navy's anxiety about film and security see PRO, ADM 116/1446, AD8/M07158, 22 September 1915, AD15/M45151/15, 4 October 1915.

23. The hand-cranked, tripod-mounted cameras then available were heavy and bulky, film spools were short, and both focal lengths and lens apertures were limited. Well-defined and singular objects – artillery pieces, men drawn up in ranks, ships – could be photographed at relatively close range from a fixed position in good weather. Trying to take shots of distant, dispersed and/or fast-moving objects as the occasion demanded – ships firing at sea, men advancing over the top – was much more problematic. Apart from the physical dangers involved in being caught up in the action, there was the risk, even the likelihood, that the resulting film would be underexposed, overexposed, out of focus, or otherwise unsatisfactory. Reeves, *Official British Film Propaganda*, pp. 97–101, 146.

24. S. D. Badsey, '*Battle of the Somme*: British War Propaganda', *Historical Journal of Film, Radio and Television*, 3 (1983), p. 103; Brownrigg, *Indiscretions*, pp. 51–52; Reeves, *Official British Film Propaganda*, pp. 92–93.

25. PRO, INF 4/2, Brooke Wilkinson TS, pp. 304–6.

26. *The Times*, 31 December 1915, p. 10; *Evening News*, 30 December 1915, p. 5.

27. Masterman, *C. F. G. Masterman*, p. 284; see Reeves, *Official British Film Propaganda*, pp. 92–93, 142–45.
28. Badsey, 'Battle of the Somme', pp. 107–8; Reeves, *Official British Film Propaganda*, pp. 157–59.
29. *Bioscope*, 17 August 1916, p. 579; PRO, INF 4/2, Brooke Wilkinson TS, pp. 298–99.
30. Badsey, *'Battle of the Somme'*, p. 108.
31. Badsey, *'Battle of the Somme'*, pp. 108, 109–10; *The Times*, 11 August 1916, p. 3.
32. *Manchester Guardian*, 11 August 1916, p. 7. Neither *Britain Prepared* nor *Battle of the Somme* was, in fact, entirely the real thing, as both films contained staged scenes. See Reeves, *Official British Film Propaganda*, pp. 90, 101–5.
33. R. Low, *The History of the British Film, 1918–1929* (London, 1948), p. 47; Robertson, *British Board of Film Censors*, p. 44.
34. PRO, CAB 27/17, The Cinema and its Relation to the Government, T. L. Gilmour minute, 13 October 1917; see INF 4/2, Brooke Wilkinson TS, p. 300.
35. PRO, FO 395/38/232794/8403, Gowers to FO, 17 November 1916.
36. Reeves, *Official British Film Propaganda*, pp. 61–63. Aitken and Brade had already forged a close working relationship. See Lord Beaverbrook, *Men and Power, 1917–1918* (London, 1956), p. 44.
37. Though full of self-promotion and therefore somewhat unreliable, cameraman Geoffrey Malins' war memoirs indirectly indicate greater military involvement in film work from the latter part of 1916 onward. See Malins, *How I Filmed the War*, pp. 76, 80, 93, 122–23, 222–23, 250.
38. Reeves, *Official British Film Propaganda*, pp. 164–66.
39. *Daily Mail*, 23 December 1916, p. 3. Evidence suggests a number of scenes in this film were in fact staged. Reeves, *Official British Film Propaganda*, p. 165.
40. *Evening News*, 9 June 1917, p. 4; see Reeves, *Official British Film Propaganda*, pp. 167–68, 232.
41. See House of Lords Record Office, Beaverbrook Papers, BBKE 14, Beaverbrook to Greene, 16 May 1917, Greene to Beaverbrook, 19 May 1917; Reeves, *Official British Film Propaganda*, p. 64.
42. On the shift to shorter formats see Reeves, *Official British Film Propaganda*, pp. 65–66, 175–77.
43. *Cinema News and Property Gazette*, 16 August 1917.
44. The War Office cinema committee and the cinema branch of the Department of Information were separate and in some ways competing organizations. Even when the military film propaganda organization was absorbed into a new Ministry of Information under Lord Beaverbrook in March 1918, other government departments and bodies such as the National War Aims Committee continued to sponsor films of their own. Reeves, *Official British Film Propaganda*, pp. 70–71, 77–78, 117–18.
45. Riddell, *War Memoirs*, p. 340.
46. Brownrigg, *Indiscretions*, p. 100; Reeves, *Official British Film Propaganda*, p. 110.

Charteris, to be fair, did agree to try and speed up the vetting process; ibid., p. 110.

47. Reeves, *Official British Film Propaganda*, pp. 119–30.

48. *Bioscope*, 14 November 1918, supplement, pp. vi–vii; Brownrigg, *Indiscretions*, p. 100.

49. See P. H. Taylor, 'British Official Attitudes towards Propaganda Abroad, 1918–39', *Propaganda, Politics and Film, 1918–45*, N. Pronay and D. W. Spring, eds (London, 1982), pp. 23–49; M. Grant, *Propaganda and the Role of the State in Inter-War Britain* (Oxford, 1994).

50. Brownrigg, *Indiscretions*, pp. 54–55.

51. ADM 1/19195, p. 4; see annual *Navy List, Air Force List, Army List, War Office List*, 1920s; AIR 41/9, p. 3.

52. On the interwar army, see B. Bond, *British Military Policy between the Two World Wars* (Oxford, 1980), ch. 2. On the navy, see Carew, *Lower Deck*, passim. On the anxieties of the RAF (which to be fair very much broke with tradition in the form of short-service commissions) see A. Boyle, *Trenchard* (London, 1962), chs 12–13.

53. These films included *The Battle of Jutland* (1926), *Zeebrugge* (1924), *Ypres* (1925), *Mons* (1926), *The Somme* (1927), and *The Battle of the Coronel and Falkland Islands* (1927). See PRO, ADM 167/75, Admiralty Board Minute 2389, 3 November 1927, ADM 167/76, Naval Facilities for the Production of Films (Memorandum); MacKenzie, *Propaganda and Empire*, p. 81. On the popularity of war films see K. Bamford, *Distorted Images: British National Identity and Film in the 1920s* (London, 1999), pp. 128–29.

54. PRO, ADM 116/2490, enclosure to CP 19392/31, Agreement between Admiralty and Astra-National Productions Ltd, 30 June 1926.

55. PRO, ADM 167/75, Admiralty Board Minute 2389, 3 November 1927, in reference to ADM 167/76, Naval Facilities for the Production of Films (Memorandum). On the number of cinemas in operation see S. Rowson, 'A Statistical Survey of the Cinema Industry in Great Britain in 1934', *Journal of the Royal Statistical Society*, 99 (1936), p. 77.

56. *OHMS* (1937) was the first film made with the cooperation of the army. *Kinematograph Weekly*, 28 January 1937, p. 28. See also *Daily Express*, 15 December 1930, p. 5.

57. Boyle, *Trenchard*, p. 342.

58. On 'gentlemanly ritual and elegance' see M. Hastings, *Bomber Command* (London, 1979), caption and picture, RAF Boscome Down; see also J. James, *The Paladins: A Social History of the RAF up to the Outbreak of World War II* (London, 1990), pp. 142–43, 183. On the uniforms and training of Other Ranks see T. E. Lawrence, *The Mint* (London, 1956); James, *Paladins*, pp. 113, 182.

59. On RAF promotional activities see Boyle, *Trenchard*, pp. 359–60.

60. M. Paris, *From the Wright Brothers to Top Gun: Aviation, Nationalism and Popular Cinema* (Manchester, 1995), p. 105.

61. Ibid.; Bamford, *Distorted Images*, pp. 162–63. *Flight Commander* did, however,

generate protests from the Chinese government, which did not appreciate scenes of a Chinese village being bombed. See *Index to the Correspondence of the Foreign Office, 1927*, pt 1 (London, 1969), p. 341.

62. PRO, AIR 2/514, minute 1, C3 to DDC, 19 January 1932.

63. H. E. Browning and A. A. Sorrell, 'Cinema and Cinemagoing in Great Britain', *Journal of the Royal Statistical Society*, 117 (1954), p. 134; *Kinematograph Year Book 1939* (London, 1939), p. 9.

64. C. L. Mowat, *Britain between the Wars, 1918–40* (London, 1956), p. 523.

65. On the place of the cinema in society in the 1930s see J. Richards, *The Age of the Dream Palace: Cinema and Society in Britain, 1930–1939* (London, 1984); P. Stead, 'The People and the Pictures: The British Working Class and Film in the 1930s', *Propaganda, Politics and Film, 1918–45*, N. Pronay and D. W. Spring, eds (London, 1982), ch. 3.

66. MacKenzie, *Propaganda and Empire*, pp. 80–81; S. C. Shafer, *British Popular Films 1929–1939: The Cinema of Reassurance* (London, 1997), pp. 20, 27.

67. J. Weels, *The Royal Navy: An Illustrated Social History* (Phoenix Mill, 1994), p. 140.

68. Carew, *Lower Deck*, p. 176. See ADM 1/19195, CNI 1086/45, pp. 2–3.

69. Gifford, *British Film Catalogue*, entry 8900; see also I. Hay and S. King-Hall, *The Middle Watch: A Romance of the Navy* (London, 1931).

70. PRO, ADM 1/2490, Admiralty Policy in Regard to Naval Facilities for the Production of Films, Memorandum for the Board, 2 June 1932.

71. PRO, ADM 116/2679, CP17880/31, Stapleton to DNC, 12 August 1931. On the more developed relationship between Hollywood and the USN see L. Suid, *Sailing on the Silver Screen: Hollywood and the US Navy* (Annapolis, MY, 1996), chs 1–3.

72. PRO, ADM 116/2679, CP17833/31; see *Daily Telegraph*, 9 November 1931, p. 6.

73. R. Low, *The History of British Film, 1929–1939: Film Making in 1930s Britain* (London, 1985), p. 356.

74. PRO, ADM 116/2490, CP4537/32, First Lord minute, 15 April 1932, DNI minute, 6 April 1932.

75. *The Times*, 19 January 1932, p. 5.

76. PRO, ADM 1116/2490, extract 2952 from Board Minutes, 2 June 1932; ibid., Admiralty Policy in Regard to Naval Facilities for the Production of Films, Memorandum for the Board, 2 June 1932.

77. See PRO, FO 371/19098, J5935/5935/16, M4928/35, Barnes to FO, 10 October 1935.

78. Low, *British Film, 1929–1939*, p. 318.

79. *The Times*, 17 December 1930, p. 10.

80. *Daily Express*, 9 November 1931, p. 9; *The Times*, 11 November 1931, p. 10; *Daily Herald*, 9 November 1931, p. 12; *Daily Telegraph*, 9 November 1931, p. 6.

81. Gifford, *British Film Catalogue*, entries 9239, 8900; PRO, ADM 116/2490, CP17692/32, DNI minute, 15 September 1932. On the relative popularity of *The Flag Lieutenant*, see J. Sedgwick, 'Cinema-Going Preferences in Britain in the

1930s', *The Unknown 1930s: An Alternative History of the British Cinema 1929–39*, J. Richards, ed. (London, 1998), p. 24.

82. See *The Times*, 20 September 1933, p. 15; ibid., 22 September 1933, p. 14; ibid., 26 September 1933, p. 16; *Kinematograph Weekly*, 21 September 1933, p. 1.

83. PRO, ADM 167/89, Board Memorandum 3139, 15 November 1933; ibid., Viscount Lee Memorandum.

84. PRO, ADM 167/88, Board Minute 3139, 30 November 1933.

85. PRO, ADM 116/2679, CP13991/34, 22 June 1934; *Kinematograph Weekly*, 9 May 1935, p. 12; C. S. Forester, *Brown on Resolution* (London, 1929).

86. BFI, *Born for Glory* pressbook. The main changes asked for in the script involved greater technical accuracy in the use of gunnery terms and procedures. See BFI, S7495, *Forever England* screenplay, E38, 70, 80, 86, 89, 99, 103.

87. J. Mills, *Up in the Clouds, Gentlemen Please* (London, 1980), p. 123; see BFI, *Born for Glory* pressbook.

88. PRO, ADM 116/2679, CP13991/34.

89. Mills, *Up in the Clouds*, p. 126; BFI, S7495, screenplay of *Forever England*. In light of the navy's role in this production the BBFC in effect passed responsibility for censorship to the Admiralty. See BFI Special Collections, BBFC Scenario Reports, 1934, p. 287, Scenario Report on *Brown on Resolution*, 11 April 1934.

90. *Spectator*, 24 May 1935, p. 874; *Daily Telegraph*, 20 May 1935, p. 6; *The Times*, 16 May 1935, p. 14; *Daily Mirror*, 17 May 1935, p. 26; *Daily Express*, 16 May 1935, p. 13; see *Monthly Film Bulletin*, 16 May 1935, p. 51.

91. Gifford, *British Film Catalogue*, entry 9770. On the Silver Jubilee Review see P. Ransome-Wallis, *The Royal Naval Reviews, 1935–1977* (London, 1982), pp. 9–34.

92. *Kinematograph Weekly*, 19 November 1936, p. 39; ibid., 12 November 1936, p. 51; 22 October 1936, p. 41. The navy also was involved in making *Our Island Nation* (MGM-British, 1937), a documentary with some fictional connecting sequences, directed by Lieutenant-Commander J. L. F. Hunt (retd). See *Sight and Sound*, 6 (1937), p. 148; K. R. M. Shortt, *Screening the Propaganda of British Air Power: From RAF (1935) to The Lion Has Wings (1939)* (Trowbridge, 1997), p. 2 n. 9.

93. *Daily Telegraph*, 26 April 1937, p. 7; see, e.g., 'Bartimeus', *Naval Occasions* (London, 1914); idem, *An Awfully Big Adventure* (London, 1929).

94. Ransome-Wallis, *Naval Reviews*, p. 36

95. *Daily Telegraph*, 26 April 1937, p. 7; *Manchester Guardian*, 23 April 1937, p. 12; *The Times*, 26 April 1937, p. 12; *Kinematograph Weekly*, 29 April 1937, p. 43; *Daily Express*, 23 April 1937, p. 4. For a completely negative review see *Monthly Film Bulletin*, 30 April 1937, p. 76. On RN ship participation see *Kinematograph Weekly*, 14 Jan. 1937, p. 95. Cinemas and local naval and cadet units cooperated in publicizing the film. See, e.g., *Kinematograph Weekly*, 22 December 1937, p. 44. It was recognized, however, that *Our Fighting Navy* would probably not go down well in Latin America, and publicity material for the film was

withdrawn from the Latin American market. See – in lieu of the files themselves, not preserved – *Index to the Correspondence of the Foreign Office, 1937*, pt 1 (London, 1969), p. 507, P1772/P2605/1772/150.

96. *Today's Cinema*, 27 October 1939, pp. 4–5; 3 November 1939; see *Picturegoer*, 27 April 1940, p. 304; *Monthly Film Bulletin*, 30 November 1939, p. 202. See also Gifford, *British Film Catalogue*, entry 10674. P. L. Mannock, writing in the *Daily Herald*, thought that the stiff-upper-lip tone of the film was too much of a good thing. 'A frightfully decent Melodrama,' he wrote, 'but in treatment an emotional blockade.' *Daily Herald*, 8 March 1940, p. 11. *Sons of the Sea* was one of a number of spy films which came into vogue in 1939. See J. Chapman, 'Celluloid Shockers', *The Unknown 1930s: An Alternative History of the British Cinema 1929–39*, J. Richards, ed. (London, 1998), pp. 93–96.

97. BFI, *All at Sea* pressbook. See *Monthly Film Bulletin*, 31 October 1939, p. 185.

98. *Today's Cinema*, 18 October 1939, p. 9. See *Picturegoer*, 3 February 1940, p. 20; *Monthly Film Bulletin*, 31 October 1939, p. 185.

99. On the role of Colonel Hanna see J. Richards, 'The British Board of Film Censors and Content Control in the 1930s: Images of Britain', *Historical Journal of Film, Radio and Television*, 1 (1981), pp. 100–1. On the BBFC in these years see also J. Richards, 'The British Board of Film Censors and Content Control in the 1930s: Foreign Affairs', *Historical Journal of Film, Radio and Television*, 2 (1982), pp. 39–48; N. Pronay, 'The Political Censorship of Films in Britain between the Wars', *Propaganda, Politics and Film, 1918–45*, N. Pronay and D. W. Spring, eds (London, 1982), ch. 4.

100. BFI Special Collections, BBFC Scenario Reports Nos 70, 70a, May 1936. On *Hail and Farewell* see BFI, *Hail and Farewell* pressbook; *Kinematograph Weekly*, 8 October 1936, p. 30; *The Times*, 21 December 1936, p. 10; *Monthly Film Bulletin*, 31 October 1936, p. 170.

101. On the creation of DPR, see PRO, WO 32/4587.

102. L. H. Suid, *Guts and Glory: Great American War Movies* (Reading, MA, 1978), pp. 24–25.

103. *Film Weekly*, 22 January 1937, p. 10; see BFI script 4373, *OHMS*, 31 July 1937.

104. See *Manchester Guardian*, 21 January 1937, p. 18; *Film Weekly*, 22 January 1937, p. 10.

105. See BFI Special Collections, BBFC Scenario Reports, 75, 1936; *Manchester Guardian*, 21 January 1937, p. 18.

106. *The Times*, 21 January 1937, p. 10.

107. *Manchester Guardian*, 21 January 1937, p. 18; *The Times*, 21 January 1937, p. 10; *Kinematograph Weekly*, 28 January 1937, p. 28; see also *Monthly Film Bulletin*, 31 January 1937, pp. 10–11; *Glasgow Herald*, 23 January 1937, p. 7.

108. Gifford, *British Film Catalogue*, entry 10169; see *Daily Express*, 23 January 1937, p. 4; *Film Weekly*, 22 January 1937, p. 10; *Monthly Film Bulletin*, January 1937, pp. 10–11; *Kinematograph Weekly*, 18 March 1937, p. 45; 8 April 1937, p. 38; 15 April 1937, p. 39. See also Sedgwick, 'Cinema-Going Preferences', p. 34. *OHMS* also provoked a formal protest by the Chinese government to the Foreign

Office – the file on which, alas, was not retained. See *Index to the Correspondence of the Foreign Office, 1936*, pt 1 (London, 1969), p. 466.

109. *Film Weekly*, 17 April 1937, p. 7; *The Times*, 8 April 1937, p. 14. On production of *The Gap* see PRO, WO 32/2689; see also PRO, WO 32/4587, encl. 1A, report to PUS, 3 April 1937, p. 8; Gifford, entry 10246.

110. *The Times*, 8 April 1937, p. 14; *Film Weekly*, 17 April 1937, p. 7. The Nazi press took great exception to *The Gap*. For the (unpreserved) FO files on the subject see *Index to the General Correspondence of the Foreign Office 1937*, pt 1 (London, 1969), p. 507.

111. BFI, *Farewell Again* pressbook.

112. BFI, *Farewell Again* pressbook, reviews; *Monthly Film Bulletin*, 31 August 1937, p. 165.

113. *Spectator*, 14 May 1937, p. 903; *Daily Express*, 7 May 1937, p. 4; *Daily Telegraph*, 10 May 1937, p. 5. Dixon, unlike Allot, thought that the film 'treats of the Tommy without degenerating into slobbering sentiment on the one hand or howling farce on the other'. See also *The Times*, 10 May 1937, p. 12; *Film Weekly*, 15 May 1937, p. 27.

114. Gifford, *British Film Catalogue*, entry 10256. See also Sedgwick, 'Cinema-Going Preferences', p. 34. On Flora Robson in *Farewell Again* see K. Barrow, *Flora* (London, 1981), p. 108. On TA involvement in publicizing the film see, e.g., *Kinematograph Weekly*, 18 November 1937, p. 50, 2 December 1937 p. 44.

115. On *Four Feathers* see R. C. Sherriff, *No Leading Lady* (London, 1948), p. 293; PRO, FO 395/655, P917/143/150, Wilkinson to Kennedy, 11 March 1939. On *The Drum* see BFI, *The Drum* pressbook.

116. On problems with *The Drum* see Richards, *Dream Palace*, p. 137. On problems with *The Four Feathers* see PRO, FO 395/655, P553/143/150, P1237/143/150. *OHMS* had prompted an official complaint by the Chinese government (as had *The Flight Commander*): this time apparently to no avail. See, in lieu of the destroyed file, *Index to the Correspondence of the Foreign Office, 1936*, pt 1 (London, 1969), p. 466. On the anti-Chinese scenes see Robertson, *British Board of Film Censors*, pp. 67, 70.

117. Gifford, *British Film Catalogue*, entries 10461, 10607. On *The Drum* see *The Times*, 5 April 1938, p. 14; *Telegraph*, 11 April 1938, p. 7; *Daily Express*, 8 April 1938, p. 10. On *The Four Feathers* see *The Times*, 18 April 1939, p. 12; *Daily Express*, 21 April 1939, p. 12; *Daily Telegraph*, 24 April 1939, p. 4. On TA recruiting see, e.g., *Kinematograph Weekly*, 20 October 1939, p. 24. The War Minister, Leslie Hore-Belisha, along with a number of senior military and naval figures, attended the premiere of *The Four Feathers*. *The Times*, 18 April 1939, p. 9.

118. PRO, FO 395/660, P2899/281/150, PR2 list, 1 July 1939; see L. Wood (ed.), *The Commercial Imperative in the British Film Industry: Maurice Elvey, a Case Study* (London, 1987), p. 25; *Monthly Film Bulletin*, 30 April 1939, p. 68.

119. *Monthly Film Bulletin*, June 1935, p. 71; see Shortt, *Screening Propaganda*, p. 2.

120. *Monthly Film Bulletin*, 31 January 1939, p. 63. On RAF publicity efforts see PRO, AIR 2/4038, Publicity Committee progress report no. 27, 31 March 1939;

Paris, *Wright Brothers to Top Gun*, p. 107. The Admiralty certainly thought that the RAF was well ahead in terms of publicity. See ADM 1/19195, CNI 1086/45, 25 July 1945, p. 3. Another reason for the absence of features supported by the Air Ministry may have been a desire to avoid the public embarrassment suffered by the Admiralty in the 1932 court case over royalties. See PRO, AIR 2/514. On the RAF's generally positive relations with the press, see AIR 19/43–44.

121. PRO, AIR 2/2812, Report of the Publicity Committee set up to consider and formulate proposals as to the publicity measures required in the interests of the Royal Air Force, 29 September 1937, pp. 5, 2.

122. On the development of the DPR, see AIR 41/9, p. 5; AIR 2/4038.

123. Though the navy did help with *All at Sea* and *The Middle Watch*, and possibly *Luck of the Navy* (Associated British, 1938) – see BFI, *Luck of the Navy* pressbook – there is no evidence of Admiralty cooperation in, for instance, *Jack Ahoy!* (Gaumont, 1934) – where only studio sets were used; see J. Lukins (comp.) *The Fantasy Factory: Lime Grove Studios, London* (London, 1996), p. 36 – *Trust the Navy* (St George's, 1935), or War Office help with *Josser in the Army* (British International, 1932), *Many Tanks, Mr Aitkins* (First National, 1938), or comedy in general.

124. See AIR 2/2812, p. 2; Paris, *Wright Brothers to Top Gun*, p. 104; on *Things to Come* see C. Frayling, *Things to Come* (London, 1995), p. 76. On *Shadow of the Wing* see Shortt, *Screening Propaganda*, pp. 5–6.

125. To judge by the high proportion of comedies made. See Shafer, 'Cinema-Going Preferences', p. 30.

126. See *Kinematograph Weekly*, 27 April 1939, p. 58; PRO, AIR 2/4038, Publicity Committee progress report no. 27, 31 March 1939, p. 7. On recruiting problems see M. Smith, *British Air Strategy between the Wars* (Oxford, 1984), pp. 176, 220.

127. *Kinematograph Weekly*, 19 November 1936, p. 39; ibid., 14 January 1937, p. 95; *Monthly Film Bulletin*, 28 February 1937, p. 30; see Gifford, *British Film Catalogue*, entry 10179.

128. On the change to the new uniforms see James, *Paladins*, p. 182.

129. PRO, AIR 2/4038, Publicity Committee, progress report no. 27, 31 March 1939, pp. 7–8.

130. See B. Dean, *Mind's Eye: An Autobiography, 1927–1972* (London, 1973), p. 214; J. Richards and D. Sheridan, *Mass-Observation at the Movies* (London, 1987), FR 198, p. 197; A. Randall and R. Seaton, *George Formby* (London, 1974), pp. 72–74; D. Bret, *George Formby* (London, 1999), pp. 74–78; Gifford, *British Film Catalogue*, entry 10539; *Kinematograph Weekly*, 11 January 1940, p. E1; *The Times*, 16 January 1939, p. 10; *Daily Telegraph*, 16 January 1939, p. 4; *Monthly Film Bulletin*, 30 September 1938, p. 218.

131. *Q Planes*, a Harefield (Columbia) film produced by Irving Asher and Alexander Korda, and directed by Tim Whelan, starred Laurence Olivier, Valerie Hobson and Ralph Richardson. *Spies of the Air*, released two months later, featured Barry K. Barnes, Roger Livesey and Joan Marion. See Gifford, *British Film*

Catalogue, entries 10582, 10599; *Kinematograph Weekly,* 11 Jan. 1940, p. 7; *Monthly Film Bulletin,* 31 May 1939, p. 93.

132. There were fifteen films in which the services took a hand, as against thirty-five in which they did not. Gifford, *British Film Catalogue,* passim.

133. On the origins of the MoI see I. McLaine, *Ministry of Morale: Home Morale and the Ministry of Information in World War II* (London, 1979), ch. 1. See also P. M. Taylor, 'If War Should Come: Preparing the Fifth Arm for Total War', *Journal of Contemporary History,* 16 (1981), pp. 27–51.

134. See, e.g., G. P. Thomson, *Blue Pencil Admiral: The Inside Story of the Press Censorship* (London, 1947), pp. 1, 2, 171. On the relative failure of efforts to centralize government publicity see Grant, *Propaganda and State,* ch. 7.

135. On tensions over censorship see, e.g., Thomson, *Blue-Pencil Admiral,* passim; PRO, INF 1/178; AIR 2/4207; AIR 2/5090; AIR 5322; AIR 2/6163; ADM 1/20123.

136. See, e.g., PRO, INF 1/860, Mountbatten to Bracken, 10 September 1942.

137. On the progress of the MoI films division see J. Chapman, *The British at War: Cinema, State and Propaganda, 1939–1945* (London, 1988), chs 1–3. See also P. M. Taylor, 'Techniques of Persuasion: Basic Ground Rules of British Propaganda during the Second World War', *Historical Journal of Film, Radio and Television* 1 (1981), pp. 57–75; J. C. Robertson, 'British Film Censorship Goes to War', *Historical Journal of Film, Radio and Television,* 2 (1982), pp. 49–64. As Sidney Gilliat pointed out in a BBC interview, formal requests for cooperation in films involving the services went via the MoI. National Film and Televison Archive, C. Frayling, 'Filming for Victory: British Cinema, 1939–1945' (BBC 1, 24 September 1989). As we shall see, however, such requests were often pro forma, coming *after* a commercial company and a service ministry had begun to talk.

138. Chapman, *British at War,* chs 5–6; see also PRO, ADM 1/12044, Duncan to Alexander, 1 January 1942. The navy also had a film unit, but it was used only for in-house training films. See 'Film Progress in the Services', *Documentary News Letter,* 4 (1943), pp. 210–14.

Notes to Chapter 2: On Target: The Royal Air Force and Feature Films, 1939–1945

1. On public anxiety over bombing at the start of the war, see PRO, CAB 102/848, MoI monograph, p. 1. On concerns about war in the air during the 1930s see U. Bailer, *The Shadow of the Bomber: The Fear of Air Attack and British Politics, 1932–1939* (London, 1980); I. F. Clarke, *Voices Prophesying War: Future Wars, 1763–3749* (Oxford, 1992), pp. 153–62. On air power theory see D. MacIsaac, 'Voices from the Central Blue: The Air Power Theorists', *Makers of Modern Strategy: From Machiavelli to the Nuclear Age,* P. Paret, ed. (Princeton, 1986), ch. 21. On *Things to Come* see C. Frayling, *Things to Come* (London, 1995).

2. I. Dalrymple, 'The Crown Film Unit, 1940–43', *Propaganda, Politics and Film, 1918–45,* N. Pronay and D. W. Spring, eds (London, 1982), p. 209; see M. Powell,

A Life in Movies: An Autobiography (London, 1986), p. 329; BFI, NFT Interviews, M. Powell, 1971; *Daily Film Renter*, 6 November 1939, p. 2; I. Dalrymple in I. Christie (ed.), *Powell, Pressburger and Others* (London, 1978), p. 26; K. Kulik, *Alexander Korda: The Man Who Could Work Miracles* (New Rochelle, NY, 1975), pp. 232–33. Churchill had acted as an adviser in the mid 1930s on Korda's ill-fated story of flight, *Conquest of the Air*. See Churchill College, Cambridge, Churchill Papers, CHAR 8/514/16, Cunynghame to Churchill, 15 May 1935; ibid., CHAR 8/514/84–91, Churchill's comments on 'Conquest of the Air' scenario, 10 June 1935. On Churchill as film fan see D. J. Wenden, 'Churchill, Radio and Cinema', *Churchill*, R. Blake and W. R. Louis, eds (Oxford, 1993), p. 226; D. J. Wenden and K. R. M. Short, 'Winston S. Churchill: Film Fan', *Historical Journal of Film, Radio and Television*, 11 (1981), pp. 197–214.

3. Dalrymple in E. Sussex, *The Rise and Fall of the British Documentary* (Berkeley, 1975), p. 124.

4. Powell, *Life*, pp. 332–34; see K. R. M. Shortt, *Screening the Propaganda of British Air Power* (Trowbridge, 1997), p. 24; J. Falconer, *RAF Bomber Command in Fact, Film and Fiction* (Phoenix Mill, 1996), p. 82. On Treasury agreement to support the making of the film see PRO, TS/27/474.

5. Shortt, *Screening Propaganda*, p. 22.

6. See M. Middlebrook and C. Everitt, *The Bomber Command War Diaries: An Operational Reference Book, 1939–1945* (Harmondsworth, 1985), p. 22. The Kiel Raid, however, continued to figure prominently in wartime publicity for Bomber Command over the next twelve months and beyond. See, e.g., T. Stanhope Sprigg, *The Royal Air Force* (London, 1941), pp. 26, 60–62.

7. Shortt, *Screening Propaganda*, p. 20.

8. Powell, *Life*, p. 335.

9. Ibid., p. 330. In an interview Powell went further, calling it 'an outrageous piece of propaganda'. National Film and Television Archive, 'The South Bank Show: Michael Powell', 26 October 1986. See also Watt in Sussex, p. 120. See C. Chapman, *The British at War: Cinema, State and Propaganda, 1939–1945* (London, 1998), p. 60; C. Coultass, *Images for Battle: British Film and the Second World War, 1939–1945* (London, 1989), pp. 20–23; A. Aldgate and J. Richards, *Britain Can Take It: The British Cinema in the Second World War* (2nd edn Edinburgh, 1994), p. 23.

10. M-O FR–24, 'The Cinema in the First Three Months of the War,' in J. Richards and D. Sheridan, *Mass-Observation at the Movies* (London, 1987), p. 167.

11. *Picturegoer*, 13 January 1940, p. 28; see *Monthly Film Bulletin*, 6 (1939), p. 201; Sussex, *Rise and Fall of British Documentary*, p. 120.

12. *Spectator*, 3 November 1939, p. 619. See also M-O FR 24 in Richards and Sheridan, p. 167; *Documentary News Letter*, 1 (1940), p. 8; *The Times*, 31 October 1939, p. 4. Harry Watt was wrong, however, in implying that actors playing officers were deliberately given spotless white overalls while Other Rank aircrew wore dark colours; see Watt in Sussex, *Rise and Fall of British Documentary*, p. 120. White overalls were used because the documentary footage of the real

Kiel raiders which followed the staged sequence showed some of the aircrew dressed in pre-war white coveralls – including some NCOs. On the Kiel Raid see J. Terraine, *The Right of the Line: The Royal Air Force in the European War, 1939–1945* (London, 1985), pp. 99–100.

13. *The Times*, 14 November 1939, p. 5; see ibid., 3 November 1939, p. 9, 21 October 1939, p. 3.

14. Richards and Sheridan, *Mass-Observation*, pp. 153–54.

15. *Yorkshire Post*, 28 November 1939, p. 3; *Daily Telegraph*, 31 October 1939, p. 3. *Manchester Guardian* (London edn), 31 October 1939, p. 7; *Daily Express*, 31 October 1939, p. 11; *The Times*, 31 October 1939, p. 4; *Picturegoer*, 16 December 1939, p. 14; *Today's Cinema*, 31 October 1939, p. 10.

16. Chapman, *British at War*, p. 62. On the popularity of *The Lion Has Wings* in the UK, see *Kinematograph Weekly*, 11 January 1940, p. E1; G. Morgan, *Red Roses Every Night* (London, 1948), p. 26; J. Poole, 'British Cinema Attendance in Wartime: Audience Preference at the Majestic, Macclesfield, 1939–1946', *Historical Journal of Film, Radio and Television*, 7 (1987), p. 20. On the film in the USA see N. J. Cull, *Selling War: The British Propaganda Campaign Against American 'Neutrality' in World War II* (New York, 1995), p. 49. On RAF help with publicity, see, e.g., *Kinematograph Weekly*, 4 January 1940, p. 18, 11 January 1940, p. 26.

17. H. Watt, *Don't Look at the Camera!* (London, 1974), pp. 130–34; Watt in Sussex, *British Documentary*, p. 118.

18. BFI, NFT Interviews, H. Watt, 1974; see note 17; *Manchester Guardian*, 2 July 1940, p. 6; *Daily Express*, 25 June 1940, p. 6. On the merits of *Squadron 922* as a piece of filmmaking, see *New Statesman and Nation*, 8 June 1940, pp. 724–25.

19. See, e.g., PRO, AIR 14/1451, minutes 2 and 3.

20. PRO, INF 1/857, A. P. Ryan memo, 4 June 1941. See P. M. Taylor, 'Film as a Weapon during the Second World War', *Statecraft and Diplomacy in the Twentieth Century*, D. Dutton, ed. (Liverpool, 1995), p. 135. Despite involvement in prewar comedies, the Air Ministry did not lend a hand in the making of the low-budget and low-brow Butcher Films RAF comedy *Garrison Follies*, released in the summer of 1940. On this film see *Monthly Film Bulletin*, 31 July 1940, p. 109.

21. D. Niven, *The Moon's a Balloon* (London, 1971), p. 203. The playwright Terence Rattigan also had a difficult time joining the RAF, only managing to gain a favourable impression by mentioning that he was the author of *French Without Tears* (which, for some reason, seems to have been regarded as evidence of moral fibre). G. Wansell, *Terence Rattigan* (London, 1995), p. 109; see also J. Le Mesurier, *A Jobbing Actor* (London, 1984), pp. 48–49.

22. Watt, *Don't Look at the Camera*, p. 130.

23. PRO, AIR 2/5325, 2B, note from ACAS(G) to PS to S of S, 14 May 1941. See also AIR 2/5325, memo to MoI, April 1941.

24. PRO, AIR 14/80, Harris to HQ, 12 September 1040. See also AIR 2/5325, ACAS(G) to PS to S of S, 14 May 1941.

25. The hypothetical case explained below (see n. 26) was probably similar to what transpired in filming a few scenes of a 75 Squadron Wellington on the ground and in the air for *The Day Will Dawn* (Niksos, 1942) and of a Lancaster for *Millions Like Us* (Gainsborough, 1943), in which the love interest of the principal character is an RAF air gunner.

26. PRO, AIR 41/9, AHB Narrative on Press and Publicity, pp. 2–3.

27. On 'Britain's RAF', *March of Time*, 7, no. 2 (October 1940), see *Kinematograph Weekly*, 31 October 1940, p. 29; *Monthly Film Bulletin*, 30 November 1940, p. 179. On *The March of Time* series and British propaganda in the USA see Cull, *Selling War*, pp. 46, 212 n. 49; R. Fielding, *The March of Time, 1935–1951* (New York, 1978), p. 254. In 1942, when *The Battle of Britain* was made as part of the US Army's 'Why We Fight' series, director Frank Capra was supplied with existing footage (including some from *The Lion Has Wings* as well as a number of short documentaries), apparently without Air Ministry involvement. On *The Battle of Britain* see A. Calder, *The Myth of the Blitz* (London, 1992 edn), pp. 245–50; T. W. Bohn, 'An Historical and Descriptive Analysis of the "Why We Fight" Series' (unpublished Ph.D. thesis, University of Wisconsin, 1968).

28. *Kinematograph Weekly*, 7 November 1940, p. 1. For a defence of the Air Ministry position, see H. Chevalier in *Kinematograph Weekly*, 28 November 1940, p. 33.

29. Richards and Sheridan, *Mass-Observation*, p. 365; *Kinematograph Weekly*, 7 November 1940, p. 1.

30. *Kinematograph Weekly*, 9 January 1941, p. 86.

31. Ibid., 27 March 1941, p. 21. See ibid., 16 January 1941, p. 39, 5 December 1940, p. 23.

32. Ibid., 16 October 1941, p. 29. On Leslie Howard's role in the making of the picture see L. R. Howard, *A Quite Remarkable Father* (New York, 1959), pp. 281–82. On 1426 Enemy Aircraft Flight see M. J. F. Bowyer, *Action Stations*, i, *Wartime Military Airfields of East Anglia, 1939–1945* (Cambridge, 1979), p. 105.

33. *Daily Express*, 22 August 1942, p. 2; *Daily Herald*, 22 August 1942, p. 2. Even those critics who were unsure if Howard's account of R. J. Mitchell's career was true to life evidently thought it ought to be. See *The Times*, 20 August 1942, p. 2; *Daily Telegraph*, 24 August 1942, p. 2; *Manchester Guardian*, 6 October 1942, p. 3; *Spectator*, 28 August 1942, p. 194; *Monthly Film Bulletin*, 30 September 1942, p. 111. Even *Documentary News Letter*, the organ of the documentary movement whose critics habitually disliked commercial dramas, grudgingly admitted that the film had 'many good points'. *Documentary News Letter*, September 1942, p. 128.

34. *Kinematograph Weekly*, 14 January 1943, p. 47; 1943 M-O Directive replies in Richards and Sheridan, *Mass-Observation*, pp. 223, 229, 233–34, 239, 242, 246, 287, 248, 256, 262, 265, 269, 270, 280, 284, 288; J. P. Mayer, *British Cinemas and their Audiences: Sociological Studies* (London, 1948), p. 177; V. Hodgson, *Few Eggs and No Oranges: A Diary* (London, 1976), p. 369.

35. M. Gilbert, *Winston S. Churchill*, vi, *Finest Hour, 1939–1941* (London, 1983),

p. 770; see also Churchill to Beaverbrook, 8 July 1940, in W. S. Churchill, *Second World War*, iii, *Their Finest Hour* (London, 1949), p. 567.

36. See Middlebrook and Everitt, *War Diaries*, chs 5–6.

37. This is not to suggest that Fighter Command received no PR support at all in the domestic context. HMSO, for example, published an Air Ministry pamphlet on the Battle of Britain in 1941, and support was afforded for various commercial publishing efforts. See PRO, INF 1/249, planning committee, 6 March 1941; C. Graves, *The Thin Blue Line* (London, 1940); A. B. Austin, *Fighter Command* (London, 1941). An inspiring letter, written by a Battle of Britain fighter pilot killed in action and first published in *The Times*, became both a pamphlet and a short film under the title *An Airman's Letter to his Mother*. See Coultass, *British at War*, pp. 57, 200 n. 60; Falconer, *Bomber Command*, pp. 84–86.

38. PRO, AIR 49/9, p. 4; see AIR 14/1451, minute 2, Lawrence to Bootham, 21 November 1941; A. Harris, *Bomber Command*, p. 156.

39. PRO, AIR 14/80, HQ to Groups, 4 December 1939.

40. See, e.g., S/L S. Sprigg, *The Royal Air Force* (London, 1941); 'The Aeroplane', *The Royal Air Force at War* (London, 1941); *Winged Words: Our Airmen Speak for Themselves* (London, 1941). The Air Ministry also did its best to suppress unfavourable reports on the RAF. See PRO, AIR 2/6555, enclosure 27A.

41. See PRO, AIR 14/1451, minute 43, D/SASO to AOA, 17 July 1942; AIR 2/5325, minute 2, enclosure 2B, ACAS(G) to PS to S of S, 14 May 1941; E. Bishop, *The Guinea Pig Club* (London, 1963), pp. 27–28.

42. F. J. Assersohn, 'Propaganda and Policy: The Presentation of the Strategic Air Offensive in the British Mass Media, 1939–45' (unpublished MA Thesis, Leeds University, 1989), pp. 5–6, 10, 15–16, 19, 19–22; see PRO, CAB 102/848, 'A People at War: Thought and Mood on the Home Front', S. Taylor, p. 5; see also, e.g., N. Macmillan, *Air Strategy* (London, 1941), pp. 125, 128.

43. PRO, INF 1/249, planning committee, 20 March 1941; see M-O, FR 142, 27 May 1940.

44. PRO, AIR 14/1451, minute 14.

45. *Winged Words*, pp. 99–100. On the RAF and radio broadcasts see S. Nicholas, *The Echo of War: Home Front Propaganda and the Wartime BBC, 1939–45* (Manchester, 1996), pp. 201–2.

46. See *Winged Words*, pp. 140, 149, 160–61, 170, 174, 230, 252.

47. M. Renault, *Terror by Night: A Bomber Pilot's Story* (London, 1982), p. 41; see M. Hastings, *Bomber Command: The Myth and Reality of the Strategic Air Offensive, 1939–45* (London, 1979), pp. 83–85.

48. PRO, AIR 14/1451, minute 14.

49. PRO, AIR 14/1451, Lawrence to Bootham, 21 November 1940.

50. *House of Commons Parliamentary Debates*, 5th series, vol. 364, col. 187.

51. PRO, INF 1/210, Bomber Command Film outline; see also INF 5/78, Fletcher to Betjeman, 8 November 1940. On Watt's claim to having taken the initiative see Watt, *Camera*, p. 146; Watt in Sussex, *British Documentary*, p. 128. On the

likelihood that the initiative originated within the Air Ministry, see K. R. M. Short, 'RAF Bomber Command's *Target for Tonight* (1941)', *Historical Journal of Film, Radio and Television*, 17 (1997), pp. 182–84. The Air Ministry may also have been influenced by the effectiveness of German propaganda films as presented in the MoI study *Film as a Weapon*, shown to senior service figures in March 1941. See P. M. Taylor, 'Film as a Weapon during the Second World War', *Statecraft and Diplomacy in the Twentieth Century*, D. Dutton, ed. (Liverpool, 1995), p. 148.

52. PRO, INF 1/210, Bomber Command film outline.

53. BFI, NFT Interviews, H. Watt, 1974.

54. PRO, INF 5/78, Lawrence to Williams, 29 January 1941; ibid., Watt to Williams, 7 February 1941. On the Griersonian tradition and its influence see Sussex, *British Documentary*, passim; Chapman, *British at War*, passim.

55. Comparing Watt's complaints with the kind of bureaucratic problems outlined in the AHB history of DPR is instructive. See Watt, *Camera*, pp. 146, 148–49; Watt in Sussex, *British Documentary*, pp. 129–30; PRO, AIR 41/9, pp. 2–4. On the filming and costs of *Target for Tonight* – a four-reeler originally supposed to be only two reels in length – see Short, '*Target*', pp. 186–89. On the Wellington which played 'F for Freddie' at Mildenhall see Bowyer, *Action Stations*, i, p. 162.

56. PRO, INF 1/210. Script for 'A Target is Bombed', shots 258–59, 261. The rear-gunner's comment is missing from the filmed version, but the destruction of the target is just as vivid as described.

57. Q. Reynolds, *By Quentin Reynolds* (London, 1963), p. 228; see Short, '*Target*', p. 194.

58. *Spectator*, 1 August 1941, p. 106; *New Statesman*, 2 August 1941, p. 111; *Picturegoer*, 16 August 1941, p. 3; *Kinematograph Weekly*, 31 July 1941, p. 13, 24 July 1941, p. 6; see *Manchester Guardian*, 25 July 1941, p. 3; *The Times*, 24 July 1941, p. 6; *Daily Express*, 24 July 1941, p. 1; *Sight and Sound*, 10 (1941), p. 48; Watt, *Camera*, pp. 151–52; Short, '*Target*', p. 195.

59. P. Holt, *Target for Tonight. The Book of the Famous Film Target for Tonight: The Record in Text and Pictures of a Bombing Raid on Germany* (London, 1941); PRO, INF 1/210, Griggs to Williams, 16 July 1941.

60. *Kinematograph Weekly*, 14 August 1941, p. 4; see ibid., 8 January 1942, p. 37.

61. Richards and Sheridan, *Mass-Observation*, answer 2 to 1943 M-O Directive; see ibid., pp. 372, 218; Paris, *Wright Brothers to Top Gun*, pp. 143–44. On the psychological eagerness to believe the message see Edgar Anstey in *Spectator*, 5 May 1944, p. 406; F. Hardy, 'The British Documentary Film', *Twenty Years of British Film, 1925–1945* (London, 1947), p. 57. Watt himself shared this feeling, Watt, *Camera*, p. 146.

62. See Hastings, *Bomber Command*, p. 103; M. Pedan, *A Thousand Shall Fall* (Stittsville, ON, 1979), p. 280; Short, '*Target*', p. 194; *Documentary News Letter*, 2 (1942), p. 147; *Kinematograph Weekly*, 4 September 1941, p. 37, 11 September 1941, p. 33, 18 September 1941, p. 33, 2 October 1941, p. 42. On *Target for Tonight*

in America and elsewhere see Short, '*Target*', pp. 196–99; Cull, *Selling War*, p. 137.

63. K. Buckman, 'The Royal Air Force Film Production Unit, 1941–45', *Historical Journal of Film, Radio and Television*, 17 (1997), pp. 219–20; PRO, AIR 2/5325, enclosure 2 B, Memorandum on Publicity for the RAF, p. 4, ACAS(G) to PS to S of S, 14 May 1941; Imperial War Museum Department of Film, B6/1, History of the Royal Air Force Film Production Unit, 1946, p. 1.

64. C. Webster and N. Frankland, *The Strategic Air Offensive Against Germany, 1939–1945*, iv (HMSO, 1961), p. 205.

65. PRO, AIR 8/440, Churchill to Portal, 19 September 1941.

66. D. Richards, *Portal of Hungerford* (London, 1977), pp. 89–90.

67. PRO, AIR 41/40, AHB Narrative: The RAF Bombing Offensive Against Germany, ii, June 1941-February 1942, p. 65. On the centrality of strategic bombing to the RAF see S. Robertson, *The Development of RAF Strategic Bombing Doctrine, 1919–1939* (Westport, CT, 1995).

68. *Bomber Command: The Air Ministry Account of the Bomber Command's Offensive Against the Axis* (HMSO, 1941), p. 124. See also P. F. M. Fellowes (ed.), *Britain's Wonderful Air Force* (London, 1942), ch. 5 (which included, interestingly, a still from *Target for Tonight*, p. 118); *We Speak from the Air: Broadcasts by the RAF* (HMSO, 1942); Assersohn, 'Presentation of Strategic Air Offensive', passim.

69. *Kinematograph Weekly*, 27 March 1941, p. 33.

70. R. Harrison, *Rex: An Autobiography* (London, 1974), pp. 74–75. Harrison became a Flying Control Officer.

71. *Daily Express*, 14 November 1941, p. 3; see *Kinematograph Weekly*, 28 November 1941.

72. PRO, INF 1/249, Planning Committee minutes, 16 December 1940.

73. *Kinematograph Weekly*, 31 July 1941, p. 17; PRO, T 162/1002, 'Big Blockade', file E43147.

74. See, e.g., J. Slessor, *The Central Blue: The Autobiography of Sir John Slessor, Marshal of the RAF* (London, 1957), ch. 14.

75. M. Balcon, *Michael Balcon Presents … A Lifetime of Films* (London, 1969), p. 136.

76. *The Times*, 14 January 1942, p. 6; see *Manchester Guardian*, 31 March 1942, p. 3; *Monthly Film Bulletin*, 28 February 1942, p. 13; *New Statesman*, 17 January 1942, p. 40; *Spectator*, 6 January 1942, p. 58; *Documentary News Letter*, 3 (1942), p. 67. On Ealing publicity efforts see BFI, *The Big Blockade* pressbook. On the problems of putting the film together see C. Crichton in B. McFarlane, *An Autobiography of British Cinema as Told by the Filmmakers and Actors who Made it* (London, 1997), p. 152. *The Big Blockade* was not mentioned at all in the Mass-Observation surveys. See Richards and Sheridan, *Mass-Observation*, passim. The Ministry of Economic Warfare regarded the film as a failure. W. N. Medlicott, *The Economic Blockade*, ii (HMSO, 1959), p. 52. United Artists, the distributors, were even sued in Argentina by the Germans for illegally

incorporating footage from a captured Nazi film, 'Baptism of Fire'. PRO, FO 371/37739, file 664, 1944; FO 371/33595, file 5019, 1943.

77. *Daily Telegraph*, 29 December 1941, p. 3. For a more positive response see *Monthly Film Bulletin*, 31 October 1941, p. 156; see, with reference to RAF cooperation, PRO, AIR 20/2950, DPR Progress Report, 30 September 1941, p. 5; H. M. Glancy, *When Hollywood Loved Britain: The Hollywood 'British' Film, 1939–45* (Manchester, 1999), p. 120. Sidney Bernstein, as MoI Films Division representative, was more concerned to persuade 20th Century Fox to change the plot in order to keep the hero alive – a Yank dying for England might send the wrong signals – than anything else: though he did strive to make *Eagle Squadron* (a Universal picture about American fighter pilots in the RAF destined for the US market) less inauthentic than it might otherwise have been. See C. Moorehead, *Sidney Bernstein* (London, 1984), p. 156. In contrast to the high-brow critics, the average cinemagoer appears to have engaged in willing suspension of disbelief when viewing US portrayals of England. *A Yank in the RAF* tied for second place at the box office in February 1942, and *Eagle Squadron* for third in September. *Mrs Miniver* was the most popular film of the year. *Kinematograph Weekly*, 14 January 1943, p. 47; see also Poole, 'British Cinema Attendance', p. 22.

78. PRO, INF 1/625, Williams to Beddington, 25 May 1941. *Eagle Squadron*, eventually made by Universal in 1942, used existing documentary material purchased from the MoI. It too was a hit. Glancy, *Hollywood Loved Britain*, pp. 122–27.

79. PRO, AIR 28/625, RAF Polebrook operations record book, 11 October 1941; *Kinematograph Weekly*, 16 October 1941, p. 29; see also PRO, AIR 41/9, films section, p. 4; *Monthly Film Bulletin*, 30 June 1942, p. 69.

80. *Daily Express*, 13 June 1942, p. 2; *Daily Mail*, 12 June 1942, p. 2; see *The Times*, 15 June 1942, p. 8; *News Chronicle*, 13 June 1942, p. 2.

81. Ibid. On the Flying Fortress in RAF service see J. Terraine, *The Right of the Line: The Royal Air Force in the European War, 1939–1945* (London, 1985), pp. 279–80.

82. J. Bennett and S. Godwin, *Godfrey: A Special Time Remembered* (London, 1983), p. 72. See also *Monthly Film Bulletin*, 30 April 1942, p. 42, where the BFI critic labelled it 'an exceedingly good flying-war film'.

83. Powell, *Life*, pp. 384–85, 387–88. See K. Gough-Yates, *Michael Powell in Collaboration with Emeric Pressburger* (London, 1971), p. 8. Also NFTA, 202268A, 'All Our Yesterdays: Michael Powell' interview, 23 April 1972. On the resistance genre see Chapman, *British at War*, ch. 10.

84. Pilot Officer A. Wilson was killed over Germany while serving as a tail gunner in November 1940.

85. BFI, *One of Our Aircraft is Missing* pressbook; *Kinematograph Weekly*, 4 September 1941, p. 15, 11 September 1941, p. 21, 18 September 1941, p. 17; Powell, *Life*, p. 391; Powell in Gough-Yates, *Powell*, p. 7.

86. The flying sequences of the two films are so similar that they have led even a seasoned observer to conclude that Powell must have used footage from

Watt's film. See Falconer, *Bomber Command*, p. 86. Repeated close observation suggests this is not in fact the case.

87. Falconer, *Bomber Command*, p. 87.

88. Hugh Williams, while later serving in the British Army in North Africa, was struck by the way in which a decorated fellow-officer appeared to think appearing in *One of Our Aircraft is Missing* made Williams more of a hero than himself – an incident which suggests that fiction was being confused with fact and, by extension, that the cast had been extremely convincing. H. Williams to M. Williams, 14 March 1943, in K. Dunn (ed.), *Always and Always: The Wartime Letters of Hugh and Margaret Williams* (London, 1995), p. 87. It is perhaps significant that the RAF Film Unit, in making *Journey Together* in 1945, chose to use actors already in the air force rather than repeat Watt's formula. See Buckman, 'RAF Film Unit', p. 234.

89. See Mass-Observation, film topic box 2, file 2H, report by Len England, 15 September 1941; *New Statesmen*, 2 August 1941, p. 111. Jack Warner was so overwhelmed by the accent – though he professed enthusiasm in front of the Englishman who had brought him the film – that he had *Target for Tonight* dubbed before it was released in the USA. See *Daily Express*, 17 November 1941, p. 2; Cull, *Selling War*, p. 137.

90. On Pressburger's successful efforts to distill British character see K. Macdonald, *Emeric Pressburger: The Life and Death of a Screenwriter* (London, 1994), pp. 127, 229–31.

91. See D. Powell, *Films since 1939* (London, 1947), p. 22.

92. *The Times*, 25 April 1942, p. 6, 21 April 1942, p. 2; E. Pressburger, *One of Our Aircraft is Missing* (HMSO, 1942); *Kinematograph Weekly*, 12 March 1942, pp. 32–33, 25 September 1941, p. 14; BFI, *One of Our Aircraft is Missing* press-book.

93. Richards and Sheridan, *Mass-Observation*, pp. 231, 240, 282; *New Statesman*, 2 May 1942, p. 288; *Daily Mirror*, 22 April 1942, p. 3; *Sunday Pictorial*, 26 April 1942, p. 8; *News Chronicle*, 22 April 1942, p. 3; see *Kinematograph Weekly*, 26 March 1942, p. 45; *Glasgow Herald*, 26 December 1942, p. 2; *Daily Express*, 25 April 1942, p. 2; *Sight and Sound*, 11 (1942), p. 18. Typically, the documentary movement types objected to this attempt to dilute the purity of their form. See 'Feature Film Propaganda', *Documentary News Letter*, May 1942, p. 67. Yet C. A. Lejeune, a strong supporter, admitted that it was better than most popular pictures. *Observer*, 26 April 1942, p. 7.

94. *New Statesman*, 2 May 1942, p. 288; *The Times*, 22 April 1942, p. 6.

95. See *Kinematograph Weekly*, 14 January 1943, p. 47; Morgan, *Red Roses Every Night*, p. 46; Poole, 'British Cinema Attendance', p. 22.

96. See, e.g., *Bomber Command Continues: The Air Ministry Account of the Rising Offensive Against Germany, July 1941-June 1942* (HMSO, 1943); L. Cheshire, *Bomber Pilot* (London, 1943), p. 56; H. Hawton, *The Men Who Fly* (London, 1944), p. 8, passim; Assersohn, 'Presentation of Strategic Air Offensive', passim. There was also still great sensitivity to anything which might be regarded as

criticism of the RAF. See, e.g., PRO, AIR 8/619; AIR 8/759; AIR 2/6555; AIR 20/2951, ACAS/(G)/CB/8794, ACAS(G) to VCAS, 10 February 1944; R. Boothby, *Boothby: Recollections of a Rebel* (London, 1978), p. 178.

97. Wartime Social Survey, *The Cinema Audience: An Inquiry Made by the Wartime Social Survey for the Ministry of Information*, L. Moss and K. Box (new series no. 37b, June-July 1943).

98. *Kinematograph Weekly*, 25 June 1942, p. 22, 2 July 1942, p. 17; BFI, E. Betts Papers, 'The Shelterers' Verdict', *Sunday Express*, 20 April 1941; Reg Whitley in *Daily Mirror*, 16 April 1943, p. 7; see Chapman, *British at War*, pp. 79–80.

99. See PRO, PREM4/3/15, Sinclair to Churchill, 22 June 1944; AIR 8/761; AIR 2/7852.

100. Wansell, *Rattigan*, pp. 120–25; T. Rattigan, *The Collected Plays of Terence Rattigan* (London, 1953), p. xiv; ibid., *Flare Path: A Play in Three Acts* (London, 1943), p. 54. On friction with DPR see A. Harris, *Bomber Offensive* (London, 1947), p. 156; PRO, AIR 2/7852. His suspicion of outside publicity makers can only have been deepened by the comparative failure of a radio broadcast he was asked to make which – he later claimed – had been written for him by the Political Warfare Executive. See Harris, *Bomber Offensive*, p. 115; PRO, INF 1/293, HI Special Report No. 27, 7 August 1942.

101. See Harris, *Bomber Offensive*, pp. 104, 157.

102. LHC, King-Hall Papers, box 3, *National News Letter*, 308, 4 June 1942, p. 2; see N. Frankland, *The Bombing Offensive Against Germany: Outlines and Perspectives* (London, 1965), p. 97; PRO, AIR 2/7852; INF 1/293, HI Special Report 38, 3 March 1943; INF 1/292, HI weekly reports 1942–44, passim; Assersohn, ch. 3. When Harris attempted to get the Air Ministry to be more forthright in 1943 (on the grounds that people could cope with the truth if they thought it a means to victory) he was rebuffed. See AIR 2/7852.

103. See E. Anstey in *Spectator*, 5 May 1944, p. 406.

104. On the aborted dams film project see PRO, AIR 2/5546. Hawks instead went on to make *To Have and Have Not* for Warner Brothers. See T. McCarthy, *Howard Hawks* (New York, 1997), chs 24–26. On Gibson being enlisted to publicize his own achievement see R. Morris, *Guy Gibson* (London, 1994), pp. 221–26.

105. An ambitious Korda production featuring the RAF and USAAF, tentatively entitled 'Rendezvous', never got past the planning stage. See *Kinematograph Weekly*, 15 July 1943, p. 19.

106. These included *Millions Like Us* (1943) and – probably for Fighter Command – *The Gentle Sex* (1943), in which boyfriends in the RAF are killed on operations.

107. See C. Coultass, *Images for Battle: British Film and the Second World War, 1939–1945* (Newark, NJ, 1989), pp. 145–46.

108. On *The Way to the Stars* see A. Aldgate and J. Richards, *Britain Can Take It: The British Cinema in the Second World War* (2nd edn, Edinburgh, 1994), ch. 12; see also Powell, *Films Since 1939*, p. 30; R. J. Minney, *'Puffin' Asquith* (London, 1973), pp. 111–15; M. Redgrave, *In My Mind's Eye* (London, 1983),

pp. 171–73; J. Mills, *Up in the Clouds, Gentlemen Please* (London, 1980), p. 193; D. Tomlinson, *Luckier Than Most* (London, 1990), pp. 82–83. On *The Way to the Stars* as 'the' RAF film of the war, see, e.g., G. Perry, *The Great British Picture Show* (London, 1974), p. 112; National Film and Television Archive, 8008.98AA, Christopher Frayling, 'Filming for Victory: British Cinema, 1939–1945', 24 September 1981, D. Powell comment on *Way to the Stars*.

109. It is worth noting in this regard that references to saturation attacks were fairly forthright – if somewhat brief – in the first two postwar films to feature Bomber Command: *A Matter of Life and Death* (Archers, 1946) and *Appointment in London* (Mayflower, 1953).

110. On the making of *Journey Together* see Buckman, 'RAF Film Unit', pp. 232–40; Falconer, *Bomber Command*, p. 91. On the (generally positive) critical reaction see, e.g., *Manchester Guardian*, 5 February 1946, p. 3; *Spectator*, 19 October 1945, p. 359; *New Statesman*, 6 October 1945, p. 228; see also IWM Department of Film, B6/1, History of the Royal Air Force Film Production Unit, p. 6.

111. On rivalry between the commands see PRO, AIR 20/2950.

112. PRO, INF 1/249, home planning committee, 1 May 1941; INF1/86. On Joubert's efforts to raise the profile of Coastal Command and the resources allocated to it, see Terraine, *Right of the Line*, p. 419ff.

113. PRO, INF 6/24, p. 1.

114. *Monthly Film Bulletin*, 31 October 1942, p. 125; see *Spectator*, 23 October 1942, p. 383; *Daily Telegraph*, 19 October 1942, p. 2; *New Statesman*, 17 October 1942, p. 256; *The Times*, 5 October 1942, p. 6; *Daily Herald*, 15 October 1942, p. 3; *Daily Express*, 17 October 1942, p. 2; Dalrymple, 'Crown Film Unit', p. 215.

115. Coultass, *Images for Battle*, pp. 99–100; Paris, *Wright Brothers to Top Gun*, pp. 147–48.

116. On RAF cooperation with cinema managers in boosting the profile of both film and command, see, e.g., *Kinematograph Weekly*, 18 February 1943, p. 28, 11 March 1943, p. 52, 18 March 1943, p. 38.

117. See, e.g., *House of Commons Parliamentary Debates*, 5th series, vol. 378, col. 1032, 11 March 1942; see also PRO, AIR 20/447.

118. *Documentary News Letter*, March 1943, p. 191; *Monthly Film Bulletin*, 28 February 1943, p. 13; *Spectator*, 19 March 1943, pp. 267–68. On the making of *Operational Height* see Buckman, 'RAF Film Unit', pp. 224–28; PRO, INF 6/103.

119. Buckman, 'RAF Film Unit', pp. 228–31; Chapman, *British at War*, p. 155; Coultass, *Images for Battle*, p. 166.

120. *The Times*, 4 September 1944, p. 8; see *Monthly Film Bulletin*, 30 September 1944, p. 99.

121. Hillary had written the script while serving as an Air Ministry adviser to Ealing in 1942. See Balcon, *Michael Balcon Presents*, p. 143.

122. *Daily Express*, 2 July 1944, p. 2; *Monthly Film Bulletin*, 30 April 1944, p. 39; see D. Farrar, *No Royal Road* (London, 1947), pp. 109–13; *Kinematograph Weekly*, 6 April 1944, p. 31; *Daily Mirror*, 30 June 1944, p. 7.

123. Farrar, *No Royal Road*, pp. 113–14; C. Crichton and D. Farrar in McFarlane,

Autobiography, pp. 152, 183–84. See *Daily Express*, 2 July 1944, p. 2; *The Times*, 3 July 1944, p. 8. On the animus towards war films see, e.g., P. L. Mannock in *Kinematograph Weekly*, 25 March 1943, p. 33. Ealing did, to be fair, try and capitalize on the positive trade reviews in its press publicity. See BFI, *For Those in Peril* pressbook.

124. *Spectator*, 19 October 1945, p. 359; see *Manchester Guardian*, 5 February 1946, p. 3; *New Statesman*, 6 October 1945, p. 228; *Kinematograph Weekly*, 4 October 1945, pp. 26, 39.

125. *Daily Mirror*, 5 October 1945, p. 7. One of the actors involved, however, was later informed that *Journey Together* 'has proved very successful'. PRO, INF 12/100, Catch to Watling, 15 January 1947. *Journey Together* may have suffered from the stigma of appearing to be another government-sponsored feature documentary at a time when popular taste was very much in favour of escapism (witness the success of the Gainsborough melodramas of the mid 1940s and 'romantic' war films such as *Way to the Stars* (Two Cities, 1945) and *The Captive Heart* (Ealing, 1946). On the desire for escapism see, e.g., T. Massicks, 'Why Documentaries Fail in Suburban Theatres', *Kinematograph Weekly*, 11 January 1945, p. 90; see also Morgan, *Red Roses*, p. 70. For the popularity of 'romantic' war pictures in 1945–46 see BFI Special Collections, Bernstein Papers, box 5, file A, Report on 1946–47 Questionnaire, p. 21. On the escapist and sensual Gainsborough melodramas – hated by critics but commercially successful – see P. Cook (ed.), *Gainsborough Pictures* (London, 1997); S. Aspinall and R. Murphy (eds), *Gainsborough Melodrama* (London, 1983); S. Harper, *Picturing the Past: The Rise and Fall of the British Costume Film* (London, 1994), ch. 9; National Film and Television Archive, 8014632AB, 'Limelight: The Film Years', BBC, 26 August 1991.

126. P. Ustinov, *Dear Me* (London, 1977), p. 147; see PRO, AIR 2/5667, enclosures 1A–10C, 44A; IWM Department of Film, B6/1, History of the Royal Air Force Film Production Unit, p. 7.

127. P. Ustinov in McFarlane, *Autobiography*, p. 585; see Ustinov, *Dear Me*, pp. 147–50; PRO, AIR 2/5667, encl. 52A, Lod to Lawrence, 13 June 1945.

128. PRO, AIR 2/5567, passim.

129. *Daily Mirror*, 8 November 1946, p. 2; *Daily Mail*, 8 November 1946, p. 4; *News Chronicle*, 9 November 1946, p. 2; *Daily Express*, 8 November 1946, p. 2; *Guardian*, 9 November 1946, p. 5. On the director's intentions see BFI, NFT Interviews, P. Ustinov, 1990. *School for Secrets* appears to have been a success at the box office. See *Kinematograph Weekly*, 18 December 1947, p. 13.

130. In May 1940, the DPR had nineteen people on its staff. By January 1941 the figure had risen to thirty-seven; by January 1942 to sixty-four; and by January 1943 to eighty-five. *Air Force List*.

131. PRO, AIR 2/5325, enclosure 26 A, Bracken to Sinclair, 25 August 1941, enclosure 1A, Cooper to Sinclair, 28 April 1941.

132. PRO, ADM 1/19195, Report by Rear Admiral R. K. Dickson on history of Naval Information, 25 July 1945, p. 4.

133. Mass-Observation Archive, M-O FR 887, p. 1.
134. PRO, AIR 20/2950, undated memorandum, *c.* 1942, p. 1; see IWMSA, H. Stewart, 4579/6, TS, p. 64.

Notes to Chapter 3: Mightier Yet: The Royal Navy and Feature Films, 1939–1945

1. See G. P. Thomson, *Blue Pencil Admiral: The Inside Story of the Press Censorship* (London, 1947), pp. 6, 11; PRO, ADM 1/20123.
2. On *Cavalcade of the Navy*, see *Today's Cinema*, 11 October 1939, p. 9; *Monthly Film Bulletin*, 31 October 1939, p. 185; on *All at Sea* see *Monthly Film Bulletin*, 31 October 1939, p. 185; BFI, *All at Sea* pressbook.
3. See J. Richards and D. Sheridan, *Mass-Observation at the Movies* (London, 1987), pp. 154–55. *Monthly Film Bulletin*, 30 November 1939, p. 21; N. J. Cull, *Selling War: The British Propaganda Campaign Against American 'Neutrality' in World War II* (New York, 1995), p. 212 n. 49; R. Fielding, *The March of Time, 1935–1951* (New York, 1978), p. 254; Southampton University, Mountbatten Papers, MB1/A76, passim.
4. See PRO, ADM 1/19195, CNI 1086/45, pp. 4, 5.
5. W. S. Churchill, *The Gathering Storm* (Boston, 1948), p. 563; M. Gilbert, *Winston S. Churchill*, vi, *Finest Hour, 1939–1941* (London, 1983), pp. 96, 151–54, 169–70.
6. See *Kinematograph Weekly*, 1 February 1940, p. 27; 29 February 1940, p. 4; 21 March 1940, p. 31; 11 April 1940, p. 14; see also L. Wood (ed.), *The Commercial Imperative in the British Film Industry: Maurice Elvey, a Case Study* (London, 1987), p. 26.
7. M-O, FR163, Len England memo on 'For Freedom', 3 June 1940, p. 2.
8. *The Times*, 15 April 1940, p. 4; *Daily Herald*, 12 April 1940, p. 4; see M-O, FR163; Richards and Sheridan, *Mass-Observation*, pp. 355, 380, 399; *Kinematograph Weekly*, 11 April 1940, p. 9, 25 April 1940, pp. 3, 36, 38, 11 July 1940, p. 19; *Daily Telegraph*, 15 April 1940, p. 4; 18 April 1940, p. 22; *Monthly Film Bulletin*, 30 April 1940, p. 54.
9. *Kinematograph Weekly*, 9 January 1941, p. 26; see J. Chapman, *The British at War: Cinema, State and Propaganda, 1939–1945* (London, 1998), p. 181.
10. BFI, *Convoy* pressbook; M. Balcon, *Michael Balcon Presents ... A Lifetime in Films* (London, 1969), p. 129; see D. Morgan in B. McFarlane, *An Autobiography of British Cinema: As Told by the Filmmakers and Actors who Made it* (London, 1997), p. 419.
11. BFI Special Collections, Clive Brooke Collection, box 83, 'The Eighty-Four Ages' TS, p. 238.
12. BFI, *Convoy* pressbook, poster.
13. *Daily Mirror*, 5 July 1940, p. 9; *Sunday Express*, 14 July 1940, p. 8.
14. *Daily Express*, 5 July 1940, p. 3; see BFI, *Convoy* script, S4380.
15. *Daily Herald*, 5 July 1940, p. 7; *Daily Express*, 5 July 1940, p. 3; *Daily Mirror*, 5 July 1940, p. 9; see *Daily Telegraph*, 8 July 1940, p. 3; *The Times*, 8 July 1940,

p. 6; *Spectator*, 12 July 1940, p. 35; *New Statesman*, 13 July 1940, p. 40; *Monthly Film Bulletin*, 30 June 1940, p. 82; *Today's Cinema*, 12 June 1940, p. 10; *Picturegoer*, 20 July 1940, p. 14.

16. Reviews quoted in BFI, *Convoy* pressbook.

17. *Picturegoer*, 14 September 1940, p. 17; *Kinematograph Weekly*, 9 January 1941, p. 26, 20 February 1941, p. 6; see also J. Poole, 'British Cinema Attendance in Wartime: Audience Preference at the Majestic, Macclesfield, 1939–1946', *Historical Journal of Film, Radio and Television*, 7 (1987), p. 20.

18. *Kinematograph Weekly*, 9 January 1942, pp. 51, 85.

19. *Picturegoer*, 24 May 1941, p. 10.

20. M. Wilding, *Apple Sauce: The Story of My Life* (London, 1982), p. 34.

21. Balcon, *Michael Balcon Presents*, p. 133.

22. *Daily Mail*, 7 November 1941, p. 4; *Daily Telegraph*, 6 November 1941, p. 4, 6 November 1941, p. 3.

23. *Daily Mail*, 20 November 1941, p. 3; *Daily Express*, 8 November 1941, p. 2; *Daily Herald*, 7 November 1941, p. 3; *Manchester Guardian*, 6 November 1941, p. 3; *The Times*, 10 November 1941, p. 8; *Daily Telegraph*, 10 November 1941, p. 3; C. A. Lejeune, *Chestnuts in Her Lap* (London, 1947), pp. 63–64.

24. *The Times*, 10 November 1941, p. 8; *Daily Express*, 8 November 1941, p. 2; *Daily Herald*, 7 November 1941, p. 3.

25. *Monthly Film Bulletin*, 30 September 1942, p. 111; F. Thorpe and N. Pronay, *British Official Films in the Second World War: A Descriptive Catalogue* (Oxford, 1980), p. 111; C. Coultass, *Images for Battle: British Film and the Second World War, 1939–1945* (Cranbury, NJ, 1989), p. 73.

26. Richards and Sheridan, *Mass-Observation*, pp. 364–80. The classic study of *Ships with Wings* is contained in A. Aldgate and J. Richards, *Britain Can Take It: The British Cinema in the Second World War* (2nd edn, Edinburgh, 1994), ch. 14.

27. G. Ramsey, *Ships with Wings: The Illustrated Book of the Great Film* (London, 1942); see *Kinematograph Weekly*, 8 January 1942, p. 6; see also *Picturegoer*, 29 November 1941, p. 3.

28. PRO, ADM 1/19195, report on the history of Naval Information by Rear Admiral R. K. Dickson, CNI 1086/45, 25 July 1945.

29. G. P. Thomson, *Blue Pencil Admiral: The Inside Story of the Press Censorship* (London, 1947), p. 12; see J. L. Hodson, *Home Front* (London, 1944), p. 315.

30. Balcon, *Michael Balcon Presents*, p. 134.

31. PRO, ADM 1/12044, minute by Director Press Division, 5 January 1942. For some reason it was forgotten – or perhaps not even known in DPD – that in 1941 a branch dealing with the development of AA weapons had made a drama-documentary entitled *The Gun* for the specific purpose of showing US audiences the importance of the Bofors Gun in convoy defence. See E. Terrell, *Admiralty Brief* (London, 1958), pp. 116–26.

32. On the semi-clandestine making of *The Gun*, see Terrell, *Admiralty Brief*, pp. 116–28. On *Submarine Patrol*, for which permission to film came from the

C-in-C Mediterranean rather than the Admiralty, see Imperial War Museum Sound Archive, D. Prosser, 4844/9.

33. Imperial War Museum Sound Archive, H. Stewart, 4579/6. TS, p. 64. On RN training film production see 'Film Progress in the Services', *Documentary News Letter*, 4 (1943), pp. 210–14.

34. P. Macnee and M. Cameron, *Blind in One Ear* (London, 1988), pp. 121, 123; K. More, *More or Less* (London, 1978), p. 89; M. Redgrave, *In My Mind's Eye* (London, 1983), pp. 149–50. More was nevertheless able to bluff his way through the interview and became a sub-lieutenant, RNVR, as did Alec Guinness. A. Guinness, *Blessings in Disguise* (London, 1985), pp. 108–9. Guinness subsequently became aware of the contempt in which regular RN officers held the acting profession. Ibid., p. 128. On Newton's drunkenness in the RN see, e.g., H. Wilcox, *Twenty-Five Thousand Sunsets* (London, 1967), p. 131.

35. *Kinematograph Weekly*, 9 April 1942, p. 23, 16 April 1942, p. 35, 8 January 1942, p. 100. It is possible that *Mediterranean Crossing* was axed because the Admiralty had already agreed to another submarine film, *We Dive at Dawn*. *Kinematograph Weekly*, 19 March 1942, p. 41. An earlier feature involving minesweeping had also failed to make it to the screen, presumably on security grounds. See Chapman, *British at War*, p. 69. As early as 1940 a 'naval epic' being planned by Alexander Korda to complement *The Lion Has Wings* never got beyond the planning stages. See *Kinematograph Weekly*, 4 January 1940, p. 1.

36. On public concern over shipping losses see, e.g., PRO, INF 1/292, pt 1, Home Intelligence weekly reports no. 38 (18–25 June 1941).

37. PRO, INF 1/213, Brooking to Beddington, 28 November 1941, 'HM Escort' enclosure.

38. Ibid., *Western Approaches* script, 17 June 1942.

39. Ibid., Dalrymple to Beddington, 11 August 1942.

40. The full story of *Western Approaches* can be found in Aldgate and Richards, *Britain Can Take It*, ch. 11. On problems filming the *Graph* see J. Cardiff, *Magic Hour* (London, 1996), p. 78.

41. See C. Fisher, *Noël Coward* (New York, 1992), p. 15; P. Ziegler, *Mountbatten: The Official Biography* (London, 1985), pp. 89, 100; G. Payne and S. Morley (eds), *The Noël Coward Diaries* (London, 1982), p. 6.

42. N. Coward, *Future Indefinite* (London, 1954), p. 208; Payne and Morley, *Coward Diaries*, p. 7; G. Campbell, *Of True Experience* (New York, 1947), p. 211.

43. Coward, *Future Indefinite*, pp. 208, 216–19; see Payne and Morley, *Coward Diaries*, pp. 9–10; A. Havelock-Allan and R. Neame in McFarlane, *Autobiography*, pp. 291, 431. Mountbatten not only had direct contact with the Palace but was also listened to by Churchill. In addition to his RNFC work, Mountbatten was himself a keen cinemagoer. He had paid a very public visit to Hollywood during his honeymoon, something that was looked on askance at the Admiralty (Ziegler, *Mountbatten*, pp. 71–72, 117, 149), and had been involved in plotting the 1939 *March of Time* film on the navy; see Southampton University, Mountbatten Papers, MB1/A67, MB1/L180.

44. National Film and Television Archive, 202268A, 'All Our Yesterdays': M. Powell interview, 23 April 1972; see R. Neame and G. Green in McFarlane, *Autobiography*, pp. 431, 233; K. Brownlow, *David Lean: A Biography* (London, 1996), pp. 150–51; BFI, NFT Interviews, N. Coward, 1969.

45. S. Morley, *A Talent to Amuse* (London, 1974), p. 277.

46. Brownlow, *David Lean*, pp. 153–54; R. Neame and A. Havelock-Allan in McFarlane. *Autobiography*, pp. 431, 291; C. Johnson letter, May 1942, in K. Fleming, *Celia Johnson: A Biography* (London, 1991), p. 81.

47. C. Castle, *Noël* (London, 1974), p. 174; Southampton University, Mountbatten Papers, MB1/H66, p. 1; Coward, *Future Indefinite*, p. 209.

48. Ziegler, *Mountbatten*, p. 171; see National Film and Television Archive, 8,008.9-AA, 'Filming for Victory: British Cinema, 1939–1945', 24 September 1989, B. Miles; BFI, NFT Interviews, N. Coward, 1969.

49. Southampton University, Mountbatten Papers, MB1/A48, Reports of the Visits of Mr. Noel Coward to the various Fleet Establishments, 21 July 1938. This is reproduced in *Sight and Sound*, 59 (1990), pp. 183–84.

50. J. Mills, *Up in the Clouds, Gentlemen Please* (London, 1980), p. 176; Wilding, *Apple Sauce*, pp. 34–35; J. Mason, *Before I Forget* (London, 1981), pp. 130–31.

51. National Sound Archive, V1596, 'South Bank Show: Richard Attenborough'. Coward also took trouble in casting the wives. See, e.g., Fleming, *Celia Johnson*, p. 89.

52. M. Powell, *Million Dollar Movie* (New York, 1995), p. 259; see A. Havelock-Allan in McFarlane, *Autobiography*, p. 291; see also J. Mills in National Sound Archive, NP 6708 WR BD1, M. Dean, 'Noel Coward: A Private Life', 1984.

53. Payne and Morley, *Coward Diaries*, p. 15.

54. PRO, ADM 1/19195, CNI 1086/45, p. 5; *Daily Express*, 29 August 1941, p. 1.

55. Payn and Morley, *Coward Diaries*, p. 10. On the 1940 uniform affair see *Sunday Pictorial*, 10 March 1940, p. 3; *Daily Telegraph*, 19 February 1940, p. 3.

56. Southampton University, Mountbatten Papers, HB1/H66, p. 2; *Daily Express*, 17 September 1941, p. 1, 30 September 1941, p. 3; Mountbatten Papers, MB1/A48, Coward to Mountbatten, 17 September 1941; Payne and Morley, *Coward Diaries*, p. 10–11, C. Moorehead, *Sidney Bernstein: A Biography* (London, 1984), p. 149.

57. See Southampton University, Mountbatten Papers, MB1/C58/2, Mountbatten to Coward, 1 January 1942.

58. National Film and Television Archive, 8,0008–9AA, C. Frayling, 'Filming for Victory: British Cinema, 1939–1945', B. Miles interview; Southampton University, Mountbatten Papers, MB1/H66, p. 3, MB1/L180.

59. Payne and Morley, *Coward Diaries*, p. 15; see Ziegler, *Mountbatten*, p. 171; Southampton University, Mountbatten Papers, MB1/C58/1, Mountbatten to Coward, 21 November 1941, MB1/C58/13, Mountbatten to Coward, 21 February 1942; MB 1/C58/5, memo, 22 January 1942.

60. See Ziegler, *Mountbatten*, p. 171; Southampton University, Mountbatten Papers, MB1/C58/7, Mountbatten to Littlejohn, 30 January 1942, Mountbatten to Torrington, 17 February 1942, MB1/C58/4, note, 21 January 1942, MB1/C58/6,

Mountbatten and President, Board of Trade, January 1942; MB1/C58/17, Mount-batten to Coward, 30 April 1942. See MB1/C58/14, Mountbatten to C. H. de Mewlbery, 31 March 1942, for his strenuous – though ultimately unsuccessful – efforts to keep Clark from being posted. He was replaced by Lieutenant C. R. E. Compton; Coward, *Future Indefinite*, p. 215.

61. Brownlow, *David Lean*, p. 157; *Kinematograph Weekly*, 16 April 1942, p. 35.

62. Mills, *Up in the Clouds*, p. 178; see R. Neame in McFarlane, *Autobiography*, p. 431.

63. Payne and Morley, *Coward Diaries*, p. 15; Mills, *Up in the Clouds*, pp. 176–77; see Brownlow, *David Lean*, p. 160; National Sound Archive, B1808/2, 'Dilys Powell's History of the British Cinema [4]: The War', D. Lean and J. Mills comments on Coward during *In Which We Serve*.

64. National Sound Archive, V1094, 'South Bank Show: Noël Coward', 1 March 1992, D. Lean comments; see BFI, NFT Interviews, N. Coward, 1969; TV On-tario, BPN 180201, E. Yost interview with R. Attenborough, 1979; Brownlow, *David Lean*, pp. 160, 162; J. Mills in McFarlane, *Autobiography*, p. 414.

65. Coward, *Future Imperfect*, p. 224.

66. Brownlow, *David Lean*, p. 166; B. Wright in E. Sussex, *The Rise and Fall of the British Documentary Movement* (Berkeley, 1975), p. 139.

67. Brownlow, *David Lean*, p. 163; see B. Wright in Sussex, *British Documentary*, p. 139; Coward, *Future Imperfect*, p. 226; *Kinematograph Weekly*, 16 April 1942, p. 35, 7 May 1942, p. 32.

68. TV Ontario, BPN 180201, E. Yost interview with R. Attenborough, 1979; see Wilding, *Apple Sauce*, pp. 35–36; Payne and Morley, *Coward Diaries*, p. 15.

69. Mills, *Up in the Clouds*, p. 178.

70. Aldgate and Richards, *Britain Can Take It*, p. 198; Coward, *Future Imperfect*, pp. 226–27; Wilding, *Apple Sauce*, p. 35; see *Kinematograph Weekly*, 16 April 1942, p. 35, 7 May 1942, p. 32, 14 May 1942, p. 50, 21 May 1942, p. 38, 28 May 1942, p. 26, 11 June 1942, p. 27, 25 June 1942, p. 24.

71. See Ziegler, *Mountbatten*, pp. 122–23.

72. Ibid., pp. 127–28. Coward also appears to have copied Mountbatten's account of how he was swept overboard and what he did underwater. See W. Pattinson, *Mountbatten and the Men of the 'Kelly'* (Wellingborough, 1986), pp. 109–11.

73. Coward, *Future Imperfect*, p. 231; see BFI, *In Which We Serve* pressbook.

74. Southampton University, Mountbatten Papers, MB1/C58/21, Mountbatten to Coward, 2 October 1942; MB1/L180, Jarrett to Mountbatten, 24 September 1942; Coward, *Future Imperfect*, p. 231; see Ziegler, *Mountbatten*, p. 172.

75. *Documentary News Letter*, October 1942, p. 143; *Daily Express*, 24 September 1942, p. 3; *Daily Mirror*, 25 September 1942, p. 7; *Spectator*, 2 October 1942, p. 311; *Picturegoer*, 17 October 1942, p. 2; see *Sight and Sound*, 11 (1942), p. 68; *Manchester Guardian*, 2 February 1943, p. 3; *The Times*, 24 September 1942, p. 6; *Daily Mirror*, 25 September 1942, p. 7; C. Cook (ed.), *The Dilys Powell Film Reader* (Manchester, 1991), pp. 4–6; D. Powell, *Films Since 1939* (London,

1947), pp. 25–28; Lejeune, *Chestnuts*, pp. 79–80. On the popularity of the *Mirror* see P. Kimble, *Newspaper Reading in the Third Year of the War* (London, 1942).

76. J. P. Mayer, *British Cinemas and their Audiences: Sociological Studies* (London, 1948), p. 195, see pp. 172, 175, 177, 179185, 193, 205, 214, 227, 228; Richards and Sheridan, *Mass-Observation*, pp. 267, 269, 271, 276, 278, 280, 282, 283, 286; Whitebait in *New Statesman*, 26 September 1942, pp. 204–5; *Kinematograph Weekly*, 13 January 1944, p. 34.

77. Southampton University, Mountbatten Papers, MB1/H66, Mountbatten to Coward, 11 September 1953. See, e.g., *Daily Express*, 24 September 1942, p. 3; P. Ziegler (ed.), *Personal Diary of Admiral the Lord Louis Mountbatten: Supreme Allied Commander, South-East Asia, 1943–1946* (London, 1988), p. 5; Southampton University, Mountbatten Papers, MB1/C20, 'The Strange Case of Lord Beaverbrook', MB1/A48, Smith to Coward, 30 October 1942.

78. Ziegler, *Mountbatten*, p. 172, see also chs 9–10; R. Whinney, *The U-Boat Peril* (London, 1989), p. 201. On exploitation of the film for recruiting and publicity purposes, see *Kinematograph Weekly*, 25 February 1943, p. 32, 25 March 1943, p. 42, 1 April 1943, p. 49, 8 April 1943, p. 37.

79. See Mass-Observation, FR 886, Civilian Attitudes to the Navy compared with the Army and RAF, 30 September 1941; PRO, INF 1/292, pt 1, weekly Home Intelligence reports, nos 34 (21–28 May 1941), 35 (29–5 May 1941).

80. PRO, INF 1/292, pt 1, weekly home intelligence report no. 34 (21–28 May 1941); see report no. 7 (11–18 November 1940).

81. Ibid., pt 2, report no. 59, 19 November 1941.

82. PRO, INF 1/293, memo on recruitment for the RN, 5 December 1941.

83. PRO, INF 1/292 pt 2, report no. 63, 17 December 1941.

84. Ibid., report no. 65, 31 December 1941.

85. Ibid., report no 72, 18 February 1942; N. Nicolson (ed.), *Diaries and Letters*, ii, *The War Years, 1939–1945* (London, 1967), p. 211; see Thomson, *Blue-Pencil Admiral*, p. 141; K. Macdonald, *Emeric Pressburger* (London, 1994), p. 187.

86. Dalrymple in Sussex, *British Documentary*, p. 139; PRO, ADM 1/19195, CNI 1086/45, p. 6.

87. The Admiralty did, to be sure, attempt to promote minesweepers – 'All the valour of a Battle-Cruiser' – in print form. See *His Majesty's Minesweepers* (London, 1943), ch. 1 title. Any thoughts about a film featuring a corvette were doubtless buried by the development in 1942 of a film to be directed by Howard Hawks for Universal featuring a Royal Canadian Navy corvette. *Corvette K–225* eventually appeared on screens in 1943. See T. McCarthy, *Howard Hawks* (New York, 1997), pp. 349–51.

88. The submarine, indeed, had already been the subject of one British feature before the war (*Men Like These*) and would be the subject of two more in the 1950s (*Morning Departure* and *Above Us the Waves*). It was no accident that so many American films were also about submarines. See L. Suid, *Sailing on the Silver Screen: Hollywood and the US Navy* (Annapolis, MY, 1996), chs 2–3, 8.

89. See PRO, INF 1/292, pt 2, Home Intelligence weekly report nos 38 (18–25 June 1941), 90 (25 June 1942).

90. I. Dalrymple and B. Wright in Sussex, *British Documentary*, p. 139. Two, however, was enough: hence, in all probability, the decision not to support the request for help from British National for a film about submarines in the Mediterranean. See *Kinematograph Weekly*, 16 April 1942, p. 35.

91. *Kinematograph Weekly*, 19 March 1942, p. 41; see *Kinematograph Weekly*, 11 June 1942, p. 27.

92. *We Dive at Dawn* pressbook; see K. Edwards, *We Dive at Dawn* (London, 1939).

93. Mills, *Up in the Clouds*, p. 178; PRO, ADM 173/17521, P614 log, 18–20 April 1942.

94. More recently the U–331 had sunk the battleship *Barham* at sea in the Mediterranean in November 1941.

95. See *Kinematograph Weekly*, 28 May 1942, p. 26.

96. *Guardian*, 22 May 1943, p. 4, 10 August 1943, p. 3; *The Times*, 20 May 1943, p. 6; *Spectator*, 28 May 1943, p. 499; *New Statesman*, 29 May 1943, p. 352; *Daily Telegraph*, 24 May 1943, p. 2; *Monthly Film Bulletin*, 30 June 1943, p. 62; *Kinematograph Weekly*, 22 April 1943, p. 29.

97. *Daily Mirror*, 21 May 1943, p. 7; *Picturegoer*, 26 June 1943, p. 2; *Daily Herald*, 28 June 1943, p. 2; *Daily Express*, 22 May 1943, p. 2. The story was also adapted by Marjory Williams in *Picturegoer*, 10 July 1943, p. 14.

98. Richards and Sheridan, *Mass-Observation*, pp. 246, 258, 265, 267, 268, 276, 277, 278, 286; see G. Morgan, *Red Roses Every Night* (London, 1948), p. 74.

99. Dalrymple in Sussex, *British Documentary*, p. 139.

100. I. Dalrymple, 'The Crown Film Unit, 1940–43', *Propaganda, Politics and Film, 1918–45*, N. Pronay and D. W. Spring, eds (London, 1982), p. 216.

101. R. Loyd in McFarlane, *Autobiography*, p. 368.

102. PRO, INF 6/25.

103. PRO, INF 1/199, receipts from commercial distribution of films, summary, May 1944. *Close Quarters* was not even mentioned once in the Mass-Observation or later surveys. For quoted reviews see *Daily Herald*, 26 June 1943, p. 2; *Kinematograph Weekly*, 1 July 1943, p. 20; *Daily Express*, 28 June 1943, p. 2; *Daily Telegraph*, 28 June 1943, p. 2; *The Times*, 23 June 1943, p. 6; see also *Monthly Film Bulletin*, 31 July 1943, p. 73.

104. PRO, ADM 167/114, Board Minute 3839, 4 December 1942; ADM 16/116, Report of the Naval Publicity Committee.

105. Moorehead, *Sidney Bernstein*, p. 148.

106. See Balcon, *Michael Balcon Presents*, p. 148; Chapman, *British at War*, pp. 188–89; C. Coultass, 'Film and Reality: The *San Demetrio* Episode', *Imperial War Museum Review*, 5 (1990), pp. 79–85.

107. British Library, Add Ms 52578, Cunningham Diary, 11 December 1945.

108. See PRO, ADM 1/19195, CNI 1086/45, 25 July 1945, pp. 6–7; Thomson, *Blue-Pencil Admiral*, p. 12. The Admiralty did not have much to do with wartime

naval comedies such as a British International remake of *The Middle Watch* (1939), *Sailors Three* (Ealing, 1940), *Sailors Don't Care* (Butcher's, 1940) and *Bell-Bottom George* (Columbia British, 1943). See D. Bret, *George Formby: A Troubled Genius* (London, 1999), pp. 129–33; BFI, *Sailors Three* script, S232; *Monthly Film Bulletin*, 31 October 1943, p. 159; ibid., 30 September 1940, p. 147; ibid., 31 December 1939, p. 218.

109. Powell, *Life*, pp. 419, 400–1.

110. INF 6/600, script, 'The Volunteer'; see Powell in K. Gough-Yates, *Michael Powell in Collaboration with Emeric Pressburger* (London, 1971), p. 8; Powell in I. Christie (ed.), *Powell, Pressburger and Others* (London, 1978), p. 32.

111. Powell, *Life*, p. 421.

112. Ibid., pp. 400, 422, 432.

113. G. O'Conner, *Ralph Richardson: An Actor's Life* (London, 1982), p. 107.

114. *The Times*, 1 November 1943, p. 8; see *Monthly Film Bulletin*, 30 November 1943, p. 122.

115. PRO, ADM 1/19195, CNI 1086/45, 25 July 1945, pp. 7–9; *Documentary News Letter*, 4 (1943), pp. 211–12; K. F. Bean, 'Naval Reflections', *Sight and Sound*, 13 (1944), pp. 33–35; J. Baxter, 'War Films Should be Given a Rest as Popular Subjects', *Kinematograph Weekly*, 14 January 1943, p. 103; P. L. Mannock, 'A Plea for More Escapism', *Kinematograph Weekly*, 25 June 1942, p. 22; C. M. Woolf, 'Let Us Have Fewer War Themes', *Kinematograph Weekly*, 2 July 1942, p. 17; see ibid., 8 January 1942, p. 87, 3 June 1943, p. 10.

116. In the aftermath of the Channel Dash, for example, confidence in the navy was quickly renewed even as the RAF continued to be criticized. See PRO, INF 1/292, pt 2, HI weekly report no. 73, 25 February 1942.

Notes to Chapter 4: Civilians in Uniform: The British Army and Feature Films, 1939–1945

1. See C. Seymour-Ure and J. Schoff, *David Low* (London, 1985); see also Chapter 1 above.

2. B. Bond, *British Military Policy between the Two World Wars* (London, 1980), ch. 2. The social and educational background – and thus cultural attitudes – of officers did change over time, but very slowly. See C. B. Otley, 'The Social Origins of British Army Officers', *Sociological Review*, 18 (1970), pp. 213–49; idem, 'The Educational Background of British Army Officers', *Sociology*, 7 (1973), pp. 191–209. A sense of the rather stultifying atmosphere of garrison life can be gleaned from David Niven's experience as a young professional officer in the Highland Light Infantry. See D. Niven, *The Moon's a Balloon* (London, 1971), pp. 53–93.

3. See Chapter 1.

4. I. Hay, *Arms and the Men* (London, 1950), p. 323.

5. E. T. Williams and H. M. Palmer (eds), *Dictionary of National Biography, 1951–1960* (Oxford, 1971), pp. 79–80; see also J. H. Beith, *The King's Service: An*

Informal History of the British Infantry Soldier (London, 1938). This was re-printed in abridged form by Penguin as *The British Infantryman* for the services in 1942. See Bristol University Library, editorial correspondence, DM 1107 00.0359. On the cantankerous Tommy 'Old Bill' see B. T. and V. Holt, *In Search of the Better 'Ole* (Portsmouth, 1985).

6. See *Kinematograph Weekly*, 29 February 1940, p. 37, 8 January 1940, p. 39; *Monthly Film Bulletin*, 31 December 1940, p. 181; Holt, *Better 'Ole*, pp. 159–60; see B. Bairnsfather, *Old Bill and Son* (London, 1940). Even as work continued at Denham Studios on *Old Bill and Son*, Butcher Films was making a similar comedy drama, this time without War Office help, entitled *Pack Up Your Troubles*, directed by Oswald Mitchell. Though there were several sub-plots, the main storyline bore a strong resemblance to the Dalrymple effort, in that a young volunteer (Reginald Purdell), later joined by an Old Sweat from the Great War, combine to outwit the Germans and escape across No Man's Land and back to the BEF. Supposed to be 'a richly humourous picture of the Army of today' (*Kinematograph Weekly*, 14 November 1940, p. 26), *Pack Up Your Troubles* clearly fitted the tendency to situate the new war in the context of the old. See *Monthly Film Bulletin*, 30 April 1940, p. 54.

7. On the change in public mood and Beith's inability to grasp the consequences see E. T. Williams and H. M. Palmer (eds), *Dictionary of National Biography, 1951–1960* (London, 1971), p. 80; PRO, CAB 102/848, pp. 1–5. On the lukewarm reception of *Old Bill and Son* see Holt, *Better 'Ole*, p. 165; *Picturegoer*, 22 February 1941, p. 14.

8. See PRO, INF 1/292, pt 2, Home Intelligence reports nos 35 (28 May–4 June 1941), 38 (11–18 June 1941); Mass-Observation, FR 73, report on some army questions – June 1941; A. Calder, *The People's War: Britain, 1939–45* (London, 1969), pp. 248–49.

9. Hay, *Arms and Men*, p. 320.

10. Ibid., pp. 323–25. Writing as Ian Hay, Beith had collaborated in 1929 with Stephen King-Hall on *The Middle Watch*, the first of a series of successful naval farces, and with Anthony Armstrong on the army comedy *Orders are Orders* in 1932.

11. *Kinematograph Weekly*, 12 February 1942, p. 28; see *Monthly Film Bulletin*, 28 February 1942, p. 14; J. Chapman, *The British at War: Cinema, State and Propaganda, 1939–1945* (London, 1998), pp. 141, 190. On the Army Film Unit see I. Grant, *Cameramen at War* (Cambridge, 1980), pp. 8–11.

12. See *Kinematograph Weekly*, 14 January 1943, p. 47; see also J. Poole, 'British Cinema Attendance in Wartime: Audience Preference at the Majestic, Macclesfield, 1939–1946', *Historical Journal of Film, Radio and Television*, 7 (1987), p. 22. *Somewhere in Camp* was followed later in the year by a sequel, *Somewhere on Leave*. See *Monthly Film Bulletin*, 31 December 1942, p. 154.

13. 'Boomerang' [Alan Wood], *Bless 'Em All: An Analysis of the British Army, its Morale, Efficiency and Leadership* (London, 1942), p. 16; Liddell Hart Centre, Adam Papers, viii, ch. 5, p. 2; Mass-Observation, FR723, Civilian and Service

Morale, 4 June 1941; ibid., TC29, box 2, file A, Report on Morale and Training in the Army – 11 June 1941; ibid., file D, Crete—Syria—Parliamentary Debate: Reaction in a Large North Country Emergency Hospital, 14 June 1941; PRO, INF 2/292, pt 2, Home Intelligence weekly reports nos 38 (11–18 June 1941), 47 (20–27 August 1941); INF 1/293, memo on recruitment for the RN, 5 December 1941; S. Milligan, *Adolf Hitler: My Part in His Downfall* (London, 1971), pp. 31–32, 57; A. Cotterell, *Oh, It's Nice to be in the Army!* (London, 1941), p. 19. On the Bingham affair see *The Times*, 15 January 1941, p. 7; *House of Commons Parliamentary Debates*, 5th series, vol. 367, cols 304–5. On the officer-man gulf see, e.g., 'Should the Colonel Dine with his Sergeant? "Familiarity" Charge', *Daily Express*, 10 May 1940, p. 3.

14. National Library of Scotland, Elliot Papers, box 8, file 1, W. Elliot to Mrs. Elliot, 29 August 1941.

15. Chapman, *British at War*, pp. 143–44; see *Kinematograph Weekly*, 12 February 1942, p. 28; *Monthly Film Bulletin*, 28 February 1942, p. 14; I. Dalrymple, 'The Crown Film Unit, 1940–43', *Propaganda, Politics and Film, 1918–45*, N. Pronay and D. W. Spring, eds (London, 1982), p. 215.

16. PRO, CAB 102/848, p. 16; INF 1/292, pt 2, HI weekly report no. 73 (18–24 February 1942); see ibid., pt 3, HI weekly report no. 91 (21–30 June 1942); J. L. Hodson, *Home Front* (London, 1944), p. 98; February 1942 BIPO survey concerning Japanese success in G. Catrill (ed.), *Public Opinion, 1935–1946* (Princeton, 1951), p. 1062; D. Dilks (ed.), *The Diaries of Sir Alexander Cadogan, 1938–1945* (London, 1971), 9 February 1942, p. 433; P. J. Grigg, *Prejudice and Judgment* (London, 1948), p. 355.

17. Elliot, Conservative MP for Kelvingrove, had been a strong supporter of Appeasement, very much in line with public opinion in 1938 but very much against the popular tide of 1940. When Churchill replaced Chamberlain, Elliot was dropped at once from the Cabinet (he had most recently been Minister of Health), the post of DPR being something of a consolation prize. See National Library of Scotland, Elliot Papers, box 8, file 1, W. Elliot to Mrs Elliot, 6 November 1940, 8 January 1941, 10 January 1941, 13 January 1941. See also E. T. Williams and Helen M. Palmer (eds), *Dictionary of National Biography, 1951–1960* (London, 1971), p. 333.

18. PRO, WO 259/62, enclosure 1A; Churchill College Cambridge, Grigg Papers, 9/7/13, Bernard Paget (Commander-in-Chief Home Forces) to P. J. Grigg (War Minister), 29 October 1942; see N. Nicolson (ed.), *Harold Nicolson: Diaries and Letters, 1939–1945* (London, 1967), p. 213. On the efforts of the Adjutant-General see Liddell Hart Centre, Ronald Adam memoir (unpublished). On the tensions surrounding ABCA see S. P. MacKenzie, *Politics and Military Morale: Current-Affairs and Citizenship Education in the British Army, 1914–1950* (Oxford, 1992), ch. 5.

19. M. Joseph, *The Sword in the Scabbard* (London, 1942), p. 211; IWM, 86/207/1, R. E. Tritton Diary, 25 September 1941, 20 October 1940.

20. B. Forbes, *A Divided Life* (London, 1992), p. 259; D. Bogarde, *Snakes and Ladders*

(London, 1978), pp. 20–21; S. Granger, *Sparks Fly Upwards* (New York, 1981), pp. 57–58; Imperial War Museum Sound Archive, R. Boulting, 4627, TS pp. 51–52; see also A. Guinness, *Blessings in Disguise* (London, 1985), pp. 101–3; D. Farrar, *No Royal Road* (London, 1947), p. 83.

21. M. Balcon, *Michael Balcon Presents ... A Lifetime of Films* (London, 1969), p. 137.

22. *Daily Express*, 11 April 1942, p. 2; see *Monthly Film Bulletin*, 30 April 1942, p. 41.

23. See Chapman, *British at War*, pp. 172–73; P. Huston, *Went the Day Well?* (London, 1992), pp. 21–22.

24. Nicolson, 24 February 1942, p. 213; see Chapman, *British at War*, p. 173.

25. On the making of *The Next of Kin* see PRO, AVIA 22/2701; J. Richards, *Thorold Dickinson: The Man and his Films* (London, 1986), pp. 93–104; A. Aldgate and J. Richards, *Britain Can Take It: The British Cinema in the Second World War* (2nd edn, Edinburgh, 1994), ch. 5. See also *Picturegoer*, 4 April 1942, p. 5. Security was one of the few areas in which film was thought to have possibilities in military circles this early in the war. See Imperial War Museum Sound Archive, D. Macdonald, 4654, TS p. 6.

26. The fact that civilian actors were paid more than the actors in uniform, who had to manage on their army pay, was a source of considerable annoyance to Lieutenant Jack Hawkins, who played the brigade major. J. Hawkins, *Anything for a Quiet Life* (London, 1973), pp. 64–65.

27. PRO, WO 165/96, DAK, monthly progress report for the Army Council, February 1942, p. 2.

28. Balcon, *Michael Balcon Presents*, p. 149.

29. *Sunday Times*, 17 May 1942, p. 4; *Observer*, 17 May 1943, p. 5; *Kinematograph Weekly*, 21 May 1942, p. 30; *Daily Express*, 16 May 1942, p. 2; *Daily Herald*, 14 May 1942, p. 3.

30. PRO, 165/96, DAK monthly progress report for the Army Council, December 1942, p. 5.

31. M-O, FR 1342, audience survey, *Next of Kin*, May 1942; see PRO, INF 1/29, pt 2, HI weekly report no. 89 (2–9 June 1942); see also Poole, 'Cinema Attendance', p. 22.

32. On *Went the Day Well?* see Aldgate and Richards, *Britain Can Take It*, ch. 6; P. Huston, *Went the Day Well?* (London, 1992).

33. It is not mentioned in the *Kinematograph Weekly* survey of the successful films of 1942 or 1943. *Kinematograph Weekly*, 14 January 1943, p. 47, 13 January 1944, p. 52. Reviews are summarized in Huston, *Went the Day Well?*, pp. 53–55.

34. See D. Farrar in B. McFarlane, *An Autobiography of British Cinema: As Told by the Filmmakers and Actors who Made it* (London, 1997), p. 183. On the other hand Cavalcanti had to work mostly with actors under contract to Ealing, so that using English actors more readily convincing as Nazis – Eric Portman comes to mind – may simply have not been an option.

35. PRO, INF 2/292, pt 3, HI weekly report no. 91; see ibid., HI weekly reports

nos 100, 102, 103; see CAB 102/848, S. Taylor, 'A People at War: Thought and Mood on the Home Front', p. 10.

36. PRO, WO 163/161, WO committee on morale, report for May-July 1942; see ibid., August-October 1942. Though see also Hodson, *Home Front*, pp. 138, 142.

37. Nicolson, *Diaries*, p. 213; 'listless and lazy', PRO, WO 259/62, enclosure 1A, The 'Spirit' of the Army; 'years of soft living'; INF 2/292, pt 3, HI weekly report no. 91. For radical reformist criticism see, e.g., the *Daily Mirror* position outlined in A. C. H. Smith, *Paper Voices: The Popular Press and Social Change, 1935–1965* (London, 1975), pp. 66–69, 82. For less strident criticism see, e.g., M. Joseph, *Sword*, pp. 201–9. On traditionalist fury over such attacks see, e.g., WO 259/62, Paget to Grigg, 14 March 1942, Utterson-Kelso to Templer, 6 March 1942. On the nature of the wartime army and official efforts to cope see J. A. Crang, 'A Social History of the British Army, 1939–45' (unpublished Edinburgh University Ph.D. thesis, 1993).

38. See LHC, Adam Papers, viii, ch. 12, p. 10.

39. IWM, 186/207/1, Tritton diary, 31 March 1943, 27 July 1943; see also, e.g., H. P. Croft, *My Life of Strife* (London, 1948), pp. 324–25, Hodson, *Home Front*, p. 274.

40. IWM, 186/207/1, Tritton Diary, 31 March 1943. On Lawson see E. T. Williams and C. S. Nicholls (eds) *Dictionary of National Biography 1961–1970* (Oxford, 1981), pp. 634–35.

41. Imperial War Museum Sound Archive, R. Boulting, 4627, TS p. 20. On Wintringham see D. Fernbach, 'Tom Wintringham and Socialist Defence Strategy', *History Workshop*, 14 (1982), pp. 63–91; Smith, *Paper Voices*, pp. 66–69. Elliot, as already noted, was an old-guard Tory MP, who complained about 'the loss of caste which hangs around any job that brings one into contact with the Press'. National Library of Scotland, Elliot Papers, box 8, file 1, W. Elliot to Mrs. Elliot, 8 January 1941. Lawson – about to succeed to the title of 4th Baron Burnham – ran a paper that was considered very much a Conservative organ. Neither, as far as can be ascertained, had any film experience. Lord Croft, joint Under-Secretary of State for War, admitted that he found people from the film trade 'not easy people' to deal with. Croft, *Life*, p. 323.

42. D. Badder, 'Powell and Pressburger: The War Years', *Sight and Sound*, 48 (1978), p. 10; see M. Powell, *A Life in Movies* (London, 1986), p. 399.

43. Outline in I. Christie (ed.), *Powell and Pressburger: The Life and Death of Colonel Blimp* (London, 1994), pp. 3–16; see D. Low, *Low's Autobiography* (London, 1956), p. 273. A survey of the various interpretations of the 'Blimp Affair' can be found in J. Chapman, '*The Life and Death of Colonel Blimp* (1943) Reconsidered', *Historical Journal of Film, Radio and Television*, 15 (1995), pp. 31–34.

44. Grigg, in an unusual move, had been elevated from the civil service post of Permanent Under-Secretary at the War Office to the political position of War Minister by Churchill, a vacant seat being found for him. Having worked with

generals for years, Grigg thought that much of the wartime criticism of the
army was baseless, and as a neophyte politician proved extremely thin-skinned
when hectored in Parliament. He was also extremely suspicious of left-wing
ideas. See, e.g., P. J. Grigg, *Prejudice and Judgement* (London, 1948), ch. 9;
Churchill College Cambridge, Grigg Papers, 9/6/11, letter of 23 February 1941;
Hodson, *Home Front*, p. 23.

45. Grigg to Powell, 22 May 1942, in Christie, *Blimp*, pp. 27–28.
46. From the dedication – cut from the finished film – in the shooting script.
    Christie, *Blimp*, p. 76.
47. Grigg to Powell, June 1942, Powell to Grigg, n.d. in Christie, *Blimp*, pp. 28–29.
48. Gates to Powell, 25 June 1942, Bracken to Powell, 7 July 1942, Powell to Grigg,
    n.d. in Christie, *Blimp*, pp. 40–41, 30–31.
49. Powell, *Life*, p. 406. It is also possible that Powell received help from the navy.
    The journalist J. L. Hodson noted in his diary on 12 August 1942 that 'A film
    director who has been trying without success to persuade the army to loan
    him a hundred soldiers, said to me: "the Admiralty have now loaned us
    machine-guns, etc., because they feel we are friends"'. Hodson, *Home Front*,
    p. 137.
50. PRO, PREM 4/14/15, Grigg to Churchill, 8 September 1942.
51. PRO, CAB 65/31, WCM 126(42), 21 September 1942; PREM 4/14/15, PM's
    personal minute M381/2, Churchill to Bracken, 17 September 1942, Bracken to
    Churchill, 15 September 1942, PM's personal minute M357/2, Churchill to
    Bracken, 10 September 1942.
52. On the script and critical reactions see Chapman, '*Blimp* Reconsidered', p. 40;
    Richards and Aldgate, pp. 64–65; see also A. L. Kennedy, *The Life and Death
    of Colonel Blimp* (London, 1997); K. Macdonald, *Emeric Pressburger: The Life
    and Death of a Screenwriter* (London, 1994), p. 208.
53. Richards and Aldgate, *Britain Can Take It*, pp. 72–73.
54. PRO, CAB 65/38, 67(43), 10 May 1943.
55. Chapman, '*Blimp* Reconsidered', p. 30.
56. *Documentary News Letter*, 4, no. 5, 1943, p. 219; *New Statesman*, 12 June 1943,
    p. 384; E. W. and M. Robson, *The Shame and Disgrace of Colonel Blimp: The
    True Story of the Film* (London, 1944), pp. 5–6; D. Low, *Low's Autobiography*
    (London, 1956), p. pp. 273–74.
57. See, e.g., *Daily Herald*, 12 June 1943, p. 2; *Daily Telegraph*, 14 June 1943, p. 2;
    Observer, 13 June 1943, p. 3; *Monthly Film Bulletin*, 30 June 1943, p. 61.
58. *Daily Express*, 12 June 1943, p. 2. For other positive comments see *Kinemato-
    graph Weekly*, 24 June 1943, pp. 44–45.
59. Richards and Sheridan, *Mass-Observation*, pp. 222, 224, 225, 232, 239, 259, 261,
    262, 263, 265, 272, 282, 284; V. Hodgson, *Few Eggs and No Oranges: A Diary*
    (London, 1976), p. 339; PRO, PREM 4/14/15, Hodge to Sendall, 19 August 1943;
    Kinematograph Weekly, 13 January 1944, p. 32.
60. *A Canterbury Tale* (Archers, 1944) was made with official approval and help.
    Powell, *Life*, p. 441, 437–48.

61. Interview with H. Watt in G. Brown, *Der Produzent: Michael Balcon und der englische Film* (Berlin, 1981), pp. 187–88; H. Watt, *Don't Look at the Camera!* (London, 1974), p. 194.

62. On *Nine Men* see Chapman, *British at War*, p. 278 n. 22; Watt, H., 'Casting *Nine Men*', *Documentary News Letter*, 4 (1943), pp. 179–80. On the 'pulling together' theme see G. Jackson in B. McFarlane, *An Autobiography of British Cinema* (London, 1997), p. 321.

63. See BFI, S192, final shooting script, *Nine Men*. Thirty years later Watt admitted to being rather queasy about the graphic hand-to-hand fighting sequences. BFI, NFT Interviews, H. Watt, 1974.

64. G. Jackson in B. McFarlane, *Autobiography*, p. 320; Watt, *Don't Look at the Camera*, p. 194. Balcon admitted that it was 'a modest undertaking'. Balcon, *Michael Balcon Presents*, p. 142.

65. IWM, 186/207/1, Tritton diary, 23 June 1942.

66. *Daily Express*, 20 February 1943, p. 2; see, e.g., *Picturegoer*, 20 February 1943, p. 2; *Kinematograph Weekly*, 28 January 1943, p. 22, 4 February 1943, p. 5; also *Daily Express*, 7 April 1943, p. 3. On audience reaction see Richards and Sheridan, *Mass-Observation*, pp. 226, 243, 244, 247, 263.

67. *Monthly Film Bulletin*, 28 February 1943, p. 13; *Kinematograph Weekly*, 28 January 1943, p. 27; *The Times*, 27 January 1943, p. 6; *Spectator*, 29 January 1943, p. 99; *New Statesman*, 30 January 1943, p. 76. For summaries of other reviews see *Kinematograph Weekly*, 11 February 1943, p. 2.

68. *Kinematograph Weekly*, 4 February 1943, p. 15; H. Watt interview in Brown, *Produzent*, p. 190; BFI, NFT Interviews, H. Watt, 1974.

69. IWM, A. D. Melville diary, 5 March 1943.

70. On the production of *Desert Victory* see PRO, INF 1/221; IWMSA, R. Boulting, 4627, TS, pp. 18–28; R. Boulting in McFarlane, *Autobiography*, p. 77. On the AFPU in North Africa see I. Grant, *Cameramen*, chs 2–3. On the first War Office showing, for which Grigg and Lawson, among others, were present, see Hodson, *Home Front*, p. 305.

71. Hodson is usually credited as narrator as well as writer, but in the fiftieth anniversary video edition produced in association with the Imperial War Museum it is clearly Genn who does most of the talking. On Hodson's role see Hodson, *Home Front*, p. 290–91.

72. Newspaper review excerpts can be found in *Kinematograph Weekly*, 18 March 1943, pp. 32–33; see also *Monthly Film Bulletin*, 31 March 1943, p. 25.

73. Richards and Sheridan, *Mass-Observation*, pp. 275, 245; see ibid., pp. 225, 226, 228, 236, 241, 249, 257, 260, 262, 264, 266, 267, 279, 281, 283, 284; see also Poole, 'Cinema Attendance', p. 24.

74. PRO, INF 1/199, Receipts from commercial distribution of films, May 1944.

75. The Monty mystique was already being built up by Captain Geoffrey Keating of the APFU, who took credit for the way Montgomery was portrayed in *Desert Victory*. David Macdonald, on the other hand, thought that the commander of the Eighth Army had no interest in the desert cameramen until

after its success. The film certainly fed the general's vanity. N. Hamilton, *Monty: Master of the Battlefield, 1942–1944* (London, 1983), p. 173; IWMSA, D. Macdonald, 4654, TS, p. 19.

76. Richards and Sheridan, *Mass-Observation*, p. 257; see A. Kuhn, 'Desert Victory and the People's War', *Screen*, 22 (1981), pp. 45–68.

77. For reviews, see, e.g., *Daily Telegraph*, 17 March 1944, p. 3, *Daily Herald*, 17 March 1944, p. 3, *Daily Express*, 17 March 1944, p. 3, On *Tunisian Victory* see Aldgate and Richards, *Britain Can Take It*, ch. 13; C. Coultass, 'Tunisian Victory: A Film Too Late?', *Imperial War Museum Review*, 1 (1986), pp. 64–73; A. Aldgate, 'Creative Tensions: *Desert Victory*, the Army Film Unit and Anglo-American Rivalry, 1943–5', *Britain and the Cinema in the Second World War*, P. M. Taylor, ed. (London, 1988), ch. 8.

78. M-O, FR 1083, Summary Report on ATS Campaign, 28 January 1942; R. Terry, *Women in Khaki: The Story of the British Woman Soldier* (London, 1988), p. 125; F. Pile, *Ack-Ack* (London, 1949), p. 188; Hodson, *Home Front*, p. 118; G. Baraybon and P. Summerfield, *Out of the Cage: Women's Experiences In Two World Wars* (London, 1987), pp. 165–66; see P. Summerfield, *Reconstructing Women's Wartime Lives: Discourse and Subjectivity in Oral Histories of the Second World War* (Manchester, 1998), pp. 73 n. 38, 164; T. Harrison, 'Appeals to Women', *Political Quarterly*, 13 (1942), p. 277.

79. These included a more photogenic Director of the ATS, a less dowdy uniform, and commissioning a public report on measures to improve conditions in the service. J. M. Cowper, *The Auxiliary Territorial Service* (London, 1949), pp. 236–38; see Terry, *Women in Khaki*, pp. 127–32; see also Pile, *Ack-Ack*, p. 193.

80. *Kinematograph Weekly*, 20 August 1942, p. 43, 13 August 1942, p. 26B, 6 August 1942, p. 17, 4 June 1942, p. 18; R. Howard, *In Search of My Father: A Portrait of Leslie Howard* (London, 1981), p. 125; R. John in McFarlane, *Autobiography*, p. 329. After Howard fell ill, Maurice Elvey completed shooting according to Howard's instructions. L. Wood, *The Commercial Imperative in the British Film Industry: Maurice Elvey, a Case Study* (London, 1987), p. 27. Brunel was far from pleased at being replaced, on the initiative of Derrick De Marney, over what he thought was unfair criticism of the initial rushes taken at the tiny upper studio at Highbury, but agreed to serve as production assistant to his friend Leslie Howard. A. Brunel, *Nice Work: The Story of Thirty Years in British Film Production* (London, 1949), pp. 192–93.

81. See BFI, *The Gentle Sex* pressbook.

82. Howard may, in fact, have been trying to reprise his recent screen roles as a charming misogynist (*Pygmalion, Pimpernel Smith*) in order to indicate a shift in attitude as the film progresses. If so, the transformation appears at best incomplete. On the problems of trying to reconcile traditional images of women with the demands of war in *The Gentle Sex* see A. Lant, *Blackout: Reinventing Women for Wartime British Cinema* (Princeton, 1991), pp. 93–99. See also S. Harper, 'The Representation of Women in British Feature Films,

1939–45', *Britain and the Cinema in the Second World War*, P. M. Taylor, ed. (London, 1988), p. 172.

83. IWM, 92/15/1, Melville Diary, 8 April 1943.

84. *Spectator*, 16 April 1943, p. 359; *Manchester Guardian*, 27 July 1943, p. 3; *Daily Telegraph*, 12 April 1943, p. 2; *Kinematograph Weekly*, 22 April 1943, p. 38–39; *Daily Mirror*, 7 April 1943, p. 5; *Daily Herald*, 10 April 1943, p. 2; *Daily Express*, 10 April 1943, p. 2, 7 April 1943, p. 3; see also, e.g., *Monthly Film Bulletin*, 30 April 1943, pp. 37–38; *The Times*, 7 April 1943, p. 6; Lejeune, *Chestnuts*, pp. 95–96.

85. Richards and Sheridan, *Mass-Observation*, pp. 267, 260, 262, 266, 278, also 234, 237, 248, 250, 252, 257, 261, 264, 266, 270, 275, 280, 281, 282, 286, 288, 289; see also Poole, 'Wartime Cinema Attendance', p. 24.

86. PRO, WO 163/161, morale report, August-October 1942.

87. Ibid., App. A to MC/P(43)1; see morale report, November 1942 to January 1943; INF 1/292, pt 3, HI weekly reports 102, 103, 105, 106, 112, 119, 129, 130, 132, 137, 138, 143, 146, 146, 148 (September 1942-August 1943).

88. E. Ambler, *Here Lies: An Autobiography* (London, 1985), pp. 184–85.

89. P. Ustinov, *Dear Me* (London, 1977), p. 118, ch. 8; Ustinov in McFarlane, *Autobiography*, p. 585–86; Ambler, *Here Lies*, pp. 159, 162, 185.

90. Ambler, *Here Lies*, p. 185. Peggy Ashcroft had a small role in the film. See M. Billington, *Peggy Ashcroft* (London, 1988), pp. 105–6.

91. PRO, WO 163/161, MC/M(43)4, 26 April 1943.

92. Ambler, *Here Lies*, p. 185. Peter Ustinov states in his memoirs that *The New Lot* was shown not only during but long after the war. It seems likely, however, that he was in fact thinking of *The Way Ahead*. Ustinov, *Dear Me*, p. 199.

93. Ambler, *Here Lies*, pp. 185–86.

94. TV Ontario, 79/80B, Cass B SP 31388, Elwy Yost interview with David Niven for 'Saturday Night at the Movies', 28 June 1979; Niven, *Moon's a Balloon*, pp. 226, 221, 211, 204.

95. Granger, *Sparks Fly Upward*, pp. 73–75. Though it did do occasional war films (e.g. *We Dive at Dawn*), Gainsborough made most of its money from costume melodramas, and was thus one of the least likely studios to take on such a project. On industry attitudes to war films in this period see, e.g., *Kinematograph Weekly*, 14 January 1943, p. 103.

96. See S. Morley, *The Other Side of the Moon: The Life of David Niven* (London, 1985), p. 125.

97. Ambler, *Here Lies*, p. 186.

98. TV Ontario, 79/80B, Cass B SP 31388, Elwy Yost interview with David Niven for 'Saturday Night at the Movies', 28 June 1979; see also BFI Special Collections, Carol Reed Papers, box 12, cutting of 6 May 1944, *Evening News* interview with Niven.

99. PRO, INF 1/224, Niven to O'Donnell, 27 November 1942; see E. Linklater, *Fanfare for a Tin Hat* (London, 1970), pp. 185–250.

100. PRO, INF 1/224, Beddington to Del Guidice, 11 November 1942, Del Guidice to Beddington, 7 November 1942, Niven to O'Donnell, 27 November 1942.
101. PRO, INF 1/224, Niven to O'Donnell, 27 November 1942; see Ambler, *Here Lies*, p. 186.
102. Ambler, *Here Lies*, p. 187; see Ustinov, *Dear Me*, p. 130.
103. Ambler, *Here Lies*, p. 187n.
104. TV Ontario, 79/80B, Cass B SP 31388, Elwy Yost interview with David Niven for 'Saturday Night at the Movies', 28 June 1979.
105. N. Wapshott, *The Man Between: A Biography of Carol Reed* (London, 1990), pp. 163–64; PRO, INF 1/224, Niven to Beddington, 27 March 1943; IWM, Tritton diary, 86/207/1, 1 April 1943; see Tam to Margaret, 20 March 1943, in K. Dunn (ed.), *Always and Always: The Wartime Letters of Hugh and Margaret Williams* (London, 1995), p. 89.
106. PRO, INF 1/224, negotiations with J. Arthur Rank, March 1943, final contract between Two Cities and MoI.
107. I. Carmichael, *Will the Real Ian Carmichael . . .* (London, 1979), p. 153; G. Green in McFarlane, *Autobiography*, p. 233; Ambler, *Here Lies*, pp. 187–89; Ustinov, *Dear Me*, 131–32; Morley, *Other Side of the Moon*, pp. 127–28; PRO, INF 1/224, Bromhead minute, 29 June 1943; see Wapshott, *Man Between*, p. 165. Niven's services were eventually bought at the cost of virtually handing over control of the film in America to Goldwyn. See INF 1/224, Del Guidice to May, 12 October 1943.
108. Other feature films based on this premise included *Millions Like Us* (Gainsbrough, 1943), about women in industry, and *The Bells Go Down* (Ealing, 1943), about men in the fire service. One of the differences between *Nine Men* and *The Way Ahead* was the higher proportion in Watt's film of working-class as against middle-class or lower middle-class characters. See C. Coultass, *Images for Battle: British Film and the Second World War, 1939–1945* (Newark, NJ, 1989), p. 161. On the decision *not* to emphasize home life in the manner of *In Which We Serve*, see Boston University Library, Special Collections, Eric Ambler Papers, Ambler to Frend, 16 October 1951, 'Notes on *The Cruel Sea*', p. 9.
109. S. Holloway, *Wiv a Little Bit o'Luck* (London, 1967), p. 261.
110. J. Carney, *Who's There? The Life and Career of William Hartnell* (London, 1996), p. 97. Hartnell was so good in the role that he would be called to reprise it in several postwar features and a television series. Ironically, he himself had hated the six months he was in the army in 1941. Ibid., pp. 88, 125, 131–33, 136.
111. This is examined in detail in V. Porter and C. Litewski, 'The Way Ahead: Case History of a Propaganda Film', *Sight and Sound*, 50 (1981), pp. 114–15.
112. 'The Beginning' was substituted for 'The End' after the first showing. See BFI Special Collections, Carol Reed Papers, box 12, cutting from *Yorkshire Post*, 12 June 1944.
113. *Daily Telegraph*, 20 December 1943, p. 3; see *Daily Express*, 18 December 1943, p. 2; *The Times*, 20 December 1943, p. 6.

114. PRO, WO 163/162, morale committee report, August-October 1943. Matters did improve in 1944. See ibid., February-April 1944.

115. PRO, INF 1/292, pt 4, HI weekly reports, 14 April 1944, 27 April 1944, 4 May 1944, 2 June 1944; see CAB 102/848, S. Taylor, 'A People at War: Thought and Mood on the Home Front', p. 23.

116. IWM, 86/207/1, Tritton diary, 28 May 1944.

117. BFI Special Collections, Carol Reed Papers, box 12, pressbook for *The Way Ahead*.

118. C. A. Lejeune, *Chestnuts in Her Lap* (London, 1947), p. 123. Reviews of *The Way Ahead* can be found in BFI Special Collections, Carol Reed Papers, box 12, press clippings album; see also *Monthly Film Bulletin*, 30 June 1944, p. 68.

119. PRO, INF 1/224, Bracken to Niven, 14 July 1944; BFI Special Collections, Carol Reed Papers, box 12, Beddington to Reed, 1 July 1944, 'Bob' (Combined Operations HQ) to Reed, 10 June 1944, Burnham to Reed, 9 June 1944; see also INF 1/224, Calder-Marshall to Reed, 5 June 1944.

120. PRO, INF 1/224, royalties statement, 2 February 1946; see also *Kinematograph Weekly*, 11 January 1945, p. 45; G. Macnab, *J. Arthur Rank and the British Film Industry* (London, 1993), p. 87. The fate of the film in America was another matter entirely. See Porter and Litewski, 'The Way Ahead', p. 116.

121. J. P. Mayer, *British Cinemas and their Audiences: Sociological Studies* (London, 1948), pp. 92, 172, 175, 177, 185, 201, 203, 205, 214, 225, 227, 234, 239; see also Poole, 'Cinema Attendance', p. 25.

122. Niven, *Moon's a Balloon*, p. 225.

123. The enormous bureaucratic difficulties in producing *The True Glory* are followed in detail in two articles: F. Krome, '*The True Glory* and the Failure of Anglo-American Film Propaganda in the Second World War', *Journal of Contemporary History*, 33 (1998), pp. 21–34; J. Chapman, '"The Yanks Are Shown to Such Advantage": Anglo-American Rivalry in the Production of *The True Glory* (1945)', *Historical Journal of Film, Radio and Television*, 16 (1996), pp. 533–54.

124. For the British these voices included those of Leslie Banks, Richard Attenborough, Leslie Dwyer, Celia Johnson and Jimmy Hanley.

125. *Daily Telegraph*, 2 August 1945, p. 5; *Daily Herald*, 2 August 1945, p. 3; *The Times*, 2 August 1945, p. 6; see Chapman, *British at War*, p. 152.

126. *Daily Herald*, 2 August 1945, p. 3.

127. I. Jarvie, 'The Burma Campaign on Film: *Objective Burma* (1945), *The Stillwell Road* (1945) and *Burma Victory* (1945)', *Historical Journal of Film, Radio and Television*, 8 (1988), pp. 59–66.

128. *The Times*, 25 October 1945, p. 6; *Daily Telegraph*, 29 October 1945, p. 3; see *Daily Herald*, 25 October 1945, p. 3; *Daily Express*, 25 October 1945, p. 3; I. Jarvie, 'Fanning the Flames: Anti-American Reaction to *Operation Burma*', *Historical Journal of Film, Radio and Television*, 1 (1981), pp. 117–37.

129. Jarvie, 'Burma Campaign on Film', p. 65.

Notes to Chapter 5: The Services and the Cinema, 1945–1970

1. See PRO, AIR 2/12261, enclosure 1C; *Air Force List, Navy List, Army List,* 1946–50. The Central Office of Information, successor to the wartime Ministry of Information, divested itself of all vetting functions concerning commercial features and other departments in 1946, and concentrated on production propaganda. See W. Crofts, *Coercion or Persuasion? Propaganda in Britain after 1945* (London, 1989).
2. PRO, WO 32/16022, sample Air Ministry film contract.
3. D. Gifford, *The British Film Catalogue, 1895–1970* (Newton Abbot, 1973), entries 10965, 10833, 10858, 10863; BFI Special Collections, Bernstein Papers, box 5, file A, Report on 1946–47 Bernstein Questionnaire; H. E. Browning and A. A. Sorrell, 'Cinemas and Cinema-Going in Great Britain', *Journal of the Royal Statistical Society,* 117 (1954), pp. 133–65.
4. The various possibilities are discussed in J. Ramsden, 'Refocusing "The People's War": British War Films of the 1950s', *Journal of Contemporary History,* 33 (1998), pp. 35–63; J. Chapman, 'Our Finest Hour Revisited: The Second World War in British Feature Films since 1945', *Journal of Popular British Cinema,* 1 (1998), pp. 63–75. See also B. Forbes, L. Gilbert, G. Green, M. Hordern, in B. McFarlane, *An Autobiography of British Cinema: As Told by the Filmmakers and Actors who Made it* (London, 1997), pp. 191, 221, 233, 307.
5. See S. Harper and V. Porter, 'Cinema Audience Tastes in 1950s Britain', *Journal of Popular British Cinema,* 2 (1999), p. 67.
6. On *They Who Dare* see D. Bogarde, *Snakes and Ladders* (London, 1978), p. 136.
7. *Kinematograph Weekly,* 19 December 1946, p. 46; BFI, *The Captive Heart* pressbook.
8. In the interim there had also appeared *The Small Back Room* (1949), a Powell and Pressburger adaptation of a novel involving a troubled bomb-disposal expert in which the army comes off better than the boffins. Help for this film, however, came from the Ministry of Supply rather than the War Office. BFI, *The Small Back Room* pressbook.
9. *Spectator,* 7 April 1950, p. 461.
10. Gifford, *British Film Catalogue,* entry 11439; *Kinematograph Weekly,* 14 December 1950, p. 10; *New Statesman,* 15 April 1950, p. 428; *Daily Express,* 31 March 1950, p. 6; see *Daily Herald,* 31 March 1950, p. 6; *The Times,* 30 March 1950, p. 8.
11. *Kinematograph Weekly,* 17 December 1953, p. 11; *The Times,* 14 August 1953, p. 10; *Daily Express,* 14 August 1953, p. 3; *Spectator,* 14 August 1953, p. 173; *Daily Herald,* 14 August 1953, p. 4; see *New Statesman,* 22 August 1953, p. 207.
12. PRO, DEFE 10/405, PRC/M(57)10, 31 October 1957. On recruiting drives see, e.g., C. Harding and B. Lewis (eds), *Talking Pictures: The Popular Experience of Cinema* (Bradford, 1993), p. 51. On promotional activities into which such drives could fit, see A. Burton and S. Chiball, 'Promotional Activities and

Showmanship in British Film Exhibitions', *Journal of Popular British Cinema*, 2 (1999), pp. 83–99.

13. T. Johnson and D. Del Vecchio, *Hammer Films: An Exhaustive Filmography* (Jefferson, NC, 1996), pp. 119–21. *The Steel Bayonet*, perhaps because it was too grittily realistic, was not a box office success story.

14. PRO, WO 32/16917, facilities for 'Dunkirk', 1957; WO 32/16478, facilities for *I Was Monty's Double*, 1957; WO 32/16026, facilities for *No Time to Die*, 1957; BFI, *No Time to Die* pressbook; *Ice Cold in Alex* pressbook.

15. *Kinematograph Weekly*, 18 December 1958, pp. 6–7. On *Ice Cold in Alex* see also J. Mills, *Up in the Clouds, Gentlemen Please* (London, 1980), pp. 230–32; A. Quayle, *A Time to Speak* (London, 1990), p. 340.

16. *Who Goes There?* (London Films, 1952) or *Orders Are Orders* (Group 3, 1954).

17. PRO, WO 32/16027, enclosure 18A, Shortt to Percival, 3 May 1957; Roy Boulting interview, *Oldie*, January 2000, p. 26. The War Office had consistently and more or less successfully thwarted efforts from various companies to make films about certain problematic wartime intelligence operations. See WO 32/16025; WO 32/16232; WO 32/17807.

18. BFI, NFT Interview, Boulting Brothers, 1969. On APFU clashes with the regular army see also F. Young, *Seventy Light Years* (London, 1999), pp. 54–55.

19. S. Boyd-Bowman, 'War and Comedy', *National Fictions: World War Two in British Films and Television*, G. Hurd, ed. (London, 1984), p. 40.

20. *The Times*, 6 March 1956, p. 7.

21. *Kinematograph Weekly*, 13 December 1956, pp. 6–7; *Daily Herald*, 17 February 1956, p. 6; *Daily Telegraph*, 18 February 1956, p. 8; *The Times*, 20 February 1956, p. 6. On the filming of *Private's Progess* see I. Carmichael, *Will the Real Ian Carmichael* ... (London, 1979), pp. 281–82; T. Thomas with T. Daum, *Terry-Thomas Tells Tales* (London, 1990), pp. 90–91.

22. On *The Army Game* see T. Vahimayi (ed.), *British Television: An Illustrated Guide* (London, 1996), p. 6; B. Sendall, *Independent Television in Britain*, i, *Origin and Foundations, 1946–62* (London, 1982), p. 334; M. Lewisohn, *Radio Times Guide to TV Comedy* (London, 1998), p. 43.

23. PRO, WO 32/16027, enclosure 18A, Shortt to Percival, 3 May 1957. On the making of *Bridge Over the River Kwai* see K. Brownlow, *David Lean: A Biography* (London, 1996), chs 26–27.

24. J. Carney, *Who's There? The Life and Career of William Hartnell* (London, 1996), p. 133.

25. See BFI, *Carry on Sergeant* pressbook; S. Hibbin and N. Hibbin, *What a Carry On: The Official Story of the Carry On Film Series* (London, 1988), pp. 7–8, 19; R. Davies (ed.), *The Kenneth Williams Diaries* (London, 1993), p. 141.

26. *Kinematograph Weekly*, 18 December 1958, p. 6; Hibbin and Hibbin, *What a Carry On*, p. 14, passim; see *Monthly Film Bulletin*, September 1958, p. 112; M. Jordan, 'Carry On ... Follow that Stereotype', *British Cinema History*, J. Curran and V. Porter, eds (London, 1983), pp. 312–27.

27. On *The League of Gentlemen* see *Kinematograph Weekly*, 15 December 1960,

p. 9; B. Forbes, *Notes for a Life* (London, 1974), pp. 288, 290, 292, 295; B. Forbes in McFarlane, *Autobiography*, p. 191; J. Hawkins, *Anything for a Quiet Life* (London, 1973), pp. 137–38. On *I Only Arsked* see Johnson and Del Vecchio, *Hammer Films*, pp. 150–52.

28. Neither was a hit, *A Hill in Korea* – which was shot in Portugal – being released at precisely the wrong moment during the Suez Crisis. See M. Caine, *What's It All About?* (London, 1992), pp. 101–6. On *Bitter Victory* see T. Steverson, *Richard Burton* (Westport, CT, 1992), pp. 112–14. There was also *Carrington VC* (1954), adapted from the stage courtroom drama by Dorothy and Campbell Christie and directed by Anthony Asquith, which could be read as both a critique and an affirmation of military virtue. See D. and C. Christie, *Carrington VC: A Play in Three Acts* (London, 1954). The film was well received by reviewers but did not score at the box office. See R. J. Minney, *'Puffin' Asquith* (London, 1973), pp. 168–69; *Kinematograph Weekly*, 15 December 1955, pp. 4–6; *Daily Telegraph*, 11 December 1954, p. 8; *Daily Express*, 10 December 1954, p. 6; *The Times*, 9 December 1954, p. 7.

29. On *Yesterday's Enemy* see Johnson and Del Vecchio, *Hammer Films*, pp. 162–63; *Kinematograph Weekly*, 17 December 1959, p. 6; see *Films and Filming*, September 1959, p. 24. On *The Long and the Short and the Tall* see M. Balcon, *Michael Balcon Presents ... A Lifetime in Films* (London, 1969), pp. 191–92, and, e.g., *Spectator*, 24 February 1961, p. 262.

30. The Hammer publicity people rather cannily invited senior officers who had served in Burma for a special showing of *Yesterday's Enemy* in the hope of eliciting some useful quotes. Either positive or negative assessments could be turned to advantage. They got what they needed from Major-General (retd) H. L. Davies, who had served in the campaign and who commented: 'I have never been so impressed or gripped by a film. The character portrayal is magnificent, and there is a realism and authenticity about the background that is quite frightening.' Johnson and Del Vecchio, *Hammer Films*, p. 162.

31. BFI, Cinema (Granada TV, 1964–75) Collection, J. Mills interview TS, 1971, p. 8, for earlier War Office concerns see pressbook, BFI.

32. *Kinematograph Weekly*, 15 December 1960, p. 10; see Mills, *Up in the Clouds*, p. 245.

33. M. Powell, *Million Dollar Movie* (London, 1992), pp. 414, see 409–13; see J. Howard, *Michael Powell* (London, 1996), pp. 141–42.

34. See K. Woolward, *Morning Departure: A Drama in Three Acts* (London, 1948).

35. Ibid.

36. J. Mills in McFarlane, p. 416; see P. J. Kemp, *The T-Class Submarine* (London, 1990), pp. 112–14.

37. *New Statesman*, 4 March 1950, p. 244; *Daily Herald*, 24 February 1950, p. 2; *Manchester Guardian*, 4 April 1950, p. 5; *The Times*, 24 February 1950, p. 2; *Daily Telegraph*, 27 February 1950, p. 6.

38. R. W. Baker in McFarlane, *Autobiography*, p. 49; see *Kinematograph Weekly*, 14 December 1950, p. 10. On letters to the Admiralty see PRO, ADM 1/22255.

39. On the St-Nazaire Raid see J. Dorrian, *Storming St Nazaire* (London, 1998).

40. On the evolution of the DNI from the CNI and changing attitudes toward publicity see PRO, ADM 1/20322, ADM 1/19195.

41. D. Castell, *Richard Attenborough: A Pictorial Film Biography* (London, 1984), p. 51.

42. *Daily Herald*, 18 July 1952, p. 4; *Daily Express*, 16 July 1952, p. 6; *Manchester Guardian*, 19 July 1952, p. 5; *Daily Telegraph*, 21 July 1952, p. 6; *The Times*, 21 July 1952, p. 6; see also *New Statesman*, 2 August 1952, p. 134.

43. *Kinematograph Weekly*, 18 December 1952, p. 10.

44. Balcon, *Michael Balcon Presents*, p. 179.

45. N. Monsarrat, *The Cruel Sea* (New York, 1951), p. 413.

46. Boston University Library, Special Collections, Eric Ambler Papers, 'Notes on *The Cruel Sea*', Ambler to Frend, 16 October 1951, p. 8.

47. Indeed, as the editor of *Picturegoer* noted, what had begun as a highly graphic novel ended up as a film mild enough to be granted a 'U' certificate. See G. Perry, *Forever Ealing* (London, 1981), p. 159.

48. Balcon, *Michael Balcon Presents*, p. 179; PRO, ADM 53/133507, HMS *Portchester Castle* log book, July 1952; *Picturegoer*, 19 July 1952, p. 10; Hawkins, *Quiet Life*, p. 102.

49. D. Sinden, *A Touch of the Memoirs* (London, 1982), p. 160; see Hawkins, *Quiet Life*, p. 104.

50. Hawkins, *Quiet Life*, pp. 103–4; Sinden, *Memoirs*, pp. 159–60. The accident was the result of Broome showing off.

51. N. Monsarrat, *Life is a Four-Letter Word*, ii, *Breaking Out* (London, 1970), p. 327.

52. B. Forbes in McFarlane, *Autobiography*, p. 191; D. Bogarde, *Snakes and Ladders* (London, 1978), p. 134. Officer-and-gentleman typecasting was not confined to films about the navy. 'The last air film I appeared in was *The Dam Busters* [1955],' burly Robert Shaw complained in the mid 1960s, 'and I came up for an audition as one of the pilots. They took a look at my jib and my brawn and waved me away. "Not officer material," they said. I played a sergeant.' L. Mosley, *The Battle of Britain: The Making of a Film* (London, 1969), p. 138.

53. A. Storey, *Stanley Baker: Portrait of an Actor* (London, 1977), p. 59.

54. Ericson's time in one of the more wretched corners of the merchant service, as explained in the book, was not referred to in the script. As with other things cut from the book, this was probably done mainly in order to condense a 416-page novel into a 126-minute film. (On the paring down of the story see Monsarrat, *Life*, ii, p. 326; Boston University Library, Special Collections, Eric Ambler Papers, 'Notes on *The Cruel Sea*', Ambler to Frend, 16 October 1951, pp. 7–9.) The effect, however, when combined with the casting of Jack Hawkins, was to make him appear a navy professional. The reference to Bennett having been a second-hand car salesman was something Ambler added when he changed the first lieutenant from an Australian into an Englishman. On Hawkins becoming typecast see Hawkins, *Quiet Life*, p. 94.

55. Monsarrat, *Breaking Out*, p. 334; see Hawkins, *Quiet Life*, p. 100.

56. *New Statesman*, 4 April 1953, p. 397; *Spectator*, 27 March 1953, p. 373.

57. *Kinematograph Weekly*, 17 December 1953, p. 10; G. Brown, *Der Produzent: Michael Balcon und der englische Film* (Berlin, 1981), p. 32.

58. BFI, *Single-Handed/Sailor of the King*, script S3299.

59. *Kinematograph Weekly*, 17 December 1953, pp. 10–11; *Daily Herald*, 24 July 1953, p. 6; *Spectator*, 12 June 1953, p. 757.

60. On naval support for *Above Us the Waves* see Sinden, *Memoirs*, pp. 207–10.

61. *Kinematograph Weekly*, 15 December 1955, p. 4; *New Statesman*, 16 April 1955, pp. 534–35; *Monthly Film Bulletin*, May 1955, p. 67; *Films and Filming*, May 1955, p. 18; *Manchester Guardian* (Manchester edn), 17 May 1955, p. 5; *Daily Mirror*, 23 April 1955, p. 15.

62. The UK reviews were lukewarm at best (see *Daily Telegraph*, 17 July 1954, p. 8; *The Times*, 19 July 1954, p. 11; *Spectator*, 16 July 1954, p. 82; *Daily Herald*, 16 July 1954, p. 7) and the film did not do well at the box office (see *Kinematograph Weekly*, 15 December 1955, pp. 4–5, 9).

63. C. E. L. Phillips, *Cockleshell Heroes* (London, 1956), pp. 250–52; see *The Times*, 3 May 1955, p. 14, 17 November 1955, p. 14; *Daily Herald*, 18 November 1955, p. 6; *Kinematograph Weekly*, 13 December 1956, p. 6.

64. *Kinematograph Weekly*, 13 December 1956, p. 9. For general positive critical reactions in the UK see *Daily Telegraph*, 10 March 1956, p. 8; *The Times*, 12 March 1956, p. 12; *Daily Herald*, 9 March 1956, p. 6; *New Statesman*, 17 March 1956, p. 242. It had been a delicate task bringing *The Man Who Never Was* to the screen in view of the way in which senior figures – including Mountbatten and Churchill – insisted on having a say in how they were portrayed. See Southampton University Library, Mountbatten Papers, MB1/I435; Churchill College, Cambridge, Churchill Papers, CHUR 4/60B, item 559.

65. Problems arose – as they had in *Western Approaches* – over the inability of a submarine to surface at an exact spot relative to the tracking vessel. B. Forbes, *A Divided Life* (London, 1992), p. 16; see J. Cardiff, *Magic Hour* (London, 1996), p. 78.

66. *Kinematograph Weekly*, 18 December 1958, p. 7.

67. *The Times*, 16 July 1956, p. 5.

68. *Kinematograph Weekly.*, 13 December 1956, p. 6; *Daily Telegraph*, 14 July 1956, p. 8; *Daily Herald*, 13 July 1956, p. 6; *Films and Filming*, September 1956, p. 27; *Spectator*, 20 July 1956, p. 99; R. Tantich, *John Mills* (London, 1993), p. 89. See A. Thorne, *The Baby and the Battleship* (London, 1956).

69. Powell, *Million Dollar Movie*, p. 260.

70. *The Gift Horse*, *The Cruel Sea* and *The Key* all featured captains suffering acutely from the burdens of command.

71. Powell, *Million Dollar Movie*, p. 269.

72. Ibid., p. 292; see also pp. 269–71, 282, 284–92; E. Millington-Drake, *The Drama of Graf Spee and the Battle of the River Plate: A Documentary Anthology*,

1914–1964 (London, 1964), memo on film, pp. 409–10; C. Challis, *Are They Really So Awful? A Cameraman's Chronicles* (London, 1995), p. 245.

73. Powell, *Million Dollar Movie*, p. 308.

74. *Daily Express*, 24 September 1956, p. 7; Powell *Million Dollar Movie*, p. 322; see Millington-Drake, *Graf Spee*, p. 409; Burton and Chibnall, 'Promotional Activities', p. 87.

75. *Picturegoer*, 1 December 1956, p. 16; see *Kinematograph Weekly*, 12 December 1957, 6; see also *The Times*, 30 October 1956, p. 3; *Daily Telegraph*, 3 November 1956, p. 8; *New Statesman*, 3 November 1956, p. 548; *Spectator*, 9 November 1956, p. 644; *Monthly Film Bulletin*, December 1956, p. 148; *Sight and Sound*, 26 (1956/57), p. 501; Howard, *Powell*, pp. 137–38.

76. H. Wilcox, *Twenty-Five Thousand Sunsets* (London, 1967), p. 196.

77. Southampton University, Mountbatten Papers, MB1/L188, 'Yangtse Incident' file; Wilcox, *Sunsets*, pp. 197–98. For another close call see R. Todd, *In Camera* (London, 1989), pp. 105–6.

78. *Daily Herald*, 2 April 1957, p. 3; *Films and Filming*, May 1957, p. 24; *New Statesman*, 6 April 1957, p. 440; see *Daily Telegraph*, 6 April 1957, p. 9; *The Times*, 2 April 1957, p. 3; *Glasgow Herald*, 21 July 1957, p. 5; *Sight and Sound*, 26 (1957), p. 209; see pressbook, BFI.

79. Wilcox, *Sunsets*, p. 200.

80. Ibid. On reaction to *The Silent Enemy*, filmed on location in Gibraltar with Admiralty assistance, see *Kinematograph Weekly*, 18 December 1958, p. 7; *The Times*, 5 March 1958, p. 3; *Daily Telegraph*, 8 March 1958, p. 4; *Films and Filming*, May 1958, pp. 22–23.

81. PRO, DEFE 10/246, sub-committee on public relations, ACP(PR)2, 5 May 1958.

82. *Girls at Sea*, a colour film produced and partially directed by Gilbert Gunn, was released late in 1958 with little reaction even in the provinces. See *Films and Filming*, December 1958, p. 21; BFI, *Girls at Sea* pressbook. *Carry on Admiral*, directed by Val Guest, had premiered in April of the previous year, and did well enough for its title to be reworked for the first of the true 'Carry On' films, *Carry on Sergeant*, the following year. See P. Rogers in Hubbin and Hubbin, *What a Carry On*, p. 7; see also BFI, *Carry on Admiral* pressbook.

83. See BFI, *The Ship That Died of Shame* information folder; see also N. Monsarrat, *The Ship That Died of Shame and Other Stories* (London, 1959), p. 225; J. Cook, 'The Ship that Died of Shame', *All Our Yesterdays*, C. Barr, ed. (London, 1986), pp. 362–67; T. O'Sullivan, 'Not Quite Fit for Heroes: Cautionary Tales of Men at Work – *The Ship That Died of Shame* and *The League of Gentlemen*', *Liberal Directions: Basil Dearden and Postwar British Film Culture*, A. Burton, T. O'-Sullivan, P. Wells, eds (Trowbridge, 1997), pp. 173–81; *Daily Mirror*, 23 April 1955, p. 15; *Daily Express*, 22 April 1955, p. 3.

84. Johnson and Del Vecchio, *Hammer Films*, pp. 135–36, 148–50; *Kinematograph Weekly*, 18 December. 1958, p. 7; see D. Tomlinson, *Luckier Than Most* (London, 1990), p. 119; *Glasgow Herald*, 14 July 1958, p. 3.

85. On *The Navy Lark* see *Films and Filming*, November 1959, p. 25; *The Times*,

19 October 1959, p. 6. On *The Bulldog Breed* see *Kinematograph Weekly*, 15 December 1960, p. 143.

86. See PR, DEFE 10/246, PRC/P(57)18. On the growing bias against traditional war films see, e.g., John Gillett, 'Westfront 1957', *Sight and Sound*, 27 (1957), p. 126; Anthony Carew in *Daily Herald*, 10 October 1958, p. 6.

87. Christopher Lee, who played an RN S-boat commander in *Cockleshell Heroes*, recalled that 'We shot all the submarine sequences off the coast of Portugal, using British submarines from the Portuguese navy – the only ones that were right for the period, because the British submarines from that period (1955, ten years after the war) were no longer correct, technically'. R. W. Pohle Jr and D. C. Hart, with the participation of C. Lee, *The Films of Christopher Lee* (Metuchen, NJ, 1983), p. 45. This may have been only partially correct – *Cockleshell Heroes* was filmed in Portugal because of weather and labour difficulties in Bordeaux; see *The Times*, 3 May 1955, p. 14 – but it is illustrative of the basic problem.

88. See, e.g., Gillett, 'Westfront', p. 126; A. Carew in *Daily Herald*, 10 October 1958, p. 6.

89. J. Spraos, *The Decline of the Cinema: An Economist's Report* (London, 1962), p. 24.

90. BFI, *Sink the Bismarck!* press information folder, pp. 32–34, 37–38, 47; K. More, *More or Less* (London, 1978), p. 179.

91. *Kinematograph Weekly*, 15 December 1960, p. 8; see *Daily Telegraph*, 13 February 1960, p. 11; *The Times*, 10 February 1960, p. 5; *Spectator*, 19 February 1960, p. 255; *New Statesman*, 13 February 1960, p. 219.

92. See, e.g., PRO, AIR 20/9127, RAF Participation in Public Events, summary as of 1 September 1951, p. 3.

93. *Daily Telegraph*, 24 March 1952, p. 6; see *The Times*, 21 March 1952, p. 2; *Manchester Guardian*, 22 March 1952, p. 3; *Daily Herald*, 21 March 1952, p. 4; *Spectator*, 21 March 1952, p. 366; *New Statesman*, 29 March 1952, p. 373; *Monthly Film Bulletin*, May 1952, p. 63.

94. *Kinematograph Weekly*, 18 December 1952, p. 10; see *Picturegoer*, 5 April 1952, p. 16.

95. *Kinematograph Weekly*, 17 December 1953, p. 10; *The Times*, 24 June 1953, p. 4; *Daily Telegraph*, 27 June 1953, p. 8; *Daily Herald*, 26 June 1953, p. 4; *New Statesman*, 4 July 1953, p. 17; see also Burton and Chibnall, 'Promotional Activities', p. 87.

96. J. Falconer, *RAF Bomber Command in Fact, Film and Fiction* (Phoenix Mill, 1996), pp. 92–93.

97. *Kinematograph Weekly*, 17 December 1953, p. 10; Bogarde, *Snakes and Ladders*, p. 135; *The Times*, 16 February 1953, p. 10; see *Daily Telegraph*, 16 February 1953, p. 10; *Spectator*, 13 February 1953, p. 181; *New Statesman*, 21 February 1953, p. 206; *Monthly Film Bulletin*, February 1953, p. 30.

98. R. Morris, *Guy Gibson* (London, 1994), p. 314.

99. See PRO, AIR 2/12261, enclosure 84A, Kruse to Ware, 17 November 1955.

100. Falconer, *Bomber Command*, p. 93; Todd, *In Camera*, pp. 68–69; BFI, *Dambusters* pressbook. As in *Appointment in London*, the Avro Lincolns then in service, which looked like Lancasters from a distance, were used to fill out flight line shots.

101. *Kinematograph Weekly*, 15 December 1955, p. 4; *Films and Filming*, July 1955, p. 14; *New Statesman*, 21 May 1955, p. 720; *Daily Herald*, 20 May 1955, p. 4; see *The Times*, 17 May 1955, p. 3; *Daily Telegraph*, 21 May 1955, p. 8; *Spectator*, 20 May 1955, p. 650.

102. *Kinematograph Weekly*, 13 December 1956, p. 6; *Daily Herald*, 6 July 1956, p. 6; see *Spectator*, 13 July 1956, p. 67. Bader himself disliked the film.

103. PRO, DEFE 10/246, Annex C, Note by Air Ministry, 4 (d).

104. On the making of *The Sound Barrier* see Brownlow, *David Lean*, ch. 22. An absence of Air Ministry involvement in the production is suggested in PRO, PREM 11/123.

105. BFI, *Conflict of Wings* pressbook.

106. *Spectator*, 2 April 1954, p. 386; *Daily Mail*, 2 April 1954, p. 6; *Daily Mirror*, 1 April 1954, p. 2; see also *News Chronicle*, 2 April 1954, p. 6.

107. See *Kinematograph Weekly*, 16 December 1954, pp. 9, 206; see BFI, *The Sea Shall Not Have Them* Information Folder. On *The Purple Plain* see BFI, *Purple Plain* pressbook; R. Parrish, *Hollywood Doesn't Live Here Anymore* (Boston, 1988), pp. 74–81.

108. PRO, AIR 20/9663, enclosure 8A, Bottomley Report, p. 8.

109. DEFE 10/405, PRC/P(57)18, 28 October 1957.

110. Gifford, *British Film Catalogue*, entry 12414; *Kinematograph Weekly*, 12 December 1957, p. 6; *Daily Herald*, 13 September 1957, p. 6; *Glasgow Herald*, 18 November 1957, p. 5; *The Times*, 16 September 1957, p. 3; see *Films and Filming*, November 1957, p. 25; *Monthly Film Bulletin*, November 1957, p. 139.

111. *Daily Telegraph*, 3 October 1959, p. 9; see pressbook, BFI.

112. A. Yule, *Sean Connery* (London, 1993), p. 65; see pressbook, BFI.

113. See PRO, AIR 19/1134, relations with BBC and ITV, 1959–65.

114. P. Pirelli, 'Statistical Survey of the British Film Industry', *British Cinema History*, J. Curran and V. Porter, eds (London, 1984), p. 372.

115. On *633 Squadron*, *Mosquito Squadron*, and *The Pathfinders* see Falconer, *Bomber Command*, pp. 94–96, 106; see also BFI, *633 Squadron* pressbook. On *The Battle of Britain* see Mosley, ch. 3; PRO, AIR 18162; Young, *Light Years*, pp. 122–25. Lancaster models were used in *The Guns of Navarone* (1961) and *Operation Crossbow* (1965) as well as *The Pathfinders*.

116. National Sound Archive, V1596, Melvyn Bragg, South Bank Show Special: Richard Attenbrough (interview).

117. D. Castell, *Richard Attenborough* (London, 1984), p. 76; see pressbook, BFI.

118. See R. Murphy, *Sixties British Cinema* (London, 1992).

119. *The Bofors Gun* was based on a stage play by Joe McGrath, *The Hill* on a play by Ray Rigby and R. S. Allen. On *How I Won the War* see N. Sinyard, *The Films of Richard Lester* (London, 1985), pp. 48–53.

120. Chapman, 'Our Finest Hour', p. 67. The air films of the sixties were also popular, as was the American D-Day epic *The Longest Day* (Fox, 1962), for which producer Darryl F. Zanuck obtained some logistical assistance from Mountbatten and the Chiefs of Staff in return for emphasizing the British role. See M. Gussow, *Don't Say Yes Until I Finish Talking: A Biography of Darryl F. Zanuck* (New York, 1971), p. 220.

121. Perilli, 'Statistical Survey', p. 373. The complex relationship between the decline of film and the rise of television – and more recently the video cassette player – is discussed in D. Docherty, D. Morrison, M. Tracey, *The Last Picture Show? Britain's Changing Film Audiences* (London, 1987).

122. Vahimaya, *British Television*, p. 215.

123. It was significant that Operation Market-Garden had a strong American presence, thus allowing Attenborough access to American financing. It is also worth noting that even with MoD help, a score of museums and foreign forces had to be scoured to find enough Second World War era vehicles and aircraft to make the film look authentic. See J. Hacker and D. Price, *Take Ten: Contemporary British Film Directors* (Oxford, 1991), pp. 80–82. The previous year the MoD had allowed Associated General Films to use runways and a hanger at St Mawgans, a Nimrod base, as a backdrop for scenes in *The Eagle Has Landed*, even though in this film it is the Germans who are (more or less) the heroes. BFI, *The Eagle Has Landed*, press information folder, p. 13.

124. The army equivalent to Royal Navy support for the 1970s BBC drama series *Warship*, for example, involved lending a hand with the popular 1990s Carlton drama series *Soldier Soldier*. See, e.g., J. G. Lewis, *Soldier Soldier: Diary of a Soldier* (London, 1997), p. 93.

Notes to Conclusion

1. Admiral Williams, whose career path had involved naval aviation, not Admiralty public relations, had retired as NATO Deputy Supreme Commander, Atlantic.

2. G. Macdonald Fraser, *The Hollywood History of the World* (London, 1988), p. 224; see P. Stead, *Film and the Working Class: The Feature Film in British and American Society* (London, 1989), pp. 131–32. For the theoretical angle on this see P. Corrigan, 'Film Entertainment as Ideology and Pleasure: Towards a History of Audiences', *British Cinema History*, J. Curran and V. Porter, eds (London, 1984), p. 26; J. Mayne, *Cinema and Spectatorship* (London, 1993), pp. 80–81, 92–93. See in addition J. Curran, 'The New Revisionism in Mass Communications Research: A Reappraisal', and D. Morley, 'Populism, Revisionism and the "New" Audience Research', in *Cultural Studies and Communications*, J. Curran, D. Morley, V. Walkerdine, eds (London, 1996), chs 11–12.

3. See *Documentary News Letter*, May 1943, p. 67.

4. No effort was made by Howard to model himself on the real R. J. Mitchell,

whose career was heavily modified for the screen not only for dramatic purposes but also to make the story more in line with the standard Howard persona.

5. The similarity between the terms used by critics and by surveyed cinemagoers in describing why certain films appealed to them is quite striking. Compare J. Richards and D. Sheridan, *Mass-Observation at the Movies* (London, 1987), passim; J. P. Mayer, *British Cinemas and their Audiences* (London, 1948), and responses to MoI shorts in PRO, INF 1/293, Home Intelligence Special Report No. 28, 22 Aug. 1942, with reviews. On the period-specific of 'real' on film and the willingness of people to attend pictures because they believe on the basis of advance publicity that they will conform to expectations as regards narrative content, see J. Ellis, *Visible Fictions* (London, 1992), pp. 30–31, 50; J. Trevelyan, *What the Censor Saw* (London, 1973), p. 156. Films or parts of films that were in fact very realistic but did not conform to audience expectations of the real on screen, such as swearing, could at least for a time disconnect the audience from the characters on screen. See M. Beresford, 'Realism and Emotion', *Sight and Sound*, 14 (1945), pp. 13–14; R. Manvell, 'They Laugh at Realism', *Documentary News Letter*, March 1943, p. 188. Conversely, somewhat unrealistic working-class accents and manners could still be appreciated by lower-class audiences as long as characters were portrayed in a positive light. See, e.g., Richards and Aldgate, p. 216 n. 66.

6. The phrase coined by Roger Durgnat for the title of his book *A Mirror for England: British Movies from Austerity to Affluence* (London, 1970); see V. Porter, *On Cinema* (London, 1985), p. 40.

7. Macdonald Fraser, *Hollywood History*, pp. 239–40.

8. Actors who became partly typecast in war roles included Jack Hawkins, John Gregson, John Mills, Trevor Howard and Kenneth More. One of the key differences between wartime and postwar films was that NCOs and Other Ranks were gradually relegated to the background in the fifties. This may well have been a reflection of middle-class bias now that the war was won J. Ramsden, 'Refocusing "The People's War": British War Films of the 1950s', *Journal of Contemporary History* 33 (1998), p. 56. It may also have had something to do with the fact that the plots were based on books written by officers (i.e. their own stories). It is also important to remember that the wartime films themselves highlighted but did not question the class structure as such. See A. Marwick, *Class: Image and Reality in Britain, France and the USA since 1930* (London, 1980), p. 227.

9. Macdonald Fraser, *Hollywood History*, p. 224.

10. Political and Economic Planning (P. E. P.), *The British Film Industry* (London, 1952), p. 85; see Porter, *On Cinema*, p. 42.

11. B. Forbes in McFarlane, *Autobiography*, p. 85.

12. On the issue of 'staged' footage from theses films being used in TV documentaries see N. Frankland, *History at War* (London, 1998), pp. 181–95. Even before the TV documentaries of the 1960s, footage used in *Desert Victory* appeared

in the establishing sequences of both *Ice Cold in Alex* (Associated British, 1958) and *Danger Within* (British Lion, 1959), the latter a POW film set in 1943 Italy. Scenes from *Target for Tonight* were used in episode twelve (Whirlwind: Bombing Germany, September 1939-April 1944) of the Thames Television series *The World at War* (1973–74) to satirize the gap between the rhetoric and reality of bombing *circa* 1941.

13. See, e.g., J. Chapman, *The British at War: Cinema, State and Propaganda, 1939–1945* (London, 1997), p. 187.

14. The opinions expressed in this section, which are to some extent subjective, arose from analyzing undergraduate reactions to the films and estimating the frequency with which they are rebroadcast on TV.

15. A position manifest in everything from Dilys Powell's *Films Since 1939* (London, 1947) to Charles Drazin's *The Finest Years: British Cinema of the 1940s* (London, 1998).

Bibliography

PRIMARY SOURCES

Public Record Office

ADM 1, 53, 116, 167, 173.
AIR 2, 8, 14, 19, 20, 28.
AVIA 22.
CAB 65, 27, 102. DEFE 10, 53.
FO 371, 395.
INF 1, 2, 4, 5, 6, 12.
PREM 4, 11, 12.
T 162.
TS 27.
WO 32, 163, 165, 258, 259.

Private Papers

Adam, R., Liddell Hart Centre for Military Archives.
Ambler, E., Department of Special Collections, Boston University Library.
Balcon, M., Special Collections, British Film Institute.
Beaverbrook (Max Aitkin, 1st Lord Beaverbrook), House of Lords Record Office.
Brooke, C., Special Collections, British Film Institute.
Churchill, W. S. C., Churchill College Cambridge.
Cunnigham, A., British Library.
Elibank (A. Murray, 1st Viscount Elibank), National Library of Scotland.
Elliot, W. E., National Library of Scotland.
Grigg, P. J., Churchill College Cambridge.
King-Hall, S., Liddell Hart Centre for Military Archives.
Meville, A. D., Imperial War Museum.
Mountbatten (1st Earl Mountbatten), University of Southampton.
Reed, C., Special Collections, British Film Institute.
Tritton, R. E., Imperial War Museum.
Urban, C., Science Museum Library.

Interviews

Asquith, A., BFI Special Collections, Granada TV, 1964–75.
Attenborough, R., TV Ontario, BPN 180201, 1979/80.
Baker, S., BFI Special Collections, Granada TV, 1964–75.
Balcon, M., BFI, National Film Theatre, 1969.
Boulting, R., IWM Sound Archive, 4627/1–6, TS.
Boulting, R. and J., BFI, National Film Theatre, 1969.
Coward, N., BFI, National Film Theatre, 1969.
Howard, T., BFI Special Collections, Granada TV, 1964–75.
Macdonald, D., IWM Sound Archive, 4654/1–3, TS.
Mills, J., BFI, BECTU History Project 401.
——, BFI Special Collections, Granada TV, 1964–75.
Niven, D., TV Ontario, 79/80B, Cass B SP 31388.
O'Neill, D., IWM Sound Archive, 3971/104, TS.
Powell, M., BFI, National Film and Television Archive, 202268A.
——, BFI, National Film Theatre, 1971.
Prosser, D., IWM Sound Archive, 4844/1–9, TS.
Stewart, H., IWM Sound Archive, 4579/1–6, TS.
Ustinov, P., BFI, National Film Theatre, 1990.
Watt, H., BFI, National Film Theatre, 1974.

Unpublished Documents

Bernstein Questionnaires, Special Collections, BFI Library.
BBFC Scenario Reports, Special Collections, BFI Library.
B6/1, History of the Royal Air Force Film Production Unit, 1945, IWM Department of Film.
Mass-Observation File Reports 66, 163, 723, 445, 1083, 1120, TC 29 box 2 files A, D, Tom Harrisson Mass-Observation Archive.

Unpublished Scripts

S7495 *Forever England*; S4373 *OHMS*; S4380 *Convoy*; S232 *Sailors Three*; S1591 *Ships With Wings*; S10867 *They Were Not Divided*; S313 *Yangtse Incident*.

Pressbooks, Press Sheets, Information Folders, etc. (BFI Library)

Above Us the Waves; All at Sea; Angels One Five; The Battle of the River Plate; The Bofors Gun; Brown on Resolution; The Captive Heart; Carry on Admiral; Carry on Sergeant; Conflict of Wings; Convoy; The Cruel Sea; The Dam Busters; The Drum; Dunkirk; Farewell Again; For Those in Peril; The Gentle Sex; The Gift Horse; Girls at Sea: Hail and Farewell; In Which We Serve; Ice Cold in Alex; It's in the Air, *Jack Ahoy!*; *Journey Together*; *Long and the Short and the Tall*; *Luck of the Navy*; *The Middle Watch*; *Morning Departure*; *Nine Men*; *No Time to Die!*; *OHMS*; *On the Fiddle*; *One of Our Aircraft is Missing*; *Operation Bullshine*; *The Purple Plain*; *The Sea Shall Not Have Them*; *The Ship That Died of Shame*; *Ships With Wings*; *Single-Handed*; *Sink the Bismarck!*; *The Small Back Room*; *We Dive at Dawn*; *Yangtse Incident*.

Film Programmes

Above Us the Waves; *The Dam Busters*; *Zeebrugge*.

Newspapers and Magazines

Bioscope; *Cinema News and Property Gazette*; *Cinema Today*; *Daily Express*; *Daily Herald*; *Daily Mail*; *Daily Mirror*; *Daily Telegraph*; *Documentary News Letter*; *Evening News*; *Film Weekly*; *Films and Filming*; *Glasgow Herald*; *Kinematograph Weekly*; *Manchester Guardian*; *Monthly Film Bulletin*; *New Statesman and Nation*; *News Chronicle*; *Observer*; *Picturegoer*; *Sight and Sound*; *Spectator*; *Sunday Express*; *Sunday Times*; *The Times*.

Books

Anon., *The Admiralty Account of Naval Air Operations, Prepared for the Admiralty by the Ministry of Information*, HMSO, 1943.

Anon., *The Battle of Britain: An Air Ministry Record*, HMSO, 1941.

Anon., *Bomber Command: The Air Ministry Account of the Bomber Command's Offensive Against the Axis*, HMSO, 1941.

Anon., *Bomber Command Continues: The Air Ministry Account of the Rising Offensive Against Germany, July 1941–June 1942*, HMSO, 1942.

Anon., *The British Army*, London, 1940.

Anon., *Coastal Command: The Air Ministry Account of the Part Played by Coastal Command in the Battle of the Seas, 1939–1942*, HMSO, 1942.

Anon., *His Majesty's Minesweepers*, HMSO, 1943.

Anon., *Winged Words: Our Airmen Speak for Themselves*, London, 1941.

Anon., *The Royal Air Force at War*, London, 1940.

Ambler, E., *Here Lies: An Autobiography*, London, 1985.

Austin, A. B., *Fighter Command*, London, 1941.

Balcon, M., E. Lindgren, F. Hardy and R. Manvell, *Twenty Years of British Film, 1925–1945*, London, 1947.

Balcon, M., *Michael Balcon Presents ... A Lifetime of Films*, London, 1969.

Beaverbrook [Lord], *Men and Power, 1917–1918*, London, 1956.

Bennett, J. with S. Gordon, *Godfrey: A Special Time Remembered*, London, 1983.

Bishop, E., *The Guinea Pig Club*, London, 1963.

Bogarde, D., *Snakes and Ladders*, London, 1978.

'Boomerang', *Bless 'Em All: An Analysis of the British Army, its Morale, Efficiency and Leadership*, London, 1942.

Boothby, R., *Boothby: Recollections of a Rebel*, London, 1978.

Brownlow, K., *How It Happened Here*, London, 1968.

Brownrigg, D., *Indiscretions of the Naval Censor*, New York, 1920.

Brunel, A., *Nice Work: The Story of Thirty Years in British Film Production*, London, 1949.

Caine, M., *What's it All About?*, London, 1992.

Cantril, G. (ed.), *Public Opinion, 1935–1946*, Princeton, 1951.

Cardiff, J., *Magic Hour*, London, 1996.

Carmichael, I., *Will the Real Ian Carmichael . . .* London, 1979.

Challis, C., *Are They Really So Awful? A Cameraman's Chronicles*, London, 1995.

Cheshire, L., *Bomber Pilot*, London, 1943.

Christie, I. (ed.), *The Life and Death of Colonel Blimp*, London, 1994.

——, *Powell, Pressburger and Others*, London, 1978.

Cook, C. (ed.), *The Dilys Powell Film Reader*, Manchester, 1991.

Cotterell, A., *Oh, It's Nice to be in the Army!*, London, 1941.

——, *What! No Morning Tea?*, London, 1941.

Coward, N., *Autobiography*, London, 1986.

Croft, H. P., *My Life of Strife*, London, 1948.

Davies, R. (ed.), *The Kenneth Williams Diaries*, London, 1993.

Dean, B., *Mind's Eye: An Autobiography*, London, 1973.

Dickson, W. K. L., *The Biograph in Battle: Its Story in the South African War Related with Personal Experiences*, Trowbridge, 1995.

Dunn, K. (ed.), *Always and Always: The Wartime Letters of Hugh and Margaret Williams*, London, 1995.

Edwards, K., *We Dive at Dawn*, London, 1939.

Farrar, D., *No Royal Road: Autobiography*, London, 1947.

Forbes, B., *Notes for a Life*, London, 1974.

——, *A Divided Life*, London, 1992.

Forester, C. S., *Long Before Forty*, London, 1967.

——, *Brown on Resolution*, London, 1929.

Frankland, N., *History at War*, London, 1998.

Gibson, G., *Enemy Coast Ahead*, London, 1946.

Granger, S., *Sparks Fly Upward*, New York, 1981.

Graves, C., *The Avengers*, London, 1941.

Grigg, P. J., *Prejudice and Judgment*, London, 1948.

Guiness, A., *Blessings in Disguise*, London, 1985.

Harding, C. and B. Lewis (eds), *Talking Pictures: The Popular Experience of the Cinema*, Castleford, 1993.

Harris, R., *Rex: An Autobiography*, London, 1974.

Hawkins, J., *Anything for a Quiet Life*, London, 1973.

Hawton, H., *The Men Who Fly*, London, 1944.

Hay, I. and S. King-Hall, *The Middle Watch: A Romance of the Navy*, London, 1931.

Hay, I., *Arms and the Men*, London, 1950.

——, *The British Infantryman*, London, 1942.

Hibbin, S. and N. Hibbin (eds), *What a Carry On: The Official Story of the Carry On Film Series*, London, 1988.

Hodgson, V., *Few Eggs and No Oranges: A Diary*, London, 1976.

Hodson, J., *Home Front: Being Some Account of Journeys, Meetings and What was Said To Me in and about England during 1942–1943* (London, 1944).

Holloway, S., *Wiv a Little Bit o' Luck* (London, 1967).

Hordern, M with P. England, *A World Elsewhere: The Autobiography of Sir Michael Hordern*, London, 1993.

Joseph, M., *The Sword in the Scabbard*, London, 1942.

Kimble, P., *Newspaper Reading in the Third Year of the War*, London, 1942.

Lawrence, T. E., *The Mint*, London, 1956.

Lejeune, A. (ed.), *The C. A. Lejeune Film Reader*, Manchester, 1997.

Lejuene, C. A., *Chestnuts in Her Lap*, London, 1947.

——, *Thank You For Having Me*, London, 1971.

Linklater, E., *Fanfare for a Tin Hat: A Third Essay in Autobiography*, London, 1970.

Low, D., *Low's Autobiography*, London, 1956.

Macmillan, N., *Air Strategy*, London, 1941.

Malins, G., *How I Filmed the War*, London, 1993.

Mason, J., *Before I Forget*, London, 1981.

Mayer, J. P., *Sociology of Film: Studies and Documents*, London, 1946.

——, *British Cinemas and their Audiences: Sociological Studies*, London, 1948.

Macnee, P. and M. Cameron, *Blind in One Ear*, London, 1988.

Massey, R., *A Hundred Different Lives: An Autobiography*, Toronto, 1979.

McFarlane, B., *An Autobiography of British Cinema: As Told by the Filmmakers and Actors who Made it*, London 1997.

Middlebrook, M. and C. Everitt, *The Bomber Command War Diaries: An Operational Reference Book, 1939–1945*, Harmondsworth, 1985.

Milligan, S., *Adolf Hitler: My Part in His Downfall*, London, 1971.

Millington-Drake, E., *The Drama of the Graf Spee and the Battle of the Plate: A Documentary Anthology 1914–1964*, London, 1964.

Mills, J., *Up in the Clouds, Gentlemen Please*, London, 1980.

Mitchie, A. A., *The Air Offensive Against Germany*, New York, 1943.

Monsarratt, N., *The Cruel Sea*, London, 1951.

——, *Life is a Four-Letter Word*, ii, *Breaking Out*, London, 1970.

Montagu, E., *The Man Who Never Was: The Story of Operation Mincemeat*, London, 1954.

More, K., *More or Less*, London, 1978.

Morgan, G., *Red Roses Every Night: An Account of London Cinemas under Fire*, London, 1948.

Morley, R. and S. Stokes, *Robert Morley: A Reluctant Autobiography*, New York, 1966.

Nicolson, N. (ed.), *Harold Nicolson: The War Years, 1939–1945*, ii, *Diaries and Letters*, London, 1967.

Niven, D., *The Moon's a Balloon*, London, 1971.

Olivier, L., *Confessions of an Actor: An Autobiography*, New York, 1982.

Parkinson, D. (ed.), *Mornings in the Dark: The Graham Greene Film Reader*, Manchester, 1993.

Parrish, R., *Hollywood Doesn't Live Here Anymore*, Boston, 1988.

Payne, G. and S. Morley (eds), *The Noël Coward Diaries*, London, 1981.

Pedan, M. *A Thousand Shall Fall*, Stittsville, ON, 1979.

Penguin Film Review, 1946–1949, i, London, 1977.

Political and Economic Planning (PEP), *The British Film Industry*, London, 1952.

Powell, D., *Films Since 1939*, London, 1947.

Powell, M., *A Life in Movies*, London, 1986.

——, *Million Dollar Movie*, London, 1992.

Quayle, A., *A Time to Speak*, London, 1990.

Ramsey, G., *Ships With Wings: The Illustrated Book of the Great Film*, London, 1942.

Rattigan, T., *The Collected Plays of Terence Rattigan*, London, 1953.

——, *Flare Path: A Play in Three Acts*, London, 1943.

Redgrave, M., *In My Mind's Eye: An Autobiography*, London, 1983.

Reynolds, Q., *By Quentin Reynolds*, London, 1963.

Richards, J. and D. Sheridan, *Mass-Observation at the Movies*, London, 1987.

Robson, E. W. and M. Robson, *The Shame and Disgrace of Colonel Blimp: The True Story of the Film*, London, 1944.

Sinden, D., *A Touch of the Memoirs*, London, 1982.

Slessor, J., *The Central Blue*, London, 1957.

Sussex, E., *The Rise and Fall of British Documentary: The Story of the Film Movement Founded by John Grierson*, Berkeley, 1975.

Terrell, E., *Admiralty Brief: The Story of Inventions that Contributed to Victory in the Battle of the Atlantic*, London, 1958.

Thorne, A., *The Baby and the Battleship*, London, 1956.

Thomas, T. with T. Daum, *Terry-Thomas Tells Tales: An Autobiography*, London, 1990.

Thomson, G. P., *Blue Pencil Admiral: The Inside Story of the Press Censorship*, London, 1947.

Todd, A., *The Eighth Veil*, London, 1980.

Todd, R., *In Camera: An Autobiography Continued*, London, 1989.

Tollemache, E. D. H., *The British Army at War*, London, 1941.

Tomlinson, D., *Luckier Than Most*, London, 1990.

Trevelyan, J., *What the Censor Saw*, London, 1973.

Ustinov, P., *Dear Me*, London, 1977.

Watt, H., *Don't Look at the Camera!*, London, 1974.

Wilcox, H., *Twenty-Five Thousand Sunsets*, London, 1967.

Wilding, M., *Apple Sauce: The Story of My Life*, London, 1982.

Williams, F., *Nothing So Strange: An Autobiography*, London, 1970.

Wood, E., *From Midshipman to Field Marshal*, London, 1912.

——, *Winnowed Memories*, London, 1917.

Woodward, K., *Morning Departure: A Drama in Three Acts*, London, 1948.

Young, F. as told to P. Busby, *Seventy Light Years: An Autobiography*, London, 1999.

Zielger, P. (ed.), *Personal Diary of Admiral the Lord Louis Mountbatten: Supreme Allied Commander, South-East Asia, 1943–1946*, London, 1988.

SECONDARY SOURCES

Radio and Television Programmes

BBC Radio, 'Dilys Powell's History of the British Cinema', 4, 'The War', National Sound Archive.

BBC TV, M. Bragg, 'The South Bank Show: Richard Attenborough', National Sound Archive/National Film and Television Archive.

BBC TV, M. Dean, 'Noël Coward: A Private Life', National Sound Archive.

BBC TV, M. Bragg, 'The South Bank Show: Noël Coward', National Sound Archive/National Film and Television Archive.

BBC TV, M. Bragg, 'The South Bank Show: Michael Powell', National Film and Television Archive.

BBC TV, M. Frayling, 'Filming for Victory: British Cinema 1939–1945', National Film and Television Archive.

Unpublished Theses

Allison, M. J., 'The National Service Issue, 1899–1914', Ph.D., University of London, 1975.

Assershohn, F. J. 'Propaganda and Policy: the Presentation of the Strategic Air Offensive in the British Mass Media, 1939–45', M. A., Leeds University, 1989.

Bohn, T. W. 'An Historical and Descriptive Analysis of the "Why We Fight" Series', Ph.D., University of Wisconsin, 1968.

Crang, J. A. 'A Social History of the British Army, 1939–45', Ph.D., Edinburgh University, 1993.

Books

Anderegg, M., *David Lean* (Boston, 1984).

Aldgate, A. and J. Richards, *Britain Can Take It: The British Cinema in the Second World War* (2nd edn, Edinburgh, 1994).

Armes, R., *A Critical History of British Cinema* (London, 1978).

Aspinall, S. and R. Murphy (eds), *Gainsborough Melodrama* (London, 1983).

Balfour, M., *Propaganda in War, 1939–1945: Organisations, Policies and Publics in Britain and Germany* (London, 1979).

Bamford, K., *Distorted Images: British National Identity and Film in the 1920s* (London, 1999).

Barnes, J., *Filming the Boer War* (London, 1992).

——, *The Beginnings of the Cinema in England, 1894–1901*, 5 vols (Exeter, 1996).

Barr, C., *Ealing Studios* (3rd edn, Berkeley, 1998).

Barrow, K., *Flora: An Appreciation of the Life and Work of Dame Flora Robson* (London, 1981).

Betts, E., *The Film Business: A History of British Cinema, 1896–1972* (London, 1973).

Billington, M., *Peggy Ashcroft* (London, 1988).

Bond, B., *British Military Policy between the Two World Wars* (Oxford, 1980).

Bowyer, C., *The Wellington Bomber* (London, 1986).

Bowyer, M. J. F., *Action Stations*, i, *Wartime Military Airfields of East Anglia, 1939–1945* (Cambridge, 1979).

——, *Fighting Colours: RAF Fighter Camouflage and Markings, 1937–1975* (Cambridge, 1975).

Boyle, A., *Trenchard* (London, 1962).

Braun, E., *Deborah Kerr* (New York, 1978).

Braybon, G. and P. Summerfield, *Out of the Cage: Women's Experiences in Two World Wars* (London, 1987).

Bret, D., *George Formby: A Troubled Genius* (London, 1999).

Brewer, S. A., *To Win the Peace: British Propaganda in the United States during World War II* (Ithaca, NY, 1997).

Brown, G., *Der Produzent: Michael Balcon und der englische Film* (Berlin, 1981).

Brownlow, K., *David Lean: A Biography* (London, 1996).

Carew, A., *The Lower Deck of the Royal Navy, 1900–39* (Manchester, 1981).

Carney, J., *Who's There? The Life and Career of William Hartnell* (London, 1996).

Castell, D., *Richard Attenborough: A Pictorial Film Biography* (London, 1984).

Castelli, L. P. with C. L. Cleeland, *David Lean: A Guide to References and Sources* (Boston, 1980).

Chapman, J., *The British at War: Cinema, State and Propaganda, 1939–1945* (London, 1998).

Christie, I., *Arrows of Desire: The Films of Michael Powell and Emeric Pressburger* (London, 1985).

Cook, P. (ed.), *Gainborough Pictures* (London, 1977).

Coultass, C., *Images for Battle: British Film and the Second World War* (Cranbury, NJ, 1989).

Cowper, J. M., *The Auxiliary Territorial Service* (London, 1949).

Crofts, W., *Coercion or Persuasion? Propaganda in Britain after 1945* (London, 1989).

Cull, N. J., *Selling War: The British Propaganda Campaign Against American 'Neutrality' in World War II* (New York, 1985).

Curran, J. and V. Porter (eds), *British Cinema History* (London, 1983).

Curran, J., D. Morley, V. Walkerdine (eds), *Cultural Studies and Communications* (London, 1996).

Dickinson, M. and S. Street, *Cinema and State: The Film Industry and the British Government, 1927–84* (London, 1985).

Dixon, W. W. (ed.), *Re-Viewing British Cinema, 1900–1992* (Albany, NY, 1994).

Docherty, D. Morrison, M. Tracey, *The Last Picture Show? Britain's Changing Film Audiences* (London, 1987).

Drazin, C., *The Finest Years: British Cinema of the 1940s* (London, 1998).

Durgant, R., *A Mirror for England: British Movies from Austerity to Affluence* (London, 1970).

Ellis, J., *Visible Fictions: Cinema, Television, Video* (London, 1992).

Evans, M. and K. Lunn, *War and Memory in the Twentieth Century* (Oxford, 1997).

Falk, Q., *The Golden Gong: Fifty Years of the Rank Organization, its Films and its Stars* (London, 1980).

Fielding, R., *The March of Time, 1935–1951* (New York, 1978).

Fischer, C., *Noël Coward* (New York, 1992).

Fleming, K., *Celia Johnson: A Biography* (London, 1991).

Fowler, K. J., *David Niven: A Bio-Bibliography* (Westport, CT, 1985).

Frayling, C., *Things to Come* (London, 1995).

Freeman, R. A., *The British Airman* (London, 1989),

Garrett, G., *The Films of David Niven* (London, 1975).

Gifford, D., *The British Film Catalogue, 1895–1970: A Guide to Entertainment Films* (Newton Abbott, 1973).

Gilbert, M. S., *Winston S. Churchill*, iii, vi (London, 1971, 1983).

Glancy, H. M., *When Hollywood Loved Britain: The Hollywood 'British' Film, 1939–45* (Manchester, 1999).

Gledhill, C. and G. Sawnson (eds), *Nationalising Femininity: Culture, Sexuality and British Cinema in the Second World War* (Manchester, 1996).

Grant, I., *Cameramen at War* (Cambridge, 1980).

Grant, M., *Propaganda and the Role of the State in Inter-War Britain* (Oxford, 1994).

Gussow, M., *Don't Say Yes Until I Finish Talking: A Biography of Darryl F. Zanuck* (New York, 1971).

Hacker, J. and D. Price, *Take Ten: Contemporary British Film Directors* (Oxford, 1991).

Hallows, I. S., *Regiments and Corps of the British Army* (London, 1991).

Harper, S., *Picturing the Past: The Rise and Fall of the British Costume Film* (London, 1994).

Harries-Jenkins, G., *The Army in Victorian Society* (London, 1977).

Haste, C., *Keep the Home Fires Burning: Propaganda in the First World War* (London, 1977).

Hawton, H., *The Men Who Fly* (London, 1944).

Harley, J. E., *Worldwide Influence of the Cinema* (Los Angeles, 1940).

Hastings, M., *Bomber Command* (London, 1979).

Higham, C. and R. Moseley, *Princess Merle: The Romantic Life of Merle Oberon* (New York, 1983).

Higson, A. (ed.), *Dissolving Views: Writings on British Cinema* (London, 1996).

——, *Waving the Flag: Constructing a National Cinema in Britain* (Oxford, 1995).

Hirschhorn, C., *Gene Kelly* (New York, 1984).

Hoare, P., *Noël Coward* (New York, 1996).

Holden, A., *Laurence Olivier* (New York, 1988).

Holt, T. and V. Holt, *In Search of the Better 'Ole* (Portsmouth, 1985).

Hough, R., *Bless Our Ship: Mountbatten and the* Kelly (London, 1991).

Houston, P., *Went the Day Well?* (London, 1992).

Howard, J., *Michael Powell* (London, 1996).

Howard, L. H., *A Quite Remarkable Father* (New York, 1959).

Howard, T. and J. Stokes (eds), *Acts of War: The Representation of Military Conflict on the British Stage and Television since 1945* (Aldershot, 1996).

Hurd, G. (ed.), *National Fictions: World War Two in British Films and Television* (London, 1984).

James, J., *The Paladins: A Social History of the RAF up to the Outbreak of World War II* (London, 1990).

Johnson, T. and D. Del Vecchio, *Hammer Films: An Exhaustive Filmography* (Jefferson, NC, 1996).

Kelly, A., *Cinema and the Great War* (London, 1997).

Kemp, Paul J., *The T-Class Submarine* (London, 1990).

Kennedy, A. L., *The Life and Death of Colonel Blimp* (London, 1997).

Kirkham, P. and D. Thoms (eds), *War Culture: Social Change and Changing Experience in World War Two Britain* (London, 1995).

Knight, V., *Trevor Howard: A Gentleman and a Player* (London, 1986).

Knightly, P., *The First Casualty: From the Crimea to Vietnam. The War Correspondent as Hero, Propagandist and Myth* (New York, 1975).

Korda, M., *Charmed Lives: A Family Romance* (New York, 1979).

Kuhn, A. and J. Stacey (eds), *Screen Histories: A Screen Reader* (Oxford, 1999).

Kulik, K., *Alexander Korda: The Man Who Could Work Miracles* (New Rochelle, NY, 1975).

Landy, M., *British Genres: Cinema and Society, 1930–1960* (Princeton, 1991).

Lant, A., *Blackout: Reinventing Women for Wartime British Cinema* (Princeton, 1991).

Lipscomb, F. W., *The British Submarine* (London, 1975 edn).

Low, R., *The History of the British Film, 1906–1914* (London, 1948).

——, *The History of the British Film, 1914–1918* (London, 1948).

——, *The History of the British Film, 1918–1929* (London, 1948).

——, *The History of British Film, 1929–1939: Film Making in 1930s Britain* (London, 1985).

Low, R, and R. Manvell, *The History of the British Film, 1896–1906* (London, 1948).

Lukins, J., *The Fantasy Factory: Lime Grove Studios, London* (London, 1996).

Lysaght, C. E., *Brendan Bracken* (London, 1979).

Macnab, G., *J. Arthur Rank and the British Film Industry* (London, 1993).

Marwick, A., *Class: Image and Reality in Britain, France and the USA since 1930* (London, 1980).

Macdonald, K., *Emeric Pressburger: The Life and Death of a Screenwriter* (London, 1994).

Macdonald Fraser, G., *The Hollywood History of the World* (London, 1988).

MacKenzie, J. M., *Propaganda and Empire: The Manipulation of British Public Opinion, 1880–1960* (Manchester, 1984).

Marder, A. J., *From Dreadnought to Scapa Flow: The Royal Navy in the Fisher Era, 1904–1919*, i, *The Road to War, 1904–1914* (London, 1961).

——, *The Anatomy of British Sea Power: A History of British Naval Policy in the Pre-Dreadnought Era, 1880–1905* (New York, 1940).

Masterman, L., *C. F. G. Masterman: A Biography* (London, 1939).

Mayne, J., *Cinema and Spectatorship* (London, 1993).

McCarthy, T., *Howard Hawks: The Grey Fox of Hollywood* (New York, 1997).

Mclaine, I., *Ministry of Morale: Home Morale and the Ministry of Information in World War II* (London, 1979).

Medlicott, W. N., *The Economic Blockade*, ii (HMSO, 1959).

Messinger, G. S., *British Propaganda and the State in the First World War* (Manchester, 1992).

Miles, P. and M. Smith, *Cinema, Literature and Society: Elite and Mass Culture in Interwar Britain* (London, 1987).

Minney, R. J., *'Puffin' Asquith: A Biography of the Hon. Anthony Asquith, Aesthete, Aristocrat, Prime Minister's Son and Film Maker* (London, 1973).

Moorehead, C., *Sidney Bernstein: A Biography* (London, 1984).

Morley, S., *A Talent to Amuse: A Biography of Noël Coward* (Boston, 1984).

——, *The Other Side of the Moon: The Life of David Niven* (London, 1985).

——, *Dirk Bogarde: Rank Outsider* (London, 1996).

Morris, R., *Guy Gibson* (London, 1994).

Mosley, L., *The Battle of Britain: The Making of a Film* (London, 1969).

Moss, Robert F., *The Films of Carol Reed* (London, 1987).

Moyes, P. J. R., *Bomber Squadrons of the RAF and their Aircraft* (London, 1976).

Munn, M., *Stars at War* (London, 1995).

——, *Trevor Howard: The Man and his Films* (London, 1989).

Murphy, R. (ed.), *The British Cinema Book* (London, 1997).

Murphy, R., *Realism and Tinsel: Cinema and Society in Britain, 1939–1948* (London, 1989).

——, *Sixties British Cinema* (London, 1992).

Nicholas, S., *The Echo of War: Home Front Propaganda and the Wartime BBC, 1939–45* (Manchester, 1996).

Noakes, L., *War and the British: Gender, Memory and National Identity* (London, 1998).

Oakley, C. A., *Where We Came In: Seventy Years of the British Film Industry* (London, 1964).

O'Conner, G., *Ralph Richardson: An Actor's Life* (London, 1982).

Opie, R., *Rule Britannia: Trading on the British Image* (Harmondsworth, 1985).

Orbanz, E., *Journey to a Legend and Back: The British Realistic Film* (Berlin, 1977).

Paret, P. (ed.), *Makers of Modern Strategy: from Machiavelli to the Nuclear Age* (Princeton, 1986).

Paris, M., *From the Wright Brothers to Top Gun: Aviation, Nationalism and Popular Cinema* (Manchester, 1995).

Park, J., *British Cinema: The Light That Failed* (London, 1990).

Pattinson, W., *Mountbatten and the Men of the Kelly* (Wellingborough, 1986).

Perry, G., *The Great British Picture Show* (London, 1974).

——, *Forever Ealing* (London, 1981).

Petrie, D., *The British Cinematographer* (London, 1996).

Phillips, C. E. L., *Cockleshell Heroes* (London, 1956).

Pohle, R. W. and D. C. Hart, with C. Lee, *The Films of Christopher Lee* (Metuchen, NJ, 1983).

Porter, V., *On Cinema* (London, 1985).

Randall, A. and R. Seaton, *George Formby* (London, 1974)

Ransome-Wallis, P., *The Royal Naval Reviews, 1935–1977* (London, 1982).

Rawlings, J. D. R., *Fighter Squadrons of the RAF and their Aircraft* (London, 1976).

Redgrave, C., *Michael Redgrave: My Father* (London, 1995).

Reeves, N., *Official British Film Propaganda during the First World War* (London, 1986).

Richards, D., *Portal of Hungerford* (London, 1977).

Richards, J., *Visions of Yesterday* (London, 1973).

——, *The Age of the Dream Palace: Cinema and Society in Britain, 1930–1939* (London, 1984).

——, *Thorold Dickinson: The Man and his Films* (London, 1986).

——, *Films and British National Identity: From Dickens to Dad's Army* (Manchester, 1997).

—— (ed.), *The Unknown 1930s: An Alternative History of the British Cinema, 1929–39* (London, 1998).

Richards, J. and A. Aldgate, *Best of British: Cinema and Society, 1930–1970* (Oxford, 1983).

Robertson, J. C., *The British Board of Film Censors: Film Censorship in Britain, 1896–1950* (London, 1985).

——, *The Hidden Camera: British Film Censorship in Action, 1913–1972* (London, 1989).

Robertson, S., *The Development of RAF Strategic Bombing Doctrine, 1919–1939* (Westport, CT, 1995).

Royle, T., *War Report: The War Correspondent's View of Battle from the Crimea to the Falklands* (London, 1987).

Salwolke, S., *The Films of Michael Powell and the Archers* (Lanham, MD, 1997).

Schafer, S. C. *British Popular Films, 1929–1939: The Cinema of Reassurance* (London, 1997).

Short, K. R. M., *Feature Films as History* (London, 1981).

—— (ed.), *Film and Radio Propaganda in World War II* (London, 1983).

——, *Screening the Propaganda of British Air Power: From RAF (1935) to The Lion Has Wings (1939)* (Trowbridge, 1997).

Simkins, P., *Kitchener's Army: The Raising of the New Armies, 1914–16* (Manchester, 1988).

Sinyard, N., *The Films of Richard Lester* (London, 1985).

Skelley, A. R., *The Victorian Army at Home: The Recruitment and Terms and Conditions of the British Regular, 1859–1899* (London, 1977).

Slide, A., *'Banned in the USA': British Films in the United States and their Censorship, 1933–1960* (London, 1998).

Smith, M., *British Air Strategy Between the Wars* (Oxford, 1984).

Smithers, R. (ed.), *Imperial War Museum Film Catalogue*, i, *The First World War Archive* (Westport, CT, 1994).

Spiers, E. M., *The Army and Society, 1815–1914* (London, 1980).

——, *The Late Victorian Army, 1868–1902* (Manchester, 1992).

Spraos, J., *The Decline of the Cinema: An Economist's Report* (London, 1962).

Stead, P., *Film and the Working Class: The Feature Film in British and American Society* (London, 1989).

Steverson, T., *Richard Burton: A Bio-Bibliography* (Westport, CT, 1992).

Stewart, I. and S. L. Carruthers (eds), *War, Culture and the Media: Representations of the Military in 20th Century Britain* (Trowbridge, 1996).

Storey, A., *Stanley Baker: Portrait of an Actor* (London, 1977).

Street, S., *British National Cinema* (London, 1997).

Suid, L., *Guts and Glory: Great American War Movies* (Reading, MA, 1978).

——, *Sailing on the Silver Screen: Hollywood and the US Navy* (Annapolis, 1996).

Summerfield, P., *Reconstructing Women's Wartime Lives: Discourse and Subjectivity in Oral Histories of the Second World War* (Manchester, 1998).

Swann, P., *The British Documentary Film Movement, 1926–1946* (Oxford, 1989).

Tabori, P., *Alexander Korda* (New York, 1966).

Tanitch, R., *John Mills* (London, 1993).

Taylor, P. M. (ed.), *Britain and the Cinema in the Second World War* (London, 1988).

Terraine, J., *The Right of the Line: The Royal Air Force in the European War, 1939–1945* (London, 1985).

Thorpe, F. and N. Pronay, *Official British Films of the Second World War: A Descriptive Catalogue* (Oxford, 1980).

Tunbridge, P., *History of Royal Air Force Halton, No. 1 School of Technical Training* (London, 1995).

Vahamayi, T., *British Television: An Illustrated Guide* (London, 1996).

Virilio, P., *War and Cinema: The Logistics of Perception* (London, 1989).

Wansell, G., *Terence Rattigan* (London, 1995).

Wapshott, N., *The Man Between: A Biography of Carol Reed* (London, 1990).

Warren, P., *British Film Studios: An Illustrated History* (London, 1995).

Webster, C. and N. Frankland, *The Strategic Air Offensive Against Germany, 1939–1945*, 4 vols (HMSO, 1961).

Wells, J., *The Royal Navy: An Illustrated Social History* (Phoenix Mill, 1994).

Whitley, M. J., *Destroyers of World War Two* (London, 1988).

Wilmut, R., *Tony Hancock, 'Artiste'* (London, 1978).

Wood, L. (ed.), *The Commercial Imperative in the British Film Industry: Maurice Elvey, a Case Study* (London, 1987).

Yass, M., *This is Your War: Home Front Propaganda in the Second World War* (London, 1983).

Young, P. and P. Jesser, *The Media and the Military: From the Crimea to Desert Strike* (New York, 1997).

Yule, A., *Sean Connery: Neither Shaken nor Stirred* (London, 1993).

Ziegler, P., *Mountbatten: An Official Biography* (London, 1985).

Articles

Aldgate, T., 'Comedy, Class and Containment: The British Domestic Cinema of the 1930s', *British Cinema History*, J. Curran and V. Porter, eds (London, 1983), pp. 257–71.

——, 'Ideological Consensus in British Feature Films, 1935–1937', *Feature Films as History*, K. R. M. Short, ed. (London, 1981), pp. 94–112.

Badder, D., 'Powell and Pressburger: The War Years', *Sight and Sound*, 48 (1978), pp. 8–12.

Badsey, S. D., 'Battle of the Somme: British War-Propaganda', *Historical Journal of Film, Radio and Television*, 3 (1983), pp. 99–115.

Barr, C., 'War Record', *Sight and Sound*, 58 (1978), pp. 260–65.

Bean, K. F., 'Naval Reflections', *Sight and Sound*, 13 (1944), pp. 33–35.

Beresford, M., 'Realism and Emotion', *Sight and Sound*, 14 (1945), pp. 13–15.

Boyd-Bowman, S., 'War and Comedy', *National Fictions*, G. Hurd, ed. (London, 1984), pp. 39–42.

Brownrigg, H. E. and A. A. Sorrell, 'Cinemas and Cinema-Going in Great Britain', *Journal of the Royal Statistical Society*, 117, pt 2 (1954), pp. 133–65.

Buckman, K., 'The Royal Air Force Film Production Unit', *Historical Journal of Film, Radio and Television*, 17 (1997), pp. 219–44.

Burton, A. and S. Chibnall, 'Promotional Activities and Showmanship in British Film Exhibition', *Journal of Popular British Cinema*, 2 (1999), pp. 83–99.

Chapman, J., 'Celluloid Shockers', *The Unknown 1930s: An Alternative History of the British Cinema 1929–39*, J. Richards, ed. (London, 1998), pp. 75–97.

——, 'Our Finest Hour Revisited: The Second World War in British Feature Films since 1945', *Journal of Popular British Cinema*, 1 (1998), pp. 63–75.

——, '*The Life and Death of Colonel Blimp* (1943) Reconsidered', *Historical Journal of Film, Radio and Television*, 15 (1995), pp. 19–54.

——, '"The Yanks Are Shown to Such Advantage": Anglo-American Rivalry in the production of *The True Glory* (1945)', *Historical Journal of Film, Radio and Television*, 16 (1996), pp. 533–54.

Coultass, C., 'British Feature Films and the Second World War', *Journal of Contemporary History*, 19 (1984), pp. 7–22.

——, '*Tunisian Victory*: A Film Too Late?', *Imperial War Museum Review*, 1 (1986), pp. 64–73.

——, 'British Cinema and the Reality of War', *Britain and the Cinema in the Second World War*, P. M. Taylor, ed. (London, 1988), pp. 84–100.

——, 'The Ministry of Information and Documentary Film, 1939–45', *Imperial War Museum Review*, 4 (1989), pp. 103–11.

——, 'Film and Reality: The *San Demetrio* Episode', *Imperial War Museum Review*, 5 (1990), pp. 79–85.

Crang, J. A., 'The British Soldier on the Home Front: Army Morale Reports, 1940–45', *Time to Kill: The Soldier's Experience of War in the West, 1939–1945*, P. Addison and A. Calder, eds (London, 1997), pp. 60–76.

Curran, J., 'The New Revisionism in Mass Communication Research: A Reappraisal', *Cultural Studies and Communications*, J. Curran, D. Morley, V. Walkerdine, eds (London, 1996), ch. 11.

Dalrymple, I., 'The Crown Film Unit, 1940–43', *Propaganda, Politics and Film, 1918–45*, N. Pronay and D. W. Spring, eds (London, 1982), pp. 209–20.

Dawson, G., 'History-Writing on World War II', *National Fictions*, G. Hurd, ed. (London, 1984), pp. 1–7.

Ellis, J., 'The Quality Film Adventure: British Critics and the Cinema, 1942–1948', *Dissolving Views*, A. Higson, ed. (London, 1986), pp. 66–93.

Fernbach, T., 'Tom Wintringham and Socialist Defence Strategy', *History Workshop*, 14 (1982), pp. 63–91.

Forman, H., 'The Non-Theatrical Distribution of Films by the Ministry of Information', *Propaganda, Politics and Film, 1918–45*, N. Pronay and D. W. Spring, eds (London, 1982), pp. 221–33.

Gifford, D., 'Filmography: Gainsborough and Related Films, 1924–1950', *Gainsborough Pictures*, P. Cook, ed. (London, 1997), ch. 11.

Gillett, B. E., 'A. C. 2 at the Teachies', *Sight and Sound*, 13 (1944), pp. 61–63.

Harper, S., 'The Representation of Women in British Feature Films, 1939–45', *Britain and the Cinema in the Second World War*, P. M. Taylor, ed. (London, 1988), pp. 168- 202.

——, 'The Years of Total War: Propaganda and Entertainment', *Nationalising Femininity*, C. Gledhill and G. Swanson, eds (Manchester, 1996), pp. 193–212.

——, '"Nothing to Beat the Hay Diet": Comedy at Gaumont and Gainsborough', *Gainsborough Pictures*, P. Cook, ed. (London, 1997), pp. 80–98.

Harper, S. and V. Porter, 'Cinema Audience Tastes in 1950s Britain', *Journal of Popular British Cinema*, 2 (1999), pp. 66–82.

Harrisson, T., 'Appeals to Women', *Political Quarterly*, 13 (1942), pp. 265–79.

——, 'Films and the Home Front: The Evaluation of their Effectiveness by Mass-

Observation', *Propaganda, Politics and Film, 1918–45*, N. Pronay and D. W. Spring, eds (London, 1982), pp. 234–48.

Higson, A., 'Addressing the Nation: Five Films', *National Fictions*, G. Hurd, ed. (London, 1984), pp. 22–26.

Hiley, N., '"Let's Go to the Pictures": The British Cinema Audience in the 1920s and 1930s', *Journal of Popular British Cinema*, 2 (1999), pp. 39–53.

Hiley, N. P., '*The British Army Film, You!* and *For the Empire*: Reconstructed Propaganda Films, 1914–1916', *Historical Journal of Film, Radio and Television*, 5 (1985), pp. 165–82.

Jarvie, I., 'Fanning the Flames: Anti-American Reaction to *Objective Burma* (1945)', *Historical Journal of Film, Radio and Television*, 1 (1981), pp. 117–37.

——, 'The Burma Campaign on Film: *Objective Burma* (1945), *The Stilwell Road* (1945) and *Burma Victory* (1945)', *Historical Journal of Film, Radio and Television*, 8 (1988), pp. 55–73.

Jordon, M., 'Carry On ... Follow that Stereotype', *British Cinema History*, J. Curran and V. Porter, eds (London, 1983), pp. 312–27.

Krome, F., '*Tunisian Victory* and Anglo-American Film Propaganda in World War II', *The Historian*, 58 (1996), pp. 517–29.

——, '*The True Glory* and the Failure of Anglo-American Film Propaganda in the Second World War', *Journal of Contemporary History*, 33 (1998), pp. 21–34.

Kuhn, A., '*Desert Victory* and the People's War', *Screen*, 22 (1981), pp. 45–68.

McCormack, J. V., 'The Army and the Press in War', *Journal of the Royal United Services Institution*, 98 (1953), pp. 269–73.

McIsaac, D., 'Voices from the Central Blue: The Air Power Theorists', *Makers of Modern Strategy*, P. Paret, ed. (Princeton, 1986), ch. 21.

Medhurst, A., '1950s War Films', *National Fictions*, G. Hurd, ed. (London, 1984), pp. 35–38.

Morley, D. 'Populism, Revisionism and the "New" Audience Research', *Cultural Studies and Communications*, J. Curran, D. Morley, V. Walkerdine, eds (London, 1996), ch. 12.

Murfett, M. H., 'Admiral Sir Henry Bradwardine Jackson (1915–1916)', *The First Sea Lords*, M. H. Murfitt, ed. (Westport, CT, 1995), pp. 91–100.

Murphy, R., 'Rank's Attempt on the American Market, 1944–9', *British Cinema History* (London, 1983), pp. 164–78.

——, 'British Film Production, 1939 to 1945', *National Fictions*, G. Hurd, ed. (London, 1984), pp. 14–16.

——, 'The British Film Industry: Audiences and Producers ', *Britain and the Cinema in the Second Word War*, P. M. Taylor, ed. (London, 1988), pp. 31–41.

Otley, C. B., 'The Social Origins of British Army Officers', *Sociological Review*, 18 (1970), pp. 213–49.

——, 'The Educational Background of British Army Officers', *Sociology*, 7 (1973), pp. 191–209.

Poole, J., 'British Cinema Attendance in Wartime: Audience Preference at the

Majestic, Macclesfield, 1939–1945', *Historical Journal of Film, Radio and Television*, 7 (1987), pp. 15–34.

Porter, V. and C. Litewski, 'The Way Ahead: Case History of a Propaganda Film', *Sight and Sound*, 50 (1981), pp. 110–16.

Pronay, N., 'The First Reality: Film Censorship in Liberal England', *Feature Films as History*, K. R. M. Short, ed. (London, 1981), pp. 113–37.

——, 'The News Media at War', *Propaganda, Politics and Film*, N. Pronay and D. W. Spring, eds (London, 1982), pp. 173–208.

——, 'The Political Censorship of Films in Britain Between the Wars', *Propaganda, Politics and Film, 1918–45*, N. Pronay and D. Spring, eds (London, 1982), pp. 98–125.

——, 'The British Post-Bellum Cinema: A Survey of the Films Relating to World War II Made in Britain between 1945 and 1960', *Historical Journal of Film, Radio and Television*, 8 (1988), pp. 39–54.

Pronay, N. and J. Croft, 'British Film Censorship and Propaganda Policy during the Second World War', *British Cinema History*, J. Curran and V. Porter, eds (London, 1983), pp. 144–63.

Ramsden, J., 'British Society in the Second World War', *Britain and the Cinema in the Second World War*, P. M. Taylor, ed. (London, 1988), pp. 15–30.

——, 'Refocusing "The People's War": British War Films of the 1950s', *Journal of Contemporary History*, 33 (1998), pp. 35–63.

Reeves, G., '*Tumbledown* (Charles Wood) and *The Falklands Play* (Ian Curteis): The Falklands Faction', *British Television Drama in the 1980s*, G. W. Brandt, ed. (Cambridge, 1993), pp. 140–61.

Richards, J., 'The British Board of Film Censors and Content Control in the 1930s: Images of Britain', *Historical Journal of Film, Radio and Television*, 1 (1981), pp. 95-116.

——, 'The British Board of Film Censors and Content Control in the 1930s: Foreign Affairs', *Historical Journal of Film, Radio and Television*, 2 (1982), pp. 39–48.

——, 'National Identity in British Wartime Films', *Britain and the Cinema in the Second World War*, P. M. Taylor, ed. (London, 1988), pp. 42–61.

Robertson, J. C., 'British Film Censorship Goes to War', *Historical Journal of Film, Radio and Television*, 2 (1982), pp. 49–64.

Rowson, S., 'A Statistical Survey of the Cinema Industry in Great Britain in 1934', *Journal of the Royal Statistical Society*, 99 (1936), pp. 67–119.

Sedgwick, J., 'Cinema-Going Preferences in Britain in the 1930s', *The Unknown 1930s*, J. Richards, ed. (London, 1988), ch. 1.

——, 'Film "Hits" and "Misses" in mid-1930s Britain', *Historical Journal of Film, Radio and Television*, 18 (1998), pp. 333–51.

Short, K. R. M., 'RAF Bomber Command's *Target for Tonight*', *Historical Journal of Film, Radio and Television*, 17 (1997), pp. 181–218.

Stead, P., 'The People and the Pictures: The British Working Class and Film in the 1930s', *Propaganda, Politics and Film, 1918–45*, N. Pronay and D. W. Spring, eds (London, 1982), pp. 77–97.

——, 'The People as Stars: Feature Films as National Expression', *Britain and the Cinema in the Second World War*, P. M. Taylor, ed. (London, 1988), pp. 62–83.

Suid, L., 'The Battle of the Atlantic in Feature Films', *To Die Gallantly*, T. J. Runyan and J. M. Copes, eds (Boulder, CO, 1994), pp. 311–21.

Taylor, P. M., 'Techniques of Persuasion: Basic Ground Rules of British Propaganda during the Second World War', *Historical Journal of Film, Radio and Television*, 1 (1981), pp 57–65.

——, 'If War Should Come: Preparing the Fifth Arm for Total War', *Journal of Contemporary History*, 16 (1981), pp. 27–51.

——, 'British Official Attitudes towards Propaganda Abroad, 1918–39', *Propaganda, Politics and Film, 1918–45*, N. Pronay and D. W. Spring, eds (London, 1982), pp. 23–49.

——, 'Film as a Weapon during the Second World War', *Statecraft and Diplomacy in the Twentieth Century*, D. Dutton, ed. (Liverpool, 1995), pp. 135–54.

Towle, P., 'The Debate on Wartime Censorship in Britain, 1902–14', *War and Society: A Yearbook of Military History*, B. Bond and I. Roy, eds (London, 1977), pp. 102–16.

Watt, H. 'Casting Nine Men', *Documentary News Letter*, 4 (1943), pp. 179–80.

Wenden, D. J. 'Churchill, Radio, and Cinema', *Churchill*, R. Blake and W. R. Louis, eds (Oxford, 1993), pp. 215–39.

Wenden, D. J. and K. R. M. Short, 'Winston S. Churchill: Film Fan', *Historical Journal of Film, Radio and Television*, 11 (1991), pp. 197–214.

Index

Illustrations are shown in **bold**